"To Toil the
Livelong Day"

"To Toil the Livelong Day"

·

AMERICA'S WOMEN AT WORK, 1780–1980

·

Edited by Carol Groneman
and Mary Beth Norton

Cornell University Press

ITHACA AND LONDON

First published 1987 by Cornell University Press.

International Standard Book Number (cloth) 0–8014–1847–x
International Standard Book Number (paper) 0–8014–9452–4
Library of Congress Catalog Number 86–47975

Printed in the United States of America

Librarians: Library of Congress cataloging information appears on the last page of the book.

The paper in this book is acid-free and meets the guidelines for permanence and durability of the Committee on Production Guidelines for Book Longevity of the Council on Library Resources.

To
William P. Groneman and the
memory of Eileen Crowe Groneman
and to
Clark and Catharine Norton

Contents

Part 4   1940–Present

Acknowledgments

The articles in this book have been selected from among hundreds of papers presented at the Sixth Berkshire Conference on the History of Women, held at Smith College, June 1–3, 1984. The conference and thus the book were made possible by the hard work of Dorothy Green, the conference coordinator; Mary McFeely, chair of the local arrangements committee; and the members of the program committee (which the editors cochaired): Iris Berger, Edith Couturier, Ellen DuBois, Barbara Harris, Deborah Hertz, Judy Jeffrey Howard, Alice Kessler-Harris, Asunción Lavrin, Marjorie Lightman, JoAnn McNamara, Ruth Milkman, Joan Nestle, Barbara Ramusack, Margaret Rossiter, Marylynn Salmon, Kathryn Kish Sklar, Carroll Smith-Rosenberg, Amy Swerdlow, Louise Tilly, Judy Walkowitz, and Lillian Williams.

The editors also express their thanks to Gerald R. Lynch, president, and Theodore Gill, former dean of faculty, of John Jay College of Criminal Justice, who provided Carol Groneman with released time to prepare for the conference; to Jacqueline A. Jaffe for suggesting the title of the book; to Cornell University for the use of its mainframe computer; and to Lori Schechter, whose dual expertise in computing and women's studies proved invaluable in the early stages of organizing the conference.

"To Toil the Livelong Day"

Introduction

Carol Groneman and
Mary Beth Norton

The long-term trend of women entering the paid labor force passed a critical point in the last decade: working for wages has now become the norm for women rather than the exception. Not only have the numbers been increasing, but the kinds of women working and the types of jobs they perform have changed dramatically. In 1890, 40 percent of single women and 5 percent of married women worked for wages; today, two-thirds of single women and an astonishing 53 percent of married women do so. In the late nineteenth century, most paid women workers were domestic servants; in the late twentieth century, clerical and sales work have replaced domestic service to become the leading occupations for women.

One thing has not changed, however. The sexual division of labor, with the consequent low wages paid to women, remains firmly entrenched. Throughout this century, women have never earned, on the average, more than sixty-four cents for every dollar men earned. The justification for these low wages has often rested on the assumption, even when contradicted by the evidence, that women are secondary wage earners and work only for "pin money."

Sharp distinctions exist between the kinds of jobs women and men do. Seventy per cent of women workers are concentrated in just twenty job categories, only a few more occupations than in 1900, and those

3

employed in less female-dominated industries are clustered in the lowest-skilled, lowest-paid jobs.

Race further stratifies the occupational structure. Domestic work continued to be the major occupation for black and Hispanic women until the 1960s, and their average wage today lags behind white women's wages. The median annual income of full-time women workers is $11,702 for whites, $10,914 for blacks, and $9,887 for Hispanics. Despite affirmative action legislation, job discrimination against racial minorities continues.

The historic roots of these divisions of labor are discussed in the following collection of seventeen essays, originally presented at the Sixth Berkshire Conference on the History of Women, held at Smith College in June 1984. They are presented in four chronological sections, and the thematic connections are described below. One of the major contributions of these articles is the challenge they pose to traditional labor history and to women's history.

Until recently, labor historians have assumed that working women acted just like working men. Preindustrial artisan workshops, working-class saloons and political clubs, and male-dominated unions, scholars argued, were the center of working-class culture and the locus of the development of working-class consciousness. These essays suggest that to understand the female half of the working class, we must look more broadly at kin and community networks, at different kinds of leisure activities, and at women's particular experience of work, family, and union and strike activity. Direct comparison of male and female experiences provides new insights not only into women's labor history but into labor history in general. In addition, when the traditional labor history model based on the experience of working men is reconceptualized, *unpaid* work—both in the home and on the farm—takes on a new importance.

Scholars who have drawn the central issues of labor history from men's experience have developed a series of simple dichotomous categories: working men are active, permanent, and organized; working women are passive, temporary, and unorganized. Such distinctions both overgeneralize and assume that all women workers are young, single, temporarily employed, and thus uncommitted to organization. Deconstruction of these dichotomies, suggests Carole Turbin, leads to a new analysis not only of women's work but of men's work as well.

The essays in this volume also pose a challenge to dominant themes in women's history based mainly on the experiences of middle-class and elite women: for example, the docine of "separate spheres." Gender as a category has to be further refined by examination of class and race. Working-class and immigrant women in cities, women on farms in the Northeast and on the frontier, and blacks before and after slavery—the majority of women—did not operate within the confines of separate spheres. In particular, Nancy Grey Osterud concludes that women on upstate New York dairy farms did not turn to female networks or create female subcultures but enlarged the dimensions of sharing in their relations with men through joint patterns of sociability. Kathy Peiss argues that while private and public leisure activities for women and men were separate, that separation was not unbridgeable. These studies suggest that outside the urban middle class, we need to locate the majority of women within families and in relation to men.

Other essays raise serious questions about the traditional notion of a "working-class sisterhood." Dolores Janiewski describes the racial division between black and white women tobacco workers in the South. Mary Blewett notes the conflict among female shoemakers based on their relationship to the mode of production—home or factory. And, according to Kathy Peiss, leisure itself separated married and single working-class women.

Nevertheless, women frequently overcame such divisions. The recognition of *interdependence*—of worker with family and community, of women workers with their male counterparts, of women workers with women reformers—is also stressed in this volume. The mutually supportive working-class community described by Carole Turbin and the relationship between female and male slaves, examined by Christie Farnham, underscore the importance of these interactions. In fact, Laurel Thatcher Ulrich argues that the New England family farm economy was actually characterized by interdependence, calling into question the simple preindustrial, agricultural model of self-sufficient farms.

All of the essays deal with the ways in which gender—and to some extent race and ethnicity—shaped the experience of working women. Whether they worked in their own or other people's homes, on farms or in factories, gender influenced society's and women's own attitudes about norms of acceptable behavior, relationships to other workers and to the family, and the kinds of jobs and wages available. To highlight additional major themes that connect the articles, we must look at three categories: unpaid and paid housework and unionized work.

Unpaid Domestic Work

The seven essays in this collection that discuss women's unpaid domestic work span the period from 1780 to the present. In spite of the many changes the United States has undergone since the Revolutionary era, certain thematic unities link the experience of domestically employed women across boundaries of time, space, race, and class.

First, women's household labor has always been defined and determined by the culturally shaped "needs" of their families. A woman's own interests have long been subordinated to those of her husband and children; she and they have traditionally perceived their demands on her time as superior to other possible claims. This was as true for Laurel Thatcher Ulrich's eighteenth-century New England housewives, who were supposed to stay at home instead of "gadding about," as it is for Sarah Elbert's twentieth-century women living in farm families in upstate New York, who are expected to devote their primary energies to maintaining the family farming enterprise and passing it on intact to the next (male) generation. Even slave and white working-class women put their families ahead of themselves. If the demands of their masters or employers sometimes preempted those of their families, the women's own priorities remained unchanged. (Phyllis Palmer demonstrates that women's adherence to this principle has also affected them in their role as employers of domestic servants, for they have tended to assume that their hired workers should behave like housewives rather than like paid employees; that is, that their labor should be defined by a series of necessary tasks rather than by a work day of predetermined length.)

Second, the sexual division of labor prevailed in all the families described in these seven essays. Throughout the history of the United States, its residents have distinguished between men's and women's work and the respective contributions of each sex to the household. In rural homes, men were responsible for heavy outdoor labor (including planting and harvesting), the primary care of livestock, and financial management; women for child care, gardening, cooking and cleaning, and occasionally assisting the men at their chores. Women's work was essential to the maintenance of all the rural households, and men's and women's tasks were complementary. But several authors, among them Corlann Bush and Christie Farnham, warn us that *complementary* and *essential* were not the equivalent of *equal*. This was the unpleasant truth brought home to the upstate New York farm wife Meg Lewis when her husband, Ted, unilaterally decided to sell their farm to their son, thus rendering her years of managing the bloodlines of their stock irrelevant to the family's income and forcing her to seek outside employment.

Laurel Thatcher Ulrich's portrait of eighteenth-century New England households and the sexual division of labor therein bears little resemblance to the classic picture of the self-sufficient, patriarchal colonial home. She shows that households depended on each other for subsistence and that work and produce were regularly shared and bartered. Further, she suggests that women may have had independent roles in pervasive informal trading networks. She describes a society in which mothers managed their daughters' labor, and kinship ties created crucial links in a chain of exchanges. Paid work, such as Martha Moore Ballard's midwifery, existed within the context of a vast trading network and should be seen as a variant of it rather than as an aberration in women's traditional domestic role. In the world of the eighteenth-century rural New England housewife, there was no sharp division between work performed for the household and that done for the market. Any item produced or skill obtained had potential value in both realms.

Likewise, the women from shoemaking families described in Mary Blewett's essay—contemporaries of those studied by Ulrich—contributed to the family enterprise through their labor. As American shoe manufacturing expanded after 1780, women acquired a new responsibility: shoebinding, or sewing the uppers, while the male members of the family (aided by apprentices) performed the rest of the jobs associated with producing a finished shoe. Women did not earn separate wages for this work until after 1810; instead, they functioned entirely within the context of a family business. These artisan homes maintained the sexual division of labor characteristic of farm households; women's participation in the production of goods for the market involved only one task, which was explicitly defined as "women's work." Moreover, both mothers and daughters were supervised by men in this endeavor, and domestic work occasionally had to be subordinated to the demands of sewing enough shoe uppers to keep their menfolk fully occupied.

The sexual division of labor was so pervasive that it was perpetuated even among slave families on antebellum plantations, where it had no explicit economic base. Christie Farnham points out that despite recent assertions to the contrary, black husbands and wives did observe gender distinctions in their intrafamilial work assignments. Farnham criticizes many current studies of the contemporary and historical black family for their unspoken assumptions concerning the "proper" roles of men and women. She relates the family forms the slaves adopted in North America to their West African heritage, showing that slave women's work roles were crucial in shaping their lives and those of their families. Adult slave women, she provocatively contends, had no need to marry because they were not financially dependent on black men.

Their own work, for which their masters compensated them with minimal subsistence, could sustain them and their children. As a result, unlike white women, they could form unions for love alone; furthermore, they did not have to remain in unsatisfactory marital relationships. This positive element of choice in their lives, Farnham argues, helped to create the female-headed black household that has been condemned as "pathological" by twentieth-century observers.

Nancy Grey Osterud's study of gender relations in a white farming community in upstate New York in the late nineteenth century presents a contrasting picture of intense mutual dependence between husbands and wives. The key to understanding the pattern of the sexual division of labor in the Nanticoke Valley lies in the nature of its economy. Dairying, more than any other type of farming, required nearly equal contributions from men and women—men in their role as caretakers of livestock, women in their role as milkers and as cheese and butter makers. Men's and women's labor was highly interdependent, yet some customary distinctions were maintained. Just as the work roles of slave women shaped their family lives, so the work roles of these dairy farmers affected theirs. Families socialized together rather than in sex-segregated units, and extended kin ties were of great importance in providing links to the community as a whole.

Corlann Bush discovers still a different pattern—and one that changed sharply over time because of the introduction of new technology—among the farm families of the early twentieth century in the Palouse region of northern Idaho and eastern Washington. Before the invention of a tractor that could work those steep slopes, men's and women's efforts were both essential to a succesful harvest. Until well into the 1930s, huge teams of horses driven by large numbers of hired men pulled the combines that harvested the wheat crop. Those men had to be fed (five meals a day) by a farm's resident women. As in eighteenth-century rural New England, daughters and hired girls worked under adult women's supervision; as in shoemaking families, women's unpaid labor was essential to the production of goods for the market. But the introduction of the crawler Caterpillar tractor changed all that. Absent the need to feed those male laborers, women's work on the Palouse farms came to resemble that found elsewhere: it was invisible, no longer so clearly complementary to men's, and more wholly under men's direction. Bush points out a significant paradox: although feminist historians today may lament the loss of such a crucial function for women, the Palouse women welcomed the new ease and leisure in their lives. Thus she reminds us that we must take our subjects' own perceptions into account when we make historical judgments and that technological developments often affect the sexes differently.

To such themes as women's sacrifice of self-interest to the family farm, the sexual division of labor, the invisibility of women's contributions to the farm household, and the importance of kinship ties, Sarah Elbert adds another consideration in her article on modern farm families in upstate New York: the impact of the changing life cycle of the family on the farm as an enterprise. The work demands placed on men, women, and children of both sexes shift as time passes and the farm and the family enter different phases of the cycle. A young, childless couple who start a farm incur heavy debts and work long hours; eventually, children are available to assist their parents in chores deemed appropriate for their age and sex; and ultimately the property will be transferred to a new generation, probably to one designated son. The divergent shapes of the farm family at these various stages suggest that past scholarship has presented too static a view of rural households, that they must be traced over time if their workings are to be fully understood.

Although these articles concentrate on women's work lives, they also pay attention to work's apparent antithesis: leisure. In rural households, leisure activities were tightly connected to work and thus are often difficult to distinguish from it. In early Maine, among the major leisure activities, work bees—quilting, spinning, or cornhusking frolics—offered a vehicle for socializing as well as for completing essential work. In the Nanticoke valley in the late nineteenth century, social activities likewise focused on work bees, church organizations, and visits among extended kin. Kathy Peiss shows that married working-class women in the cities also centered their leisure time on household and family, perhaps sitting on the front stoop to gossip with friends while watching their children at play. The domestic work of adult women was accordingly (and quite literally) "never done." A woman employed in her home rarely had the luxury of time away from her duties to her family.

Peiss's article also demonstrates that in urban areas leisure activities were as sex-segregated as was employment. Accordingly, she argues, recent contentions that working-class culture and consciousness grew out of the male world of the saloon and lodge erroneously omit the female half of the working-class population from consideration. Patterns of leisure-time use for young, unmarried, employed women revolved around new forms of entertainment, such as public dances, movie theaters, and vaudeville houses, and involved socializing with both male and female peers. Peiss concludes, therefore, that labor historians will have to rethink their developing paradigms of working-class formation if they are fully to explain this important phenomenon. And, in general, she reminds us once again of the ways in which new findings in women's history should force historians to reassess their views of men as well.

Paid Domestic Work

Four articles in this volume consider paid labor in the home. Such an emphasis is appropriate, because domestic service has been one of the major sources of employment for women throughout American history. Yet the household was a peculiar context for paid labor, as the essays on this topic clearly demonstrate. The tasks performed in the household were normally unpaid; that is, wives and daughters were never formally compensated for their labors on behalf of their husbands, fathers, and brothers. Therefore hired female domestic workers and their employers had to contend constantly with two ambiguities inherent in the circumstances of household employment. First, women were being paid to do work that, when performed by female members of the family, had no generally recognized or agreed-upon value. Second, since—unlike industrial labor—household work had never been organized into carefully defined time periods, it was difficult to determine precisely the proper length of a work day or the tasks it should encompass.

Consequently, levels of compensation and job requirements were problematic for both employers and workers. Employers wanted maximum hours of work, demanding of their employees what their families demanded of them: an unlimited commitment to the household's welfare. Since housewives did the same or similar work for nothing, they coupled those expectations with a reluctance to pay more than minimum wages. Servants, by contrast, sought pay adequate to compensate them for the heavy and essential work they performed, along with clearly delimited working hours in which they would complete only certain defined tasks. Because the employers were usually in the stronger position and their definitions of the job tended to prevail, domestic service held little attraction for women with other work options. As a direct result, domestic service became increasingly race- as well as sex-segregated, with black and Hispanic women dominating the ranks of hired household workers in the United States once the great wave of European immigration (which had provided generations of Irish, Scandinavian, and German female servants for American homes) ceased in the early decades of the twentieth century.

In the eighteenth century, as was noted earlier, paid household work was part of a wider system of exchanges among households in general and their womenfolk in particular. Thus when the midwife Martha Moore Ballard supervised the childbirth of her clients, she was frequently compensated in goods rather than cash, and her paid work took place in a wholly female context. But a century later, as Janet Golden shows in her study of wet nurses, male doctors had begun to intrude into the formerly all-female world of childbearing and child rearing, by promulgating standards for wet nurses and by instructing mothers on dealing with them. Wet nurses could not easily be replaced, and their presence was crucial to the survival of their infant charges. Thus they were unique among domestic servants and in a position of considerable potential power when they negotiated the terms of their employment. Yet the occupation itself was marginal and temporary, and it obliged an impoverished nursing mother to surrender her own baby to the not-so-tender care of others. It was not, then, a job that many women willingly sought. Similarly, a new mother would only reluctantly employ a wet nurse, not wanting to bring into her home a woman who—almost by definition—was "immoral." Wet nurses were thus perhaps the most anomalous and problematic of all domestic servants, and one can sense the frustrations of the physicians who kept trying (and failing) to create orderly relations among all those concerned.

Attempts to systematize the household are also the subject of Phyllis Palmer's article on domestic employment in the District of Columbia. Before World War II, she demonstrates, some white reformers tried to make housework more closely resemble industrial labor by establishing model contracts with regulated hours and clearly stated terms of employment. Although the reformers' goals coincided with those of black domestic laborers—who wanted to limit their hours of work—the efforts met with little success. The attempt to introduce social science into the home failed because the housewives who employed domestic workers could not see parallels between their households and industrial workplaces. Faced with the choice of either meeting the demands of their families or regularizing the hours of their servants, they opted for the former and resisted attempts to limit their claims on their employees' time.

To present black domestic workers' viewpoints on the same question, Elizabeth Clark-Lewis uses the recollections of women who migrated to Washington, D.C., before 1921 and paints a richly detailed portrait of their lives. Their reminiscences reveal the ways in which race and gender intersected to restrict the job opportunities open to them as female migrants from the South who hoped to better themselves and assist their families in the process. The ties of kin and religion important to rural women employed in their own households did not break when they moved to the city; for many years these women continued to contribute to the households and churches into which they had been born. Clark-Lewis's essay discloses the value that black domestic workers placed on being able to control their own hours. For them, the transition from live-in to live-out work was momentous: live-out work allowed them privacy, time to themselves, and the opportunity to participate in church activities. What might seem to an outside observer an unimportant shift—for they were still employed in domestic service—had major positive consequences in their view. Thus once again we are reminded that we must try to understand women's past experiences as they themselves understood them, in addition to assessing them by our own contemporary standards.

Vicki L. Ruiz demonstrates that Mexican and Mexican-American women workers in El Paso, Texas, have experienced the same types of job discrimination as the black domestic servants of Washington, D.C. Ethnicity and gender have combined, historically and in the contemporary world, to restrict Hispanic women's occupational choices. Because they have so few other options, many are willing to enter domestic service in El Paso, with the result that an already unequal balance of power is tipped further in favor of the employer. The consequences are low prevailing wages and difficult working conditions. To the domestic workers (as to the Wisconsin clerical workers described in Cynthia Costello's essay) perhaps just as important a consequence is a lack of respect from their employers. The Hispanic women of El Paso want—and deserve—better treatment. But the sex- and race-segregated character of the labor market has prevented the success of all attempts to regularize working hours or establish adequate minimum wages for domestic workers.

Ruiz's and Clark-Lewis's studies both point up an intriguing fact: the structure of women's employment often has unforeseen and unrecognized effects on society at large. In El Paso, Ruiz observes, at least half the riders on the city's public transit system are commuting domestic workers. Were the government to crack down on those who hire "illegal" Mexican maids from across the border, the bus system might collapse. And in Washington, Clark-Lewis notes that live-in workers placed their meager savings in the mutual benefit associations known as penny savers clubs. When women began to live out and do day work, they had the time to visit banks and saw the use of those institutions as more appropriate to their new status as salaried employees. Thus the clubs were weakened as the women withdrew their money for deposit in banks. The workers' new free time on Sundays also enabled them to participate much more fully in church activities and even to rise to leadership positions in their congregations. For women who had so little, this seemed an enormous benefit.

Unionized Work

Traditionally, historians of unionized work have focused on male craft or industrial unions. Seven essays in this volume look at women workers in unions, from collar, corset, and shoe workers in the nineteenth and early twentieth centuries, to factory workers in the tobacco and auto industry in the 1930s and 1940s to contemporary clerical workers. As Carole Turbin suggests, we must explore "under what conditions some women were able to form unions," not simply why there were so few organized women. Additionally, we must ask under what conditions some women were able to participate in and win strikes, shape the activity of the strike or the union, and create successful all-female unions or gender-specific union strategies.

Three themes run through these seven essays. First, from the struggle of nineteenth-century women shoemakers to the efforts of the United Auto Workers Women's Bureau in the 1950s, conventional notions of femininity have conflicted with the union and strike activity of women. In order for women to participate in unions or in strikes, they had to challenge the assumption that women's place was in the home. Collective action required women to be active in the public arena, to be assertive and not passive. Operating within the accepted notions of femininity, as in the "demure" form of picketing adopted by the Kalamazoo corsetmakers described by Karen Mason, could lead to the defeat of a strike. On the other hand, by enabling women to challenge the dominant ideology, a strike, such as that outlined by Cynthia Costello, could bring its participants self-confidence, independence, and a new view of themselves as workers and as women.

Women have traditionally been employed in the secondary labor market, in low-skilled, low-paid jobs that male union leaders often thought to be unorganizable. This sex segregation of jobs, a second theme of the essays, sometimes led to divisions among women workers, as well as between women and men. In the 1860 shoe workers' strike, as Mary Blewett shows us, factory girls tried to establish a gender alliance with women homeworkers by demanding increased wages for all women workers. Their efforts were defeated by male strike leaders, who organized the homeworkers in support of the family wage. Sex segregation of jobs was also supported by cultural forms. As Ann Schofield demonstrates, the definition of gender widened to include occupational segregation for women as acceptable and desirable. Moreover, sex segregation was not the only way in which workers were divided: the tobacco workers discussed by Dolores Janiewski, for example, were segregated racially as well as sexually.

Third, many of these essays speak, implicitly or explicitly, about the creation of class consciousness. Costello underscores the inconsistent and contradictory nature of a working-class consciousness, which combines a critique of the system with a belief in some of its dominant elements. Turbin argues that previous studies have neglected the ways in which family life and relationships may *encourage* women's awareness and activism.

Mary Blewett analyzes the experience of women shoe workers, first as homeworkers in the late eighteenth century and increasingly as factory workers by the middle of the nineteenth century. The assumption by labor historians that the artisan shop was the source of working-class culture and consciousness ignores the very real development of women workers' class and gender consciousness as exemplified in the strategy developed by women factory workers in the 1860 shoe workers' strike. Male strikers sought to mitigate the threat to the preindustrial family wage system by proposing increases in male wages only. The factory girls of Lynn wanted an alliance with the female homeworkers, advocating increased wages for both home and factory shoe production as an alternative to the family wage. The sexual division of labor supported by the male artisans made it difficult for them to regard women as fellow workers and to recognize in the experience of working women what would eventually confront all workers under industrial capitalism.

Carole Turbin criticizes labor historians' use of models based solely on the study of male workers. To correct the view that all working women were young, single, and uncommitted to their jobs, she examines the widows, working wives, and self-supporting single women among the Troy collar workers who provided leadership in the union and the strikes. Furthermore, she shows that collar workers, as a group, were a permanent part of the labor force; their participation in work life, while intermittent and interrupted, was not temporary. Finally, in the industrial context of Troy, New York, the sexual division of labor was sometimes advantageous; female collar workers and male iron workers in the same families could support each other's labor activity because a strike in one industry did not threaten a family's entire subsistence.

In addition to the economic conditions that perpetuated the sex segregation of jobs, cultural forms also supported the division. The labor press of the late nineteenth and early twentieth centuries, Ann Schofield argues, inculcated an ideology of gender that reinforced prevailing cultural concepts regarding masculinity and femininity. The stories might be about working girls and their triumphs, but the underlying themes and structural relationships were patriarchal. These polarized stereotypes of men and women were internalized by women workers because they helped to resolve the disparity between traditional concepts of women and the reality of their working lives. Provocatively, Schofield suggests that these working women unconsciously colluded in maintaining their own oppression through the acceptance of such ideal types.

Karen Mason examines the ways in which the internalized notions of proper feminine behavior could affect strike tactics. The two union organizers in the Kalamazoo corsetmakers' strike of 1912 represented opposing views of the relationship between femininity and union activity. One made gender an issue in the strike by emphasizing women's vulnerability and their need to be protected against sexual exploitation, shifting the focus of the strike from economic to moral issues; the other favored aggressive picketing and the demand for higher wages as a way to deal with exploitation. Mason also shows how, in contrast to earlier historical examples of cross-class alliances such as the middle-class-dominated Women's Trade Union League's support for the shirtwaist makers' strike in New York City, class ties were stronger than gender ties in Kalamazoo.

A different form of cross-class alliance was fostered by the Food and Tobacco Workers (CIO) in the late 1930s and early 1940s. Dolores Janiewski explains that because white, male-dominated unions had made no effort to change the sex and race segregation of occupations in the southern tobacco industry, blacks—particularly black women—were deeply suspicious of unions. In order to organize black women in the tobacco factories, the Food and Tobacco Workers had to develop tactics specifically designed to appeal to them. For example, they sought support from local black ministers, held meetings in black churches, and promoted racial integration within their own ranks. Although the left-wing union did not ultimately prevail over the forces of postwar conservatism, it had provided black women with a "public space where they could simultaneously address the issues of class, gender, and race."

A legitimate platform for women's issues was also provided by the Women's Bureau of the United Auto Workers in the post–World War

II period. The Women's Bureau, according to Nancy Gabin, ensured the survival of gender-conscious protest and increased the visibility of women in the UAW, although it was unable to bring about fundamental change in the structure and organization of work in the auto factories. Gabin challenges the standard view of scholars concerning the impermanence of advances made by women workers during the war and posits the survival and vitality of feminist goals and purposes within the Women's Bureau from 1945 to the early 1960s. The conflict between traditional notions of femininity and unionism, however, continued to have force: articles in the union's newspaper about married women union leaders, for example, always described both their domestic and union roles in an attempt to counter the notion that employment and union activity were unfeminine.

The same contradictions affected the fifty-three women office workers interviewed by Cynthia Costello in her study of a contemporary strike at the Wisconsin Education Association Insurance Trust. The strike created ambivalence for some workers as they struggled with the disparity beweeen their conventional female roles and the assertiveness called for by collective action, but it was the actual participation in the strike, Costello reminds us, that forged a critical consciousness for many of them. Their class consciousness of their treatment by management fused with a gender consciousness of the male-dominated hierarchy at the Insurance Trust. Yet because working-class consciousness is often contradictory, their awareness and sense of connection extended to other working *women* but not necessarily to the labor movement itself.

The seventeen essays in this volume demonstrate the dramatic increase in recent years in the sophistication of historical inquiry into the subject of women and work. It is now understood that unpaid labor and wage labor form a continuum rather than a dichotomy, with many intermediate stages linking, not separating, the two poles. The study of women's work is not simply an extension of the study of men's labor; models developed from the experience of working men must be reconceptualized so that they apply to women. These new models lead to an increased understanding of men's work, as well.

Recent scholarship demonstrates that women's work has always been linked in some way to their families. These essays expand those connections to explore the relationship of work, kin, and community. The nature of women's domestic responsibilities—coupled with their race, ethnicity, marital status, and ties to kin and community—has largely determined the sort of labor they did, whether paid or unpaid, performed inside or outside the household. Accordingly, these articles develop new paradigms for understanding the complex nature of the work of women over the past two centuries. This reconceptualization poses an exciting challenge both to the history of labor and to the history of women.

· *Part* *1* ·

1780–1880

1

Housewife and Gadder: Themes of Self-sufficiency and Community in Eighteenth-Century New England

Laurel Thatcher Ulrich

In her novel *Northwood,* published in 1827, Sarah Josepha Hale (the future editor of *Godey's Lady's Book*) described a Thanksgiving dinner served in the household of the prosperous New Hampshire farmer she called "Squire Romolee." On two tables pushed together in the parlor were a roasted turkey, a goose, a pair of ducklings, a chicken pie, and a sirloin of beef flanked by a leg of pork and a joint of mutton, all embellished with vegetables, pickles, and preserves. On a side table stood plum pudding, custards, pies of every description, several kinds of rich cake, sweetmeats, fruit and currant wine, cider, and ginger beer. When a visiting Englishman asked Squire Romolee how he could claim temperance after eating such a dinner, the happy farmer replied, "Well, well, I may at least recommend industry, for all this variety you have seen before you on the table, excepting the spices and salt, has been furnished from my own farm and procured by our own labor and care."[1]

Although Hale gave the punch line to Squire Romolee, she devoted most of her chapter to the women's "labor and care." Mrs. Romolee and her daughters not only churned, pickled, roasted, and baked with supreme skill; they spun and wove their own linens, raised the geese

---

1. Mrs. S. J. Hale, *Northwood: A Tale of New England* (Boston, 1827), 1:108–16.

that filled their featherbeds, and in spare moments ornamented their house with simple art. Over the mantel in the chamber where the Englishman slept was a "family record" painted and lettered by Sophia.[2]

Hale's description is more than an amusing fantasy. Its essential point, that the early American economy rested on family self-sufficiency, underlies most interpretations of women's work in early America. While Hale and her contemporaries emphasized the character- and body-building virtues of home production, twentieth-century scholars have stressed gender integration through shared responsibility for family support. As mutual labor within self-sufficient rural households declined, so the argument goes, separate spheres were born.[3] Even those historians who reverse the argument, emphasizing the subordination of women in a male-dominated household economy, have not questioned the original model. The essential question has been the relation of husbands and wives within a unified "family economy."[4]

Economic historians, on the other hand, have mounted a formidable attack on the whole notion of self-sufficiency. We now know that few families had the land, the tools, or the labor to produce and process all their own food and clothing. Interdependence rather than independence is the theme of current scholarship, though historians continue to argue over its meaning. Was trade shaped by outside markets or by family need? Did entrepreneurial or communal values predominate?[5] As yet, however, few of these studies have had anything to say about women.

In this regard, a second heroic housewife in Hale's *Northwood* is worth considering. Mrs. Watson, "the gossip of the neighborhood," combined the worst and the best features of neighborliness. She was a charitable soul, always ready to nurse the sick or watch with the dying, but she was also a busybody given to telling fortunes in tea leaves. She

2. Hale, *Northwood*, 1:83.

3. E.g., Nancy Cott, *The Bonds of Womanhood: "Women's Sphere" in New England, 1780–1835* (New Haven, Conn., 1978); Ann Douglas, *The Feminization of American Culture* (New York, 1978); and most recently, Ruth Schwartz Cowan, *More Work for Mother: The Ironies of Household Technology from the Open Hearth to the Microwave* (New York, 1983).

4. John Mack Faragher, *Women and Men on the Overland Trail* (New Haven, Conn., 1979), chap. 2.

5. E.g., Carole Shammas, "How Self-Sufficient Was Early America?" *Journal of Interdisciplinary History* 13 (Autumn 1982): 247–72; Joyce Appleby, "Commercial Farming and the 'Agrarian Myth' in the Early Republic," *Journal of American History* 68 (March 1982): 833–49; Michael Merrill, "Cash Is Good to Eat: Self-Sufficiency and Exchange in the Rural Economy of the United States," *Radical History Review* 3 (Winter 1977): 42–71; Winifred B. Rothenberg, "The Market and Massachusetts Farmers, 1750–1855," *Journal of Economic History* 41 (June 1981): 283–314.

was "reputed one of the neatest women and best managers in the village," though Hale cautioned that "those women who have neither her sleight to work, nor constitution to endure fatigue, must not imitate the worst part of her examples—gadding."[6] In Mrs. Romolee the novelist celebrated the virtues of home production, but in Mrs. Watson she remembered the essential and sometimes troubling interdependence that underlay it.

Robert Gross has suggested that increased production in early-nineteenth-century New England was accompanied by growing distrust of communal work. Work exchanges between neighbors now seemed inefficient, while neighborhood work frolics appeared to cost more in refreshment than they gained in productivity.[7] Hale's portraits reflect this anxiety, yet they also convey forgotten details of a world that was passing. She was wrong in thinking the Romolees could achieve such abundance outside the market, but she was right in placing them in the best house in the village.[8] She was also right in making an extravagant (and seemingly wasteful) display of food the mark of their prosperity.

But Hale's portraits are most suggestive in their limning of female roles. Her emphasis on the mother–daughter relationship in the Romolee household, as well as her unforgettable (if somewhat backhanded) acknowledgment of the authority of Mrs. Watson, have the ring of memory. Sarah Hale herself was born in a New Hampshire village in 1788, and she spent the first forty years of her life there before widowhood and the success of *Northwood* propelled her to Boston. Letters and diaries from her mother's generation portray a world in which gentility and industry were indeed compatible, in which servants were daughters and daughters were servants, in which the same neighbors who came to drink tea came to nurse the sick and lay out the dead—in short, a world in which self-sufficiency was sustained by neighborliness, and vice versa.

Historians have given far too little attention to the social character of women's work in early New England. In Hale's novel Mrs. Romolee and Mrs. Watson, the housewife and the gadder, stand in splendid isolation. In life they were one, as a quick survey of three eighteenth-century diaries shows.

Martha Ballard, a Hallowell, Maine, midwife, was clearly a gadder.

6. Hale, *Northwood*, 2:178–90.

7. Robert A. Gross, "Culture and Cultivation: Agriculture and Society in Thoreau's Concord," *Journal of American History* 69 (June 1982): 45–46.

8. As Gross has argued ("Culture and Cultivation," 46), "it was the rich—the large landholders and the men who combined farming with a profitable trade—who could aspire to independence."

Between 1790 and 1799 she was home less than half the days of the year. Yet she also spun her own linen, grew her own cabbages, and raised enough turkeys to last from August to Thanksgiving.[9] Elizabeth Phelps of Hadley, Massachusetts, the wife of a country squire, was a "good housewife." She made her own sausage and soap, manufactured textiles and candles, and entertained an endless stream of visitors. Yet she also managed to leave home one day in three.[10] Elizabeth Wildes, a young bonnetmaker from Arundel (now Kennebunkport), Maine, also combined housekeeping and gadding. She had three young children at home and a husband at sea, yet she went visiting almost as often as Mrs. Phelps; and when she was confined by illness or work, a host of relatives and neighbors came to her.[11] Given differences of geography, occupation, and age, the evidence of the three diaries is remarkably similar. In 1790 there were only 77 days in the entire year when Martha Ballard neither left home nor received visitors; for Elizabeth Wildes there were 100; Elizabeth Phelps recorded visits or visitors on 200 of the 235 days she wrote in her diary.[12]

Because these women were New Englanders, it is easy to imagine them walking from house to house around a village green. Not so. In 1790, Martha Ballard lived near her husband's sawmill, a third of a mile and across two brooks from her nearest neighbor, a bachelor trader. The meeting house and the handful of houses around it were more than three-quarters of a mile away, by water or land; folks on both sides of the Kennebec River were accounted "neighbors." Elizabeth Phelps lived on a 600-acre estate two miles outside Hadley, while Elizabeth Wildes lived a mile and a half from the meeting house in a sparsely settled area of Arundel.[13] The distances were not impossible, but neither were they inconsequential. In all three towns, interaction with neighbors was the result of intent rather than accident. Women walked; they rode sidesaddle, sometimes carrying a child or neighbor behind them on a pillion; and they traveled by canoe.[14] Though Mrs. Phelps, the wealthiest of the three, had access to a one-horse vehicle called a chaise, she drove it herself.

9. Martha Moore Ballard Diary, 1785–1812, manuscript, Maine State Library, Augusta (hereafter MMB).

10. "The Diary of Elizabeth (Porter) Phelps," ed. Thomas Eliot Andrews, *New England Historical and Genealogical Register* 118:1–30, 108–27, 217–36, 297–308; 119:43–60, 127–40, 205–23, 289–307; 120:57–63, 123–35, 203–14, 293–304 (hereafter EPP).

11. Elizabeth Perkins Wildes Diary, 1789–93, manuscript, Maine Historical Society, Portland.

12. EPP, 120:62.

13. E. E. Bourne, "The Bourne Family" (1855), typescript, Brick Store Museum, Kennebunk, Maine, 222–24; EPP, 120:61.

14. EPP, 120:60, 118:5; MMB, 24 August 1786.

Fifty years later, New Englanders found all this coming and going marvelous indeed. Elizabeth Wildes's son, in a family history written in 1855, wondered at his mother's ability to bounce along on horseback. "Men and women in the last century were different from the race of the present," he declared. The theme was repeated in a history of Winthrop, Maine, published in the same year. "The first settlers in a new country cultivate the social affections," the author wrote, following with a long story about a woman who, when invited to visit her neighbor on baking day, was persuaded to carry her dough with her. "What a spectacle it would now present to see a horse, saddled and pillioned, carrying a gentleman and lady on his back, the gentleman having before him a kneading trough, in which was dough for a batch of bread!" he exclaimed.[15] Necessity as much as the "social affections" motivated some such visits; many Maine houses in this period lacked ovens.

There is not space here to explore all the nuances of community interdependence in rural New England, but even a brief survey demonstrates that women were fully involved in at least three forms of economic interaction. They traded goods and services with their neighbors; they engaged in labor transactions; and they joined in communal work.

Family subsistence in early America was achieved by hundreds of transactions with neighbors. Consider again that marvelous Thanksgiving dinner assembled in the home of Squire Romolee. Though few eighteenth-century fireplaces could accommodate the menagerie Hale described, contemporary sources demonstrate that a genuine feast did include more than one kind of meat. Martha Ballard's favorite combination was a "line" (loin) of veal and a leg of pork. The pork was usually the product of the autumn slaughtering, but the veal, killed in spring or early summer, was eaten fresh—and unless a family were large enough to consume a sixty-pound animal at once, they had no choice but to share with neighbors, as Martha Ballard did when she sent a side of veal to one family in May and in June "borrowed" a quarter of veal from another.[16]

This was neighborliness in support of self-sufficiency. Families extended their own supply by sharing with others. Neighborly support also allowed home production of textiles. "Mrs. Peirce put in a piece of overshot," Elizabeth Phelps wrote in June of 1778. The neighbor was doing not the weaving but the warping, the difficult preliminary threading of the loom. Once that task was completed, a woman or her

15. Bourne, "Bourne Family," 222–23; David Thurston, *A Brief History of Winthrop* (Portland, Maine, 1855), 20–21.

16. Darret and Anita Rutman note the same pattern in seventeenth-century Virginia, in *A Place in Time* (New York, 1984), 36.

daughters could do the weaving. In this way the specialized skills of a
few women helped to sustain the general productivity of others.[17]

The interweaving of home production and trade is apparent in a
brief entry in Martha Ballard's diary. "Mr. Woodward & his wife here
at Evening," she wrote on December 18, 1789. "I let her have 1 lb. of
Cotten for Combing worsted." Although the Ballards raised flax, they
did not own sheep, nor does cotton grow on the Kennebec. That simple
exchange between neighbors involved an elaborate network of barter
and trade stretching to the Caribbean. The wool Mrs. Woodward card-
ed probably came from Mrs. Cummings, who paid a medical bill in
"sheep's wool" in August, though it may have been part of the wool
Martha Ballard's son got "on board Capt. Dana's vessel" in September.
The cotton could have come from "Captain Norcross' Lady," who gave
Martha Ballard two pounds of cotton and a pound of tea in May, or
from Ezra Hodges, who paid his wife's midwifery bill with the same
commodity in June.

Thus West Indian cotton and Massachusetts wool helped to sustain
a village economy characterized by home production. Once Mrs.
Woodward had finished carding the worsted, Martha Ballard's daughter Dolly did the spinning and weaving, though Polly Savage, another
neighbor, warped the loom. Meanwhile Martha Ballard was cutting
and drying pumpkins that Mrs. Woodward had given her.[18] Not all
such transactions made their way into written records, however. On
June 21, 1787, for example, Martha Ballard reported that Mrs. Pollard
had "sent home 5 lb of poark which shee Borrowed 12 of April 1786,"
but the entry for April 12 records no such transaction, simply reading,
"I went to Mr. Williams'. Mrs. Pollard came home with me."

Jack Larkin has suggested that surviving rural account books were
an effort on the part of a few New Englanders "to achieve a greater
measure of control over and to have more information about, an economic life still stunningly concrete."[19] The concreteness if not the control is reflected in the diary of Abner Sanger of Dublin, New Hampshire, who on one day noted that Mrs. Ichabod Rowel had received "a
brown earthern quart bowl (6 times) full of Indian meal" and on another that Deacon John Knowlton's wife had balanced "13 ounces of
good butter" with "9 ounces of tallow" and "a little scoop of rennet

---

17. EPP, 118:305.

18. MMB, 30 May, 5 June, 12 and 23 August, 29 September, 16 and 19 October, 18
December 1789.

19. Jack Larkin, "The World of the Account Book: Some Perspectives on Economic
Life in Rural New England in the Early 19th Century," paper presented at the Keene
State College Symposium on Social History, Keene, New Hampshire, 13 October 1984.

bag."[20] Little scoops are hard to quantify and even "quart" bowls must have varied, since Sanger thought it important to specify the "brown earthen" bowl in his entry.

Such accounts are far removed from the double-entry ledgers of merchants with their debits and credits assembled on opposite pages. In rural diaries it is seldom possible to see both sides of a transaction, though an occasional "reckoning" survives. "Mrs. Savage here," Martha Ballard wrote on April 15, 1788. "Shee & I made a settlement on account of her spinning and the wolen wheel, my being with her when sick & 1 pair of shoes & medicine I let her have when her children were sick & we wer Evin in our accounts. I lett her have 4 lb of flax which she has not paid for." The range of products traded, if not the written accounting, was typical. A stream of feathers, ashes, baby chicks, seedlings, and old clothes linked households in rural New England.

Patterns of village trade are so unstudied (and so difficult to study) that many questions remain. Did men and women trade freely with one another, accumulating "family" rather than personal accounts, as in the Sanger diary? Or did women primarily trade with women and men with men, as the Ballard diary suggests? One merchant eager to establish a potash works at Thomaston, Maine, assumed that there were some products that women routinely controlled. "Ashes in general being the women's perquisite certain articles of goods must be kept on hand for payment which will induce them to save as many as they can & often to send them to the works," he wrote.[21] The success of his operation depended upon his ability to divert ashes from household use (in soapmaking) and from neighborhood trade.

The notion of married women trading and reckoning with their neighbors has no place in prevailing models of the preindustrial family economy, yet it conforms well with statistical evidence assembled in recent literature. In a meticulous study of agricultural production in eighteenth-century Massachusetts, Bettye Hobbs Pruitt found that "widows' portions"—those curious passages in early wills which provide allotments of food, fuel, and fiber for a widow's support—typically included far more grain than one woman could consume. Presumably she was expected to trade it to supply other needs. "That such a strategy was not spelled out in wills merely suggests that salable or

20. Abner Sanger Diary, 7 May, 6 October 1794, manuscript, Library of Congress. Lois Stabler of Keene, New Hampshire, allowed me to use her typsescript of the original. She has since published *Very Poor and of a Lo Make: The Diary of Abner Sanger* (Portsmouth, N.H., 1986).

21. Thomas Vose to Henry Knox, 14 December 1789, Henry Knox Papers, Massachusetts Historical Society, Boston.

exchangeable surpluses were so fully incorporated into the notion of subsistence as to be inseparable from it and hence hidden, from our eyes at least," Pruitt writes.[22] Whatever forms it took, female trade was an integral part of economic life.

Women were also involved in exchanges of labor. Again it is not a question of "self-sufficiency" versus "community" but of both. Dependence upon family labor inevitably meant dependence on neighbors. Hale caught the Romolees of *Northwood* in a charmed instant when their daughters were old enough to work but too young to marry. Such richness could not last. Family labor was born helpless and destined to leave. Prosperous households such as the Romolees might keep their daughters at home, but eventually the girls would marry. Nor, given the wide availability of land and the almost universal opportunity to marry, could they fully appropriate the labor of their neighbors' daughters. A bewildering number of young women—Pene, Lucy, Dolly, Polly, Jerusha, Sally, Becca, Fanny, and Submit, in addition to daughters Betsey and Thankful—march through the pages of Elizabeth Phelps's diary. Without surnames or more detailed entries it is difficult to determine which were workers and which merely visitors. Probably many were both.

Since there were few bound servants in New England, most household workers even in wealthy families were the sons or daughters of neighbors. Few stayed long. In 1791, Elizabeth Wildes employed Hannah and Betsy Hutchings, Lydia Kilpatrick, Molly Watson, and Molly Wildes in addition to her sisters, Sally and Abiel Perkins. Between 1785 and 1800 thirty-nine young women lived and worked for some period in Martha Ballard's house; almost all were the daughters of local men in the middle range of the tax list. The social origins of workers helps to explain their comings and goings. Most young women alternated work at home with work "abroad," spending a week or two spinning at a neighbor's house, going home to help with the hay, moving on to a sister's house where there was sickness, going back to the first house or on to another to spin or wash. The promise of self-sufficiency and the reality of insufficiency kept people as well as goods in motion.

A young daughter's labor might be used to balance her mother's accounts, as when Martha Ballard included "2 Days Work of Dolly" when she settled with Mrs. Weston, the wife of a local merchant.[23]

---

22. Bettye Hobbs Pruitt, "Self-Sufficiency and the Agricultural Economy of Eighteenth-Century Massachusetts," *William & Mary Quarterly*, 3d ser., 41 (1984): 348.

23. MMB, 16 January 1787.

Dolly Ballard was then barely fourteen; within three years she had completed an apprenticeship with Mrs. Densmore, a dressmaker, and was working on her own, sometimes in her mother's house, sometimes in the homes of neighbors. Martha Ballard paid most of her helpers directly, occasionally in cash, more often in clothing or credit at a store.[24]

A brief diary kept in Eastport, Maine, in the summer of 1801 explains the system. Mary Yeaton worked at home, helping her mother with the sewing and her father with the reaping, though she longed to return to Portsmouth, New Hampshire, where she had been living with friends. "You speak as tho I ought to stay here," she told her mother. "If you will point out any means for my support I'll thank you. You know very well I can not look to my father for clothing, etc." When her father worried about her becoming dependent on her friends, she insisted she was not. "I told him . . . I was industrious, and endeavored to support myself; that he had not had it in his power to do much for me for some time, and I could sew for my western friends and by this means supply myself."[25]

Since few fathers had the means "to do much" for their daughters, girls balanced obligations to their families (and especially to their mothers) with the necessity of providing for themselves, much as they would do a generation later when they went to the mills. Such a system ensured broad-based but low-level production as well as continuity from one generation to the next but made it difficult even for an unusually energetic woman to sustain specialized work. It is no accident that Elizabeth Wildes was able to weave and market cotton coverlets during the years her daughters were available to help. Nor is it surprising that Martha Ballard's midwifery practice reached its height while her daughters still lived at home. Once the daughters were gone, however, that sort of enterprise depended upon the availability of hired help.[26]

"Lydia went off last night," Elizabeth Phelps reported in a letter to her daughter Betsey, who was visiting in Boston. "Silence Furgunson came last night to tarry . . . & this day we have been hard at it I can tell

24. Thomas Dublin notes a similar pattern in nineteenth-century store accounts for hatmaking: "Apparently daughters made hats for the family account for a number of years and then, when they reached a certain age, their parents allowed them to make hats on their own account, perhaps to generate dowries" ("Women and Outwork in a Nineteenth-Century New England Town," in *The Countryside in the Age of Capitalist Transformation*, ed. Steven Hahn and Jonathan Prude [Chapel Hill, N.C., 1985], 57–58).

25. Mary Yeaton Diary, typescript, Maine State Library, Augusta, 29 June and 4 October 1801.

26. Laurel Thatcher Ulrich, "Martha Ballard and Her Girls: Women's Work in Eighteenth-Century Maine," forthcoming; Bourne, "Bourne Family," 244–47.

you. made a cheese—churned—got dinner for between .20. & .30. persons, made between .20. & .30. mince-pies . . . but we shall all be rested by the morning I hope."[27] The mistress of the best house in the village parted with her daughters at serious cost to herself. The industrious gentility Sarah Hale so much admired was in large measure a consequence of the instability of servants. In another generation Catharine Beecher would make a virtue of Mrs. Phelps's (and Mrs. Romolee's) necessity. Without servants there was little choice but to "educate" young ladies in their mothers' kitchens.

Communal work was the most picturesque form of economic interdependence in rural New England—and to nineteenth-century moralists the most troubling. Berrying, nutting, breaking wool, fishing, husking, house or barn raising, and quilting joined work with sociability. On February 11, 1792, after a male relative had "drawd some Flowers" on a quilt, Elizabeth Wildes sent him to get "Mrs. Green and Abiel to come here to quilting. We had a frollick." "Frolic" rather than "bee" was the common term. In his single days in Keene, New Hampshire, Abner Sanger reported "quilting frolics," "election frolics," "drunken frolics," and on one summer day "a cow-tord frolic"—presumably a spontaneous game of tag or toss with two girls who were working near him in a field.[28]

Like other sober citizens, Martha Ballard worried about the behavior of the young folks who frequented the large gatherings. Drinking was a concern and perhaps also, though she never expressed it directly, the high premarital pregnancy rates in the town.[29] On November 10, 1790, she described a quilting that took place at her own house. Fifteen "ladies" arrived about three o'clock in the afternoon and quilted until seven, when twelve "gentlemen" arrived to take tea. The young people

27. Elizabeth Porter Phelps to Elizabeth W. Phelps, 4 November 1797, Phelps Family Papers, Amherst College Library, Amherst, Mass. (I am grateful to Edward McCarron for this reference.)

28. Sanger Diary, 21 May, 18 June 1778; 27 May, 28 December 1779; 7 December, 9 February 1780; 28 November 1782.

29. Marriage dates exist (in Hallowell Town Records, manuscript, Maine State Library, Augusta) for 87 women whose first child was delivered by Martha Ballard between 1785 and 1795. More than one third of these first births occurred less than 8½ months after marriage. For similar evidence from other parts of New England, see Daniel Scott Smith and Michael Hindus, "Premarital Pregnancy in America, 1640–1971: An Overview and Interpretation," *Journal of Interdisciplinary History* 4 (1975): 537–70; Robert Gross, *The Minutemen and Their World* (New York, 1976), 235; Christopher Jedrey, *The World of John Cleaveland: Family and Community in Eighteenth-Century New England* (New York, 1979), 152; and Laurel Thatcher Ulrich and Lois Stabler, " 'Girling of It' in Eighteenth-Century Keene," to appear in *Annual Proceedings* (1985), Dublin Seminar for New England Folklife.

danced after supper, "behaved exceeding cleverly," she wrote, and went home by eleven. In contrast, she noted dryly, "Mr. Densmore had a quilting & husking. My young folks there came home late." Her entry for July 7, 1788, after neighbors came to raise a sawmill, reflected both anxiety and relief. "There was a vast concorse of men and children and not many disguised with Licquor."

For women, however, births and illnesses provided the most frequent opportunities for communal work. "Monday morn just at day break Mr. Hibbard came here," Elizabeth Phelps wrote on March 21, 1790. "I went there—she had a daughter born about 10. I home directly to help wash." Mrs. Phelps was not a midwife. She was simply responding to one more obligation of neighborliness. In the midwifery accounts of Martha Ballard, "calling the women" usually marked the final stage in a labor. "Mrs. Blanchard had her women calld and was delivered at 11 hour Evn of a dagt," she wrote on December 26, 1795, three days after she herself had arrived at the Blanchard house. In midwifery as in textile production, the practiced skills of a few women intersected with the ordinary skills of the many.

Watching with the sick and laying out the dead were also activities that brought together skilled specialists, such as Martha Ballard, with other friends and neighbors. When Elizabeth Wildes had the measles in 1790, half a dozen women (in addition to a male doctor) appeared by turns at her house. "Mrs. Demsy came here and my Mother and Doc Emerson. Hannah Hutchings Sat up with me," she wrote on March 25. Although Israel Wildes was at home on one of his rare intervals between voyages, it was not he but the women who cared for his wife. When Elizabeth Phelps's mother died, Mrs. Gaylord and Sally Parsons prepared her body for burial.[30] Martha Ballard performed similar services for dozens of Hallowell families, usually with the assistance of one or two other women.

Carroll Smith-Rosenberg has written of a "female world of love and ritual" associated with such events, though her analysis tends to combine and perhaps to confuse two very different kinds of female bonding: one originating in a traditional world that organized work by gender and encouraged communal rather than individual identity, the other in a new, more sentimental hemisphere of intense personal relationships.[31] In the New England I am describing, birth, illness, and death were all group events; friends even accompanied newly married

---

30. EPP, 121:67.

31. Carroll Smith-Rosenberg, "The Female World of Love and Ritual: Relations between Women in Nineteenth-Century America," *Signs* 1 (1975): 1–29.

couples on their wedding journeys.[32] "Wedingers here," Elizabeth
Phelps wrote when one such party arrived at her house.

The realities of birth and death sometimes bent social and racial
barriers. Although paid wet-nursing was unusual in rural New
England, even a wealthy woman like Elizabeth Phelps might offer
breast milk when a child was in need. Soon after her own baby died in
December of 1776, she took in a newborn infant whose mother had
died. Apparently there was a marked social distance between the two
families: she referred to the father as "one Richmond"; and a week
after the baby arrived, she wrote, "We having heard that the mother of
those Children had the itch tho't it not safe to keep it," adding, "now
Lord I make it my prayer that I may do my duty fully however hard."
Whether keeping or giving up the baby was the harder duty is not
clear, for Elizabeth Phelps soon reclaimed the child. "We feared it
would suffer," she wrote.[33]

Physical need might also bend barriers in the opposite direction,
sending privileged women to the homes of social inferiors. "Mrs. Par-
ker had our hors to go & see the Negro woman Docter," Martha Ballard wrote on November 9, 1793. The mysterious black practitioner,
never given a name, appeared two or three times in the diary in the
1790s, then disappeared. That Martha Ballard always referred to her
as a "Docter" or "doctoress" suggests that she respected the woman's
powers as a healer even though she denied her the full dignity of a
name.[34]

In early America, of course, blacks and Indians, as well as women,
had long been associated with both healing and magic. Jon Butler has
suggested that among whites, folk medicine was "the most important
depository of occult activity."[35] Unfortunately, the magical practices of
New England women have not been studied, though again Hale's
Northwood contains a tantalizing clue. In her portrait of Mrs. Watson,

32. Ellen Rothman, *Hands and Hearts: A History of Courtship in America* (New York,
1984), 80–81.

33. EPP, 118:235, 236, 397, 398. The evidence that Elizabeth Phelps breastfed the
baby is circumstantial but strong. Having given birth and lost her child, she was capable
of nursing another child; since no other "nurse" is mentioned, and since the concern
about the "itch" implied some sort of physical intimacy, the conclusion seems reasonable.

34. Martha Ballard was usually able to provide a surname even for travelers or
strangers in the town. Like most diarists of the period, she routinely referred to the black
women she knew by first name, regardless of marital status, though she always identified
white married women as "Mrs."

35. Jon Butler, "The Dark Ages of American Occultism, 1760–1848," in *The Occult in
America: New Historical Perspectives*, ed. Howard Kerr and Charles L. Crow (Urbana, Ill.,
1983), 69.

Hale poked fun at writers who insisted on portraying country for-
tunetellers as witchlike creatures with "weather beaten, sallow, shriv-
elled skin" and "grizzled, disheveled" hair. "How I wish the ingenious
authors, rich as they are in invention, coud have afforded them a
comb!" she wrote. She insisted that her Mrs. Watson was a perfectly
respectable woman. Though too fond of tea and gossip, she was nevertheless a tidy woman and a good manager, and she was always ready
at a moment's notice to watch with the sick. Clearly, her authority as a
fortuneteller was a direct consequence of those errands of mercy and
curiosity that took her to the homes of her neighbors.[36]

Again the diaries corroborate Hale's portrait. "The Widow Lassel
was here and told our fortunes," Eliza Wilde wrote on January 22,
1790, reporting the widow's visit in the same matter-of-fact way that
she noted going to church. For the women of Kennebunk, fortunetelling was apparently just another kind of "frolick." "The Widow Lassel
and Sukey Perkins and Sally came here. Had their fortunes told," she
wrote on another day; a week later she noted that the girls had repeated the ritual without the help of their neighbor.[37] Although moralists
were as hard on female fortunetelling as on male drinking, it may have
been as much a part of preindustrial life.[38] In Mrs. Watson, Sarah Hale
preserved a forgotten form of neighborliness in early New England.

Most models of the "patriarchal family economy" ill fit the evidence
of eighteenth-century diaries, which describe a world in which wives as
well as husbands traded with their neighbors, where young women felt
themselves responsible for their own support, where matches were
made in the tumult of neighborhood frolics, and where outsiders as
well as family members were involved in the most intimate events of
life. The New England we have explored was a world neither of free-
floating individuals nor of self-contained households. It was a world in
which some women aspired to the independence of Mrs. Romolee but
all were sustained by the running about of Mrs. Watson.

Such material alerts us to a number of undeveloped themes in
women's history. First, it invites further exploration of the economic
orientation of men and women. Did the barter economy encourage
easygoing trade across gender lines, or did patterns of exchange co-

36. Hale, 2:180.
37. Wildes Diary, 31 March, 6 April 1790.
38. For a typical attack on fortunetelling, see *An Explanation of the Ten Command-
ments . . . by an Aged School-Mistress in the State of Massachusetts* (Keene, N.H., 1794), 17.
Also see David Hall, "The Uses of Literacy," in *Printing and Society in Early America*, ed.
William Joyce et al. (Worcester, Mass., 1983), 40–41.

alesce into two quite different economies, one dominated by men and characterized by developing market transactions, the other devoted to "use exchanges" of the sort increasingly more common to women?

Second, it suggests the importance of relations between women both within and beyond the family economy. If mothers rather than fathers had the chief interest in their daughters' labor, then the central theme in the development of factory employment and of public education for girls may not be increased autonomy for young women but an overall loss by older women of the responsibility to educate and to manage female workers. In this regard, more careful distinctions between elite women and their neighbors, as employers and as workers, are needed.

Third, it shows forms of female association organically related to women's work. One wonders, considering the myriad ways in which ordinary life tied women together, whether the appropriate question for the early nineteenth century is not how some women *developed* bonds of womanhood but how generations of women over time sustained and redefined those that had long existed.

Finally, it encourages closer attention to the concrete details of women's lives at every social level, to patterns of consumption, of production, and of "frolicking." If historians cannot accommodate all of Hale's fanciful feast, we at least may begin to look with new interest at the ashes in Mrs. Romolee's fireplace and the leaves in Mrs. Watson's cup.

2

The Sexual Division of Labor and the Artisan Tradition in Early Industrial Capitalism: The Case of New England Shoemaking, 1780–1860

Mary H. Blewett

Labor historians who in the 1970s investigated the connections between nineteenth-century culture and class experience came to regard the preindustrial male artisan and his work culture as the source of working-class consciousness. As Brian Palmer put it in an article in 1976: "The artisan, not the debased proletariat, fathered the labour movement. . . . The working class was born, not in the factory, but in the [artisan] workshop."[1] This metaphorical claim to hegemony in class

Research for this paper was supported by a grant from the National Endowment for the Humanities. My thanks to Tom Dublin, Paul Faler, Milton Cantor, Helena Wright, Carole Turbin, and Bruce Laurie for their support and useful criticism.

1. Bryan D. Palmer, "Most Uncommon Common Men: Craft and Culture in Historical Perspective," *Labour/Le Travailler* 1 (1976): 14. For overviews of the artisan tradition in American labor history, see Sean Wilentz, "Artisan Origins of the American Working Class," *International Labor and Working Class History* 19 (1981): 1–22; and Jim Green, "Culture, Politics and Workers' Response to Industrialization in the US," *Radical America* 16 (1982): 101–28. Among the studies reviewed by Wilentz and Green are Paul G. Faler, *Mechanics and Manufacturers in the Early Industrial Revolution: Lynn, Massachusetts, 1780–1860* (Albany, N.Y., 1981); Alan Dawley, *Class and Community: The Industrial Revolution in Lynn* (Cambridge, Mass., 1976); Thomas Dublin, *Women at Work: The Transformation of Work and Community in Lowell, Massachusetts, 1826–1860* (New York, 1979); Bruce Laurie, *Working People of Philadelphia, 1800–1850* (Philadelphia, 1980); Susan E. Hirsch, *Roots of the American Working Class: The Industrialization of Crafts in Newark, 1800–1860* (Philadelphia, 1978); and Howard B. Rock, *Artisans of the New Republic: The Tradesmen of New York City in the Age of Jefferson* (New York, 1979).

35

formation as well as human procreation is symbolic of the invisibility of
women in this conception of the working class: their invisibility as
workers and as a gender.

The artisan's workshop was indeed a male world, and much of the
new labor history assumes that the experience of female members of
artisan families who were drawn into preindustrial production was
indistinguishable from male experience. Labor historians regard the
artisan workshop as the center of preindustrial political and cultural
life and the source of the ideology and consciousness of the American
working class. Such an assumption underestimates the importance of
changes in the sexual division of labor within a craft of skilled male
artisans, such as the New England shoemakers in the late eighteenth
century. These artisans came to view women shoe workers as persons
in separate and immutable gender categories that defined both their
work and their relationship to the family and to artisan life. The artisan
tradition fostered the sexual division of labor and perpetuated the
preindustrial patterns of work and life that shaped the family wage
system of the nineteenth century. Gender categories made it difficult
for male artisans to regard women as fellow workers, include them in
the ideology and politics based on their work culture, or see in the
experience of working women what awaited all workers under industrialization. The failure of male artisans to perceive or accommodate
the interests of the women involved in shoe production weakened their
ability to resist the reorganization of work by early industrial capitalism.[2]

Women in eighteenth-century New England shoemaking families
were recruited to new work as a result of a shift in the control of profits
when markets expanded after 1780 and production increased. Before
this expansion, women had contributed as "helpmeets" to the family
economy in ways tied to their domestic duties: by boarding apprentices
and journeymen and by spinning flax into shoe thread. A cutoff of
British imports during the American Revolution stimulated efforts to
secure tariff protection and create new domestic markets. Merchants

2. For an overall discussion of the political and ideological implications of the sexual
division of labor in shoe production, see Mary H. Blewett, "Work, Gender and the
Artisan Tradition in New England Shoemaking, 1780–1860," *Journal of Social History* 17
(1983): 221–48. Similarly, Ava Baron has argued that the culture of printers contained
two communitarian traditions, one rooted in craft and the other in kinship. Kin and craft
communities were two separate sources of cultural values that influenced the development of class struggle and led to the development of contradictory strategies by printers
in dealing with women workers and capitalists ("Women and the Making of the American Working Class: A Study of the Proletarianization of Printers," *Review of Radical
Political Economics* 14 [1982]: 23–42).

began to supply capital in the form of raw materials (tanned leather) to workers in artisan shops and marketed the finished shoes in towns and cities along the Atlantic seaboard. Since merchant control over raw materials and access to markets meant merchant control of profits, artisan masters borrowed money if they could to purchase their own leather. Those shoemakers who owned no leather divided up the work among the men in their shops and augmented their own income by recruiting (unpaid) female members of their families to sew shoe uppers. Robert Gilman, traveling through Essex County in 1797, observed the early involvement of women in shoemaking work: "In our way to Salem we passed through a number of pretty little villages one of which, Lynn, is scarcely inhabited by any but shoemakers. . . . The women work also and we scarcely passed a house where the trade was not carried on."[3]

The male head of the shoemaking family assigned and controlled work on shoes in both the home and the shop. The merchant capitalists welcomed the new potential for production, but they paid no wages directly to women workers and did not supervise them. Direction of work remained in the hands of male artisans. Women simply added this new chore to their traditional household labor. The recruitment of women to shoe production was a carefully controlled assignment of work designed to fit women's role in family life and maintain gender relationships in the family, while preserving the artisan system as a training ground for the craft and part of the process of male gender formation. Apprentices continued to learn their craft as shoemakers and find their place in the gender hierarchy of the shoe shop by performing services and running errands for the master and journeymen. Women in shoemaking families were recruited to do only a small part of the work—the sewing of the upper part of the shoe—and not to learn the craft itself. They were barred from apprenticeships and group work and isolated from the center of artisan life: the shoe shop.[4]

The new work assigned to women in shoemaking families took on social connotations appropriate to female gender. "Shoebinding," a new word for this sexual division of labor, became a category of women's work in the early nineteenth century. The activity, combined with domestic chores and child care, took place in the kitchen. The shoemaker did not straddle a shoemaker's bench. She used a new tool, the shoe clamp, which rested on the floor and accommodated her long

---

3. George F. Dow, ed., *Two Centuries of Travel in Essex County* (Topsfield, Mass., 1921), 182; Dawley, *Class and Community*, 16–25.

4. For similar patterns, see Natalie Zemon Davis, "Women in the Crafts in Sixteenth-Century Lyon," *Feminist Studies* 8 (1982): 45–80.

skirt and apron while providing a flexible wooden holder for leather pieces. The binder held the clamp tightly between her knees, freeing her hands to use her awl and needle. The use of women expanded production, met the needs of both capitalist and artisan, and threatened no change in the traditional patterns of gender and craft formation. The sexual division of labor guaranteed the subordination of women by separating the work of shoebinding from additional knowledge of the craft and by maintaining separate workplaces for men and women. These patterns survived the transformation of shoe production into the factory system at midcentury and constituted a fundamental social dimension of industrial work.

As shoebinders worked in their kitchens, the demands of the artisan shop intruded upon and shaped their time. The binding of uppers by shoemakers' wives and daughters was essential to the timing and pace of the work of shoemakers. Women's work in the home combined both task labor (their domestic duties) and timed labor: the erratic but compelling need to keep all the men in the shoe shop supplied with sewn shoe uppers. One historian of shoework in nineteenth-century Lynn described the process:

> Then there would be a little delay, perhaps, until a shoe was bound, with which to start off the new lot. But generally, before the "jour" got his "stock" seasoned, one or two "uppers" were ready, and enough were usually bound ahead to keep all hands at work. And so, now and then, the order would be heard—"Come John, go and see if your mother has got a shoe bound: I'm all ready to last it."[5]

Shoebinders remained, however, socially and physically isolated from the group life of the shop. The collective nature of men's work in the artisan shop supported a militant tradition of resistance to the reorganization of production in early industrialization, but this tradition did not mirror the experience of women workers.

5. David Newhall Johnson, *Sketches of Lynn; or, The Changes of Fifty Years* (Lynn, Mass., 1880), 331. On timed and task work for women involved in preindustrial but not precapitalist work, see Lise Vogel, "The Contested Domain: A Note on the Family in the Transition to Capitalism," *Marxist Perspectives* 1 (1978): 63–67. Historians of the New England shoe industry have seen no implications for the artisan community or its ideology in the physical and social separation of the workplaces of men and women, although Paul Faler regarded the separation between the workplaces of the journeymen and the shoe boss in the central shop as the beginnings of class division (*Mechanics and Manufacturers*, 23, 27, 267). Reconstructed in the garden of the Essex Institute, Salem, are the Lye-Tapley shoe shop of Danvers and the seventeenth-century John Ward house. The kitchen of the latter is adjacent to the shop, allowing a historian to contemplate the dynamics between the two.

Binders in shoemaking families earned no wages before 1810 but simply contributed their labor to the family economy. However, the capacity of women to bind uppers for the shoe shop while also performing all kinds of domestic tasks had its limits. The domestic setting of shoebinding contradicted the increasing demands by merchant capitalists for production, but the recruitment of additional women outside the shoemaking family required some kind of a payment for their labor. After 1810, shoebinding, while still performed by hand in the home, gradually shifted to part-time outwork paid in goods (often in the new factory-made cotton textiles) and later in wages. Women's work on shoes came to be increasingly dissociated from the family labor system and done more and more by female workers outside of shoemaking families. As a result, the merchant capitalist or shoe boss assumed responsibility for hiring female workers, including those in shoemaking families, and directed their work from a central shop; his authority replaced that of shoemaking husbands and fathers.[6]

The shift in the coordination of the work process out of the hands of shoemakers and into the hands of the shoe boss represented a decline in the ability of male artisans to control their work. As shoebinding moved onto the wage labor market, its character as women's work without craft status kept wages low. These wages became part of the family wage, earnings pooled in the family's interests by its members. In New England shoemaking, the male artisan contributed the primary source of family income; it was supplemented by the much lower wages of shoebinders.

By the 1830s, shoebinders in Massachusetts outnumbered female operatives in cotton textile factories. Women shoe workers still combined sewing uppers with household tasks, a situation that continued to limit their productivity and to characterize their work as part time, intermittent, and poorly paid. In order to expand production, shoe bosses built networks of rural female outworkers in eastern Massachusetts and southern New Hampshire. This recruitment of rural New England women undercut the strikes against low wages that occurred among shoebinders in the early 1830s in the shoe towns of

---

6. Among the account books that illustrate the shift of shoebinders' work out of the family labor system are those at the Lynn Historical Society: Jonathan Boyce (1793–1813), John Burrell (1819–20), Unidentified Manufacturer's Stockbook (1830–31), and Untitled Ledger, Lynn (1790–1820), and those at the Old Sturbridge Village Archives: Samuel Bacheller Papers (1795–1845), vol. 2; James Coburn, Boxford (1804–21); Robert Brown, West Newburyport (1813–28); and Caleb Eames, Wilmington (1819–25). Alan Dawley regarded the head of the household as the coordinator of production in both kitchen and shop and offered no comment on the implications of the sexual division of labor (*Class and Community*, 16–20).

Essex County. The objective conditions of shoebinding—performed in isolation from group work and combined with domestic tasks—discouraged collective activity.[7]

Artisan shoemakers in Essex County burst into labor activity in the 1840s, organizing with other workers into workingmen's associations. They sought to include women in their activites but offered no way in which shoebinders as workers could associate themselves ideologically or strategically with the artisan protest societies. Rebellious shoemakers saw women as persons whose lives were defined primarily by family and morality. In 1844 the editor of *The Awl*, the newspaper of the Lynn Cordwainers' Society, cast women's support of labor protest in moral terms: "Thank heaven our movement is not a political one. If it were, it would not be warmed into life by the bright sunshine of woman's smiles, nor enriched by the priceless dower of her pure affections. But as it is strictly a moral enterprise, it opens to her willing heart a wide field of usefulness."[8] Oblivious of the implications of the domestic setting of shoebinding and offering no solutions for the problems that isolated outworkers faced in dealing with shoe bosses, artisan shoemakers received little support from shoebinders in the 1840s.

The expansion of markets in the developing West and the South created new demands for increased production in the early 1850s. The adaptation of the Singer sewing machine in 1852 to stitch light leather solved many of the problems of low productivity and coordination of production which characterized shoebinding as outwork. Capitalists had already centralized cutting and finishing operations in central shops, to which they added sewing machines run first by hand cranks or foot treadles and then by steam power in 1858. Because the Singer Company marketed its machines exclusively to garment manufacturers rather than immediately developing the market for home sewing machines, the initial unfamiliarity of Essex County women with the sewing

7. In 1837, 15,366 women worked as shoebinders, while 14,759 worked in cotton textile factories (Massachusetts, Secretary of the Commonwealth, *Statistical Information Relating to Certain Branches of Industry in Massachusetts for the Year Ending 1837* [Boston, 1837]). The shoebinders' societies were the "Reading, South Reading, Stoneham, Malden, Lynn and Woburn Society of Shoe Binders" in 1831 and the "Female Society of Lynn and Vicinity (Saugus) for the protection and promotion of Female Industry" in 1833–34 (Blewett, "Work, Gender and the Artisan Tradition," 225–29).

8. "Woman," *Awl*, 21 December 1844. Women shoe workers had already claimed a moral *and* political role for women in labor protest in the early 1830s. By 1845, 18,678 women in Massachusetts were working as shoebinders, compared with 14,407 in cotton textile factories; in 1855, 32,826 women worked on shoes and 22,850 in textile factories. Shoe work was part-time work performed in the home; textile work was full-time work in factories (Massachusetts, Secretary of the Commonwealth, *Statistics of the Condition and Production of Certain Branches of Industry in Massachusetts* [Boston, 1845, 1855]).

machine in the early 1850s provoked some organized resistance by shoebinders, who feared that machine operations would destroy their work:

> In 1853 . . . the first stitching machine was brought into [Haverhill]. A Mr. Pike was the first operator and so many people came from far and near to see how the great curiosity worked, that the firm was obliged to keep the factory doors locked. The women were fully excited as the men, and some of them shook their fists in Mr. Goodrich's face telling him that he was destroying their means of livelihood.[9]

Manufacturers, especially in Lynn, responded by training young women as stitchers on machines in central shops and leasing machines to women who chose to work at home. A new female factory work force was recruited from local families, but by 1860 sizable numbers of native-born, young, single New England women, once the source of industrial workers for the textile factories of the Merrimack Valley, were seeking employment in the shoe shops of eastern Massachusetts. As machine operators in steam-powered factories, they came under the direct control of their employers and the time discipline of industrial work. However, factory work offered women new opportunities for full-time employment, higher wages (three times those of home-workers) and group work, an experience that contrasted sharply with their situation as outworkers.

The mechanization of women's work and the productivity of factory stitchers changed the composition of the work force throughout the shoe industry. One factory girl working full time at her machine replaced eleven shoebinders. As a result, the number of women employed in shoe work decreased quickly in the 1850s. But higher productivity by women workers in factories stimulated the demand for additional male workers; by contemporary estimates, one sewing machine operator could supply enough work for twenty shoemakers. The new male recruits had little craft knowledge or artisan experience; they were rural migrants, Irish and German immigrants, and country shoemakers who resided in the villages and towns of eastern Massachusetts and southern New Hampshire. As a result, the sex ratio of men and women in the Lynn shoe industry sharply reversed in the 1850s from 63 percent females and 37 percent males in 1850 to 40 percent females and 60 percent males in 1860. Wages for female factory operatives rose by 41 percent between 1852 and 1860, but wages fell for female home-

---

9. Philip C. Swett, "History of Shoemaking in Haverhill, Massachusetts," manuscript, Haverhill Public Library, 16–17.

workers, unable to keep up with the productivity of centralized sewing machine operations. (Men's wages increased by only 10 percent and were severely cut during the depression of 1857.)[10] The mechanization of women's work intensified the hard conditions of all outworkers.

Intense competition among shoe manufacturers, the recruitment of large numbers of male outworkers, and the collapse of market demand for shoes in 1857 brought a crisis to the shoe industry of New England and precipitated in 1860 the largest demonstration of labor protest by American workers before the Civil War. The manufacturers blamed low wages on the laws of supply and demand, while male shoeworkers reasserted the moral and political values of the artisan tradition. The ideological emphasis on the brotherhood of the craft inherent in artisan culture prevented divisions between the new male recruits and more experienced shoemakers. The target of the strikers was the emerging factory system and the threat of mechanization and centralization to the preindustrial family wage system based on outwork. The new female factory workers seemed an alien group, while those who remained outside factory walls reaffirmed family, craft, and community values.

Significant divisions surfaced among shoe workers over the objectives of the 1860 strike in Lynn, the principal shoe town of Essex County.[11] Factory girls, realizing the power of their strategic location

10. Sex ratios and wage increases are based on the schedules for Lynn in the federal census of manufacture for 1850 and 1860 and on the statistics of industry for Massachusetts in 1855. Also see *Lynn Weekly Reporter*, 31 March, 16 and 21 April 1860; *Salem Observer*, 3 March 1860; *Marblehead Ledger*, 29 February 1860; *Tri-Weekly Publisher* (Haverhill), 3 and 10 March 1860; *New York Herald*, 22 March 1860; *Boston Journal* 28 February 1860. Helen L. Sumner noted the high productivity of the machine operators in relation to the shoemakers after the introduction of the sewing machine (*History of Women in Industry in the United States* [Washington, D.C., 1910], 172).

11. The regional shoe strike in 1860 has had attention from labor historians, but the role of women in the strike has had little systematic analysis. The most detailed account is in Philip S. Foner, *Women and the American Labor Movement: From Colonial Times to the Eve of World War I* (New York, 1979), 90–97. Foner emphasizes the heroic and exemplary aspects of the strike, especially the women's militancy and the unity between working-class men and women, but he dismisses the dissension over strike objectives as "some discussion." Overreliance by other historians on the labor press in Lynn, especially the pro-strike *Bay State*, resulted in their missing the debate over women's roles in the strike as workers and as family members (Dawley, *Class and Community*, 79–90; Faler, *Mechanics and Manufacturers*, chap. 11; Norman Ware, *The Industrial Worker, 1840–1860* [Chicago, 1964], 47; John B. Andrews and W. D. P. Bliss, *History of Women in Trade Unions* [Washington, D.C., 1911], 108). The evidence in the Boston and New York newspapers whose editors sent reporters to Lynn to cover the events as eyewitnesses reveals the conflict during the four women's meetings. See the accounts from 28 February to 6 March 1860, in *Boston Herald, New York Times, New York Herald, Boston Post, Boston Journal,* and *Boston Advertiser.*

as machine operators in centralized production, sought increases in wages for all women workers. Their productivity on steam-powered machinery was the key to shutting down the largest manufacturers in Lynn and preventing them from sending machine-sewn uppers and leather stock by express teams to country shoemakers. This tactic powerfully aided the cause of the shoemakers' regional strike. Identifying themselves with female homeworkers, the factory girls proposed a coalition to raise wages for both categories of women's work: homework and factory work. Many of the factory girls lived as boarders in the households of Lynn families but had relatively little connection with the community or its artisan culture. Their leader, twenty-one-year-old Clara H. Brown of Medford, Massachusetts, boarded with another factory stitcher in the household of a Lynn shoemaker. However, living with a young shoemaker and his wife and infant son did not deter Clara Brown from speaking for the interests of the factory girls, and it may have inspired her vision of an alliance of women working at home and in the factory.

The factory girls insisted that their proposed coalition represented the interests of *all* women workers in Lynn. They were in effect proposing an alternative to the family wage as the objective of the strike. An alliance based on gender would protect working women wherever the location of their work or whatever their marital status, and would offer homeworkers a vital and powerful link with female workers in the new factories. For example, the wage demands voted by the women strikers in 1860 included prices for homework high enough to offset the customary costs to homeworkers of furnishing their own thread and lining material, a practice that cut earnings. In return, the factory girls could anticipate that when they married, they too could do shoe work at home for decent wages. They also tried to organize machine stitchers in the shoe factories of other towns. For these new industrial workers, it was just as important to increase women's wages as it was to increase men's wages during the strike. Their support of female homeworkers offered a bridge between preindustrial patterns of work for women and the factory system. Three times during the early meetings held by home and factory workers, the majority of striking women voted for the gender alliance.

Some female homeworkers, however, identified their interests with the men of the Lynn strike committee, who sought to protect the preindustrial family wage system and decentralized work. Shoemakers, who controlled the strike committees in each New England town, sought—as they had in the 1840s—to organize women's support for the strike on the basis of female moral stature and loyalty to family interests. In addition, the men's strike committee in Lynn insisted that wage increases for men were primary. Male workers opposed efforts to raise wages for women, fearing that an increase in the wages of female factory workers might promote a centralization of all stitching operations and thereby entirely eliminate women's work in the home and its supplemental earnings. For striking shoemakers and their allies among the female homeworkers, the best protection for the family wage lay in obtaining higher wages for men's work while defending homework for women. Implicit in their defense of the family wage was the subordinated role of women's contribution to family income.

The shoemakers of Lynn and their female allies seized control of the women's strike meetings and ended the emerging coalition of women shoeworkers. They ignored the votes at the women's strike meetings, substituted a wage proposal written by homeworkers, and circulated this altered wage list in Lynn for the signatures of strikers. The factory girls confronted the betrayal of their leadership at a tumultuous meeting on March 2, 1860. Above the uproar, Clara Brown angrily demanded to know who had dared to change the women's strike objectives. During the long debate, disgruntled homeworkers characterized the factory operatives as "smart girls," motivated by selfish individualism and the desire for lavish dress, an urge "to switch a long-tailed skirt."[12] In vain, Clara Brown tried to rally the supporters of the women's alliance. She emphasized the power of the machine operatives, who as industrial workers could obtain higher wages for all women workers: "For God's sake, don't act like a pack of fools. We've got the bosses where we can do as we please with 'em. If we won't work our machines, and the out-ot-town girls won't take the work, what can the bosses do?"[13] The issue had become a test of loyalty: to the family wage or to the possibility of an alliance among female workers. Swayed by pressure from the leaders and supporters of the men's strike committee and their arguments for the family wage, the majority of women strikers at the March 2 meeting reversed themselves, voted against the factory girls, and agreed to march with the male strikers in a gaint procession through the streets of Lynn on March 7. One of the banners carried by the striking women indicated their acceptance of moral and family values as primary to their role in labor protest: "Weak in physical strength but strong in moral courage, we dare to battle for the

12. *New York Times*, 6 March 1860.
13. *New York Times*, 6 March 1860. For a detailed analysis of the strike, see chap. 5 in Mary H. Blewett, *Men, Women, and Work: A Study of Class, Gender, and Protest in the Nineteenth-Century New England Shoe Industry* (Urbana, Ill., forthcoming).

right, shoulder to shoulder with our fathers, husbands and brothers."[14]

The well-known sketches of women's participation in the Lynn strike of 1860 which appeared in *Frank Leslie's Illustrated Newspaper* depict the triumph of the artisan cause and the family wage but obscure the conflict among the women shoeworkers. The factory girls dropped out of the strike, which went on another two months but ended without a resolution of the wage issue.

The Lynn shoe workers in 1860 had failed to see the strategic potential for labor protest of female factory workers, ignored and opposed their articulated interests, and refused to recognize the implications for women of the mechanization and centralization of their work. The artisans of Lynn and their female allies fought in the 1860 strike to defend the traditions and ideology of preindustrial culture and decentralized production for men and women. This strategy cut off the new female factory work force from contributing to labor protest. The failure of the alliance among women shoe workers meant a continuation of the family wage system in which women workers were subordinated to male wage earners and divided from each other by marital status and the location of their work. The perceptions that shoemakers had developed of work and gender in the early nineteenth century made it difficult for them to regard women as fellow workers outside of family relationships, to include them as equals in the ideology and politics built on artisan life, or to represent the interests of female factory workers. The experiences of these women workers in centralized production symbolized what awaited all workers as capitalism in the New England shoe industry moved toward the factory system.

While male artisans defended their craft and its traditions between 1780 and 1860, women workers experienced the cutting edge of change in the reorganization of production: a sexual division of labor that denied women craft status; the separation of women's work from the family labor system; the loss of control over the coordination of work by artisans; the development of the family wage system; the isolation and vulnerability of the individual shoebinder in the outwork system; and the mechanization and centralization of work. The submer-

14. *Bay State* (Lynn), 8 March 1860. Marxist feminists have debated whether the family wage served the interests of patriarchy or served the ability of working-class families to resist exploitation by employers. See Heidi Hartmann, "The Unhappy Marriage of Marxism and Feminism: Towards a More Progressive Union," *Capital and Class* 8 (1979): 1–43; and Jane Humphries, "Class Struggle and the Persistence of the Working-Class Family," *Cambridge Journal of Economics* 1 (1979): 241–58. The two models appear to have operated in conflict during the Lynn strike in 1860.

sion of women's work experience within artisan culture in the new labor history has obscured the penetration of home life and household production by early industrial capitalism and has sustained the illusion of the home as a refuge from the marketplace. Artisan culture prevented men from perceiving the circumstances and accommodating the interests of women as workers, and thus weakened their ability to challenge the reorganization of production in early industrialization. The patriarchal ideology of artisan culture and the sex structuring of labor in the New England shoe industry worked together to prevent women workers from contributing to the most vital tradition of collective protest among the workers of early nineteenth-century New England.

3

Beyond Conventional Wisdom: Women's Wage Work, Household Economic Contribution, and Labor Activism in a Mid-Nineteenth-Century Working-Class Community

Carole Turbin

Recent studies of women's labor organizing have developed new perspectives on a problem that has been an important focus for analyzing women's labor activity: why did a smaller proportion of women form sustained organizations than men? In the past this question has been answered through an analysis showing links between family and work life which resulted in obstacles to women's organization. This perspective sheds light on only part of the picture, neglecting ways in which family life and relationships may encourage women's activism, organization, and consciousness. Changing the question illuminates the neglected dimension: in view of the barriers to permanent organization

I thank Houghton Mifflin Company for permission to use material from my essay "And We Are Nothing but Women: Irish Working Women in Troy," in *Women in America: A History*, ed. Carol R. Berkin and Mary Beth Norton (1979), and the *Review of Radical Political Economics* for permitting me to use material from my essay "Reconceptualizing Family, Work, and Labor Organizing: Working Women in Troy, 1860–1890," which appeared in vol. 16 (Spring 1984). The National Endowment for the Humanities, the Research Foundation of the State University of New York, and the Empire State College Foundation provided generous funding. Special thanks also to Ava Baron, Mary Blewett, Laura Anker Schwartz, Harold Benenson, Wilbur R. Miller, Michael Schwartz, Alice Kessler-Harris, William H. Sewell, Jr., and the collective and individual contributions of the Women and Work reserach group (Chris Bose, Carol Brown, Peggy Crull, Roslyn Feldberg, Nadine Felton, Myra Marx Ferree, Evelyn Nakano Glenn, Amy Kesselman, Susan Lehrer, Natalie Sokoloff, and Amy Gilman Srebnick).

for women, under what conditions were some women able to form relatively successful and permanent unions, develop an awareness of shared interests, and form strong alliances with male workers?[1] Answers to this question reveal a new dimension: the interrelationship of work and family life has an important bearing on labor activism.[2]

Studies that focus on family roles as obstacles to organization mask important aspects of women's work experience and family life, partly because they tend to view women as a homogeneous group at the lowest levels of the working class. Assuming that female wage earners were young single women who worked temporarily before marriage at least-paid, unskilled occupations, these studies argue that most women were as uncommitted to their work as they were to labor organizations.[3] While this description does fit an important group of working women, it is not the whole picture; overgeneralizing from this group results in stark contrasts between women and men and in conceptual frameworks that are simple dichotomies: "women's work is temporary and men's work is permanent," for example, or "women can be understood in terms of family roles and men can be analyzed in terms of their work experience."[4]

1. A few studies explore conditions under which women organized successfully. See Louise Tilly, "Paths of Proletarianization: Organization of Production, Sexual Division of Labor and Women's Collective Action," *Signs* 7 (1981): 400–417; and Sharon Strom, "Challenging 'Woman's Place': Feminism, the Left and Industrial Unionism in the 1930's," *Feminist Studies* 9 (1983): 359–86.

2. An earlier version of this and other arguments made in this paper appears in Carole Turbin, "Reconceptualizing Family, Work, and Labor Organizing: Working Women in Troy, 1860–1890," *Review of Radical Political Economics* 16 (1984): 1–16.

3. Analyses of why women were less likely to organize than men are important for understanding women's labor activism. See Alice Kessler-Harris, "Stratifying by Sex: Understanding the History of Working Women," in *Labor Market Segmentation*, ed. Richard C. Edwards, Michael Reich, David M. Gordon (Lexington, Mass., 1975), and "Where Are the Organized Women Workers?" in *A Heritage of Her Own: Toward a New Social History of American Women*, ed. Nancy F. Cott and Elizabeth H. Pleck (New York, 1979); Meredith Tax, *The Rising of the Women: Feminist Solidarity and Class Conflict, 1880–1917* (New York, 1980). However, barriers to women's organizing are often presented as a framework rather than part of the picture. For studies stressing factors that militate against women's sustained collective action, see Susan Estabrook Kennedy, *If All We Did Was to Weep at Home: A History of White Working Class Women in America* (Bloomington, Ind., 1979); and Leslie Woodcock Tentler, *Wage-Earning Women: Industrial Work and Family Life in the United States, 1900–1930* (New York, 1979). Studies of working-class communities discuss women's labor activism as well as barriers to organization but do not systematically examine specific conditions under which women organized successfully; see, e.g., Daniel J. Walkowitz, *Worker City Company Town* (Urbana, Ill., 1978); and Alan Dawley, *Class and Community: The Industrial Revolution in Lynn* (Cambridge, Mass., 1983).

4. The argument that the literature on the sociology of work reserves analyses of work for the study of men and those of family life for the study of women is made by Roslyn Feldberg and Evelyn Nakano Glenn, "Male and Female: Job versus Gender Models in the Sociology of Work," *Social Problems* 26 (1979): 524–38.

The exploration of differences between women and men is central to analyses of workers, but dichotomies are an inadequate framework for analyzing differences.[5] Reflecting conventional wisdom about women's work and activism, oppositional categories mask both sharp and subtle distinctions between women of different backgrounds and in different settings and occupations, and gloss over apparent contradictions and conflicting evidence. A more fruitful approach examines the significance of important exceptions and minorities that have been ignored because they were considered unrepresentative. These exceptions include women who may have identified with their occupations and women who expected to remain in the labor force continually.

Since oppositional constructs regarding gender have two sides, deconstructing dichotomies leads not only to reconceptualizing women's work and activism within a social context but also to rethinking conceptual frameworks about men and reexamining larger social reality. The results are new analyses of central issues that in the past were examined on the basis of men's experiences.[6] For example, the argument that focusing on family roles as an obstacle to labor militancy and organization overemphasizes the conservative influence of family roles on women's lives has implications for understanding the impact of family ties and relationships on men's activism and the activism of an entire community. Avoiding the characterization of women's work as temporary and of men's as permanent not only results in reconceptualizations of women's work as intermittent or interrupted but also leads to questioning the assumption that men's work was permanent in the sense of being continuous and uninterrupted throughout their adult lives. The view that working women in some communities were a permanent part of the labor force as a group (although not all individuals were employed at a given time) contributes to reanalyses of Marxist theories that view the workplace as the locus of the development of class consciousness.[7] Similarly, avoiding the characterization of women workers

5. Critiques of analyses of gender differences based on dualisms and dichotomous constructs are central to contemporary feminist theory. See, e.g., Nancy Hartsock, *Money, Sex, and Power: Toward a Feminist Historical Materialism* (New York, 1983); Catherine A. Mackinnon, "Feminism, Marxism, Method, and the State: An Agenda for Theory," *Signs* 7 (1982): 515–44; and Alice Kessler-Harris, "The Debate over Equality for Women in the Workplace: Recognizing Differences," in *Women and Work: An Annual Review*, vol. 1, ed. Laurie Larwood et al. (Beverly Hills, Calif., 1985), 141–61.

6. For a discussion of the importance of examining the implications of analyses of women for men and larger social reality, see Mary Blewett, *Men, Women, and Work: A Study in Class, Gender, and Protest in the Nineteenth-Century New England Shoe Industry* (Urbana, Ill., forthcoming).

7. Sheila Rowbotham, "The Trouble with Patriarchy," in *People's History and Socialist Theory*, ed. Raphael Samuel (London, 1981); John Foster, *Class Struggle and the Industrial Revolution: Early Industrial Capitalism in Three English Towns* (New York, 1974); Pauline

as passive and men as active corrects labor historians' tendency to emphasize male workers' resistance and to ignore ways in which working men acquiesced to employers' demands and strategies.

Constructing new conceptual frameworks that take into account distinctions and contradictions reveals subtle differences between women's and men's experiences and perceptions of the same activity, and complex connections between spheres of activity (such as family, work, and community) that are important to women and men in different ways and for different reasons. Since rethinking the analyses of women that were based on conventional wisdom leads to a reexamination of conceptualizations drawn from men's experiences and perceptions of reality, reconceptualizations about women have implications for the development of new interpretations in labor history. The following analysis of the working-class women of Troy, New York, is another step in that direction.[8]

A look at the employment patterns of working women and the impact of this employment on their lives suggests a more complex relationship between women's family and work lives than conventional wisdom assumes.[9] At first glance, statistics on Troy's collar workers support the conventional view that most nineteenth-century working

---

Hunt, *Gender and Class Consciousness* (New York, 1980); Tax, *The Rising of the Women;* Harold Benenson, "Skill Degradation, Industrial Change, and the Family and Community Bases of U.S. Working Class Response," paper presented at the Social Science History Association, Bloomington, Indiana, 1982.

8. The analysis of Troy in the 1860s and 1880s is based on Carole Turbin, "'And We Are Nothing but Women': Irish Working Women in Troy," in *Women of America: A History,* ed. Carol R. Berkin and Mary Beth Norton (Boston, 1979), and Turbin, "Reconceptualizing." Collar manufacturing is described in Horace Greeley et al., *Great Industries of the United States* (Hartford, Conn., 1873). Population statistics (drawn from 1865 New York state manuscript census schedules and 1870 federal manuscript census schedules) are more fully discussed in Carole Turbin, "Woman's Work and Woman's Rights: A Comparative Study of Women's Trade Unions and the Women's Rights Movement in the Mid-19th Century" (Ph.D. diss., New School for Social Research, 1978), chap. 5.

9. The popular view that most women wage earners were young single girls who did not depend on their income and held jobs for only a few years before marriage was first modified by studies demonstrating that most working-class families depended on women's income. Arguing that workers must be understood as members of families as well as individual wage earners, these studies examined the culture and economy of female wage earners' households. See Carol Groneman, "'She Earns as a Child, She Pays as a Man': Women Workers in a Mid-19th Century New York Community," in *Class, Sex, and the Woman Worker,* ed. Milton Cantor and Bruce Laurie (Westport, Conn., 1977). This argument is taken a step further in Mary Blewett, *We Will Rise in Our Might: The Consciousness and Protest of Nineteenth-Century Women Shoe Workers* (Urbana, Ill., forthcoming). Blewett points out that an analysis based largely on marital status and age is inadequate for understanding women's economic contribution. Focusing on women's dependence, it ignores women who supported themselves or provided for others.

women were young single girls who supplemented their families' income. Troy's highly specialized economy was dominated by two major industries: collar manufacturing and the iron industry. Both employed a significant proportion of Troy's large Irish working-class population. In 1880 most of the women in selected wards who stitched or washed, starched, and ironed detachable collars in Troy's collar factories were young and unmarried: 87.6 percent were single, 8.5 percent were widowed or separated, and 3.9 percent were wives. The average never-married collar worker was young (twenty-one) compared with the average wife (thirty-two), widow (forty-one), and separated woman (thirty-three).[10]

A closer look at working women's households reveals that analysis of age and marital status is inadequate for understanding women's economic contribution to their families. It is especially misleading in regard to never-married women, whose living arrangements were considerably more varied than conventional wisdom assumes. A more complex picture emerges when single women are analyzed in the context of the composition of their households and the sex and marital status of the household's head. Of the 87 percent who never married, a significant minority (18 percent) were over twenty-five years of age.[11] Employed daughters of all ages living with their parents were a large proportion of never-married women but not a majority. Of the 60.2 percent of single women who lived in households headed by a male whose wife was present, 11 percent were boarders who are likely to have been self-supporting. As one would expect, the average single boarder was somewhat older (twenty-four) than the average daughter living with parents (twenty). Since only 49 percent of single women were daughters of the household's head (another 2.6 percent of single women lived in households headed by a widower), only about half the unmarried collar women can be described as young single girls who were likely to be supplementing their fathers' income.

10. Percentages are based on analysis of computerized individual and household data for 745 collar women who lived in districts 129 (Ward 1), 130 (Ward 2), 145 (Ward 10), and 146 (Ward 11) of nineteenth-century Troy. Representing the total number of collar women in these districts in the 1880 manuscript census, these cases were selected for preliminary analysis out of the population of approximately 3,000 collar women because they resided in districts located in key and widely dispersed sections of the city in which collar women were a high proportion of industrially employed women. Analysis of this subpopulation is useful because it consists of individuals who lived in neighborhoods which were in themselves relatively homogeneous although they represented diverse sections of the city.

11. The average age of single women workers is low partly because a relatively large proportion (45.1 percent) were between the ages of ten and nineteen.

Analysis of single women who did not live in a household headed by a male whose wife was present underlines the importance of distinguishing between the economic contribution of never-married women in different types of households. A small but significant group (8 percent) resided with siblings, other relatives of about the same age, or unrelated individuals with whom they probably shared resources and housing costs. Like women who boarded, they were most likely self-supporting. Rarely systematically analyzed, this group represents an important variation in nineteenth-century working women's living arrangements.

The 28 percent of never-married women who lived in households headed by a widow have also rarely been analyzed as a distinct segment of the female working population. Although data on household composition and the occupations of male and female wage earners are not precise, evidence suggests that daughters in this type of household provided a substantial proportion of the family income. Daughters' contribution varied because they may have shared the responsibility of supporting brothers, sisters, and/or a widowed mother. Since it was more typical for widows not to be employed if their older children earned wages, it is more likely that daughters shared the providing responsibility with a sister and/or brother rather than with a widowed mother. In families where women were the only wage earners, employed daughters must have provided a substantial proportion of the family income, even if they shared the responsibility with another female wage earner. Given the wage differential for women and men, if one or more brothers were also employed, a daughter's contribution was probably less significant. Nevertheless, since young men's income was likely to be lower than that of older, more experienced men, the income of daughters who shared the responsibility of providing with brothers was probably essential for their family's well-being.[12] While daughters with a sister or brother who also earned wages did not have the same responsibility as widows who supported themselves and dependents, their economic contribution was more important than that of daughters living with parents. This is not to imply that daughters' contribution to fathers' income was unnecessary but to distinguish pre-

12. Mothers who managed the household economy may have valued daughters' economic contributions because their income was more predictable than that of sons. Although sons' earnings were likely to be greater, daughters contributed a larger portion of their wages and were less likely to leave the household for work in other communities or to live on their own. See Laura Anker Schwartz, "Immigrant Voices from Work, Home and Community: The Connecticut WPA Ethnic Survey" (Ph.D. diss., State University of New York, Stony Brook, 1983).

cisely between different types of contributions of never-married women: daughters who supplemented their fathers' earnings; single women who were self-supporting; and daughers who shared the responsibility of providing with a relative whose income was also comparatively low.

Returning to the total population of collar women, let us look at women's age and marital status as well as the household's composition and the head's sex and marital status. Among Troy's collar workers, daughters living with parents were the largest single group (46.9 percent) and constituted roughly half of the female working population. But even combined with the other 3.4 percent of collar women who were in similar circumstances (wives or widows living in households headed by a male wage earner), women who contributed to a male household head's earnings were 50.3 percent of the total—barely a majority. The next largest group (22.9 percent, or a little over one-fifth) were never-married women who provided for dependents or shared the responsibility of supporting family members with brothers or other female wage earners. An important minority consisted of single and widowed women who boarded (10.5 percent of the total) or self-supporting single women (6 percent) who shared lodgings with siblings or unrelated individuals. Another minority (6.3 percent) consisted of widows whose households were not headed by a male wage earner. Shifting the focus away from the age and marital status of individual women, this analysis avoids categorizing women mainly in terms of their dependence on male wage earners' income. Analysis of women's dependence is essential to understanding women's sbordination in the family, but relationships of dominance and suboination may include an interdependent relationship between family members of different ages and sexes. Working women were not only daughters, wives, and widows but also self-supporting individuals or contributors or providers in households of different composition and, as we shall see, in different settings.

Women's employment patterns also highlight women's providing role and challenge popular assumptions about the temporary character of women's work. Although women's work patterns differed from men's in part because their life cycle was different, the view that women's work was temporary while men's was permanent masks the complexities of the experience of both sexes. Many daughters who entered the labor force when they reached a suitable age had more than a few years of work ahead of them.[13] Sometimes families encouraged

13. E.g., one unmarried collar laundress aged twenty-five in 1860 was still working in the laundries in 1870, when she was thirty-six. The youngest working women in the

daughters to postpone marriage in order to contribute to the family's income. The fact that never-married collar women living in households headed by a widowed mother were considerably older than those living with both parents indicates that this was often the case in households not headed by a male wage earner.[14] Demographic factors as well as families' need for income explain the percentage of women who remained in the labor force because they married late or not at all (which was probably higher than contemporary popular reports lead us to believe). More than a few women could expect not to marry, since the relative proportion of women to men increased in the early nineteenth century, partly becuase of the westward migration of single men. Civil War casualties added to the imbalance in the sex ratio.[15] This imbalance was particularly high in Irish communities, partly because many Irish women immigrated without their families, traveling alone or with single female relatives.[16]

Women who did marry did not necessarily leave the providing role behind them. Evidence suggests that many women held jobs at several different stages of their lives. Some who married continued to earn money through work at home, some by taking in boarders, some by

---

census were fourteen, but children often left school after age twelve. Leaving school is discussed in Walkowitz, *Worker City,* and Carl F. Kaestle and Maris A. Vinovskis, "From Fireside to Factory: School Entry and School Leaving in Nineteenth-Century Massachusetts," in *Transitions: The Family and the Life Course in Historical Perspective,* ed. Tamara Hareven (New York, 1978).

14. Of single collar women between the ages of ten and nineteen who were not boarders, 70.8 percent lived with parents, compared with 24 percent whose household head was a widow. The relationship between the ages of the two groups shifts for older women. Of single women between twenty and twenty-nine, 60.6 percent lived with parents and 31 percent with a widowed mother. Among those who were over thirty, 33 percent lived with parents and 40.4 percent with a widowed mother.

15. The high proportion of women and relatively large number of single women and widows have been reported for areas throughout the Northeast, including Massachusetts and New York state. See Mary Blewett, "Work, Gender, and the Artisan Tradition in New England Shoe Making, 1780–1860," *Journal of Social History* 17 (1983): 221–48; Mary Ryan, *Cradle of the Middle Class: The Family in Oneida County, New York, 1790–1805* (Cambridge, 1981); and Alice Kessler-Harris, *Out to Work: A History of Wage-Earning Women in the United States* (New York, 1982).

16. For a discussion of Irish women in the U.S., see Hasia Diner, *Erin's Daughters in America: Irish Immigrant Women in the Nineteenth Century* (Baltimore, Md., 1983). Diner notes that although more couples with children than single women emigrated during and following the famine, significant numbers of single women traveled alone during those years. Irish women and men were more willing to remain single, in part because of traditions, inheritance patterns, and their families' household economy in Ireland, although in the U.S. they married more often and earlier. The proportion of men in Irish communities was reduced further by male occupational patterns. Irish men often found employment away from cities on canals and railroads and in difficult and dangerous occupations with high rates of fatal accidents.

assisting their husbands in their trades.[17] The percentage of women who were widows or separated in this period indicates that some returned to the work force at a later stage in life; even women who had not worked before or during marriage might have to find employment if their husbands died or left them. Preliminary analysis of census manuscripts for Troy supports these conclusions. Some collar women were employed for a good part of their lives; others worked at one time or another, or during several stages of their lives, inside or outside their homes.[18] Women's employment patterns differed from men's in that most women were not employed continually throughout their adult lives, but the term "temporary" is an inadequate description of women's work because it implies that work was a fleeting experience at only one period of women's lives. Since working-class women's employment was not necessarily limited to a few years before marriage, and in any case did not have a merely transient effect on their lives, women's work patterns can be more accurately described as interrupted or intermittent.[19]

17. Women in traditional occupations were often undocumented because their work was congruent with the view that women should not work outside the home. For a discussion of this, see Sally Alexander, "Women's Work in Nineteenth Century London: A Study of the Years 1820–1850," in *The Rights and Wrongs of Women*, ed. Juliet Mitchell and Ann Oakley (Harmondsworth, 1976), and Christine Bose, "Household Resources and U.S. Women's Work: Factors Affecting Gainful Employment at the Turn of the Century," *American Sociological Review* 49 (1984): 474–90. Recent studies of homework in urban and rural settings demonstrate that when these women's occupations are taken into account, the picture of women's work changes considerably. See, e.g., Clyde Griffen, *Natives and Newcomers: The Ordering of Opportunity in Mid-19th Century Poughkeepsie* (Cambridge, Mass., 1978). Griffen notes that the inclusion of women who took in boarders increases Poughkeepsie's rate of employment for married women from 4 percent or less to 10–14 percent for all ethnic groups. Recent studies of outwork in rural New England reveal that mill girls were not typical of the region's employed women; in many areas homework employed more women than the textile mills. See Mary Blewett, "Shared but Different: The Experience of Women Shoe Workers in the 19th Century Work Force of the New England Shoe Industry," in *Essays from the Lowell Conference on Industrial History, 1980 and 1981* (Lowell, Mass., 1981); and Thomas Dublin, "Women and the Dimension of Outwork in Nineteenth-Century New England," paper presented at the Berkshire Conference on the History of Women, Poughkeepsie, N.Y., 1981. Homework was important in Troy's specialized economy, since large numbers of married and single women of all ages were employed in the same industry. For descriptions of Troy's industries, see Arthur James Weise, *The City of Troy and Vicinity* (Troy, N.Y., 1886); and Greeley et al., *Great Industries*.

18. These data are more fully discussed in Turbin, "Women's Work," and "And We Are Nothing but Women."

19. For the argument that temporary labor force participation could permanently affect working women's lives, see Schwartz, "Immigrant Voices", and Sarah Eisenstein, *Give Us Bread but Give Us Roses: Working Women's Consciousness in the United States, 1890 to the First World War* (London, 1983). Eisenstein suggests that even transient work experience could change attitudes toward personal autonomy and marriage.

Evidence suggests networks of women employed in the collar laundries and, in later decades, in the collar industry as a whole. Collar work seems to have been a tradition in some families, partly because collar laundry work was especially attractive to Irish working-class women, who had less access to more ladylike occupations than women of native parentage. Although working conditions were far from genteel, collar laundering offered higher wages and more security than most other women's occupations.[20] Collar ironing required expertise and physical dexterity, which gave ironers the kind of pride in their work usually associated with skilled men.[21] There were other opportunities for work in Troy, but collar laundering in the 1860s and 1870s, and collar work in general in the 1880s, was a good niche in the occupational structure for women of Irish descent.[22] Just as sons often entered the same occupations as their fathers or older brothers, daughters of Troy's collar women followed female relatives into the same occupation, often working side by side in the same shop.[23]

Moreover, family members who worked at one time or another in the same industry were also part of larger networks in the city's Irish working-class community.[24] Since workers depended on friends, rela-

20. Frequent comments by laundry proprietors that good ironers were scarce and commanded high wages are found in Virginia Penny, *The Employments of Women* (Boston, 1863).

21. The complexities of women's skill are discussed in Diane Elson and Ruth Pearson, "'Nimble Fingers Make Cheaper Workers': An Analysis of Women's Employment in Third World Manufacturing," *Feminist Review* 7 (1981): 93–95. Also see Ann Phillips and Barbara Taylor, "Sex and Skill: Notes toward a Feminist Economics," *Feminist Review* 6 (1981): 79–88; and Margo Anderson Conk, *The U.S. Census and Labor Force Change: A History of Occupation Statistics* (Ann Arbor, Mich., 1980).

An incident in 1868 reveals that collar laundresses shared characteristics with skilled men that enabled them to bargain effectively with employers. Having given in to employees' demands for wage increases since 1864, laundry proprietors tried to undermine the union in 1868 by persuading nonunion ironers in the city's largest laundry to train new hands to replace workers in union shops. This tactic would not have been necessary if owners could have simply fired the union ironers and replaced them with new hands. In an interview published in the *New York Sun*, 18 September 1868, Kate Mullaney, the laundresses' president, reported that the employers' tactics failed because the nonunion ironers, "seeing what the results would finally be, for their own protection, joined the union in a body." The owners' need for experienced labor enabled the ironers to strengthen the union. For a fuller description of this episode, see Turbin, "And We Are Nothing but Women."

22. Personal communication with individuals whose relatives worked in Troy's shirt and collar industry in the early twentieth century suggests that this pattern continued until the industry's decline.

23. Women family members were often employed by the same company, with grandmothers, mothers, and daughters working in the same room in a shop. See Rutherford Hayner, *Troy and Rensselaer County, New York* (New York, 1925).

24. This discussion of Troy's closely knit Irish working-class community is drawn from Walkowitz, *Worker City.*

tives, and neighbors for job information, women's networks must have included nonkin as well as sisters-in-law, aunts, and other female relatives. Contacts at work influenced ethnic, community, and family ties and vice versa.[25] Family financial needs, the expectation among working-class families that women would contribute to the family income, and the fact that the collar industry provided relatively stable employment for Irish women combined to make the social group from which collar workers were drawn a permanent part of the labor force.

There are good reasons to conclude that women who formed a segment of the labor force perceived themselves as part of this group. The existence of networks of female friends, relatives, and neighbors suggests that individual women knew others with the same or similar work histories. Since one industry employed large numbers of women at different stage of life, females from the same household or neighborhood were probably working for wages in the collar laundries at any given time, and others had worked there in the past or expected to be employed there in the future. Moreover, the fact that the activism of collar laundresses mobilized most of the workers in the industry and was sustained over long periods of time, rather than being tied to particular labor struggles, indicates that group awareness was continuous and not limited to sporadic periods.[26] A combination of close family ties and shared experiences as workers and activists suggests that collar women were conscious of shared interests as workers.

These exceptional settings have some important implications for understanding working-class women's activism. Women's work was not uniformly unskilled, low paid, and temporary; many women sup-

25. Many studies document this pattern. See Thomas Dublin, *Women at Work: The Transformation of Work and Community in Lowell, Massachusetts, 1826–1860* (New York, 1979); Tamara Hareven, "Family Time and Industrial Time: Family and Work in a Planned Corporation Town, 1900–1924," in *Family and Kin in Urban Communities, 1700–1920*, ed. Tamara Hareven (New York, 1977); Anthony Wallace, *Rockdale: The Growth of an American Village in the Early Industrial Revolution* (New York, 1978); John T. Cumbler, *Working Class Community in Industrial America: Work, Leisure, and Struggle in Two Industrial Cities, 1880–1930* (Westport, Conn., 1979).

26. At first glance the laundresses' union seems to fit the pattern of ephemeral organizations: it did not persist in one form over several decades (as did many men's unions), and the laundresses were the only organized branch until the Joan of Arc Assembly was formed in 1885. Although after the laundry union's demise in 1870, labor activity seems to have been tied to specific conflicts, protests were not isolated events but the collective action of workers with an ongoing commitment to unions and working-class interests. Strikes were sustained for several weeks or months, mobilized most workers in the industry, and were closely tied to permanent labor organizations in the community and region. Collective action was carefully coordinated and widely publicized in the labor press, and was organized around issues central to workers' right to organize and participate in decisions about wages and conditions. For further discussion, see Turbin, "And We Are Nothing but Women" and "Woman's Work."

ported themselves and/or dependents, or provided an important part of their families' income.[27] Some nineteenth-century women's occupations required expertise and physical capacities that resulted in identification with work and a commitment that encouraged continuity of employment for both individuals and families.[28] Also, characteristics that fostered activism among male workers, such as level of skill and earnings, were not the only reasons for workers' militancy. While the shared experience of continuous wage work and conflicts with employers is important, women who were not continually employed or who never entered the labor force did not necessarily lack awareness of shared group interests. Participation in networks of friends and family members who worked at one time or another in the same occupation and shared similar ethnic identity, perceptions, and experience encouraged activism among women who were not continually employed. The fact that employment had a different place in women's lives than in men's did not mean that its effect was transitory.

These observations about women's participation in the labor force suggest a new analysis of women's labor activism. Labor historians have observed that women's labor activism differed from men's: although women were more difficult to organize, once organized—and in specific labor conflicts—they were often much more militant than men.[29] Analysis of women's unions suggests that underlying this apparent contradiction are differences in the motivation and consciousness of women from different household economies and different stages of life.[30] Two types of activists are explored here: leaders in day-to-day union operations who formed the core of participants in labor struggles, and those who were active only in specific conflicts. Analysis of the household economy, marital status, and family type of activists suggests two factors underlying these variations: the extent to which working women were responsible for their own or others' welfare, as opposed to

27. For an analysis of skilled women workers, see Ava Baron, "Women and the Making of the American Working Class: A Study of the Proletarianization of Printers," *Review of Radical Political Economics* 14 (1983): 23–42.

28. Tilly's "Paths of Proletarianization" suggests that some women tobacco workers in late nineteenth-century France developed a commitment to their occupation and a sense of solidarity similar to those of skilled men.

29. Kessler-Harris, *Out to Work.*

30. See Hunt, *Gender and Class Consciousness,* for the suggestion that this is also the case in the present. Sociologists have pointed out that analysis of points in individuals' lives reveals the dynamic interaction between families, individuals, and the historical context. See Glen Elder, "Age Differentiation and the Life Course," in Hareven, *Transitions;* and "History and the Family: The Discovery of Complexity," *Journal of Marriage and the Family* 43 (1981): 489–521.

depending on the income of male wage earners, especially fathers and brothers; and the length of their labor force participation and the extent to which they expected it to be continual. Women of different ages and marital status living in different types of households had different reasons for activism and participated in different ways.

What is known about the family situation of women activists suggests that the women who were most likely to take the lead in labor struggles were either wives living with husbands, or never-married women and widows who were self-supporting or who provided for dependents. The evidence for Troy supports this conclusion. According to Augusta Lewis, leader of New York City's female typographical union, and Susan B. Anthony, many collar laundresses had other relatives dependent on them for income.[31] The Collar Laundry Union's president, Kate Mullaney, supported her mother and two younger sisters.[32] Since Anthony's observation that "nearly all" the laundresses were supporting aged parents and younger siblings was based on a visit with the union's leadership, her comments indicate that Kate Mullaney's family was not atypical.[33] The likelihood that Lewis's observations were also based on meetings with the collar union's officials suggests that other leaders were also the only wage earners in their households. Collar women whose households included male wage earners had other reasons to be committed to unions (which will be discussed later), but it is possible that they were less active in the union's daily operation.

A look at working-class women's collective action in widely different industrial settings in different periods suggests that these examples are part of a relatively consistent pattern of women's activism in the past and present. Daniel Walkowitz notes that in late-nineteenth-century Cohoes, a textile city across the river from Troy, widows and women heading households were more active in labor protests. Louise Tilly suggests that married women in France's cotton and woolen mills in the

31. *New York Sun*, 5 July 1869.

32. Kate Mullancy and her family appear in Ward 10 (p. 26) of the manuscript census (U.S. Bureau of the Census, Ninth Census of the United States, 1870: Population of Rensselaer County, New York State). Also see *New York World*, 12 February 1870.

33. Anthony's report was based on a visit to Troy in 1870, which is described in Ida Usted Harper, *The Life and Work of Susan B. Anthony* (1898; rpt., New York, 1969). Delayed between trains, Anthony visited the union's failing cooperative laundry and met Kate Mullaney, Esther Keegan, and other leaders who, dismissed by employers after the strike, managed the cooperative enterprise. Harper notes that Anthony subsequently referred to this visit in speeches about the ballot's importance for women's bargaining position with employers. She argued that if women had been enfranchised, the collar laundresses would undoubtedly have won the strike.

late nineteenth and early twentieth centuries were more likely to be
activists than young single women, despite the fact that they were a
small percentage of the labor force. Older women also formed the
leadership in labor conflicts in nineteenth-century New England shoe
manufacturing communities.[34] While wives who lived with their husbands and widows and older single women who supported themselves
or their relatives did not form the majority of the female labor force,
they were more likely to lead young unmarried women in labor struggles.

What did wives, widows, and older single women have in common
that made them more likely to take the lead? Let us first look at widows
and older single women whose economic circumstances were much
more similar to each other's than to those of wives living with their
husbands. Older women who provided for others or were self-supporting were more likely to be activists in part because of their experience
as primary wage earners. Compared to daughters living with their
parents and wives who were protected by other family members' earnings, older women who supported relatives were more vulnerable to
the vicissitudes of the economy and the power of employers. While this
vulnerability could be a barrier to labor activity because it discouraged
risk-taking, it nevertheless gave them a greater stake in improving their
situation as wage earners. Women whose families depended on them
may have avoided the risks of participating in isolated labor conflicts,
but they may have been more likely to seek the protection of organized
collective action. Such action was especially likely among Troy's collar
women, who worked in a desirable occupation in a community where
they could count on a strong labor movement to support their efforts.

Widows and never-married women who were providers or self-
supporting had a different relationship with male authority than did
wives. As their families' primary wage earners, widows and older single
women were more independent of male authority than wives and
daughters in male-headed households. Instead of depending on others
for their well-being, they had others dependent on them. Since they
were not directly subordinate to fathers and husbands, they could control their wages and make decisions about how to protect their families,
including whether or not to join unions or participate in strikes. Experience with responsibility also set them apart from younger workers.
Accustomed to taking responsibility for their own and others' welfare
rather than deferring to fathers and husbands, they may have been

34. Walkowitz, *Worker City;* Tilly, "Paths of Proletarianization"; Blewett, *Men, Women,
and Work.*

more willing to devote time and effort to labor organizations and to take on leadership roles.

Working wives also shared some characteristics with older women who were providers or self-supporting. Although wives were not primary wage earners, as managers of the household economy they were aware of their families' need for women's income and had experience with taking responsibility for others' welfare.[35] Also, like older single women and widows, working wives were more likely to have been in the labor force longer than young single women and to expect that their employment would be continuous, if not permanent. Never-married women who shared with a widowed mother the responsibility of providing for their families did not have long years of work experience, but they probably also expected to be continually employed, although such expectations depended somewhat on the number, sex, and ages of their siblings. Younger women's chances of leaving employment (for marriage) may not have been greater than those of older women workers who looked forward to marrying or to the future employment of a younger sibling or older child, but older women—whether married, widowed, or single—were more likely to face the reality that they would have to work at several stages of their lives. Also, women who were in the labor force for longer periods or at several stages had the opportunity to develop connections with other workers, which resulted in a stronger identification with their occupation and coworkers. Having had more experience as wage earners and more opportunity to discuss their perceptions with sister workers, they probably reached conclusions about injustices in the workplace and gained familiarity with labor issues which were useful during labor conflicts.[36]

These arguments point to ways in which analyses of working women who are more vulnerable or exceptional contribute to an understanding of women's and men's activism. Examination of motivations for organizing and ingredients of success as well as barriers to it reveals that vulnerability and reluctance to organize were not the only possible consequences of women's need for income to provide for themselves and their families. In some circumstances women providers' experience with responsibility and independence may have encouraged risk-taking and activism. The characteristics essential to activism are thus not necessarily found in the group that forms the largest segment of the labor force. Leadership may come from an important minority that may not at first glance seem to share interests with the majority of

35. Schwartz, "Immigrant Voices," chaps. 9 and 10.
36. Tilly, "Paths of Proletarianization," 415–16.

workers. Also, a single factor such as vulnerability may have different effects in contrasting circumstances, revealing previously unexplored facets that may contribute to analyses of other situations. Workers who were less skilled and possessed fewer resources to fall back on during hard times and strikes may have been likely to form unions in well-organized communities in the nineteenth century partly because in these settings it was possible for workers' vulnerability to be a motivating factor in addition to or instead of inhibiting organization. This possibility suggests explanations for the development of leadership skills and motivation for activism which go beyond analyses of skilled male workers.

Although young single women living with their parents were less likely to be activists, they were by no means absent from the labor scene. Recent research suggests that shifts in young women's relations to their families and group life fostered labor activity in some circumstances. At the same time as young women's wage labor was an extension of family traditions, it also resulted in shifts in women's subordination.[37] The beginnings of increased autonomy for young women is hinted at in studies of Third World women, which suggest that a father's diminished authority over women may be replaced by male authority in the workplace.[38] There is some evidence that male family members' heightened concern about women's proper place and their attempts to exert more control over women may have been in part a response to the increased personal freedom of women wage earners. The development of women's peer groups at work, whose values sometimes conflicted with those of parents, may have been one manifestation of these changes. In a variety of settings, including early-nineteenth-century New England mills and later nineteenth-century and early-twentieth-century factories in urban areas, these groups sometimes fostered a solidarity that formed the basis for cooperation during labor struggles.[39] The argument that women's increased personal freedom heightened male concern about control may help explain conflicting assessments of the extent to which women's employment increased their autonomy or was integral to nineteenth-century working-class families' expectations in regard to women's contribution to the family's livelihood. While it is important not to underestimate the strength of family traditions and the extent of male control over women, shifts in

37. Eisenstein, *Give us Bread,* chap. 5.
38. Elson and Pearson, "Nimble Fingers," 99–100; Phillips and Taylor, "Sex and Skill," 100.
39. Dublin, *Women at Work,* 71–72; Tentler, *Wage-Earning Women,* 62.

patterns of family authority are an important avenue of investigation for understanding women's activism.

Working wives had much in common with employed daughters in that they contributed to male wage earners' income rather than being primary providers. Their family roles also most clearly differed from those of men, whose activism until recently has been taken as a model for collective action. These differences are important analytically because they suggest that ways in which women's family roles and views of themselves as women contrasted with men's explain not only the activism of young daughters and wives but also some unique characteristics of women's activism in general.[40]

Such explanations further suggest new perspectives on collective action in working-class communities. Distinguishing between obstacles to forming organizations and activism, Alice Kessler-Harris suggests that since women as a group had fewer dependents than men—and indeed could usually depend on the income of other family members—women workers could take more risks in labor struggles, including holding out longer during strikes.[41] Perhaps popular expectations about the differences in women's and men's employment patterns contributed to women's greater risk-taking in labor struggles. Occasional unemployment was probably more acceptable to young women, especially if they were contributors rather than major providers. Men probably had a greater stake in remaining in the same occupation continually because they anticipated the need to provide for their families. It seems likely that women who lived in boardinghouses or with other families could also fall back on relatives for support. Although they could not depend on family members in the same way as women who lived with their own families, some could anticipate at least a temporary return to their homes in other localities if necessary. Although young single women were less identified with work and coworkers and had less experience with labor conflicts, once organized or mobilized in specific conflicts, they had reasons for perseverance and militancy that were not shared by men. This analysis suggests that the ability to form sustained organizations should be distinguished from reasons for militancy during particular labor conflicts; women who do not participate in the daily operations of formal organizations will not necessarily refuse to take part in particular labor struggles. Moreover, evidence that certain differences in women's and men's family situa-

40. Kessler-Harris discusses some unique aspects of women's activism in *Out to Work,* 160.

41. Kessler-Harris, *Out to Work,* 160.

tions and gender roles encouraged some aspects of activism indicates that these differences are central for understanding labor conflicts.

The examination of family relationships of male and female wage-earners in Troy and other cities underlines the importance of examining workers' dependence on other relatives in any effort to understand labor activism.[42] Also, analyses of these family relations point to ways in which a city's industrial structure may foster the activism of both women and men. In such communities as textile towns, where one industry employed family members of several age groups and both sexes, family members' dependence on one another discouraged labor militancy and strikes, since even the temporary unemployment of all wage earners produced considerable family hardship.[43] In contrast, in two-industry cities such as Troy, the industrial structure encouraged militancy (although it was only one of many factors that contributed to the city's strong labor movement). Contemporary reports observed that there were often collar workers and iron molders in the same family. Therefore, workers in either industry could hold out in a labor struggle because when the male iron molders were on strike, they could depend on the income of the female collar workers, and vice versa.[44] Although this situation was unusual, it was not unique; evidence suggests similar patterns in early-twentieth-century Paterson, New Jersey, another city dominated by two major industries.[45] Since the silk and woolen mills employed mostly women and the locomotive industry employed men, workers in one industry could fall back on the income of family members in the other industry during strikes and hard times.[46] Although women's dependence and family members' reliance on each other

42. Several studies analyze the implications of family members' dependence on each other for income. See Heidi Hartmann, "The Family as the Locus of Gender, Class, and Political Struggle: The Example of Housework," *Signs* 6 (1981): 366–95; and Michelle Barrett and Mary McIntosh, "The Family Wage: Some Problems for Socialists and Feminists," *Capital and Class* 11 (1980): 51–57.

43. Hareven, "Family Time," 201–2.

44. Preliminary analysis of census data indicates that more collar laundresses were members of iron molders' families than working women in other industrial occupations. In 1865, 14 percent of the laundresses' male relatives were molders. In contrast, molders constituted only 8 percent of collar sewers' male relatives, and 5 percent of sewing women's male relatives. Although these figures are modest, they indicate that slightly more laundry women than other working women were related to molders. See Turbin, "And We Are Nothing but Women." Contemporary reports also suggest family relationships between collar women and iron molders: *New York Bureau of Labor Statistics (1887); New York World,* 19 and 20 May 1886; *Troy Daily Times,* 26 May 1886; *John Swinton's Paper,* 23 May and 23 June 1886.

45. Griffen, *Natives and Newcomers.*

46. This argument is based on unpublished work by Amy Srebnick.

sometimes discouraged labor militancy, in some circumstances dependence, or interdependence, could foster some types of activism.

This analysis suggests that women's dependent status and men's dependence on women's economic contribution must be examined not only in terms of interpersonal relations but also in the context of a city's industrial and social structure, including the character of available occupations and the labor community. While women were in a subordinate position in the family, it is not accurate to characterize women as totally dependent and men as independent. The situation of women sometimes discouraged active participation in organizations, but in certain circumstances their dependent position fostered some types of activism. Men were more independent and autonomous personally, but many depended on women's economic contribution; in some circumstances reliance on women's earnings could foster risk-taking in labor conflicts. (In Troy the fact that men did not view women as competing for their jobs, since they were employed in different industries, also fostered cooperation between workers of different sexes in labor activity.) This analysis not only emphasizes that the interrelationship of family and work life is central for understanding both women's and men's activism; it also reveals new facets of this relationship.

Exploring the conditions under which women organized relatively successfully reveals the inadequacy of characterizing differences between women and men as simple dichotomies, which submerge important exceptions and large minorities. Examining the economic contribution of a significant minority in the labor force, older single and married women, helps explain seemingly contradictory descriptions of women's activism and suggests that interdependence as well as dependence or independence should be the focus of analyses of family relationships. This demonstrates not only that analyzing working women as a homogeneous group is inadequate but also that ways in which women differ from men do not have inevitable consequences; they may have contrasting outcomes in different settings and in fact may explain seemingly conflicting evidence.

Deconstructing dichotomies and reexamining particular groups of working women encourages us to redefine commonly used terms and develop new approaches and concepts. It also reveals new and essential questions. Since this approach encompasses our understanding of gender, work, family, class consciousness, collective action, and other central concepts, these questions concern not only women but men and working-class communities. Some of these issues are currently being explored. The analysis of a particularly well-paid, skilled group of women who worked in the collar industry—collar laundresses—contributes to recent work which argues that definitions of skill have reflected male workers' experience.[47] Speculation about collar women's consciousness has important implications for understanding nineteenth-century working-class communities, since it contributes to recent arguments that class consciousness does not stem solely from work-related factors and the type of labor force participation experienced by men.[48] Although this study concerns collective action rather than consciousness, the circumstances and characteristics of women's activism indicate that important groups of working women were class conscious. And while they had some characteristics usually associated with class-conscious men, they also developed consciousness of group interests in different ways. This view contributes to a new analysis of working men's consciousness: although men's kin and friendship networks differed from women's, family and community ties must also have played a part in men's awareness of their interests as workers and members of a class.

Rethinking concepts drawn from conventional wisdom reveals new dimensions of analysis for labor studies. While studies of working women have until recently generalized from the majority who were not activists, studies of the male-dominated labor movement have centered on explanations for the activism of the minority who engaged in labor conflicts or participated in organizations. Just as the conditions under which women workers organized were ignored, so were the conditions under which men did *not* organize. Labor history has moved away from a focus on institutions to emphasize artisans and skilled workers with traditions of activism. We should look not only at important minorities such as skilled women but also to men who were less skilled and did not organize. We should question not only the assumption that women's work was temporary but also the generalization that men's work was permanent. The argument that women's employment patterns can be characterized as interrupted or intermittent leads to new questions about men's work experience and activism; for example, how did inter-

47. Ava Baron, "Contested Terrain Revisited: Technology and the Gender Definitions of Work," paper presented at the Bunting Institute, Radcliffe College, April 1986.

48. Several studies argue that gender consciousness must be included in analyses of collective identity and that class consciousness does not develop only through participation in what has been called the point of production, including relationships with employers: see Eisenstein, *Give Us Bread but Give Us Roses;* Foster, *Class Struggle;* Temma Kaplan, "Female Consciousness and Collective Action: The Case of Barcelona, 1910–1918," *Signs* 7 (1982): 548–88; Blewett, "Work, Gender, and the Artisan Tradition"; and Benenson, "Skill Degradation."

ruptions in men's labor force participation caused by illness, accidents, layoffs, and the search for better employment affect men's attitudes toward work and activism? Reconceptualizing frameworks based on dichotomies and conventional wisdom reveals new perspectives on working women, unexplored questions about male wage earners, and neglected dimensions of labor studies. It is an approach that promises to contribute to new conceptual frameworks and a new interpretation of gender, family, work, consciousness, and labor activism.

4

Sapphire? The Issue of Dominance in the Slave Family, 1830–1865

Christie Farnham

The question of dominance in the black family became a national issue in 1965 with the publication of *The Negro Family in America: The Case for National Action,* by Daniel Patrick Moynihan, who attributed the problems of the black urban poor to a "tangle of pathology" resulting from the "disorganization" of the black family. The term "disorganization," by which Moynihan meant the presence of female-headed households whose origins he claimed to find in slavery, is significant. It is a value-laden term that has become part of the jargon of social science; it implies that female-headed households are inherently disorderly because there is no male to impose his authority over the woman and her children. Female-headed households constituted for Moynihan *ispo facto* evidence of the existence of matriarchy and were by definition contrary to nature, since "the very essence of the male animal, from the bantam rooster to the four-star general, is to strut." This report is but the most prominent example of what has been termed the pathological school of black family studies, which accepts the white, middle-class nuclear family as the norm and assumes that all groups should assimilate its values. From this perspective the black family is seen as deviant, being characterized by high rates of illegitimacy, the absence of fathers, and welfare dependency—all of which are thought to undermine female–male relationships and produce adverse effects on the person-

68

ality development of the children. These views have come under increasing attack from scholars with a commitment to a pluralistic society, such as R. H. Hill and Andrew Billingsley, who emphasize the strengths of the black family, especially its coping strategies in a racist society. However, the growth of female-headed families from 17.6 percent in 1950 to 40.2 percent in 1980 (compared with 8.5 and 14.6 percent for whites)—in conjunction with statistics showing that "a Black child is twice as likely as a white child to live with neither parent, three times as likely as a white child to be born to a teenage mother, seven times as likely to have parents who separate, and three times as likely to see his or her father die"—has kept the question of dominance in the black family alive more than twenty years after Moynihan first focused national attention on this issue.[1]

However, the question of power relationships in the slave family cannot be understood apart from the African context, particularly as it affected women's work roles. Although earlier scholars rejected Melville Herskovits' emphasis on African cultural transfers, there is now a general consensus that, whereas links to African culture are not nearly so strong among Afro-Americans as among their counterparts in Latin America, such retentions are nevertheless not only numerous but fundamental to the formation of Afro-American culture. Contemporary scholars have delineated an important substratum of African retentions in such areas as music, dance, religion, folklore, and family life.[2]

1. First published by the Office of Planning and Research of the U.S. Department of Labor, the "Moynihan Report" has been widely reprinted. A readily available source and the one used here is Peter I. Rose, ed., *Slavery and Its Aftermath* (New York, 1970), 375. Moynihan's work built on the conventional wisdom of the times, as influenced by the works of E. Franklin Frazier and Stanley Elkins. Such studies as Lee Rainwater's 1968 article, "Crucible of Identity: The Negro Lower-Class Family" (*Daedalus* 95:258–64), and *Black Matriarchy: Myth or Reality*, ed. J. H. Bracey, August Meier, and Elliott Rudwick (Belmont, Calif., 1971), continued to disparage female-headed families. R. H. Hill, *The Strengths of Black Families* (New York, 1972), and Andrew Billingsley, *Black Families in White America* (Englewood Cliffs, N.J., 1968), have been germinal works for scholars, taking a more positive view of the black family and emphasizing its unique strengths. For analyses of the statistics on female-headed families and their economic ramifications, see Jacqueline Jones, *Labor of Love, Labor of Sorrow: Black Women, Work, and the Family from Slavery to the Present* (New York, 1985), 305–6; Paul C. Glick, "A Demographic Picture of Black Families" in *Black Families*, ed. Harriett Pipes McAdoo (Beverly Hills, Calif., 1981), 106–26; and Marion Wright Edelman, "An Advocacy Agenda for Black Families and Children" in McAdoo, *Black Families*, 292.

2. Melville Herskovits, *The Myth of the Negro Past* (New York, 1941). See, e.g., Albert Raboteau, *Slave Religion: The Invisible Institution* (New York, 1978); Lawrence Levine, *Black Culture and Black Consciousness: Afro-American Folk Thought from Slavery to Freedom* (New York, 1977); and Herbert Gutman, *The Black Family in Slavery and Freedom, 1750–1925* (New York, 1976).

African societies were many and varied; therefore, generalizations must be made with caution. Nevertheless, there appears to have been a basic similarity in family structures. Whether they were organized as matrilineages or patrilineages, Niara Sudarkasa makes the case for a fundamental distinction between African forms consisting of extended families—built around consanguineal cores of same-sex adult siblings with their spouses and children, living together in compounds—and Euro-American patterns of isolated households based on the husband-wife-children bond. She terms this distinction the difference between consanguinity and conjugality.[3] Although the nuclear family may not have been so typical as it was once thought to be, these two models are useful for highlighting cultural differences that influenced the development of the black family under slavery.

One of the most important differences to flow from these two models lies in the work roles of women. Most African societies were polygynous. A bride moved into the compound of her husband's kin or her husband moved into hers. In either case the lineage or kin group was of paramount importance. It was lineage elders, not husbands, who parceled out farmland to women for their individual use. Although in some parts of West Africa both men and women engaged in agriculture, elsewhere in the region, as well as in most areas to the south, farming was considered women's work. In short, there is no reason to suspect that in precolonial times women did not perform most of the agricultural labor.[4]

Women's role in cultivation derived from a sexual division of labor that assigned women the responsibility for feeding their husbands and children. Since the land was given to women for their own use, the surplus they produced often belonged to them. For example, a French missionary to the eighteenth-century Bakongo living north of the Zaire River described how "each woman has her own hut, fields, gardens, and slaves over which the husband has no rights after she takes care of his needs." Such customs continued into the nineteenth century. A German, describing the Bakongo living on the Loango coast, observed that "when they have satisfied the needs of their husband, the produce that remains from the fields and from animal husbandry is their own." During that same period it is reported that the Bakalai women of Gabon "are expected to feed their husbands . . . but to what is left or

3. Niara Sudarkasa, "Interpreting the African Heritage in Afro-American Family Organization," in McAdoo, *Black Families*, 40–44.
4. Claire C. Robertson and Martin A. Klein, "Women's Importance in African Slave Systems," in *Women and Slavery in Africa*, ed. Robertson and Klein (Madison, Wis., 1983), 9.

not needed of the fruits thus raised the men have no right. The women sell and keep for themselves the articles received." Where women controlled the agricultural surplus, internal trade markets came to form a central part of their world. Maintaining property and profits separate from those of their husbands facilitated a tradition of female entrepreneurship in which a few women even achieved wealth and status.[5]

The fact that the women of the compound were numerous and bound together by intimate ties facilitated organization in support of common interests. Women of the villages and towns, all wives of a local lineage, usually formed associations. The Igbo women of eighteenth-century Onitsha, for example, organized for the purpose of regulating trade, arranging the cooking for village meetings, and the like. Strength in numbers also provided them with some leverage in female–male relationships, enabling them to insist upon the proper treatment of wives.[6]

Polygyny, women's organizations, and the support extended by one's blood kin tended to dilute the emotional importance of marriage, which was essentially an economic transaction between two families rather than a love match that established an all-encompassing relationship, as in the conjugal model. Although some societies, like the Hausa of present-day Nigeria, required virginity in brides, most accepted premarital sex. The overarching concern of the lineage for perpetuation and the strength that numbers bring gave procreation a

5. "Chaque femme a ordinairement sa case, ses champs, ses jardins, et ses esclaves a part, sur lesquels le mari n'a aucun drôit" (J. Cuvelier, *Documents sur une mission française au Bakongo, 1766–1776* [Brussels, 1953], 51); "Was sie von ihrem Felde über den Verpflegungsbedarf für ihren Ehemann erntet, was sie aus ihrer Tierzucht gewinnt, ist ihr eigen" (E. Pechuël-Loesche, *Volkskunde von Loango* [Stuttgart, 1907], 214); Paul B. du Chaillu, *Explorations and Adventures in Equatorial Africa* (1871; rpt., New York, 1971), 338. I am indebted to Phyllis Martin for bringing these sources to my attention (and for their translation). Women's independent resources are also discussed in the secondary literature. See, e.g., LaFrances Rodger-Rose, "The Black Women: A Historical Overview," in *The Black Woman*, ed. Rodgers-Rose (Beverly Hills, Calif., 1980), 16. Women traders are discussed in Robertson and Klein, "Women's Importance," 13; George E. Brooks, "The Signares of Saint-Louis and Gorée: Women Entrepreneurs in Eighteenth-Century Senegal," in *Women in Africa: Studies in Social and Economic Change*, ed. Nancy J. Hafkin and Edna G. Bay (Stanford, Calif., 1976), 19–44. In fact, wealthier women also engaged in external trade markets, where opportunities for profits were greatest. See Karen Sacks, "An Overview of Women and Power in Africa," in *Perspectives on Power: Women in Africa, Asia, and Latin America*, ed. Jean F. O'Barr (Durham, N.C., 1982), 4.

6. Richard N. Henderson, *The King in Every Man: Evolutionary Trends in Onitsha Ibo Society and Culture* (New Haven, Conn., 1972), 217–18; Kamene Okonjo, "The Dual Sex System in Operation: Igbo Women and Community Politics in Midwestern Nigeria," in Hafkin and Bay, *Women in Africa*, 53; Sacks, "Overview," 3–4.

central focus in African life. Sterility was a calamity. The primacy of lineage and the organization of family life into collectivities of blood relatives and their spouses also meant that childbearing lacked the exclusivity attached to the conjugal model. Although biological parents had the primary responsibility for their children, there were no rigid boundaries; the parenting role was exercised by all adults, and children were taught to identify themselves as daughters and sons of the lineage rather than as cousins.[7]

The work roles of women and the sexual division of labor are in marked contrast to those of the conjugal model, whose characteristics were sharpened during the Victorian period under consideration and idealized in what Barbara Welter has termed the "cult of true womanhood," which emphasized piety, purity, submissiveness, and domesticity. The nuclear family epitomized the notion of exclusivity. Spouses were emotionally dependent on each other; resources were pooled and decisions made jointly or by the husband for the entire unit. Wives were isolated in the home, often separated from close kin and bearing sole responsibility for child care; husbands were providers and protectors, mediating between the home and the outside world. In striking contrast to the African view of sex as normal and healthy was the Victorian ambivalence, tinged with guilt and burdened with a Western cultural heritage that tended to dichotomize women into two types: the good, who were pure and passionless like the Virgin Mary; and the bad, who were sinful and seductive like Eve.[8]

Separate decision-making, property, and incomes, combined with the power that resided in women's organizations and the allies available in natal villages, provided the traditional African woman with the space to be self-reliant. Self-reliance should never be confused with equality between the sexes, however. Although many traditional societies operated with dual sex systems in which each sex managed its own affairs

7. Jeanne Noble, *Beautiful Also Are the Souls of My Black Sisters: A History of Black Women in America* (Englewood Cliffs, N.J., 1978), 26; John W. Blassingame, *The Slave Community: Plantation Life in the Antebellum South*, rev. ed. (New York, 1979), 161; Sudarkasa, "Interpreting the African Heritage," 40–42, 44; Judith Van Allen, "'Sitting on a Man': Colonialism and the Lost Political Institutions of the Igbo Women," *Canadian Journal of African Studies* 6, no. 2 (1972): 171. For an analysis of how West African women's traditional culture has been maintained under modern circumstances, see Sudarkasa, "Female Employment and Family Organization in West Africa," in *The Black Woman Cross-Culturally*, ed. Filomina Chioma Steady (Cambridge, Mass., 1981).

8. Barbara Welter, "The Cult of True Womanhood," *American Quarterly*, Winter 1966, 151–69. The impact that this idealized image of women had on black women is analyzed by Bell Hooks in *Ain't I a Woman: Black Women and Feminism* (Boston, 1981), 30–38.

and maintained its own hierarchies of power and position, such systems were meant to be complementary, not parallel—which says nothing about the relative balance of power and prestige between women and men. Separate is not equal. In general, the world that women inhabited offered labor-intensive work that largely involved taking care of the physical needs of men and children. That this work was organized and regulated by the women themselves does not erase the subordinate character of the enterprise.[9]

What happened when the consanguineal and conjugal models collided on American plantations? Reaction to the Moynihan report had the positive effect of spurring research into the slave family. Although conscious attempts were made to avoid the previous error of viewing the black family through the prism of white middle-class norms, the thrust of the research has been an effort to refute Moynihan's position by documenting the presence of males in the household. The major factor underlying this approach seems to have been a desire to substantiate the importance of the family in Afro-American culture and to attack the negative stereotype of blacks as promiscuous. Laudable as these goals are, they have had the unfortunate effect of trivializing the importance of the female-headed household.

The most important study to respond to Moynihan's allegations is Herbert Gutman's book *The Black Family in Slavery and Freedom, 1750–1925*. Documenting premarital sexual norms and naming patterns, Gutman demonstrates that Afro-American culture was not a mimetic version of white forms. He also presents evidence of a shockingly high rate of forced separations. However, he does not use this high rate to support Moynihan's contention that the separation of spouses by planters resulted in a legacy of family disorganization. On the contrary, he counters this finding with evidence demonstrating that most slaves lived in double-headed families, thereby emphasizing how slaves clung to this form of family organization despite the exigencies of the slave system.

The term "double-headed," however, calls forth an image similar to that of the two-parent nuclear family and obscures the fact that many men were not the biological fathers of all the children present in the family. Such usage avoids the issue of serial monogamy, yet serial mo-

9. Although Okonjo equates these dual sex systems with the existence of "equality of the sexes in villages as well as in national politics" ("Dual Sex System," 55), she also characterizes such societies as ones in which "men rule and dominate" (p. 45). The most important examples of the egalitarian thesis are found in Karen Sacks, *Sisters and Wives: The Past and the Future of Sexual Equality* (Westport, Conn., 1979); and Peggy Sanday, *Female Power and Male Dominance* (Cambridge, Eng., 1981).

nogamy can produce at least temporary and often permanent female-headed households. Gutman seems to share Moynihan's view that female-headed families are aberrant. When he finds, for example, that "nearly one in five children born in families that started before 1855 grew up in households headed by women who had all their children by unnamed fathers" on the Stirling plantation in Louisiana, he considers the situation "important" but "far from common." Since some of these women had large families and were never sold, these facts suggest to him that "far from revealing the legitimacy of the single-parent household, such behavior may have represented deviation from the community's norm." Nevertheless, he also finds evidence of female-headed households elsewhere—for example, eight of them on the Bennehan-Cameron plantation were established before 1830. And 9 percent of those who fled to Camp Becker during the Civil War listed themselves as single parents—and some of them were in their thirties, not teenage mothers living with their families of origin. Gutman's study attempts to demonstrate the continuance of double-headed families into the twentieth century, but although he insists that the "typical black household . . . had in it two parents," he again documents numerous exceptions.[10]

Recent research demonstrates the ubiquitousness of female-headed families in northern urban areas in the late nineteenth century, and a newly discovered 1878 survey of a portion of Dinwiddie County, Virginia, provides evidence that serial monogamy and the presence of children from pre- and extramarital unions were characteristic of the post-Emancipation family. Figures from this survey show that of those who had been married during slavery, 29.8 percent had been married more than once and 7 percent more than twice. These statistics are virtually indentical to those indicating that by 1878 31.1 percent married more than once and 7.7 percent more than twice, thus demonstrating that serial marriage was common in slave times and remained substantially unchanged after emancipation. A study of ex-slave narratives finds that 18 percent remembered having lived in single-parent households. This finding is corroborated by Paul D. Escott's work, which shows that one-fifth of the ex-slaves interviewed reported having experienced at least partial breakup of their families. Orville Vernon

10. Gutman, *Black Family*, 115–18, 180. Gutman calculates forced separations (from marriage registration books kept by the Union Army clergymen in Mississippi and Louisiana) at almost one in six over the age of twenty. Mary Frances Berry and John W. Blassingame estimate the slave marriages ended by masters at 30 percent (*Long Memory: The Black Experience in America* [New York, 1982], 73). Leonard Levy points out serious problems with the tables Gutman uses to substantiate the pervasiveness of double-headed families in 1900 ("Prize Stories," *Reviews in American History* 8 [March 1980]: 15–16).

Burton finds in his study of slavery in Edgefield, South Carolina, that "there was an accepted pattern of divorce among the slaves: long periods of relations between two slaves were replaced by alliances with others." He estimates the frequency of such divorce at 25 percent. Although Burton places little importance on African retentions as an explanation for slave society's acceptance of "divorce," the fact that it was practiced within a dominant culture to which divorce was anathema, whereas traditional African societies accepted the practice, argues for African continuities.[11] Furthermore, since it is unlikely that both spouses would find new mates simultaneously, the potential for the formation of significant numbers of female-headed households is obvious. Thus the existence of such households is sufficiently extensive to warrant their inclusion among Afro-American cultural institutions.

There are two difficulties in dealing with female-headed households: the definition of the term and the significance of the form. Are only those households to be included in which the woman never married? But since slave marriages had no legal standing, what constitutes a marriage? Despite more than fifteen years of feminist scholarship, the female-headed family has yet to be viewed as a significant institution under slavery. Contemporary scholars of all persuasions have regarded the female-headed family as transitory: a young woman will soon "settle" into marriage, giving her children a father; teenage mothers remain with their families of origin until marriage, so there is a father figure present to provide a role model; if a woman is widowed or separated from her spouse, her previous marriage constitutes evidence that she does not reject the institution. Those instances of women who never married—such as the mother of William Wells Brown, who had seven children by seven men, both black and white—are dismissed as aberrant cases that existed for the benefit of the master.[12]

11. For articles on single-parent households, see Frank F. Furstenburg, Jr., Theodore Hershberg, and John Modell, "The Origins of the Female-Headed Black Family: The Impact of the Urban Experience," *Journal of Interdisciplinary History* 6 (Autumn 1975): 218, 232; Darrel E. Bigham, "The Black Family in Evansville and Vanderburgh County, Indiana, in 1880," *Indiana Magazine of History* 75 (June 1979): 117–46; John Modell, "Herbert Gutman's *The Black Family in Slavery and Freedom, 1750–1925:* Demographic Perspectives," *Social Science History* 3 (October 1979): 45–55; Jo Ann Manfra and Robert R. Dykstra, "Serial Marriage and the Origins of the Black Stepfamily: The Rowanty Evidence," *Journal of American History* 72 (June 1985): 33; unpublished research by Stephen Crawford cited in Peter Laslett, *Family Life and Illicit Love in Earlier Generations* (London, 1977), 249; Paul D. Escott, *Slavery Remembered: A Record of Twentieth-Century Slave Narratives* (Chapel Hill, N.C., 1979), 46; Orville Vernon Burton, *In My Father's House Are Many Mansions: Family and Community in Edgefield, South Carolina* (Chapel Hill, N.C., 1985).

12. William W. Brown, *Narrative of William Wells Brown, a Fugitive Slave* (Boston, 1847), 13. Sudarkasa, for example ("Interpreting the African Heritage," 46), considers

Susanne Lebsock has taken a different view of female-headed families among free blacks in antebellum Petersburg, Virginia, half of whose households were headed by women. She sees this phenomenon as a rational response to the fact that single women retained ownership of their property, whereas married women's property reverted to their husbands: "The possibility remains that some free black women valued their relative equality and did their best to maintain it."[13] The large numbers of female-headed families under slavery indicate that for some women the maintenance of a single-parent family was an inventive approach to conditions common to the slave system and represented an expansion of women's choices. Obviously, slavery was a brutal and coercive system, and the concept of choice does not apply to those spouses torn asunder by death or forced separation, nor does it imply that the available choices included an ideal one. Nevertheless, in a system where basic needs were provided by the master, the option of heading a family offered a small measure of autonomy that some women may have found preferable to other possible arrangements. To see this choice as aberrant is to interpret female-headed families within an androcentric framework and to ignore the attempts of some women to enlarge the confines of the cage of slavery.

If female heads of households have been cast as matriarchs, the wives in double-headed families have not altogether escaped a similar charge of being "Sapphires." Named after the wife of the Kingfish on the popular *Amos 'n' Andy* radio show of the 1930s, Sapphires wore the pants in the family and treated men with contempt. Stanley M. Elkins, for example, analyzed the slave family as one in which the "'real' father was virtually without authority over his child, since discipline, parental responsibility, and control of rewards and punishments all rested in other hands." Thus the role of the slave mother was more important than that of the father. Since the father could not protect his family from the lash, Elkins saw the cardinal components of the conjugal family's conception of manhood—provision and protection—as being undermined.[14] But Africans did not view manhood in those terms. The lineage was the basic means of protection, and women themselves had a large role in providing for the family through their obligation to

---

widowhood only a phase in the life cycle, although she points out that the custom of levirate negated the institution of widowhood as a form of single-parent household in traditional West African societies.

13. Suzanne Lebsock, *The Free Women of Petersburg: Status and Culture in a Southern Town, 1784–1860* (New York, 1984), 90.

14. Stanley M. Elkins, *Slavery: A Problem in American Intellectual and Institutional Life* (Chicago, 1959), 130.

raise food. Yet if one conceptualizes the black family in terms of the nuclear middle-class white family, the slave mother is seen to slip into the power vacuum created by the emasculating effects of the slave system on the father, in consequence of which her power is unnaturally enhanced.

This view of the emasculated male which was popularized by Moynihan resulted in a particularly angry reaction, coming as it did in the midst of the Black Power movement, a movement which emphasized self-defense and pride in manhood. To counteract this interpretation, scholars sensitive to black nationalism have searched for evidence of male supremacy in both precolonial African and antebellum American societies. John Blassingame characterizes African societies as patriarchal; but, accepting the view of manhood which requires men to provide for and protect their families, he emphasizes the efforts fathers made to furnish their cabins and supplement the family diet through barter and hunting. Nevertheless, their status within the family, which Blassingame sees as resting on the authority of the husband over his wife and children, was reduced by slavery: "They could no longer exercise the same power over their families as they did in Africa." The bedrock of such a conception of manhood is the determination to stand and fight, which leads Blassingame to describe the plantation as "a battlefield where slaves fought masters for physical and psychological survival. Although unlettered, unarmed, and outnumbered, slaves fought in various ways to preserve their *manhood*" (emphasis mine). Thus, for Blassingame, Sapphire is banished, and the slave experience becomes synonymous with the male experience.[15]

The feminist movement began to impinge upon this conceptualization of the problem of dominance in the 1970s, with curious results. Eugene Genovese, for example, describes cornshucking parties in *Roll, Jordan, Roll: The World the Slaves Made*. Slaves gathered from neighboring plantations for an evening of feasting, singing, and storytelling designed to make the mountain of corn disappear faster. The men did the shucking and were served by the women. Since Genovese can find no evidence that the women complained about being excluded from the party, he concludes that "they seem to have grasped the opportunity to underscore a division of labor and authority in the family and support the pretensions of their men." He believes that "on whatever level of consciousness"—his explanation for the lack of explicit documentation—women attempted "to strengthen their men's self-esteem and to defer to their leadership." He concludes that "what has usually

---

15. Blassingame, *Slave Community*, 178, 284.

been viewed as a debilitating female supremacy was in fact a closer approximation to a healthy sexual equality than was possible for whites." Unlike Blassingame, who agrees with Elkins that husbands had lost some of their power under slavery and consequently struggled to rise to a position of parity with their wives, Genovese sees the wives as being conscious, at some level, of their unseemly superiority and there-fore as attempting to reduce themselves to the level of their husbands by becoming deferential and increasing the division of labor in slave society.[16]

By 1979, Blassingame had joined Genovese in viewing the slave family as essentially egalitarian in structure. He extolled "the transpor-tation of African familial roles [which] led to the creation of America's first democratic family in the quarters, where men and women shared authority and responsibility." Thus, in the short space of about a dec-ade, the picture of the slave family changed from one in which the wife exceeded her husband in power and authority to a situation charac-terized by egalitarian relationships. This new-found democratic family was based largely on evidence drawn from the labor force participation of black women: from the beginning of slavery most female slaves had been agricultural laborers, doing even such heavy work as plowing, cutting wood, and building fences, roads, and canals. This interpreta-tion of the family may have been influenced by the movement of American women into the work force in ever larger numbers in the 1970s and by the emphasis of the women's movement on the right of women to enter previously male-dominated professions. Many analyses in anthropology and other disciplines delineated the split between the public and private spheres of life, demonstrating how power and pres-tige inhered in the public sphere, from which women were traditionally excluded.[17]

16. Eugene Genovese, *Roll, Jordan, Roll: The World the Slaves Made* (1972; rpt., New York, 1976), 319, 500.

17. Blassingame, *Slave Community*, 178. Perhaps the best-known discussion of the domestic/public distinction is found in Michelle Rosaldo, "Women, Culture, and Society: A Theoretical Overview," in *Woman, Culture and Society*, ed. Rosaldo and Louise Lamp-here (Stanford, Calif., 1974), 17–42. A succinct statement of the problem is presented in Jean Stockard and Miriam M. Johnson, *Sex Roles: Sex Inequality and Sex Role Development* (Englewood Cliffs, N.J., 1980), 93–94. Inequities in the division of labor among slaves is analyzed by Christie Pope in "Dynamics of Family Roles: Manhood and Womanhood in Slave Society" (paper presented to the American Historical Association, Pacific Coast Branch, 1980); and by Jacqueline Jones in "'My Mother Was Much of a Woman': Black Women, Work, and the Family under Slavery," *Feminist Studies* 8 (Summer 1982): 235–69. However, Deborah G. White sees gender differences in work roles as another exam-ple of equality in a dual sex system ("Female Slaves: Sex Roles and Status in the Ante-bellum Plantation South," *Journal of Family History* 8 [Fall 1983]: 250–54).

However, the field was not a forum for slave power, either female or male. Furthermore, the fact that women worked in both the public and private spheres—that is, the field and the house—whereas men were active primarily in only one, the field, did not represent equality. Scholars have recently attempted to rectify this analysis by constructing the notion of the egalitarian slave family on a two-way movement in the division of labor. Angela Davis insists that not only did women labor in the fields but "men executed important domestic duties"; thus "the salient theme emerging from domestic life in the slave quarters is one of sexual equality." She points to the fact that "men would sometimes work in the cabin and women might tend the garden and perhaps even join the hunt." The argument that women gardened and hunted is but another instance of women participating in what white society considered to be men's work. The reverse situation—men working in the home—is but a "sometimes" activity. Thomas Webber makes the most ambitious attempt to document the presence of males in the domestic sphere. He concludes that "while it is true that in most slave households women did the cooking, washing, sewing, and cleaning and men did the gardening, constructing, and hunting roles were reversed often enough to suggest this was more a convenient division of labor than an expression of a societal norm that favored one sex over the other." He fails to explain, however, on what grounds he considers the assignment of household tasks to women to be "more convenient."[18]

The ex-slave narratives make abundantly clear that women had responsibility for what has traditionally been seen as women's work. There is no evidence, for example, that men engaged in spinning, a job that occupied much of the women's time in the evenings. More typical of the life of the ordinary slave woman is the description by the former slave Henry Baker: ". . . de wimmin plowed jes lack de men. On Wednesday night dey had tuh wash en aftuh dey washed dey had tuh cook suppah. De nex' mornin' dey would get up wid de men en dey had tuh cook breakfus 'fore dey went tuh de fiel' en had tuh cook dinner [the noon meal] at de same time en take hit wid' em."[19] Even husbands in cross-owner marriages, who saw their wives only on weekends, did not do their own laundry. A white man living in Georgia described how, on "Saturday night, the roads were . . . filled with men on their way to the 'wife house,' each pedestrian or horseman bearing his bag of

18. Angela Y. Davis, *Women, Race, and Class* (New York, 1981), 17–18; Thomas L. Webber, *Deep Like Rivers: Education in the Slave Quarter Community, 1831–1865* (New York, 1978), 194.

19. John W. Blassingame, ed., *Slave Testimony: Two Centuries of Letters, Speeches, Interviews, and Autobiographies* (Baton Rouge, La., 1977), 656.

soiled clothes."[20] The movement of women into agricultural labor did not engender egalitarian relationships, since the public sphere (if such it can be termed) was a source of neither wealth nor power. Although women took pride in their strength and competence, their labor in the public sphere meant double duty, not power parity.

Sarah Fitzpatrick, a slave born in Alabama in 1838, observed: "Love is a won'erful thing. A mother al'ays loves her chillun. Don't care whut dey do. Dey may do 'rong but it's stil' her chile. Den dere is de love uv'va 'oman fer her man, but it ain't nut'in lack a mother's love fer her chillun. I loves a man when he treats me right but I ain't never had no graveyard love fer no man."[21] Inasmuch as protection and provision were not as salient to the concept of manhood in the consanguineal model as they were in the conjugal model, it is unlikely that slaves brought from Africa insisted upon these qualities in a relationship. The slave experience itself inhibited the development of this conception, since shelter and basic provisions were provided by the masters, who also controlled to a large extent the use of physical force on the plantation. Thus there is little in the historical record to indicate that slave women considered their husbands to be unmanly. With no property to transmit or lineages to maintain, it is reasonable to suppose that companionship became a major attribute in the choice of a spouse. This may have been less true of men, however, since both consanguineal and conjugal models require women to take care of their husbands' physical needs. Robert Smalls, a former slave, explained to a congressional committee that in slavery "the colored men in taking wives always do so in reference to the service the women will render."[22]

Della Promise, a resident of rural Macon County, Alabama, explained in the early 1900s that "everybody don't git married, and if I can't git the one I want I don't want to git married. I never seen but one boy I thought I could marry, and me and him had ways too much alike, and I knowed we couldn't git along, so I just has my chillun and raises 'em myself."[23] Della Promise was exercising an option that some white professional women have only recently begun to choose. Although not universally applauded, the decision of single white professional women to raise families alone is sometimes seen as a positive approach to the problem of the paucity of men in their age and status categories, whereas the same choice by some black women—under slavery and

20. Robert Q. Mallard, *Plantation Life before Emancipation* (Richmond, Va., 1892; rpt., Detroit, 1982), 48.

21. Blassingame, *Slave Testimony*, 649.

22. Blassingame, *Slave Testimony*, 374.

23. Charles S. Johnson, *Shadow of the Plantation* (Chicago, 1934), 83.

later—has been castigated. Certainly, to be the female head of a family
was not the ideal of slave society any more than it is the ideal of today's
white professional women. But slaves, perhaps more than others, recognized that life is not always ideal. Of course, for many women—such
as those separated from spouses by force or death—circumstances, not
choice, brought them to the heads of their families. Nevertheless, a
significant if small number of women appear to have chosen not to
marry at all.

Black women were able to develop the alternative of female-headed
families when it seemed in their interest to do so, given the constraints
of slavery, because neither the slave community nor the planter class
raised sanctions against it. The female-headed family, while different
from the matricentric cell of the polygynous African family, was sufficiently similar in physical structure—a woman and her children living
together in a separate residence—that this phenomenon would not
have appeared altogether alien to slave society.

Despite occasional instances of polygamy, this form of marriage did
not take root in America; nevertheless, the consanguineal model
formed a general perspective toward marriage and family which could
become the basis of patterns of behavior developed to meet the exigencies of slavery. Of these, the prime example is the fictive kin networks,
which provided slaves—many of them torn from their blood relatives—with feelings of belonging and the protection previously provided by the lineage.

The development of a unique Afro-American culture grew out of
attempts to retain what was feasible from African values and institutions. In the process, new forms were created. Female-headed families
were viable under slavery because the planter provided the cabin,
clothing, and food rations. Slave women understood that this arrangement was not a gift; they knew that their labor paid for their upkeep
and that their children increased the value of their masters' estates.
Since African women fed their families and Afro-American women
continued to be agricultural laborers, the fact that slave women were
ultimately responsible for feeding their children would not have
seemed inappropriate.

Female-headed families were also viable in terms of child care, since
the fictive kinship system, designed in part to replace the lineages of
West African society, continued the practice of the socialization of children by the group rather than by parents alone. All adults felt some
responsibility for the children on the plantation, and this arrangement
had the added benefit of providing male role models in abundance.
Furthermore, child-care arrangements were imposed upon all moth-

ers, not just single heads of families, so that women would be free to labor in the fields. The designation of elderly women and older children to provide child care while the mothers worked removed a major obstacle that contemporary working mothers face. In fact, it was this very communal nature of the socialization of children—especially the assistance of grandmothers in caring for children resulting from the custom of prebridal pregnancy, and the assistance of older women while younger ones worked in the field—that made it possible to split off sexual relations from reproduction, much as access to the pill has separated sex from pregnancy in contemporary American society, thereby facilitating a change in sexual mores.

Blassingame points out that premarital sex was accepted among many African peoples as a normal part of courtship. Although the religious significance of sex was lost in the move to the American slave system, and Christianization developed ambivalent attitudes toward sex outside of marriage for many, the belief remained that sex is a natural act largely unconnected with sin.[24] Such a view of sexuality permitted the slave community to be more accepting of female-headed families than was possible in white society. Although null evidence is seldom reported, the fact that slave communities did not shun such women or their children supports this interpretation of slave society. In fact, their full inclusion in the community argues strongly for the acceptance of this family form.

If female-headed families did not seem totally alien or threatening to Afro-American slave society, neither did they disturb the rationale for slavery developed by the master class. Reproduction, however achieved, added to a planter's wealth. Furthermore, the female-headed family did not adversely affect the labor supply, since female heads of families were forced to work in the fields or big house in the same manner as wives. Finally, slave indifference to the white middle-class standards of female purity idealized by Victorian America appeared to corroborate negative stereotypes of black women as promiscuous, thereby making it easier for white women as well as white men to blame the exploitation of black women on the victims.

It is useful to compare the development of the female-headed family under slavery with the development of a similarly small population of single white women in America during the nineteenth century. Because the norms of white middle-class society insisted on celibacy outside of marriage, these women were never in a position to become heads of families—a tragic deprivation for some of them. The preva-

24. Blassingame, *Slave Community,* 149–91.

lent animosity toward self-reliant women required them to accept Victorian notions of purity and self-sacrifice. It was only by extending these ideals to society generally, in what has been termed social housekeeping, that they were able to maintain a precarious existence.[25] Slave women, on the other hand, through the redefinition of certain West African cultural forms that also meshed with the interests of the planter class, were able to raise a family alone. Unmarried white women, despite the image of single blessedness, were trivialized by a society that mocked them as man-hating old maids whom no man found attractive, but there is nothing in the historical record to indicate that the slave community treated female heads of families as pariahs or stigmatized their children as the illegitimate fruit of illicit unions.

"Sapphire" and "matriarch" are derogatory labels that have in common the image of women "lording it" over men. Yet black women in both double-headed and female-headed families were slaves to a double work load—both field and domestic labor. Perhaps what is so threatening, especially to a society based on conjugality, is not their power and privilege (for they had little) but their self-reliance, for self-reliance implies not so much ruling over men as the ability to manage without them.

25. Lee Virginia Chambers examines spinsters in *Liberty, a Better Husband: Single Women in America, 1780–1840* (New Haven, Conn., 1984). For English comparisons, see Martha Vicinus, *Independent Women: Work and Community for Single Women, 1850–1929* (Chicago, 1985).

· *Part 2* ·

1870–1920

5

"She Helped Me Hay It as Good as a Man": Relations among Women and Men in an Agricultural Community

Nancy Grey Osterud

On December 31, 1880, George W. Riley wrote in his diary:

Today ends another year of our lives and this is my sixteenth diary. I am able to give an account of my self every day for the past 16 years or 1840 days. Perhaps I cannot give as good a record as I ought to be able to give, but am glad that things have gone no worse for us than they have, but on the contrary have great reason to praise the giver of all good gifts that our lives have been spared and so many blessings have

This essay is based on Nancy Grey Osterud, "Strategies of Mutuality: Relations Among Women and Men in an Agricultural Community" (Ph.D. diss., Brown University, 1984), a reconstruction of the lives of women and men in one rural community between its settlement in 1790 and World War II. The Nanticoke Valley is located in western Broome County, in south-central New York State; approximately fifteen miles long and five miles wide, it is a sociocultural region defined geographically by the Nanticoke Creek, which flows into the Susquehanna River near Union. The community was settled by families from eastern New York, New England, and the British Isles. By the time of Civil War, its population had stabilized at about 3,000; a slow decline had begun by 1890, but in 1900 there were still 2,200 residents. In addition to studying public records (primarily New York State and federal manuscript censuses), I have analyzed three dozen collections of family papers and diaries, representing nearly the entire range of the socioeconomic scale and including women at different stages of life and in a variety of family situations. While the only diary quoted here is that of George Riley, his observations are typical of those recorded by other diarists and narrators. Some of these documents are in the library of the Nanticoke Valley Historical Society in Maine.

followed us during the whole time of my diary keeping together with
our whole lives. But many has been the changes, with all its disappointments and trials that this world of cares are heir to. During that time
our little seven-year-old girl have grown to womanhood, got married,
got to be a mother over four years ago. Juddie has been born and
grown to be a man in size and is a great help to us. And we have been
able to pay our debts, bought the Frost place, built a new barn on it, got
Ida and Bert on it and started. Built our wagon house, an addition on
our house, wood mill and shops, cleared and improved a good deal of
our place. Helped to build a church at Maine and have tried to do what
little I could towards helping the cause of religion along. During the
past sixteen years many afflictions have befallen us in the loss of my
father, Lucy's father, one of my half brothers and one half sister, together with scores of friends that have gone to their last resting place.
But death has not been permitted to enter into our little family, for
which we cannot be too thankful, and with all the rest we have had
many good times which is pleasant to reflect on. . . . It is a fact ever
apparent to me that during all the quarter of a century that has past in
my married life the greatest good that this world has afforded me has
been my ever true and faithful wife to stand by and help and encourage, doing all in her power to make every thing pleasant to all around.
May God bless her, guide and direct and keep and save us all is my
earnest and sincere prayer.[1]

This meditation expresses George Riley's sense of what has been
most significant and meaningful in his life. Keeping a diary was in itself
an important act; George's wish to be able to give an account of himself
echoes the Protestant tradition of self-examination, of recording one's
conduct and state of mind in order to reflect upon and assess one's
spiritual condition. But George Riley's stock-taking was not primarily
individual. It begins with George himself but shifts immediately from
first person singular to first person plural, from "I" to "we." Although
George Riley kept his own diary, he did not think of himself separately
from his immediate family.

In describing the changes that had occurred over sixteen years,
George began with the growth of his children toward adulthood. The
passage of time was marked not by some external chronology but by
the family cycle. George and Lucy's daughter, Ida, had become a woman, wife, and mother; their son, Judson, had become able to perform a
man's work. During that time the family had accumulated property
and improved it. The ideal implicit in George Riley's account is simultaneously economic and familial. The parents secured a farm that was
adequate to their family's support, and they helped their daughter and

---

1. George W. Riley diary, Nanticoke Valley Historical Society, Maine, N.Y.

her husband get established on a farm of their own nearby. The losses suffered during those sixteen years—the deaths of relatives and friends—were tempered by the recollection of the good times they had shared with neighbors and kin.

The meditation moves out from the family into the community, from temporal to spiritual concerns. There is no discontinuity in this progression, for Riley saw the ordering of human relationships in spiritual terms. Six years before, he had resolved on New Year's Day: "I hope to cultivate such a disposition that I may be a good father, a good and affectionate husband, and a reliable neighbor and citizen and above all may set such an example before my family and a dying world that I may serve the cause of salvation."[2] His closest companion and greatest help in this endeavor had been his wife, Lucy Ann. Although George's paean to his wife owes something to the contemporary sentimentalization of woman as the center of family life, "doing all in her power to make everything pleasant to all around," its context is very different from that of the popular magazines. George describes Lucy Ann as a helpmeet, not an idol; she has stood by him in "all the disappointments and trials that this world of cares are heir to."

Lucy Ann Riley's presence pervades George's diary, not only in the relatively few reflective passages but also in the daily entries that record the round of chores, seasonal farm work, and visiting that made up his world. Lucy Ann was there to "help and encourage" him in his struggles with stony fields, potato bugs, and wet hay. Equally important, he was involved in her regular tasks: carrying water on washday, sewing shirts on the machine, starting dinner while she and the children attended church. He watched over her in sickness and was present when she gave birth. The degree to which they shared farm and household labor was exceeded only by the commonality of their social activities. This was not simply a matter of joint visiting among relatives and friends; it extended into formal organizational activities in the community. George attended meetings as well as socials of the Ladies' Aid Society of the church, and Lucy Ann went to debates sponsored by the Farmers' Jubilee Club.

The Riley diary, along with other personal documents and narratives from the community, raises the question of whether women had a "separate sphere"—a set of activities and experiences not shared with men—or whether they joined with men in family and community affairs. The idea of "separate spheres" appeared during the early nineteenth century and defined the position of women in urban middle-

---

2. Riley diary.

class families. Commercialization and industrialization brought a separation between household and workplace, and between income-producing and non-income-producing labor. Women remained responsible for the home while men assumed the primary responsibility for
earning money. This distinction between men's and women's activities
was interpreted as a fundamental difference between the male and
female character. Women, who nurtured children and mediated family
relationships, were described as naturally selfless, sensitive, virtuous,
and pious; men, who competed in the rough-and-tumble world of the
capitalist marketplace and popular politics, were seen as strong-willed
and decisive, practical and rational. Ideally, women's supposed pas-
sivity and men's activity balanced each other: women were to be protected by men, while men would be softened and spiritualized by
female influence. The private life of the family was deemed responsible for maintaining stability in a time of rapid social change.[3]

Although this ideology did not fit the situations of the majority of
American women—including working-class and immigrant women in
cities, women living on farms in the Northeast and on the frontier, and
both black and white women in the slave South—it became dominant
in American culture. Ideologies do not necessarily reflect social experience but rather shape the ways people interpret their lives and interact
with one another. The notion of "separate spheres" implied that wom-
en's field of action, although distinct from that of men, was neither
incomplete nor secondary; instead of being excluded from critical
arenas of social life or subordinated to their husbands, women were
seen as having a world of their own in which they enjoyed considerable
power and autonomy. The connections between women and men and
between the family and capitalism were both obscured by this ideology
and fundamental to it.[4]

Studies of the lives of women in nineteenth-century America have
been subtly shaped by the ideology of "separate spheres" at the same
time that they have subjected it to a feminist critique. In an attempt to
see women as historical actors rather than as the passive victims of male

3. On the ideology of "separate spheres," see Nancy F. Cott, *The Bonds of Womanhood:
"Woman's Sphere" in New England, 1780–1835* (New Haven, Conn., 1977); Ann Douglas,
The Feminization of American Culture (New York, 1977); and Mary P. Ryan, *The Empire of
Mothers: American Writings on Women and the Family, 1830–1860* (New York, 1982).

4. For a brilliant analysis of the meaning of domestic ideology in the context of
changing class relations, see Mary P. Ryan, *Cradle of the Middle Class: The Family in Oneida
County, New York, 1790–1865* (Cambridge, Eng., 1981). Elizabeth Pleck, "Two Worlds in
One: Work and Family," *Journal of Social History* 10 (Winter 1976): 178–95, summarizes a
number of studies of urban women and points to the complex unity of work and family
relations.

domination, historians of women have emphasized the ways in which women created a separate culture within their societally prescribed sphere. Rooted in such experiences as childbirth and enacted primarily in friendship, this "female world of love and ritual" not only functioned as a resource for women within their marriages but also nurtured a distinctively feminine sensibility and form of cultural expression.[5] Although some scholars see the "bonds of womanhood" as providing the social basis for the feminist movement, this line of analysis most often encapsulates women within their "separate sphere," and the ways in which this ideology shaped women's relationships with men in their families and communities remain unexamined. As John Mack Faragher reminds us, the vast majority of women lived in families, and "the cultural expectation was that husbands and wives, despite their differences, would reach some ordered harmony within the bonds of marriage."[6] The feminist insight that the family is not necessarily united by common interests, that husbands and wives occupy fundamentally different positions within as well as outside the family, is crucial to our understanding of women's lives.[7] But we need to locate women within their families, in relation to men, in order to examine the processes of conflict and adjustment that defined most women's experiences.

In the Nanticoke Valley, a rural community in upstate New York, women did not occupy a "separate sphere," a gender-defined realm of experiences and activities distinct from that of men. Although women and men were not equal, they were not separate either. Women were assigned to a subordinate position within their families and kin groups, and they engaged in gender-defined and relatively devalued forms of labor in their households. The support of women's mothers, daughters, and sisters was crucial in the predictable crises of family life. But women neither elaborated the experiences they shared into a female-defined subculture nor turned to female networks as an alternative to their relationships with men. Rather, they strove to create mutuality in their marriages, reciprocity in their performance of labor, and integra-

5. The classic statement of this perspective is Carroll Smith-Rosenberg, "The Female World of Love and Ritual: Relations between Women in Nineteenth-Century America," *Signs* 1 (1975): 1–29.

6. John Mack Faragher, *Women and Men on the Overland Trail* (New Haven, Conn., 1979), 2. Faragher also developed this approach in his review article, "History from the Inside Out: Writing the History of Women in Rural America," *American Quarterly* 33 (Winter 1981): 237–257.

7. Rayna Rapp, Ellen Ross, and Renate Bridenthal, "Examining Family History," *Feminist Studies* 5 (Spring 1977): 174–200.

tion in their patterns of sociability. Individually and collectively, women in the Nanticoke Valley responded to inequality by actively enlarging the dimensions of sharing in their relationships with men.

In the rural community, the elements of conjunction between women and men outweighted those of disjunction. Socially and culturally, women were defined in direct relation to men rather than in terms of their differences from men. This situation presented women with both a problem and an opportunity. The difficulty was that the possibilities for even a relative autonomy were highly circumscribed, and the resources to which women had independent access were strictly limited. Men controlled the real property upon which rural households were based, and women had few means of support outside of the households in which they lived as daughters, wives, and mothers. Women's interactions with the men in their families and kin groups were immediate and powerful.

Women could, however, try to redefine the terms of those interactions. They could attempt to meet men as much as possible on common ground rather than in situations that were shaped by gender difference; they could focus their energies on those aspects of life in which sharing provided some basis for equality rather than on those that were marked by hierarchical divisions. Thus women emphasized the familial rather than the feminine dimensions of their lives; for example, they chose to have their husbands present at the births of their children even though midwives and female relatives presided at the delivery. Women actively and for the most part voluntarily participated in the most highly valued and least gender-marked modes of productive labor. Equally important, women could draw upon the resources of social networks beyond their immediate families. The joint patterns of sociability that women sustained in their kin groups and community organizations helped overcome the elements of gender separation that existed within conjugal households. In all these aspects of life, women adopted strategies of mutuality.

These strategies were supported by certain economic and social-structural conditions that served as a basis on which mutuality could be built and provided women with resources on which they could draw. First, there was no separation between household and workplace in this agricultural community, and women's labor was as integral to the production of farm income as it was to family subsistence. Dairy products were the most important marketable commodities produced by Nanticoke Valley farms, and women and men shared responsibility for the dairy process, organizing the work it involved in a variety of ways. This fact is especially significant in light of the conventional division of labor between women and men in farm households. In the Nanticoke Valley, as in other rural areas, men were responsible for plowing and planting the fields, cultivating and harvesting the field crops, and preparing the hay, grain, and root crops for use as animal and human food. Women were responsible for tending the vegetable garden, processing and preserving the year's supply of vegetables and fruits, and preparing meals. Men were responsible for the construction and maintenance of the house, barn, and outbuildings, for the provision of fuel for heat and cooking, and for the repair of farm and household equipment; women were responsible for cleaning the house, tending the fires, and sewing, mending, and laundering the family's clothing and household textiles.

This allocation of tasks between women and men was somewhat flexible. It varied from one family to another, depending on that mix of choice and necessity we call custom. In some families, women hoed corn and dug potatoes; in others, men cultivated the vegetable garden. Sometimes women did what was generally regarded as men's work because there weren't enough men in the household to complete it, and the family couldn't afford to hire labor. But other families seem to have departed from the conventional pattern simply as a matter of preference. And no matter how strictly some families maintained the gender division of labor, they all were willing to readjust in case of emergency—when frost jeopardized the winter vegetable supply, bugs took over the potato patch, or rain threatened the hay. On those occasions, all available hands would be pressed into service.

On July 21, 1875, George Riley wrote in his diary that his wife "helped me hay it as good as a man."[8] This phrase epitomizes George's attitude toward Lucy Ann's participation in the work of the farm. It assumes a clear division of labor by sex—haying was defined in principle as men's work—but it also asserts that the allocation of tasks between women and men was flexible: in practice, women and men stepped out of their customary work roles when the good of the farm required them to do so. On that summer day, George had been unable to hire any extra male help, so Lucy Ann put aside her usual work to join her husband in the fields, raking and turning the hay, loading it onto the wagon, and drawing it into the barn. In her husband's eyes, she had done that work "as good as a man"; the standard was male, but Lucy Ann had attained it.

The opposite phrase, "she done a good job, for a woman," would have diminished her achievement by maintaining a double standard

8. Riley diary.

that presumes that women's work is generally inferior to men's. George Riley's comment, in contrast, is entirely positive. While it assumes a division of labor based on sex, it recognizes that women are fully capable of performing tasks generally assigned to men, even those requiring substantial strength and skill. George Riley recorded the event because he found it remarkable. But his diary is filled with notations of similar occasions: the labor that women performed on family farms was so integral to the agricultural economy that their husbands and fathers had to recognize the reality and significance of their work.

The allocation of tasks between women and men was most flexible in the dairy process, perhaps because it was conducted in a domain between the fields and the house. It was generally accepted that men cared for the cattle and did the barn chores, both men and women milked, and women skimmed the cream and churned the butter.[9] In some families, however, women both milked and helped with barn chores; in others, men did all the work in the barn and also churned the butter. Within families, too, the exchange of roles between women and men was common: the allocation of particular tasks changed from day to day, depending on what else had to be done; from season to season, depending on the amount of milk being produced; and from year to year, depending on the family's available labor supply. Husbands and wives took over each other's usual tasks in the dairy when either of them was ill, away, or too busy to perform them. The flexibility of the gender division of labor in dairying may have resulted in part from the fact that the dairy process involved a chronic emergency: cows had to be milked twice a day, milk had to be skimmed after it had separated but before it had soured, and cream had to be churned within a certain range of temperatures. Few other farm processes involved so many built-in temporal constraints.

9. The division of labor by sex was customary in New England and the mid-Atlantic states, and migrants to the Nanticoke Valley probably brought it with them; during the late eighteenth and early nineteenth centuries, even the work of the dairy was as much divided between women and men as shared by them. But men's involvement with churning increased during the nineteenth century as dairying was conducted on a larger scale. Indeed, in New England men eventually took over complete responsibility for milking, and women withdrew (or were pushed) from the barn; this development did not occur in upstate New York. For analyses of women's role in dairying during the late eighteenth and early nineteenth centuries, see Joan M. Jensen, "Cloth, Butter and Boarders: Women's Household Production for the Market," *Review of Radical Political Economics* 12 (Summer 1980): 14–24; and "Churns and Butter-Making in the Mid-Atlantic Farm Economy, 1750–1850," in *Industrious Women: Home and Work in the Nineteenth-Century Mid-Atlantic Region*, ed. Glenn Porter and William H. Mulligan, Jr. (Wilmington, Del., 1982), 61–100. For New England, see Nancy Grey Osterud, *The New England Family, 1790–1840* (Sturbridge, Mass., 1978); and Nancy F. Cott, *The Bonds of Womanhood*, 19–62.

Women and men who lived and worked on farms that produced butter for the market engaged in a substantial amount of joint or closely coordinated activity. In a context that devalued women's domestic labor, women's participation in commercial dairying was vital; while women and men shared and exchanged other tasks primarily with members of their own sex, dairying provided a basis for cooperation and mutual respect across gender lines.[10] At the same time, significant differences in the spatial and temporal dimensions of women's and men's working lives arose from the more gender-specific aspects of their labor. Aside from morning and evening chores, men performed fewer distinct tasks each day than women did. Men focused their energies on one major job, while women orchestrated a variety of processes; a man might plow a field while a woman tended fires and children, cooked dinner, baked bread, ironed, and mended. On the other hand, men's work varied more than women's from one season to the next. Women complained that their work was repetitive and monotonous— "the same dull round of chores"—and seasonal tasks were more of a burden than a relief. Part of the monotony came from the fact that women's work confined them to the household and farmstead. While men came into regular contact with men on neighboring farms and in the wider community in the ordinary course of their labor, women had to create occasions for sociability; they shared work not simply to get it done more efficiently but also in order to see other women.

This difference in the temporal and spatial qualities of women's and men's lives could have provided the basis for distinctive modes of socializing: men might have participated in community-wide organizations, while women might have been restricted to more informal contacts with relatives and neighbors. To some degree, husbands and wives might have had separate social networks. They did not do so in the Nanticoke Valley. During the late nineteenth century, formal and informal social activities tended to counteract and overcome, rather than extend and reinforce, the separation between women and men arising from their gender-specific labor. Husbands and wives did not have independent circles of friends; instead, both interacted with the same small group of families in their open-country neighborhood. For every instance in which two men shared work, there was another occasion on which the two women got together, and yet another when the two couples visited. A woman might come over to help Lucy Ann Riley

10. See Nancy Grey Osterud, "The Valuation of Women's and Men's Work: Gender, Kinship, and the Market" presented at the national conference on American Farm Women in Historical Perspective, Las Cruces, New Mexico, 1985.

sew in the afternoon, and her husband might join her at the Rileys' place in the evening.

Husbands and wives also attended quilting parties together. Indeed, organized social activities almost always included both sexes, even though they were planned by groups whose membership was formally restricted to a single sex. George Riley attended meetings of the Ladies' Benevolent Society and the Ladies' Improvement Society, for example. The women who planned these gatherings could have excluded men had they chosen to do so. In fact, the women's auxiliaries of the churches were formed because women were excluded from the exercise of power in sexually mixed institutions. But women did not use these auxiliaries to create single-sex enclaves; rather, they drew men into the activities they controlled and used their auxiliary organizations to expand their power in the larger institutions. Similarly, women were not generally excluded from the social activities sponsored by men's organizations. There were women and children in the audience when the men of the Jubilee Club debated the proposition: "Is the influence of women greater than that of men?" No wonder it was "decided in the affirmative."[11]

This pattern of joint rather than segregated sociability was based on the settlement pattern and kinship system of the Nanticoke Valley. The way land was transmitted from one generation to another meant that farm families usually lived near kin, and open-country neighborhoods developed around clusters of related families. While the asymmetries of inheritance meant that the vertical links in such networks generally followed the male line—sons rather than daughters generally were given a share of their parents' land—the horizontal links that resulted from marriage were forged by women: daughters sought to marry into neighboring farm families in order to remain near their kin. Intermarriage among neighbors thus helped to balance the gender bias created by inheritance. Relatives shared resources both within and between households, and across as well as within gender and generational groupings. Women were especially active in providing mutual aid and in turn were able to rely on their families not only as a recourse in case of disaster, desertion, or death but also as a resource within their marriages. Their closeness to fathers, brothers, and cousins protected women from the arbitrary power of their husbands.

11. Riley diary, 7 January 1868. It should be noted that women remained silent during this debate, in keeping with the unstated assumptions of the ideology of women's "influence." Women did speak at meetings of the Nanticoke Valley Grange, however, and advocated woman suffrage at Grange-sponsored debates in the late nineteenth century.

Kinship ties served as a model for friendship and legitimated sexually mixed forms of sociability in neighborhood and community. Kinship also served as a model for marriage. Women in particular tried to make their marriages resemble the relationships among kin, which were characterized by reciprocal care-giving on a long-term basis that was not defined by exchange or calculations of advantage. The integration of women and men in the farm family economy and their participation in social networks that included both sexes, then, supported and reinforced one another. Both involved joint rather than separate modes of activity, and both helped mitigate the hierarchical nature of property and authority relations between husbands and wives. For women in family-centered societies characterized by deeply structural asymmetries between women and men, the elaboration of integrated modes of work and sociability could be an effective way of redressing inequality.

Although the nature of the rural economy and its dense, kin-based settlement pattern provided women with the foundation on which they constructed joint modes of work and sociability, these structural factors did not guarantee that such mutuality would automatically emerge. The degree to which husbands and wives, brothers and sisters, and friends and neighbors enjoyed relations of mutual respect and human concern testifies to the achievements of the women of the community. Not all Nanticoke Valley men were like George Riley, with so deeply internalized a sense of their duty to be a "good father, affectionate husband, and reliable neighbor." It was women's active response to the conditions in which they found themselves placed by the gender system that enlarged existing areas of commonality and created new modes of sharing between women and men. In struggling to improve their own lives, women transformed the quality of life for men as well.

6

Gender Relations and Working-Class Leisure: New York City, 1880–1920

Kathy Peiss

The history of working-class leisure in the United States has recently become a field of inquiry, as the cultural dimensions of labor receive greater attention from historians dissatisfied with purely institutional or economic studies. Scholars have included leisure in the "new labor history" to gain a richer understanding of social relations under industrial capitalism, particularly workers' response to their proletarianization. Case studies of saloons, fraternal orders, city parks, and workingmen's clubs have explored the meaning of leisure in working-class life and its relationship to class formation, identity, and struggle.

In these studies, workers' leisure is seen as inextricably shaped by an industrial mode of production, a capitalist political economy, and the evolution of class relations. With the rise of capitalist time discipline and control, "leisure" emerges as a realm differentiated from "work," a sphere of partial autonomy where an alternative or oppositional working-class culture is shared and defended. The actual forms of working-class leisure are outgrowths of laborers' experiences, necessary responses to the industrial wage system. Thus popular recreation itself is

I thank Temple University Press for granting permission to publish material that first appeared in my book *Cheap Amusements: Working Women and Leisure in Turn-of-the-Century New York.*

seen as contested terrain under capitalism, with such vital institutions of workers' culture as the saloon and lodge serving as bulwarks of defense against the encroachments of capitalists and reformers. Struggles over recreational space, although not equivalent or parallel to shop floor battles or industrial strikes, are expressions not only of ethnic, religious, and cultural values but of class conflict as well.[1]

Although historians of leisure readily acknowledge that ethnicity and religion shape workers' culture, they have been less sensitive to gender divisions. In the accounts of working-class leisure, women are largely absent, marginal, or subsumed within the social category of "workers." Primary data on working-class women's leisure admittedly are difficult to uncover, but the invisibility of women is as much a problem of conceptualization as the consequence of limited evidence. Leisure studies employ a notion of culture as a set of values, patterns of behavior, and customs shared by members of specific working-class communities and embedded in recreational institutions. Much of this work, however, assumes that leisure is *public* and *male*—the world of extrafamilial institutions and places, a world inhabited and acted upon primarily by men. Few have asked what women were doing while men attended the saloon or lodge, and what the consequences of their activities might have been in defining workers' culture, social relations, and class struggle.

Studies of leisure that use "workers" or "the working-class family" as their unit of analysis mask the ways in which gender divided much working-class social life. Working-class women's social experiences— the sexual division of labor, unequal distribution of resources, and social barriers limiting their participation in workingmen's institutional life—placed them in a relationship to leisure different from that of their male counterparts. Even when women and men shared certain values as members of the working class, that culture might take differ-

---

1. For leisure as a terrain of class conflict, see Roy Rosenzweig, *Eight Hours for What We Will: Workers and Leisure in an Industrial City, 1870–1920* (Cambridge, Eng., 1983); Francis Couvares, "The Triumph of Commerce: Class Culture and Mass Culture in Pittsburgh," in *Working-Class America*, ed. Michael Frisch and Daniel Walkowitz (Urbana, Ill., 1983). See also John T. Cumbler, *Working-Class Community in Industrial America: Work, Leisure and Struggle in Two Industrial Cities, 1880–1930* (Westport, Conn., 1979); Jon M. Kingsdale, "The 'Poor Man's Club': Social Functions of the Urban Working Class Saloon," *American Quarterly* 25 (1973): 472–89; John Alt, "Beyond Class: The Decline of Labor and Leisure," *Telos* 28 (1976): 55–80. For a historiographical overview, see Richard Butsch, "From Labor History to the Commercialization of Leisure," paper presented to the annual meeting of the Society for the Study of Social Problems, Washington, D.C., 24 August 1985. On leisure's separation from work, see E. P. Thompson, "Time, Work-Discipline, and Industrial Capitalism," *Past and Present* 38 (1967): 56–97.

ent forms and be expressed in separate recreational spaces. Indeed, with respect to women, leisure itself must be seen as a problematic category. The recreation of men and children was often predicated on women's labor. Cleaning, cooking, shopping, and decorating the home for family occasions and everyday relaxation, preparing food and tidying children for outings, organizing parties and celebrations—these were among the ways in which women served as providers of leisure for men and their families.[2]

Integrating feminist insights about gender into cultural studies should produce a more complex picture of workers' leisure. To explore some of the conceptual directions this integration might take, this essays examines women's leisure in a specific historical context, that of New York City in the years from 1880 to 1920, a period in which working-class recreation was undergoing rapid commercialization. It draws upon testimony and reports that examine the living conditions, recreational activities, and family budgets of white working-class families in those years. At the turn of the century, the American urban working class was a complex amalgam of immigrant groups and their successive generations; each had distinctive national, religious, and cultural customs. Nevertheless, many gender-based practices crossed ethnic lines; an examination of these practices suggests some of the limitations of historians' conceptualization of working-class culture.

Evidence for the separation of the sexes in everyday social activities in turn-of-the-century New York—at least among married women and men—is widespread. One extensive survey of New York workingmen's recreation in 1913 found that married men spent about half their leisure time apart from their families, although this figure varied with ethnicity, hours of labor, and type of work. "The husband comes home at night, has his dinner, and goes out with the 'men,' or sits at home to read his paper," observed an investigator of West Side families. The differences in the leisure activities of women and men is suggested by a detailed 1914 study of thirty-four families. On Sundays, men attended

2. Feminist scholars have explored sexual divisions in working-class social life; see especially Laura Oren, "The Welfare of Women in Laboring Families: England, 1860–1950," in *Clio's Consciousness Raised: New Perspectives on the History of Women*, ed. Mary S. Hartman and Lois W. Banner (New York, 1974); Ellen Ross, "'Fierce Questions and Taunts': Married Life in Working-Class London, 1870–1914," *Feminist Studies* 8 (1982): 575–602; Mary Blewett, "Work, Gender, and the Artisan Tradition in New England Shoemaking, 1780–1860," *Journal of Social History* 17 (1983): 221–48. See also Christine Griffin et al., "Women and Leisure," in *Sport, Culture, and Ideology*, ed. Jennifer Hargreave (London, 1982). A detailed discussion of working-class women's leisure appears in Kathy Peiss, *Cheap Amusements: Working Women and Leisure in Turn-of-the-Century New York* (Philadelphia, 1986).

baseball games, went fishing, or took outings to Rockaway Beach, while their wives stayed at home or took the children on walks or to local parks. In one Irish-American family, for example, the wife's recreation involved sitting on her front steps and gossiping with neighbors, as well as taking her children to the park and to the local settlement house for free movies. In contrast, her husband went out "for a shave and afterward treat[ed] his friend at one of the saloons" on Saturday nights, while on Sunday he read the newspaper and went out for a meal.[3]

Workingmen had access to a highly visible network of recreational institutions integrated into the public life of the working-class community. The saloon, which dominated the physical space of most working-class neighborhoods, was an arena in which male camaraderie resonated with financial aid, resource-sharing, and political activity. Not only did the saloon serve as a means of recuperation from the rigors of industrial labor, but its role as an employment agency, loan agency, union meeting hall, communications center, and locus for social drinking made it a hub of male working-class concerns. Similarly, fraternal societies, lodges, and clubs supported a range of recreational activities that integrated companionship and amusement with economic aid. Typically, such voluntary organizations would sponsor balls, picnics, and excursions to raise money for charitable purposes or for mutual benefit. Organized by immigrant groups, many of these associations reinforced ethnic ties as well. Labor organizations and political clubs connected leisure to larger political concerns; unions, for example, commonly used the back rooms of saloons for their meetings, combining drinking and fraternizing with union business.[4]

Historians have celebrated saloons and voluntary organizations as central to the organizational life of workers' communities, institutions that supported class interests and expressed a culture opposed to bourgeois values. At the same time, these recreational forms reinforced a distinctly masculine culture and were expressions of male privilege. The sociability of the saloons centered on discussions of work, politics,

3. Elsa Herzfeld, *Family Monographs: The History of Twenty-Four Families in the Middle-West Side of New York City* (New York, 1905), 50; George E. Bevans, *How Workingmen Spend Their Spare Time* (New York, 1913), 31; New York State Factory Investigating Commission, *Fourth Report Transmitted to Legislature, February 15, 1915*, Sen. Doc. 43 (Albany, N.Y., 1915), 1781–1808.

4. On saloons, see n. 1, and Bevans, *How Workingmen Spend Their Spare Time*, 20–21; Raymond C. Spaulding, "The Saloons of the District," in University Settlement Society of New York, *Report* (New York, 1899). On working-class voluntary organizations, see Richard H. Lane, "East Side Benefit Societies," in University Settlement Society, *Report*, 27–28; Mabel Hurd Willett, *The Employment of Women in the Clothing Trades* (New York, 1902), 131–32.

and sports. Many bars encouraged rowdy behavior and vulgar language unacceptable in other areas of social life; disorderly songs,
obscene jokes, and risqué stories circulated among the patrons. Mutuality among men was affirmed by the custom of treating one's mates to
rounds of beer or games of billiards. Within this homosocial world,
rituals of aggression and competition—through card games, drinking,
and gambling—were important mechanisms of male bonding. The
presence and availability of prostitutes were commonplace aspects of
saloon culture. Such patterns of behavior could also be found in other
amusement places frequented by men, such as pool halls, bowling al-
leys, and shooting galleries.[5]

Women had limited access to the economic and psychological benefits these institutions provided. As one investigator observed, "the men
have the saloons, political clubs, trade-unions or lodges for their recreation . . . while the mothers have almost no recreation, only a dreary
round of work, day after day, with occasionally a door-step gossip to
vary the monotony of their lives." One of the few explicit descriptions
of married women's leisure reveals its emphemeral quality, its orientation to home, and its reliance on informal kin and friendship networks:
"Many women spend their leisure sitting on the steps of their tenement
gossiping; some lean out of the window with a pillow to keep their
elbows from being scraped by the stone sills; others take walks to the
parks; some occasionally visit relatives or friends; and there is, once in a
while, a dinner party; but, on the whole, except for the men, there is
little conscious recreation."[6]

The nature of married women's leisure was dictated by the sexual
division of labor and shaped by the work rhythms of the home. One
consequence of industrialization, historians have observed, is the segmentation of work and leisure, but in these years the work of married
women—both paid and unpaid—remained largely household-based
and task-oriented. Women's work scheduling followed household
chores of cleaning, cooking, and child care, in addition to a wide range
of such wage-earning activities as keeping boarders, taking in laundry,
and sewing garments. While men took their ease at home with the

5. Aspects of the male culture of the saloon are described in investigations conducted
by the Committee of Fourteen, a New York reform organization that combatted vice and
prostitution. See, e.g., Investigator's Reports: Geo. Casey's, 251 East 39th Street, 27 June
1917; Cornerfield Brothers, 301 Eighth Avenue, 14 May 1917; Exchange, 1652 Madison
Avenue, 12 January 1917, all in Records of the Committee of Fourteen, Rare Books and
Manuscripts Division, New York Public Library, Astor, Lenox, and Tilden Foundations.

6. New York State Factory Investigating Commission, *Fourth Report*, 1667; Louise
Bolard More, *Wage-Earners' Budgets: A Study of Standards and Costs of Living in New York
City* (New York, 1907), 12.

after-dinner ritual of pipe and newspaper, women's work continued. One reporter, for example, painted the typical evening scene in an East Side home: "The mother is attending to her household work, the father is reading a paper, or he may be watching the children at play." The nature of their work gave married women less leisure than men, and the free time they had was intermittent, snatched between household chores. Doing the washing, supervising children in the tenement yard, or shopping at the local marketplace, women might find a few moments to socialize with friends and neighbors.[7]

The asymmetrical distribution of resources among family members also limited married women's access to recreation. The working-class family as a unit budgeted only a small part of its earnings for recreation as such, but a substantial portion of the household income was allocated as spending money for the breadwinner's personal use. Husbands retained the right to remove whatever spending money they desired before contributing the rest to household expenses. Workingmen spent about 10 percent of their weekly income on themselves, purchasing beer and liquor, tobacco, and movie and theater tickets. Although social custom dictated the amount of spending money a "good husband" might take, men nevertheless retained control of the financial division between their own desires and the family's welfare. "The husband brings his wages to his wife at the end of the week or fortnight," observed the investigator Elsa Herzfeld. "He gives her the whole amount and receives back carfare and 'beer' money; or he gives her as much as 'he feels like' or 'as much as he has left after Saturday night.'" Spending money allowed men to pursue a social life based on access to commercial recreation in the public domain, but married women received no spending money of their own. Typically, their expenditures were governed by family needs and dictated by the household economy. Even married women's income, earned by keeping boarders or taking in laundry, was spent on the home and family—usually to buy needed clothing for children or better food—not on personal recreation.[8]

These gender-based divisions contributed to the different recreational cultures women and men experienced. Married women's physical and economic orientation toward the household led them to construct the home as a locus for family recreation. Working-class wives

7. Paul Abelson, "The East Side Home," University Settlement Society of New York, *Report* (New York, 1897), 29.

8. Herzfeld, *Family Monographs*, 50; Bevans, *How Workingmen Spend Their Spare Time*, 75–76; More, *Wage-Earners' Budgets*, 97–98.

carefully decorated their small tenement quarters, even designating one of the multipurpose rooms the "parlor." Heavy overstuffed furniture, cheap lace curtains, pianos and carpets—often purchased on the installment plan—crowded the more prosperous working-class homes. The only recreation of some families, observed one investigator, "was the display of their furniture." The home provided a gathering place not only for the immediate family but for a woman's network of kin and neighbors. Kitchens were used for everyday socializing as well as religious and cultural observances, and house parties for birthdays or other occasions were common.[9]

The social web of female kin and neighbors also structured married women's leisure. Exchanging daily courtesies, watching the children, borrowing and lending food and other necessities were common practices integrated into women's leisure. Such customs affirmed working-class traditions of mutuality and reciprocity, values that were reinforced for men in saloons and fraternal orders. Men's institutions, however, were distinct and separate recreational spaces. Women's sociability was far more intertwined with the actual labor they performed, whether sharing household chores, helping the sick or distressed, or doing the "kinwork" involved in maintaining family ties and rituals. The distinction between women's and men's leisure may be seen, for example, in the lives of two Irish families in an upper East Side tenement: "Mrs. H. is very often in the house of Mrs. C. and they exchange many favors in the course of a day, while at night their husbands play cards and share their beer."[10]

If the workingmen's network of leisure institutions constituted an alternative culture linked to working-class interests and consciousness, as recent historians have asserted, then the place of married women in this public culture is problematic. Married women engaged in various forms of extradomestic recreation, but such activities were largely noncommercial: enjoying local parks with their children, promenading the streets, participating in church-sponsored activities and festivals. Wom-

9. Robert Coit Chapin, *The Standard of Living among Workingmen's Families in New York City* (New York, 1909), 210. On the furnishings of working-class homes, see Lizabeth Cohen, "Embellishing a Life of Labor: An Interpretation of the Material Culture of American Working-Class Homes," *Journal of American Culture* 3 (1980): 752–75. On the kitchen as gathering place, see Samuel Chotzinoff, *A Lost Paradise* (New York, 1955), 51.

10. Thomas Jesse Jones, *Sociology of a New York City Block* (New York, 1904), 100, 108–9. On women's informal networks, see Judith E. Smith, "Our Own Kind: Family and Community Networks in Providence," in *A Heritage of Her Own*, ed. Nancy F. Cott and Elizabeth H. Pleck (New York, 1979), 393–411. For the concept of kinwork, see Micaela di Leonardo, *The Varieties of Ethnic Experience: Kinship, Class, and Gender among California Italian-Americans* (Ithaca, 1984), 191–229.

en attended the balls, excursions, and social events sponsored by fraternal orders, but they participated in regular lodge or club meetings much less frequently than men. Most important, wives did not share in the celebration of the saloon as a stronghold of working-class culture, being far more aware of it as a center of male privilege. Rather than seat themselves in saloons and have their respectability questioned, drinking women more commonly "rushed the growler," buying buckets of beer to be drunk at home. Many wives voiced their opposition to the men's habit of consuming their wages in saloons instead of committing their earnings to the household, decrying in particular the practice of buying rounds. And, as has been well documented, women's interest in political or union involvement was often checked by their distaste for meetings held in saloons or unsavory halls.[11]

Married women's recreation in the public sphere was most affectd notby the traditional network of male working-class institutions but by a commercial development: the rise of the moving picture show after 1905. Movies provided the only regular form of commercial amusement for most working-class wives. Nickelodeon shows were inexpensive, and a mother could scrimp a nickel or two from the family budget to attend a matinee or evening show with her children. Movie exhibitors encouraged married women's attendance by cultivating an atmostphere of neighborliness, providing a place where kin and friends could meet for an inexpensive hour of fun and relaxation. One attraction of the movies, observed one writer, was that "the mothers do not have to 'dress' to attend them." Movie houses also doubled as local daycare centers where women could safely deposit their children for the afternoon. And if, as reformers claimed, the movies were "substitutes for the saloons," then working-class wives' support of the movies may have involved the additional motivation of protecting their families from the abuses of the workingmen's recreational world.[12] By welcoming working-class wives, such commercial establishments as movie houses may well have challenged the traditional organization of working-class recreation. For married women, participation in "public" lei-

11. Women's drinking habits are discussed in Robert DeForest and Laurence Veiller, eds., *The Tenement House Problem* (New York, 1903), 1:397; Lillian Betts, *The Leaven in a Great City* (New York, 1902), 52. Women's aversion to saloons as union meeting places is discussed in Alice Kessler-Harris, *Out to Work: A History of Wage-Earning Women in the United States* (New York, 1982), 158–59.

12. "The Nickelodeon," *Moving Picture World* 1 (1907): 140; Lewis E. Palmer, "The World in Motion," *Survey* 22 (1909): 356; M. M. Davis, *The Exploitation of Pleasure: A Study of Commercial Recreations in New York City* (New York, 1910), 16. See also Elizabeth Ewen, "City Lights: Immigrant Women and the Rise of the Movies," *Signs* 5 (supp., 1980): S45–S65.

sure activities coincided with leisure's declining basis in a semiautono-
mous working-class culture and the growth of commercialized forms of
recreation.

Working-class leisure in this period was segregated not only by
gender but by age and marital status as well. Single women participated
in the public realm of recreation to a much greater extent than their
mothers or married sisters. Accounts of reformers, social investigators,
and young women themselves resound with reports of women crowding dancehalls, attending theatrical performances, and going on Sunday excursions. In New York City, these women were typically wage
earners who worked in retail stores, domestic service, and such light
manufacturing industries as garmentmaking and bookbinding. In the
course of a day they were more likely to experience the segmentation
of labor and leisure than were most married women. If the forms of
workers' leisure were a response to the conditions of industrial labor,
mediating the experience of industrial capitalism, were such women
more closely integrated into the working-class culture expressed in
male and public leisure institutions than married women?

Important differences in the social experiences of wage-earning
women and men shaped the dimensions of young women's leisure.
The working day was arduous for both male and female wage earners,
and potential leisure hours were consumed by commuting and the
exhaustion of physical exertion. As one working girl observed, "We
only went from bed to work, and from work to bed again." However,
women on the average labored longer hours than men, and their jobs
were characterized by nonuniform working days. Domestic service allowed little free time, while the seasonal nature of many industries, low
levels of unionization, and ineffective enforcement of protective legislation limited many women's chances for leisure.[13]

Moreover, household chores placed heavy demands on women's
time after work. Many self-supporting women spent their evening
hours preparing for the next day by laundering, mending, and sewing
clothes. Louise Odencrantz reported in her study of Italian women that
"when the women or girls were visited at night they were more likely to
be found at home busy at the washtub or ironing board than out at a
dance or theater." Those who lived at home were often expected to

13. Sue Ainslie Clark and Edith Wyatt, *Making Both Ends Meet: The Income and Outlay
of New York Working Girls* (New York, 1911), 132. On the longer work day for women, see
Edward Ewing Pratt, *Industrial Causes of Congestion of Population in New York City* (New
York, 1911), 124. Working conditions of female wage earners are surveyed in Kessler-
Harris, *Out to Work*, and in Leslie Woodcock Tentler, *Wage-Earning Women: Industrial
Work and Family Life in the United States, 1900–1930* (New York, 1979).

help with the evening meal, cleaning, or caring for children. One survey of young working women found, for example, that three-quarters of those interviewed assisted with housework after their day of wage labor—unlike their working brothers.[14]

In general, single women had more spending money for recreation than working-class wives, but their resources were still more limited than men's. Sexual segmentation of the labor market, the concentration of women in semiskilled and seasonal employment, and the demands of the family economy structured women's wage labor so that few could achieve self-sufficiency. Most women did not earn a living wage—estimated to be $9 or $10 a week in 1910—and the wage differential between male and female workers was vast. Only about 15 percent of New York's women workers in 1914 lived alone, and those who did spent most of their earnings for room, board, and clothing. To pay for entertainment, many self-supporting women skimped on essentials in their weekly budgets, such as food.[15]

Financial resources were little better among the vast majority of women living with families or relatives. Most of them handed their pay envelopes unopened to their parents; according to one study, over four-fifths contributed all of their earnings to the family. In return, most daughters were given small sums of spending money, averaging twenty-five to fifty cents a week, which often had to cover clothing and transportation as well as recreation. Their spending money was much less than that allocated to sons, many of whom simply paid board to their parents and kept the rest of their earnings.[16]

Nevertheless, access to spending money and the segmentation of the work day did make involvement in public forms of leisure more likely for single women, though the formal network of working-class recreational institutions remained an alien world to most of them. Some female wage earners began to enter the back rooms of saloons after 1900 to have a free lunch or pass a sociable evening, but most avoided such places, fearing that their respectability would be compromised. Nor did young working women join lodges or mutual aid societies in large numbers. While women customarily spent five to ten cents a week on insurance, the money was usually paid into a private

14. Louise C. Odencrantz, *Italian Women in Industry: A Study of Conditions in New York City* (New York, 1919), 235; U.S. Bureau of Labor, *Working Women in Large Cities: Fourth Annual Report of the Commissioner of Labor, 1888* (Washington, D.C., 1889), 340–42.

15. Factory Investigating Commission, *Fourth Report*, 1:35; 4:1081, 1507–11, 1675–92.

16. Factory Investigating Commission, *Fourth Report*, 4:1512–13; More, *Wage-Earners' Budgets*, 87; Mary Van Kleeck, *Artificial Flower-Makers* (New York, 1913), 235.

insurance company, not a mutual aid society. Men's benefit societies were financial and social institutions rooted in working-class culture, but most of those for working women were organized by middle-class reformers, philanthropists, and "enlightened" department store owners. When working women did create their own leisure institutions, they took the form of social clubs or amusement societies. As one investigator noted, young women's organizations "seem to be largely social; they belong to little societies; they tell me they belong to a 'Heart and Hand Club,' a social club; nothing for the study of their own wage conditions at all." Sporting such outrageous names as the "Lady Flashers" and "Lady Millionaires," these clubs sponsored balls and outings and attended the entertainments of other clubs. As their names suggest, their purpose was pleasure, not economic support and mutual aid.[17]

This is not to suggest that young women's leisure did not express or reinforce a class-based identity. Particularly for unionized workers, leisure was linked to a consciousness of class interests. One woman in a newly organized shop observed, for example, that the "shorter work day brought me my first idea of there being such a thing as pleasure," and she spent that extra time with her union sisters. "I was twenty-one before I went to a theater and then I went with a crowd of union girls to a Saturday matinee performance," she observed. "I was twenty-three before I saw a dance and that was a union dance too." Dances sponsored by unions and political organizations offered not only fun and sociability but opportunities for educating workers and fostering class solidarity. One journalist described a union picnic and dance, for example: "No girl is expected to dance with a man who does not belong to a union unless he promises to join, for a picnic is also a proselyting occasion."[18]

The connections between daily social life and class interests were often close to the surface. Halls normally used for dances and concerts, for example, would be converted into communication centers during strikes:

17. New York Special Committee of the Assembly . . . to Investigate the Condition of Female Labor in the City of New York, *Report and Testimony* (Albany, N.Y., 1896), 1:85. On women's social clubs, see Herbert Asbury, *The Gangs of New York* (1927; rpt., New York, 1970), 168–69; Belle Mead, "Social Pleasures of East Side Jews" (master's thesis, Columbia University, 1904). Factory Investigating Commission, *Fourth Report*, 4:170–74, indicates young women's participation in mutual aid societies; 1:783, their attendance at saloons.

18. "Making Ends Meet on the Minimum Wage," *Life and Labor* 3 (1913): 302; Mary Gay Humphreys, "The New York Working-Girl," *Scribner's* 20 (1896): 513.

The "Grand American Palace" was packed with a strangely unaccustomed crowd. Every night "Professor" Somebody's orchestra . . . dispensed music from the little platform in the corner and some scores of work-worn immigrant boys and girls, at so much per head, struggled and giggled through the waltz and two-step. But now . . . from gaudy wall to gaudy wall were jammed girls with determined workaday faces. Strikers they were—a group of shirt-waist makers, whose strike in New York has been the biggest and most bitter strike of women in the history of American labor troubles.

Moreover, the greater social freedom young women experienced in their recreational lives at times coincided with their exposure to new ideas and possibilities for action as workers. One Jewish garment worker, who developed her political ideas before she emigrated from Austria, observed that girls were not actually involved in organizational work there. In New York, however, she quickly became active in socialist and union organizing, at the same time throwing herself into a fast-paced social life that included *landsmanschaft* dances, Yiddish theater, sports, and lectures.[19]

Nevertheless, the consciousness of young women as expressed in leisure took shape from the dynamics of gender as well as class. The "alternative culture" many women expressed was less an assertion of class-based values than a challenge to the patriarchal order of working-class life. Operating within a long-standing tradition of rowdy and disorderly female behavior, some working women used their leisure time to express a sense of personal independence, sensuality, and the rejection of parental authority; they articulated a flamboyant self-presentation through fancy dress, elaborate hairstyles, and the use of cosmetics in an age when such adornments were morally suspect. For these women, leisure was an arena of sexual experimentation and the active pursuit of romance and adventure. Staying out late at night, picking up men at theaters and public halls, using slang and verbal come-ons in the streets, enjoying sensual dances at masquerade balls— these were common cultural practices among many female wage earners.[20]

19. Miriam Finn Scott, "The Spirit of the Girl Strikers," *Outlook* 19 (1910): 392; tape I-59, New York City Immigrant Labor History Collection of the City College Oral History Project, Robert F. Wagner Archives, Tamiment Institute Library, New York University.

20. For further discussion and documentation of this cultural style, see Kathy Peiss, "'Charity Girls' and City Pleasures: Historical Notes on Working-Class Sexuality, 1880–1920," in *Powers of Desire: The Politics of Sexuality*, ed. Ann Snitow et al. (New York, 1983). On female rowdiness in the nineteenth century, see Mary Christine Stansell, "Women of the Laboring Poor in New York City, 1820–1860" (Ph.D. diss., Yale University, 1979).

At the same time, this expression of autonomy occurred in a context of dependency within leisure, as well as in the workplace and the family. Having limited spending money, most women relied on men to pay for entrance fees, drinks, and other incidentals; doing so allowed them to participate in a social life oriented toward public commercial amusements. As one observer noted, "the acceptance on the part of the girl of almost any invitation needs little explanation when one realizes that she often goes pleasureless unless she does accept 'free treats.'" Unlike working-class men, whose custom of treating affirmed reciprocity among peers, treating placed women in a position of dependency on and vulnerability to men; they bartered good looks, personality, and sexuality for companionship and amusement.[21]

While the tradition of "disorderly women" stretches back into pre-industrial society, by 1900 this cultural style was attaining greater legitimacy in leisure, not in the traditional network of working-class institutions but through the emergence of new commercialized amusements. Thousands of young women attended public dances each week in metropolitan New York; in 1910, more than 500 commercial dancehalls and 100 dancing academies competed for their patronage. The large amusement parks at Coney Island and Fort George drew female wage earners to dance pavilions and Bowery-style arcades. Vaudeville, variety houses, and moving picture shows also attracted large numbers of young women; according to one recreation report in 1910, women and girls made up one-third of the working-class audience for vaudeville and 40 percent of all moviegoers. In order to gain patronage among young women, these commercial ventures promoted a concept of leisure that linked mixed-sex companionship, romance and sensuality, and heedless fun. This cultural reorientation, observable across class lines in the early twentieth century, permitted girls to act "disorderly" but still retain respectability.[22] Excluded from the lodge and saloon but welcomed in dancehalls and amusement resorts, single women increasingly identified their social life in the public realm with commercial amusements, not with the class-based recreation of their fathers.

Working-class forms of leisure, then, held a different meaning for

---

21. Factory Investigating Commission, *Fourth Report*, 4:1685–86.

22. Davis, *Exploitation of Pleasure;* Belle Lindner Israels, "The Way of the Girl," *Survey* 22 (1909): 486–97. On leisure and the cultural reorientation in the early twentieth century, see Lewis A. Erenberg, *Steppin' Out: New York Nightlife and the Transformation of American Culture, 1890–1930* (Westport, Conn., 1981); Lary May, *Screening Out the Past: The Birth of Mass Culture and the Motion Picture Industry* (New York, 1980); John Kasson, *Amusing the Million: Coney Island at the Turn of the Century* (New York, 1978); Peiss, *Cheap Amusements.*

both married and single women than they did for men. Although involved to varying degrees in the network of working-class institutions, women did not find the same levels of social, psychological, and economic support as members of the working class that men found in their recreation. Leisure activities based in the household, family, and kinship ties, as well as emergent forms of commercial entertainment, played a more important role in their daily lives.

Historians of working-class culture cannot assume that women were simply "workers" who, like men, forged and defended distinctive forms of popular entertainment as alternatives to leisure activities imposed by the middle class or the elite. Within working-class culture there were tensions and divisions arising from the relations of gender, in addition to differences in ethnicity, religion, and age. These social relations produced among women and men different modes of cultural expression that were articulated in leisure activity. At the same time, gender had effects beyond the dichotomization of working-class culture. It would be erroneous to conclude, for example, that women weakened class solidarity by turning to new commercial amusements rather than class-based recreation; workingmen, too, were being seduced away from their traditional institutions by the movies. Moreover, private and public realms of activity were separate, but the walls were not impermeable. At times the leisure worlds of women and men mutually supported class interests: in periods of labor unrest, for example, or when, as in 1907 and 1908, the mayor threatened to close the city's nickelodeons.[23] But without larger issues to galvanize the community, women's exclusion from the traditional institutions of working-class leisure—or their marginality within them—may well have limited class consciousness and solidarity. The sexual division of leisure cut across working-class social life, and historians must rethink their conceptualization of workers' culture in that light, taking into account the complexities of consciousness rooted in differing gender-based experiences.

23. Peiss, *Cheap Amusements*, 158–59.

7

From "Sealskin and Shoddy"
to "The Pig-Headed Girl":
Patriarchal Fables for Workers

Ann Schofield

The study of culture has long intrigued yet puzzled social historians. In their search for insights into this troublesome topic, historians have turned to sociologists, who stress the relationship between fundamental symbols, values, and social cohesion; to anthropologists, particularly to Clifford Geertz, whose symbolic anthropology they have found useful in analyzing the collective behavior of inarticulate groups; and to contemporary psychoanalysts, whose concern with language and consciousness illuminates the connection between cultural ideas and forms and their internalization by individuals. To complicate this already muddy theoretical brew, politics frequently enters historical inquiry through Frankfurt school theorists who seek to answer the question of how culture encourages the maintenance of class rule.[1]

I appreciate the insightful comments of Heidi Hartmann and Alice Kessler-Harris on the original version of this paper and the closer readings given the revised article by Andrew Debicki and Elizabeth Kuznesof. Their assistance has improved it; its errors are mine alone.

1. A representative sampling of some of this literature includes Leo Lowenthal, *Literature, Popular Culture, and Society* (Englewood Cliffs, N.J., 1961); Raymond Williams, *Marxism and Literature* (New York, 1977); Clifford Geertz, "Ideology as a Cultural System," in *Ideology and Discontent*, ed. David Apter (New York, 1964); Ira H. Cohen, *Ideology and Unconsciousness: Reich, Freud, and Marx* (New York, 1982); E. Ann Kaplan "Integrating Marxist and Psychoanalytic Approaches in Feminist Literary Criticism," *Millennium:*

The critical link between history and theory, for most historians, lies at the intersection of social, ideological, and economic structures with human behavior. Theory helps us to formulate questions about historical activity which, when answered, draw us back to a more complete understanding and often a reformulation of theory.

The dialectic between theory and historical reality is well illustrated by historians of women who debate the sexual division of labor and its implications for women's status. This article attempts to expand that discussion by exploring various cultural forms for the persistence of and/or change in ideas about gender to help answer critical questions about continued female subordination despite changing material historical circumstances.

To state briefly the problematic leading in the direction of cultural analysis, one must begin with a series of influential articles in which Heidi Hartmann argues that patriachy, the hierarchical control of women by men, systematically continues to shape the socioeconomic conditions of women's employment even under capitalism.[2] Patriarchy and capitalism have historically operated as dual systems, she contends, to determine social relations oppressive to women: the "material base upon which patriarchy rests lies most fundamentally in men's control over women's labor power." Specifically, she sees even such institutions as labor unions as perpetuating patterns of male domination.

Hartmann's thesis has been applauded by feminist scholars who find the historical persistence of patriarchy the most convincing explanation for women's secondary status.[3] Others, however, feel that Hartmann's thesis fails to recognize the interacting patterns of Marxist and feminist analysis and suffers from a lack of specificity, from an underawareness of class and an overawareness of economics.[4] In many ways this debate between the proponents and opponents of patriarchy as a causal agent of women's oppression has reached a stalemate. Cultural analysis can enable us to break that stalemate by seeing patriarchy more clearly as a dynamic force in the lives and historical consciousness of both women and men.

Film Journal 6 (Spring 1980): 8–17; Stuart and Elizabeth Ewen, *Channels of Desire* (New York, 1982); Walter Benjamin, *Illuminations*, ed. Hannah Arendt (New York, 1968).

2. Heidi Hartmann, "The Unhappy Marriage of Marxism and Feminism: Towards a More Progressive Union," in *Women and Revolution*, ed. Lydia Sargent (Boston, 1981), 1–41; and "Capitalism, Patriarchy, and Job Segregation by Sex," *Signs* 1 (Spring 1976): 137–69.

3. Essays by Carol Brown, Katie Stewart, Ann Ferguson and Nancy Folbre, and Zillah Eisenstein in Sargent, *Women and Revolution*.

4. Essays by Iris Young, Christine Riddingh, Gloria Joseph, Carol Ehrlich, Sandra Harding, Azizah Al-Hibri, Lise Vogel, and Emily Hicks in Sargent, *Women and Revolution*.

Hartmann's definition of patriarchy can be expanded to include cultural forms as well as economic relationships through a demonstration of the way patriarchical relations and attitudes are constructed in the fiction written for the labor press between 1870 and 1920, years that saw a significant expansion of the female wage-labor force. Aimed at an audience caught in the throes of industrialization and endorsed, if not written, by trade union leaders, this material exemplifies the labor movement's ideology of gender[5] and, more significantly, suggests how ideal types and images were internalized by workers. Novellas, short stories, and poetry published between 1870 and 1920, a period of rapid social change, helped women to resolve the contradictions between society's ideas about them and the reality of their working lives.

Focusing on ideas about image and fantasy, about ideology and consciousness, about projection and internalization, this line of inquiry can help us explore questions about the degree to which patriarchal attitudes become part of the personal content of the lives of working-class women and men. Most especially we can examine the question of how femininity and masculinity are inscribed in fiction so that the tensions between work and home life, production and reproduction, family and individual needs are resolved for women. As one commentator has put it, popular literature fills the sociopsychological function of "ideologically supporting readers' interpretive schemes or identities . . . by providing an imaginary realm in which 'outmoded' norms and values are once again revitalized." Jochen Schulte-Sasse goes on to state that "popular literature was and is judged positively by its readers whenever it reduces or compensates for cognitive or emotive dissonances within an individual or within a social group; it was and is judged negatively (or at least meets with indifference) whenever these dissonances are not addressed or even reinforced."[6]

In short, through these stories one can enter the minds of working-class women and men at the turn of the century, when work and sex roles were in a particularly fluid state and when dissonance between traditional concepts about women and the material reality of women's lives was particularly apparent. Between 1870 and 1920, the propor-

5. Ann Schofield, "Rebel Girls and Union Maids: The Woman Question in the Journals of the AFL and IWW, 1905–20," *Feminist Studies* 9 (Summer 1983): 334–58; and "The Rise of the Pig-Headed Girl: An Analysis of the American Labor Press for its Attitudes toward Women, 1877–1920" (Ph.D. diss., State University of New York, Binghamton, 1980).

6. Jochen Schulte-Sasse, "Toward a 'Culture' for the Masses: The Socio-Psychological Function of Popular Literature in Germany and the U.S., 1880–1920," *New German Critique* 29 (Spring/Summer 1983): 85.

tion of women who worked for a wage rose from approximately 15 to 24 percent. Most of those workers were young and unmarried; many were immigrants or the children of immigrants. Unlike the female workers of earlier generations, these women increasingly found themselves employed in the manufacture of garments, shoes, cigars, and other machine-produced goods. During these same years the process of industrial work was rapidly becoming deskilled, largely as a result of such technological innovations as the sewing machine. The advent of scientific management techniques further eroded the personal relationship between employer and employee and depersonalized the workplace.[7]

Beyond the workplace, young urban working women experienced conflict between conventional values and the turbulent modern world of the streets. As several scholars have shown, dancehalls, nickelodeons, and other aspects of urban popular culture seduced young girls from the traditional world of their mothers.[8] While the stories discussed below incorporated material about women's work and public activities, the underlying themes and, indeed, the structural relationships in the stories are patriarchal. That is to say, the stories implicitly recognize the superiority of male bosses, owners, fathers, and husbands and thus reinforce prevailing cultural concepts of masculinity and femininity as they resolve the tension between old and new.

It is well to remember that the history of women seems continually cast in dichotomies: private and public, home and marketplace, production and reproduction. The tension and interrelationship between these poles is used to explain women's historical subordination to men; breaking that tension has become a goal of women's liberation. Under industrial capitalism, however, an additional polarity further defined women's secondary status: the evolution of separate, noncompeting labor markets labeled "male" and "female." The broad structural outlines of these markets are familiar: the male marked by higher wages, more skill, better benefits, more unions; the female consisting of lower-paid, less skilled, more poorly unionized work. Theorists of labor market segmentation have seen occupational segregation as a way of using

7. Daniel Nelson, *Managers and Workers: Origins of the New Factory System in the United States, 1880–1920* (Madison, Wis., 1975); David F. Noble, *America by Design: Science, Technology and the Rise of Corporate Capitalism* (New York, 1977).

8. Elizabeth Ewen, *Immigrant Women in the Land of Dollars: Life and Culture on the Lower East Side, 1890–1925* (New York, 1985); Kathy Peiss, *Cheap Amusements: Working Women and Leisure in Turn-of-the-Century New York* (Philadelphia, 1986); Joanne Reitano, "Working Girls Unite," *American Quarterly* 36 (Spring 1984): 112–34.

the sexual division of labor for the benefit of capital.[9] Critics of this theory have pointed out that it does little to explain the causes of a dual labor market and nothing to demonstrate how employers turn the sexual division of labor to their profit.[10] Nevertheless, the historical reality of occupational segregation remains. Today, when the labor market seems to be in the process of reformulation and new areas are emerging with specific gender labels, the task of understanding the history and the perpetuating mechanisms of this situation is more urgent than ever.

Several stories will illustrate the problem of adding cultural material and psychological process to theories of patriarchy and occupational segregation. The first is a novella, "Sealskin and Shoddy," by the popular fiction writer W. H. Little; it was serialized in the Knights of Labor's *Journal of United Labor* in 1888 as "new technology and new forms of industrial organization altered the structure of work, promising new opportunities to women."[11] The others are short stories by Gertrude Barnum, which appeared in the *Ladies' Garment Worker* between 1912 and 1915, written for an industry staffed by female workers. Both authors use conventions typical of the sentimental fiction of the day.

"Sealskin and Shoddy" had a phenomenal impact on its readers; according to the *Journal,* the story "lined up thousands in the order." Its appeal seems obvious, since its setting was—at least in part—the world of the industrial worker. The initial installment enticed readers by pledging that "the true womanhood of woman and manhood of man are also vividly pictured . . . in a thrilling story of a sewing girl's life; her struggles for bread against the injustice of man to man, of woman to woman; against disease, privation and death itself." True to its promise, the story does convey a distinct sense of the feminine and the masculine, but these sensibilities reflect middle-class social mores

9. Alice Kessler-Harris, "Stratifying by Sex: Understanding the History of Working Women," in *Labor Market Segmentation,* ed. Richard Edwards et al. (Lexington, Mass., 1975), 217–42.

10. Veronica Beechy, "Women and Production: A Critical Analysis of Some Sociological Theories of Women's Work," in *Feminism and Materialism,* ed. Annette Kuhn and Annmarie Wolpe (London, 1978), 155–97.

11. Susan Levine, *Labor's True Woman: Carpet Weavers, Industrialization, and Labor Reform in the Gilded Age* (Philadelphia, 1984), finds that a story written for another Knights of Labor paper in 1887 conveyed a moral lesson different from that of the conventional romance and that each character "illustrated some aspect of the order critique of the industrial system or its ideal of the cooperative industrial order." While a similar statement could be made about "Sealskin and Shoddy," my concern here is not what the story tells us about the Knights, but rather what it conveys about gender.

rather than the distinctive values and experiences of owners and workers.[12]

Gertrude Barnum, a Progressive reformer and organizer for the Women's Trade Union League and the International Ladies' Garment Workers' Union, wrote her stories for the *Ladies' Garment Worker,* a journal that appeared in English, Yiddish, and Italian editions. Like the Knights of Labor paper, the *Ladies' Garment Worker* reached a wide readership of workers, many of whom, observers claimed, were versed in the work of such classic authors as Zola, Tolstoy, and Hugo.[13] Barnum's characters exhibit autonomous behavior in choice of work and selection of mate; they find that their independent ideas and actions enhance rather than conflict with femininity.

But neither "Sealskin" nor Barnum's stories represented or mirrored the real options available to their readers. The heroine of Little's story is the privileged daughter of a wealthy family. Barnum's characters encounter a world in which opportunity and occupational mobility are equally available to women and men; only individual effort is required for success. And in both instances, occupational segregation— that is, the appropriateness of different work for women and men—is accepted as a given. Thus one of the most fundamental mechanisms for maintaining women in less advantageous economic and social roles is linked to personal feminine qualities and presented in a romantically appealing form.

"Sealskin and Shoddy" is the tale of Mamie Symington, young daughter of a Cincinnati manufacturer. When the story opens, we learn that Mamie's father, Paul Symington, is in Scotland; that Mamie has recently returned home from college; and that her mother died shortly after Mamie's birth. Mamie happens upon Lizzie Knowlton, the consumptive orphaned daughter of a genteel family whom circumstances have forced into factory labor. She befriends the young victim and, in the guise of Mary Stillson, nurses her back to health. The role of Lady Bountiful, though, does not wholly satisfy Mamie. Realizing the connection between environment and disease and determined to investigate the problem further, she disguises herself yet again—this time as Betty Broadbird, an unlettered yet goodhearted factory girl.

Stripped now of class privilege, Mamie enters a strikingly un-

12. W. H. Little, "Sealskin and Shoddy," *Journal of United Labor* 9, 12 July–1 November 1888.

13. Pauline Newman Papers, Schlesinger Library, Radcliffe College, Cambridge. I appreciate Miss Newman's permission to read and quote from her papers.

familiar world. As Betty Broadbird, she takes completed piecework to several factories, where she is cheated and victimized. Then, upon entering her own father's factory as a worker, she discovers that she is not alone in her grievances. When a crisis develops, the girls organize a "Sewing Girls Protective Association" and go on strike against Symington Clothing Company. Supported by male unionists and by a $500 contribution from Mamie Symington, the strike becomes a controversial topic in Cincinnati society. Mamie and her fellow reformers, who include the noble Hal Hinton, all agree on the righteousness of the workers' cause. Herbert Standish, manager of the Symington factory and suitor for Mamie's hand, leads the opposition.

When a young worker is driven to suicide by poverty and despair, the strike takes on a tragic tone. Standish feels compelled to inform the absent Mr. Symington about his daughter's activities; Symington, now in Peru, orders Mamie to cease her involvement with the workers' cause and her relationship with the reformers. Mamie temporarily accedes to her father's request but sends him a long explanatory letter, begging him to return home. When he does so, the conflict between capital and labor is quickly settled through the institution of a profit-sharing scheme at the Symington factory. Mamie is given 1,000 shares of stock in her father's company, and her future husband, Hal Hinton (now a professor and associate editor of *Political Economics*), becomes president of the company.

Although "Sealskin and Shoddy" closely follows the conventions of nineteenth-century sentimental fiction, its plot, its characterizations, and especially its description of the masculine and feminine can answer a number of the questions posed at the outset of this paper.

The feminine ideal as expressed in the character of Mamie Symington is a pure and noblehearted woman motivated by Christian principles. Mamie, who was "mild as an autumn sunset and loving as Cupid," is highly intuitive; strong emotion frequently leaves her in tears. Although she is physically attractive, her true beauty is rooted in her inner self: "Her lovely face was made more beautiful by her noble character, which constantly appeared in her mobile features in ever-changing aspects, each one more fascinating than its predecessor." Despite his emphasis on Mamie's character, however, the author never allows us to lose sight of her physical beauty or her own sense of herself: Mamie, we are told, "never attempted to make herself look beautiful for her own gratification." A lengthy description of her stunning appearance at one "ultra-fashionable" party is followed by the reminder that "behind her physical and artistic beauty was the greater beauty of an almost perfect character."

But Mamie's virtues are not reserved exclusively for women of a leisured, privileged class. Transformed and declassed into Mary Stillson and Betty Broadbird, she still retains those qualities, and we are reminded that "she was ever tidy and tastefully attired, even as Betty Broadbird, the poor sewing girl"—poor, in other words, but respectable, for womanly attributes transcend class.

Manhood is as clearly defined as womanhood. Stiff and stodgy Herbert Standish, the manager of the Symington factory, represents negative aspects of the male; the hero of the piece, Hal Hinton, represents the manly ideal. Standish had a mind that "seldom wandered from the shop and things shoppy," a venal quality that leads Mamie to tell him that his inherently "kindly and noble disposition" has been perverted by his "inordinate struggle for money." By contrast, the noble Hal Hinton—who has studied political economy at Harvard, in Paris, and in Heidelberg—has "a handsome face, radiant in intellectuality and beaming with good nature . . . the lines of character were strong and well-defined." Hal, of course, is as committed to improving the plight of workers as Mamie. And his rational appraisal of the industrial situation complements her consistently emotional response.

Mamie, Herbert, Hal, and other characters in "Sealskin and Shoddy" represent polarized stereotypes of nineteenth-century women and men operating in an industrial setting. Mamie, in her various incarnations, and Hal carry the promise that industrialism will not seriously alter the cherished and familiar social order: men will continue to be men; women will continue to be women. Mamie in particular stresses that work and union activity need not unsex or defeminize women. Union men, she promises, may safely "take their wives from the class of girls who recently formed the Sewing Girls' Union." She also claims, "I look upon the forming of unions among the working people of my sex as a step in the line of progress." (In so saying, she foreshadows later attempts of the American labor press to recruit female rank-and-file members by "feminizing" union participation.[14] Incorporating union experience into the female life cycle was as progressive as the bloomer costume.)

Furthermore, each relationship or interaction between Mamie and men is constructed along patriarchal lines. Mamie's reform activities are possible because of her father's wealth and status. She stops those activities at his direction and is reinstated in an influential position by his gift of stock. As the poor sewing girl Betty Broadbird, she is exploited and threatened with sexual harassment. One of her coworkers

14. Schofield, "Rebel Girls" and "Rise of the Pig-Headed Girl."

warns her about the foreman and his system of favors: "If you are cute you'll get on the right side of Mr. Haggerty and he will soon put you in the best place in the factory and you won't be docked for fines." She coyly flirts with Standish to influence his treatment of workers in the factory, and finally, she subordinates herself to Hal Hinton in the one relationship that may offer some promise of equity. Hinton, not surprisingly, is the actual organizer of the sewing girls' association—by reason of his superior knowledge of political economy—even before he assumes the presidency of the Symington Clothing Company.

All in all, Mamie deals with all the conflicts that arise throughout the story by working through patriarchal structures and relationships. The story resolves for a working-class audience the apparent contradictions of feminity: Can one be feminine and work in a factory? Can one be feminine and participate in unions? If a woman does these things, can she marry and have children? Mamie, in her life and her statements about workers, affirms her readers' femininity. Can workers emulate Mamie? On the economic level, obviously not. But on a moral level they can, in terms of their responsiveness to men, their acceptance of subordination to male power, and their perception of their structured inequity and its ideological justification.

Despite its patriarchal tone, such fiction as "Sealskin and Shoddy" did contain positive messages for women. As Nina Baym writes about the overplot of nineteenth-century women's fiction, "the story of young women discovering and asserting their powers, thereby wresting respect and recognition from a hostile and indifferent world, was immensely pleasurable to a huge number of American women."[15] Mamie's intelligence, creativity, and ability to affect situations surely made her a positive character for her female readers.

Questions about the resolution of conflict can also be asked of reformer Gertrude Barnum's stories in the *Ladies' Garment Worker,* the official journal of the International Ladies Garment Workers Union, between 1912 and 1915.[16] At first glance, these stories seem distinctively different from "Sealskin and Shoddy." The characters are always genuine working girls, the scene is usually the workplace, and the theme is frequently work-related. The fictional characters modestly object to "tough" language and gently sob over romantic disappoint-

---

15. Nina Baym, *Women's Fiction: A Guide to Novels by and about Women in America, 1820–1870* (Ithaca, 1978), 21.

16. Gertrude Barnum, "The Pig-Headed Girl," *Ladies' Garment Worker* (hereafter cited as *LGW*) 3 (April 1912): 26–27; "Ottilie's Garden," *LGW* 2 (December 1911): 19; "At the Shirt-Waist Factory," *LGW* (June 1910): 4; "The Pen and the Sword," *LGW* 2 (November 1911): 4; "In the Jacket Shop," *LGW* 5 (June 1912): 5.

ments, yet they also initiate shop floor protests and find at least part of their social identity in their own rather than in their husband's or future husband's status. In "Ottilie's Garden," for example, a girl reflects that, like a garden, a union involves hard, patient labor. The "fairies and gnomes" won't magically do the work: "There's always got to be the frosts and bugs and worms to fight." In a similar vein, an aspiring writer in "In the Jacket Shop" wants to produce "journalism and literature" to raise the consciousness of fellow workers but discovers that the best kind of literature is headed "Trade Agreement." And a dreamy factory operative in "At the Shirt-Waist Factory" receives the advice: "Stop being helpless . . . cut out appealing with soft blue eyes, and talk United States, with your tongue fair and square."

These "girls," like male workers, felt solidarity with other women on the basis of shared work experience, not through their common oppression as women. Yet Barnum's women were supportive of each other and found sisterhood in both work and friendship. After a romantic disappointment in "The Pen and the Sword," Peggy comforts Trixie, and Trixie, "curled close in her friend's comforting arms . . . closed her swollen eyes in slumber." The concepts and ideals of liberal feminism resonate through Barnum's stories—autonomy, economic self-sufficiency, and female solidarity.

One paradigmatic allegory in particular, "The Pig-Headed Girl," reflects the feminist orientation of its author. Barnum's heroine refuses to accept conventional drudgery in her parents' home or in a factory while awaiting a home of her own through marriage. She breaks from tradition and enjoys a freer lifestyle. Demanding that her work be meaningful and challenging, she asks, "Why should I accept work men wouldn't take?" She joins a union and invents a new process to be used in her trade, exclaiming, "Why should men do all the inventing?" She changes jobs—"Why not a 'rising young woman' as well as a rising young man?" She eventually marries a "man of her choice" and directs the education of her several children rather than having it "dictated by Uncle Methuselah." Unlike Mamie Symington, the pigheaded girl marches toward her goals motivated by self-interest rather than altruism.

Barnum's stories offer an alternative vision of how things could be but, given what we know of economic opportunity for women during that time, clearly were not. The pigheaded girl operates in a sort of free labor market—free, that is, from the constraints of segmentation—but her activities, and those of other characters, are still set in a patriarchal context because their goal is always marriage. Like "Sealskin and Shoddy," these stories legitimate work for women and feminize union ac-

tivity but also accept marriage, male bosses, and the reality of the power
men exercise over women. In terms of appearance, courtship mores,
and verbal interchange between women and men, Barnum promoted a
conventional ideal of respectability (one fictional worker, for example,
objects to the "tough" language she hears at a vaudeville show because
she hears enough of that at the shop), and her stories also firmly and
attractively incorporated wage work into the female life cycle. But the
primary goal for women—marriage—and the life pattern of alternating wage work and domestic work followed by the pigheaded girl constitute the domestic and reproductive circumstances that at least partially produced the segmented labor market and the secondary status
of women. The contrast between Mamie and the characters in Barnum's stories—the former, self-sacrificing but not self-supporting; the
latter, temporary wage workers—reminds us that the material conditions of women's lives may change but the social relations of patriarchy
do not.

Thus the fiction found in the labor press created and projected
patriarchal relations. These imaginative stories provided workers with
a sense of what might be possible but, more important, of what was
desirable; they help us to understand how women and men concep-
tualized femininity and masculinity and how they internalized notions
of patriarchy.[17]

Of course, the reality of working-class women's consciousness during this period was more complex than the fiction indicated. In an
effort to understand that mental world, the late Sarah Eisenstein documented the struggle of young working-class women to construct values
in keeping with changing patterns of behavior. She finds no sharp
break between traditional and modern cultural roles for women; she
rejects as well the idea that women's consciousness is formed either by
an unquestioning acceptance of the dominant social ideology or by a
distinct working-class culture. Eisenstein's work points to precisely the
kind of conflict between prescription *and* reality *and* desire for working-class women which is resolved in the fiction of the labor press. She
suggests that for working-class women "the processes of 'self-discovery'
and the emergence of a group consciousness depended on employment outside the home, and were spurred and also limited by the
character of new employment patterns." Eisenstein also reminds us
that marriage did represent "the overriding achievement in the personal lives of individual women." Marriage for young working-class

---

17. Janice Radway presents a convincing argument for the persistence of patriarchal
forms in contemporary popular texts in *Reading the Romance* (Chapel Hill, N.C., 1984).

girls represented escape from the shops as well as maturity. It provided a "sense of themselves as women." Although between 1885 and 1915 the definition of femininity had changed from the classic Victorian virtues—religious, pure, and self-sacrificing—to a more modern, self-actualized model of womanhood, marriage, the cornerstore of patriarchal society, was still promoted as an ideal goal, and "respectable" (read "bourgeois") behavior was a means to this end.[18]

Eisenstein, Elizabeth Ewen, and Kathy Peiss clearly demonstrate the challenge posed by urban and industrial life to traditional cultural values as well as to dominant social mores for women. Despite this challenge, however, patriarchy in both ideological and institutional guise persisted, in large measure because formulations of the feminine and masculine rooted in the unconscious were affirmed by fictional representations ranging from silent films to dime novels. Those representations unfortunately widened the definition of gender to include occupational segregation and secondary status in the labor market, thus securing for women a position of economic inequity well into the twentieth century.[19]

As the foregoing analysis shows, Hartmann's definition of patriarchy as "a set of social relations which has a material base and in which there are hierarchical relations between men and solidarity among them, which enable them to control women,"[20] can usefully be expanded through the study of cultural forms to understand women's unconscious collusion in maintaining their own oppression, their secondary status as laborers, and their investment in the domestic aspects of femininity. Patriarchy in both its institutional and ideological forms has historically served the needs of capital. However, its cultural manifestations in fiction also fulfill unconscious needs of readers to resolve psychological dissonance and to satisfy deeply felt desires for masculine and feminine identity. Of course, this analysis represents but one side of an important cultural drama and, given the limitations of the material, necessitates the casting of women in a passive role. Equally important are the ways in which women have often formed their own cultural

18. Sarah Eisenstein, *Give Us Bread but Give Us Roses: Working Women's Consciousness in the United States, 1890 to the First World War* (London, 1983), 9, 136–37.

19. Ewen, *Immigrant Women;* Peiss, *Cheap Amusements.* For the economic consequences of occupational segregation, see Martha Blaxall and Barbara B. Reagan, eds., "Women and the Workplace: The Implications of Occupational Segregation," *Signs* 1 (Spring 1976): suppl.

20. Hartmann, "Capitalism, Patriarchy and Job Segregation." Hartman herself indicates that "we must study the subconscious—both how these behavioral rules are internalized and how they grow out of personality structure" (169).

meanings from patriarchal material and have used culture as an arena of struggle. To understand women's historical situation, we must continue to explore the relationships between culture and ideology, ideology and consciousness, consciousness and action, and then finally see the way in which historical activity alters cultural forms. Only then will social historians understand the complicated mediation of culture among social structures, ideas, and human behavior.

8

Trouble in the Nursery: Physicians, Families, and Wet Nurses at the End of the Nineteenth Century

Janet Golden

Historians have paid little attention to the occupation of wet-nursing in the United States, although the practice continued from the colonial period into the early twentieth century.[1] Women who could not or would not breastfeed their infants typically looked to wet nurses to provide the "next best thing to mother's milk." While popular moral

Research for this article was supported in part by a Beveridge Grant from the American Historical Association. I thank Tom Broman, George Dowdall, Brian Gratton, Diana Long, Eric Schneider, and Lynn Weiner for their comments on earlier drafts.

1. References to wet-nursing appear in histories of medicine, women, and the South. Most discuss the medical and social reasons that women chose to breastfeed or to hire wet nurses; very little is said about who became wet nurses and what they experienced on the job. See, e.g., Thomas E. Cone, Jr., *History of American Pediatrics* (Boston, 1979), 56–58, 132–33; Ernest Caulfield, "Infant Feeding in Colonial America," *Journal of Pediatrics* 41 (1952): 675–81; Wyndham B. Blanton, *Medicine in Virginia in the Eighteenth Century* (Richmond, Va., 1931), 177; Mary Beth Norton, *Liberty's Daughters: The Revolutionary Experience of American Women, 1750–1800* (Boston, 1980), 90–91. On wet-nursing in the South, see Julia Cherry Spruill, *Women's Life and Work in the Southern Colonies* (Chapel Hill, N.C., 1938), 55–57; Catherine Clinton, *The Plantation Mistress* (New York, 1982), 155–56; and Sally McMillan, "Mothers' Sacred Duty: Breast-feeding Patterns among Middle- and Upper-Class Women in the Antebellum South," *Journal of Southern History* 51 (1985): 333–56. McMillan studied the journals and correspondence of seventy-eight southern women from 1800 to 1860; fourteen of them employed wet nurses, maternal nursing was the predominant and preferred form of feeding.

tracts and domestic medicine books typically chastised mothers for refusing their infants the "maternal fount," they also offered suggestions
for hiring wet nurses in cases where mothers were unable to perform
their sacred duty.[2]

This article describes the work of wet nurses from the perspective
of employers, physicians, and the wet nurses themselves and analyzes
the growing interplay of medical science and domestic mores that
transformed wet-nursing from a domestic service to a medically controlled occupation. Increasingly distinguished by their social characteristics rather than by their medical value and facing "competition"
from newly marketed infant foods, wet nurses found diminishing opportunities for private employement; during the second half of the
nineteenth century they represented an increasingly marginal sector of
the female labor force. According to the leading pediatrician Luther
Emmett Holt, by the late 1890s "at least three children out of every
four born into the homes of the well-to-do classes" were not breastfed.
Ninety percent of those denied the maternal breast, Holt asserted,
could be successfully fed with a bottle. Only the remaining 10 percent
needed a wet nurse.[3]

Significantly, the chorus of opposition grew louder as the practice
of wet-nursing declined. The advent of commercially marketed infant
foods meant that women could, with greater confidence than ever
before, choose to bottle-feed their babies. Notably, the first advertisement for a commercial infant food, published in 1869, promised "No
More Wetnurses."[4] Yet the most outspoken criticism came not from
the marketplace but from physicians. Doctors claimed that the moral
and management problems posed by wet nurses outweighed any medical advantages; they prescribed instead the use of medically formulated
infant foods. "Scientific infant feeding," as this practice came to be
called, was both the foundation of the new specialty of pediatrics and
the basis upon which physicians forged an alliance with mothers. For
just as middle- and upper-class women increasingly depended on doc-

2. See, e.g., William Buchan, *Advice to Mothers* (Philadelphia, 1804), 164–72, 180–83;
The Maternal Physician, 2d ed. (Philadelphia, 1818), 31–32.

3. L. Emmett Holt, "Infant Feeding," part of an address given before the Cleveland
Medical Society, 26 October 1900, 10, and *The Diseases of Infancy and Childhood* (New
York, 1897), 158, cited in Kathleen W. Jones, "Sentiment and Science: The Late Nine-
teenth-Century Pediatrician as Mother's Advisor," *Journal of Social History* 17 (1983): 86.
Unfortunately, exact statistics about the number of families that employed wet nurses are
not available.

4. *Hearth and Home* 1 (1869): 207, cited in Rima D. Apple, "How Shall I Feed My
Baby? Infant Feeding in the United States, 1870–1940" (Ph.D. diss., University of
Wisconsin, 1981), xviii.

tors to deliver their infants, so now they turned to medical professionals for advice about child rearing.[5]

Paradoxically, becoming experts in infant feeding forced pediatricians and other physicians to assume the domestic responsibilities that women had gratefully relinquished. When an infant was to be bottle-fed, women looked to physicians to name the produce or prescribe the formula. If artificial feeding failed, it then fell to the doctors to find wet nurses and supervise their activities. These unwanted duties account in part for the vehemence with which doctors denounced wet nurses.

In journals and memoirs doctors recounted hectic days and nights spent searching for wet nurses. The quest led from seedy maternity homes to disreputable employment offices to municipal institutions for unwed mothers. Isaac Abt, a Chicago pediatrician, recalled a midnight excursion that ended only after extended bickering with the feisty proprietress of a maternity home. Their conversation revealed that it was a seller's market: "'I've got to have a wet nurse,' I told her. 'Right away.' 'Is that so?' she drawled. Coming out on the stoop she turned and looked critically at her front windows. 'Well, I've got to have some new lace curtains.' 'You'll get them.' I promised." Abt sent the woman new lace curtains every year thereafter, a tacit admission of his dependence.[6] Private arrangements with suppliers proved vital because wet nurses sometimes failed to suit the infant or employer and had to be replaced on short notice. Dr. Clement Cleveland wrote of one family that hired thirteen wet nurses in two weeks—a practice that was not, he noted, "particularly good for the baby." It cannot have been particularly easy for the physician in charge of the case, either.[7]

Wet nurses who appeared suitable on first inspection might prove unfit upon closer examination. Doctors screened all applicants for contagious diseases, assuming that many carried syphilis, tuberculosis, and similar ailments that disproportionately afflicted the poor. Traditional assessments remained the stock-in-trade of many physicians, who judged women by noting the condition of their children; syphilitic wet nurses, for example, could be detected by lesions on their infants. Doctors also refused employment to women whose babies were still-born or had died in early infancy. Healthy babies were judged to be

5. Apple, "How Shall I Feed My Baby?" 351–74; and Jones, "Sentiment and Science," 79–96.

6. Isaac Abt, *Baby Doctor* (New York, 1944), 94. See also Jerome Walker, *The First Baby* (New York, 1881), 71–93; and Fritz B. Talbot, "An Organization for Supplying Human Milk," *New England Journal of Medicine* 199 (1928): 610.

7. Clement Cleveland, "Some Observations upon the Feeding of Infants," *Medical Record* 25 (1884): 485.

evidence of a good milk supply, although physicians also used more sophisticated tests of a candidate's milk: the same techniques that enabled physicians to formulate artificial foods allowed them to chemically analyze human milk. Leading physicians therefore took samples of a wet nurse's milk into the laboratory—even though human milk had qualities that no doctor could measure.[8]

While pediatricians busily championed the science of infant feeding, their perceptions of wet nurses and their milk remained rooted in superstition and prejudice. For most of the nineteenth century, physicians and the public at large regarded heredity as a dynamic process that began at conception and ended at weaning. Consequently, milk was thought to convey the character and emotions of its producer. One common legend told of women who nursed infants after an emotional crisis, only to see their babies fall dead in their arms. Effervesced and denatured by emotion, human milk could become a lethal substance. But even a placid woman could produce a product capable of causing grave harm.[9] Dr. Joseph Edcil Winters blamed a youngster's "secretive disposition" on his Italian wet nurse. Similarly, the popular writer Mary Terhune informed the readers of her advice book, *Eve's Daughters* (1882), of a girl "remarkably dissimilar from her family" with "rough skin, corpulent frame, harsh voice, and loud laugh" as well as "vulgar tastes such as a liking for tobacco and spirits and a relish for broad wit and low company." The explanation, according to Terhune, was her "fat, Irish, wet nurse."[10]

Despite the assertions of Winters and Terhune, concepts of lactational heredity began to disappear from the medical literature by the late nineteenth century. After all, if science allowed the claim that a child could imbibe the character of the wet nurse, what might be transmitted from an animal? Speaking for many of his colleagues, the pediatrician J. P. Crozer Griffith concluded in 1895: "There is no more possibility of a baby imbibing the character of the nurse, through the

8. On checking the health of wet nurses, see, e.g., J. Lewis Smith, *A Treatise of the Diseases of Infancy and Childhood* (Philadelphia, 1869), 52. On the scientific assessment of human milk, see, e.g., Thomas Morgan Rotch, *Pediatrics: The Hygiene and Medical Treatment of Children* (Philadelphia, 1896), 190–211.

9. Charles E. Rosenberg, "The Bitter Fruit: Heredity, Disease, and Social Thought," in *No Other Gods*, ed. Charles E. Rosenberg (Baltimore, 1976), 27; J. Lewis Smith, "Recent Improvements in Infant Feeding," *Transactions of the American Pediatric Society* 1 (1889): 89.

10. Joseph Edcil Winters, "The Relative Influences of Maternal and Wet Nursing on Mother and Child," *Medical Record* 30 (1886): 513; Marion Harland [Mary Virginia Hawes Terhune], *Eve's Daughters; or, Common Sense for Maid, Wife, and Mother* (New York, 1882), 30–32.

milk which she gives, much as we hear this talked about, than there is a danger of the child learning to 'moo' because it is fed on cow's milk."[11] Griffith tacitly admitted the persistence of the idea of milk-borne heredity even as he demonstrated its illogic. He failed to consider another question on the minds of physicians and employers: the environmental influence of the wet nurse.

The question of whether a wet nurse could pollute the home in which she worked remained moot. Dr. I. N. Love, chair of clinical medicine and diseases of children at Marion Sims Medical College, offered affecting testimony about the peril: "I recall an experience in my own family—a danger to which my little daughter of seven would have been exposed by contact with a moral leper, recommended to us as a healthy wet-nurse for our infant boy. Better by far for the latter to have been wafted to the angels than for our first-born to have breathed the same air for a day with the moral monster in the shape of a wet-nurse."[12] Love was not alone in voicing concern. In an era marked by growing alarm at the moral disorder stemming from the "dangerous classes" and by efforts to control through institutionalization those deemed deviant, suspicion of wet nurses appeared entirely rational. Physicians found it difficult to justify the placement of a wet nurse, typically the mother of an illegitimate child, in a good Christian home.[13]

Physicians used the moral dilemmas posed by wet nurses as a way of arguing against their employment, in effect substituting ethical rationales for medical common sense. Doctors, after all, knew that no formula was as good for a baby as human milk. But reliance on wet nurses raised serious questions about the proper role of physicians, undermining their claim to scientific authority and burdening them with domestic responsibilities. A wet nurse, doctors believed, forced them to become policemen in the nursery, monitoring the woman's daily regimen, rooting out misbehavior, and intervening in the skirmishes that broke out between her and her mistress. As they stepped into the fray, doctors saw their facade of expertise begin to crumble.

Faced with questions about the wet nurse's diet and the household duties she should be assigned, doctors equivocated. One stated that the wet nurse "should not be overworked by other duties" but quickly added that "she should not be kept in a state of idleness." Doctors appeared equally incapable of determining what the wet nurse should

11. J. P. Crozer Griffith, *The Care of the Baby* (Philadelphia, 1895), 178.

12. I. N. Love, "The Problem of Infant Feeding—Intestinal Diseases of Children and Cholera Infantum," *Archives of Pediatrics* 6 (1889): 585.

13. On the growing public alarm at moral disorder, see Paul Boyer, *Urban Masses and Moral Order in America, 1820–1920* (Cambridge, Mass., 1978), esp. 123–31.

eat. Some, buttressed by nutritional theories, believed they could control the content of her milk by manipulating her diet. Others simply counseled a plain menu and warned against the use of alcohol. These medical experts soon learned that it was easier to make rules than to enforce behavior.[14]

Prohibition in the nursery apparently had the same impact as it did in the public arena: those wet nurses who were inclined to drink took to tippling in secret. Dr. Will H. Wall discovered one woman who drank on the sly, thereby serving her nursling "milk-punch." (Ironically, before the heyday of the temperance movement, alcohol had sometimes been prescribed to stimulate the flow of milk.) Other forbidden intoxicants included the narcotic-laced "soothing syrups" used by wet nurses (and mothers) to keep infants quiet. Allegedly applied to combat teething pain, these nostrums allowed a wet nurse some respite from her duties.[15]

If a wet nurse threatened the well-being of her suckling by using alcohol or drugs, she would be dismissed. However, if she merely disobeyed orders, she might be kept on, especially if the infant appeared to be thriving. In either case the physician was left in a sticky situation. Firing a wet nurse meant assuming responsibility for finding an immediate replacement, an arduous task. Alternatively, tolerating minor delinquencies meant temporarily ceding power to a woman whose moral stature and behavior would ordinarily bar her employment.

Although artificial feeding succeeded in making wet nurses a "last resort," it ultimately gave them greater power. Hired by desperate families after bottle-feeding had failed, wet nurses often held a child's life in the balance. Whether they recognized their temporary dominion and acted upon it is uncertain. More critical is the fact that physicians, and some employers, believed they did. When the wet nurse entered the household, the nursery became contested terrain.

In contrast to physicians, who viewed wet nurses as a collective evil, employers judged them individually. Women's accounts of their wet nurses reverberate with the same complaints as those voiced by physicians, but the tone is more measured, and in some cases a few words of praise are sung. Physicians were caught between the needs of infants, the demands of parents, and their own professional concerns; mothers

14. Theron Wendell Kilmer, *The Practical Care of the Baby* (Philadelphia, 1903), 146. On the wet nurse's diet, see Rotch, *Pediatrics*, 211; and Griffith, *Care of the Baby*, 178.
15. Will H. Wall, "A Young Doctor's Report on a Case of 'Milk Punch' at Three Months," *Babyhood* 2 (1886): 177. On the use of alcohol, see James Stewart, *Diseases of Children* (New York, 1841), 190–91. On soothing syrups, see F. H. Getchell, *The Maternal Management of Infancy* (Philadelphia, 1868), 24; and Griffith, *Care of the Baby*, 177.

saw their babies' survival as paramount. Thus one woman wrote to the popular magazine *Babyhood* chastising her doctor for discouraging the use of wet nurses because they were unmarried. Was it not, she asked, parents' "first duty to preserve the frail life of the being that looks to them for protection?" And was it not, she further inquired, the doctor's "first duty to offer them the means of doing so?" Whatever hardships wet nurses might impose on their employers, most mothers seemed willing to pay the price.[16]

Many women, no doubt, viewed conflict with their wet nurses as merely an exaggeration of the all-too-common master–servant strife: unpleasant but not intolerable. But the fact remained that wet nurses had more bargaining power than other servants and that wet-nursing differed from other types of domestic work in both its moral dimensions and its structural arrangements. While women might look back with false nostalgia to an era when "servants knew their place," they looked forward to the time when bottle-feeding would eliminate wet nurses.[17]

Fears of moral contamination arose in connection with all servants, but wet nurses aroused even greater reservations. How could a woman who had cast aside her own baby be an appropriate companion for the family's most vulnerable and innocent member? How could a family be sure the child would not grow up to display the traits and habits of the wet nurse? Lingering reservations about lactational heredity caused employers to fear endowing their offspring with "faults bred in a stranger's blood."[18] As soon as the child could be weaned, the wet nurse was sent packing.

Although brief—typically less than a year—the job of wet nurse proved to be more lucrative and, according to some, less demanding than other domestic positions. High wages reflected both the scarcity of wet nurses, who occupied a unique corner of the labor market, and the fact that some had to pay other women to care for their own babies while they were in service. Employers found the wage structure disconcerting, fearing that high pay rewarded vice. Furthermore, some complained that wet nurses performed little domestic labor beyond their duties in the nursery, overlooking the fact that wet nurses remained at the beck and call of an infant twenty-four hours a day.[19]

16. N.N., "The Moral Objections to Wet-Nurses," *Babyhood* 3 (1887): 383.

17. On servants, see David M. Katzman, *Seven Days a Week: Women and Domestic Service in Industrializing America* (New York, 1978); and Faye E. Dudden, *Serving Women: Household Service in Nineteenth-Century America* (Middletown, Conn., 1983).

18. Materfamilias, "The Moral Objections to Wet-Nurses," *Babyhood* 3 (1887): 384.

19. Data on the wages paid wet nurses are scarce. Of the nineteen women sent out as

The issue of power lay at the heart of employers' dissatisfaction. They knew that successful wet nurses could make outrageous demands and have them met. After all, if the chambermaid left on short notice, a family could make do until her replacement was hired. If the cook threatened to leave before a dinner party, an employer could promise her higher wages and then fire her the day after the event. But if the wet nurse quit, her nursling might starve before a suitable woman was found to take her place. Aware of their dependence, employers charged that wet nurses manipulated the situation to their advantage. Perhaps some women did; most were former domestics who undoubtably knew the tricks of household combat. Alternatively, many wet nurses may have been compliant and effective workers, knowing that if they were fired they would lose the means of providing for their own babies.[20]

An interesting debate about wet nurses appeared in the "Mother's Parliament" column of *Babyhood* following one woman's account of her tribulations. Mrs. Fanny B. Workman hired a wet nurse after artificial feeding caused her infant daughter to suffer from indigestion and weight loss. Two consulting physicians recommended this step, and Mrs. Workman agreed with reluctance. In a prescient (or perhaps self-fulfilling) observation, she expressed her fear that it would be "the end of all peace in the household."[21]

The first wet nurse, dubbed "Irish Mary," seems to have possessed a dangerous combination of stupidity and guile. She never learned how to care for the Workman baby properly but quickly figured out how to

---

wet nurses from the Boston Temporary Home between 1862 and 1864 whose wages were recorded, the majority (53 percent) earned $2 or more per week, and quite possibly had their own infants' care paid for as well. The average weekly wage for female domestics in Massachusetts in 1860 was $1.58. See Temporary Home Records, Massachusetts Historical Society, and Stanley Lebergott, *Manpower in Economic Growth: The American Record since 1800* (New York, 1964), 197, Table 11.12. Physicians reported that wet nurses earned high wages. According to Grace Peckham, "Infancy in the City," *Popular Science Monthly* 28 (1885): 686, wet nurses earned $20 to $30 a month. Holt's 1897 textbook, *Diseases of Infancy and Childhood*, 159, estimated wages in New York City to be between $20 and $35 a month—significantly more than the wages paid to regular servants; see Katzman, *Seven Days a Week*, 306.

20. Of the sixty-six wet nurses sent to private service between 1873 and 1908 from the Boston Lying-In Hospital, the New England Hospital for Women and Children, and the Massachusetts Infant Asylum whose previous occupation was recorded, forty-eight (73 percent) had been in domestic service; see Janet Golden, "From Breast to Bottle: The Decline of Wet Nursing in Boston, 1867–1927" (Ph.D. diss., Boston University, 1984), 264.

21. Fanny B. Workman, "The Wet-Nurse in the Household," *Babyhood* 2 (1886): 142–44.

manipulate the cook into supplying her with forbidden foods: tea, ice water, and pickles. Mary, apparently a charismatic woman, also held sway over the other servants. Mrs. Workman fired her cook, perhaps as a warning to the other help. Mary stayed. It was a classic example of the employer's nightmare; a disobedient servant went unpunished because the infant thrived on her milk.

Mary, it seemed, could make Mrs. Workman dance to any tune she played. Yet when she spoke of leaving—sending Mrs. Workman into a frenzy—she did so because her own child had fallen ill, not in an attempt to raise her salary or increase her privileges. Mrs. Workman attempted to placate her, first by arranging for her baby to be brought to her, and later by having the baby boarded in the country and allowing Mary to visit. But when the caretaker eventually decided she could not keep the child, Mary became so distraught that her milk became unfit, and she had to leave her position. Had her intentions been solely to blackmail Mrs. Workman, she would not have reacted so strongly.

Mary's replacement, another Irish woman, lost her own baby just two weeks after beginning her job. Mrs. Workman persuaded her to forgo the funeral, believing the experience would disturb her milk. Not unmindful of the woman's grief, however, Mrs. Workman took her to the seashore to recuperate from her sorrows. The brief vacation marked a turning point. While enjoying her day of freedom, the bereaved wet nurse partook of some cucumbers and ice cream, foods evidently forbidden to her.

To Mrs. Workman it was the opening salvo in what proved to be an extended domestic uprising. Thereafter, the wet nurse fended off all attempts to control her diet. She rejected Mrs. Workman's "substantial, nourishing meals," indulging instead in peanuts, cake, and ice cream. Eventually she so neglected the Workman baby that she finally had to be dismissed. Notably, Mrs. Workman never associated the woman's insubordination with her own denial of funeral privileges. But the wet nurse's behavior may well have been motivated by bitterness.

Mrs. Workman's comments seem to echo the criticisms made by physicians, yet several elements of her story are at odds with medical accounts. Physicians assumed that wet nurses eagerly abandoned their own offspring in their greed for the high wages their employment brought. Yet Irish Mary preferred to rejoin her sick child rather than remain on the job. Certainly women became wet nurses in order to earn money, but the desire to support themselves and their offspring, rather than greed or malevolence, may well have been the reason. A second disparity between Mrs. Workman's account and the allegations of physicians can be seen in the matter of diet. Physicians condemned dietary social climbing—the wet nurse's presumed craving for expensive foods. If Mrs. Workman's experiences were typical, it would seem that wet nurses did not covet their employer's larder so much as they wished to eat as they pleased. Finally, despite doctors' complaints about the burden of wet nurse management, it appears that Mrs. Workman supervised her employees herself, with little direct intervention by medical authorities.[22]

The Workman saga moved other women to write to *Babyhood*, recounting their experiences and offering their opinions. One correspondent asked the "Nursery Problems" columnist how to find a wet nurse, making anxious reference to the Workman letter. She received an ambiguous reply: the columnist declared that Mrs. Workman had experienced "exceptional ill-luck" but nonetheless denounced wet nurses as "tyrannical, demanding stimulants and various luxuries for the sake of the milk, and threatening to desert the baby if their demands are not gratified." Other correspondents voiced similar objections, decrying wet nurses who communicated "vicious tendencies" and sinful habits.[23]

Although negative sentiment prevailed, a few women offered favorable comments. One wrote that her nineteen-year-old unmarried wet nurse was "sweet tempered, neat, and obliging." Another, who signed her letter E.B.L., described her wet nurse as a "healthy, warm-hearted, lawfully wedded wife." E.B.L had hoped to breastfeed her baby and found herself so jealous of her wet nurse that she ordered her to wean the child. Disaster struck, the infant died, and E.B.L. rued her envy. She eventually bore two other children, whom she did nurse herself, hiring the former wet nurse as a child's nurse for one of them. Summing up her feelings, E.B.L. wrote of the wet nurse, "I can truly say that a more unselfish, gentle, kind woman I have never known." Physicians apparently never considered the possibility that wet nurses would evoke feelings of envy. For individual employers, however, relations with wet nurses proved more complex and personal than doctors could predict.[24]

Wet nurses, of course, were neither an army of tyrants nor a band

22. On diet, see Edward P. Davis and John M. Keating, *Mother and Child* (Philadelphia, 1893), 91; and Nathan Oppenheim, *The Medical Diseases of Childhood* (New York, 1900), 78.

23. "Nursery Problems," *Babyhood* 2 (1886): 245–46; Materfamilias, "Moral Objections to Wet-Nurses," 383–84. Letters and comments about wet nurses appeared in other mothercraft magazines as well; see *Trained Motherhood* 4 (1899): 37; *Baby* 3 (1905): 233–40.

24. M.M., "A Warm Defender of the Wet-Nurse," *Babyhood* 5 (1889): 92; E.B.L., "A Plea for the Employment of the Wet-Nurse," *Babyhood* 6 (1890): 255–56.

of angelic women eager to save the lives of young infants. Poor women, usually without husbands and dependent on public and private charity, they accepted one of the few jobs available to them. Some went into service shortly after leaving maternity homes or hospitals; others were sent out from foundling homes, city shelters, or religious institutions serving unwed mothers. Intelligence offices and newspaper advertisements helped those without an institutional affiliation to find work. Qualified for the job solely by the recent birth of a child, the women knew wet-nursing to be a career of circumstance, not choice. Their milk earned them high wages for a short period, but the emotional toll could be greater still.[25]

Accepting a position meant agreeing to send their own babies away, a concession that earned them the epithet "mercenary." Some women may have been eager to cast off their infants, either because they could not support them or because of the stigma of illegitimacy. Others, as evidenced by their willingness to leave their positions when their babies fell ill, saw outplacement of their own infants as expedient rather than desirable. Whatever the motive, the result was often tragic. Sent to infant boarding homes—colloquially known as "baby farms"—and often poorly cared for, wet nurses' babies suffered an extraordinarily high mortality rate. Holt estimated their survival rate at "one in ten," a figure that underscored for many the essential immorality of wet nursing. All too often a poor woman's temporary abandonment of her healthy baby in order to feed a well-to-do woman's child amounted to a trading of lives.[26]

Employers and physicians rationalized their participation in this unholy exchange by blaming the wet nurses, who may in turn have held them to be the guilty parties. The whims and demands of wet nurses, so frequently referred to in the medical literature, may sometimes have sprung from a well of resentment at having to abandon their own offspring. Similarly, other accusations hurled at wet nurses can be judged from the opposite perspective. Some doctors believed that women whose babies had died became wet nurses by borrowing healthy infants to show as their own; one reportedly discovered a woman who had managed to wet-nurse for several years by using this ploy. Others accused women of disguising a failing milk supply by making judicious use of commercial infant foods and other substitutes. These subterfuges, viewed by doctors and employers as examples of guile,

25. For a demographic portrait of wet nurses, see Golden, "From Breast to Bottle," 137–76.
26. L. Emmett Holt, *The Care and Feeding of Children* (New York, 1894), 159.

might alternatively be judged clever ways to remain in a well-paying position.[27]

If wet nurses were in a better position than other domestics to manipulate their employers, they were no less vulnerable to the occupational hazards of service work. Forced to give up their babies, having only short-term prospects, toiling in isolation, often assigned poor living conditions and long hours, wet nurses had no comfortable sinecure. Furthermore, evidence suggests that, unlike "Irish Mary," who gave orders to the cook, they could be estranged from other servants, who often resented their high wages and disparaged their immoral past. Finally, wet nurses faced one particular physical hazard: just as they could infect their charges with venereal disease, they could contract such an illness from a congenitally afflicted baby. If wet nurses had left written records describing their employment, their criticisms of the profession might have been as pointed as those proffered by doctors and employers.[28]

Existing on the margins of both domestic service and medical practice, wet-nursing illustrates the dimensions of labor strife inherent in each profession. Domestic service brought together women of different social classes to negotiate the conditions of work and remuneration. While mistress and servant each had resources at her command, the balance remained tipped in favor of the mistress. With wet nurses this was not always the case. Harder to replace and occupying a more vital position within the family unit, they held greater power. The resulting difficulties—seemingly exaggerations of typical mistress–servant strife—proved far more intractable because of the wet nurse's relationship to the young infant. A woman's primary concern was the

27. On borrowed babies, see Winters, "Relative Influences," 511; Peckham, "Infancy in the City," 686. On supplemental feeding, see Louis Starr, *Hygiene of the Nursery* (Philadelphia, 1888), 126.

28. Clementina Smith to Sophie du Pont, 7 February 1887, Eleutherian Mills Historical Libarary, Wilmington, Del. Clementina's sister hired a wet nurse who was a Catholic, and apparently the other servants held "a protestant bitterness" against her. When wet nurses were used primarily in private homes, little was said about their risk of contracting a venereal disease, and only the most veiled language was employed. See, e.g., F. R. Sturgis, "On the Venereal and Genito-Urinary Diseases of Children," pt. 8, "Medico-Legal Aspects of Venereal Disease in Children," *Archives of Pediatrics* 5 (1888): 457–71; Louis Fischer, "The Management of Infant Feeding," *Pediatrics* 2 (1896): 64. When wet nurses began to be employed to feed foundlings, the syphilis problem received greater attention; see William T. Watson, "A Square Deal for the Wet Nurse," *Journal of the American Medical Association* 47 (1906): 1909–11. A play by Eugene Brieux brought this mode of transmission to public notice: see Upton Sinclair, trans., *Damaged Goods: The Great Play "Les Avaries" of Brieux* (Philadelphia, 1913).

survival of her baby, but she had to consider also the effect of the wet nurse on the entire family.

For guidance, women turned to physicians, asking them to select and supervise wet nurses and burdening them with professional and ethical dilemmas they had no desire to confront. Physicians readily admitted that wet nurses supplied a product superior to any formula; their objections centered on the gap between theoretical superiority and actual efficiency. Artificial feeding could be easily controlled; wet nurses, by contrast, posed moral problems, management difficulties, and medical challenges not easily overcome. Thus, while medical discussions of bottle feeding deliberately illuminated the scientific accomplishments of the profession, denunciations of wet nurses remained heavily laden with the rhetoric of moral pollution and household control. Doctors portrayed wet nurses as invaders in the nursery, destined to destroy the moral universe of the families they served. Underlying their invective was the recognition that they themselves could mediate but not control relations in the nursery.

In wet-nursing, as in no other domestic occupation, the labor process (breastfeeding), the labor product (human milk), and the laborer were unified. This fact forced employers and physicians to negotiate with wet nurses, exchanging privileges and high wages for cooperation. As a result the nursery was often a battleground in which wet nurses exercised their temporary power, where employers looked to professional authority for guidance, and where doctors wrung their hands in despair and sought "scientific" alternatives. Conflict within this constricted workplace revealed how the clash of professional, family, and labor values made wet-nursing a unique occupation.

· *Part 3* ·

1910–1940

9

Feeling the Pinch:
The Kalamazoo Corsetmakers'
Strike of 1912

Karen M. Mason

In February 1911, 800 employees spontaneously struck the Kalamazoo Corset Company to protest a series of wage reductions and
formed the Kalamazoo Corset Workers' Union, Local 82 of the International Ladies' Garment Workers' Union (ILGWU). The company,
apparently taken by surprise, quickly settled the strike by signing a one-
year agreement acceding to the workers' demands. A year later, however, when the agreement expired and the union presented new demands, the company was better prepared. It took a forceful stand,
dismissing union officers and agitators from their jobs and forcing a
showdown. The result was a strike that lasted from March 2, 1912, to
June 15, 1912, and attracted national attention.[1]

The history of the Kalamazoo strike is significant because it contributes to our understanding of the possibilities and limitations of organizing women workers in the early twentieth century. Less than 4 percent of women workers in the United States were members of unions in
1900, partly because male trade unionists were either indifferent or
hostile to the notion of admitting them as members. The women's
garment industry offers a prime example of this attitude: women con-

---

1. *The Ladies' Garment Worker* (*LGW*) 2 (June 1911): 40, and 3 (April 1912): 10; *Kalamazoo Telegraph-Press* (*KTP*), February–June 1912.

stituted the majority of the industry's workers, but the ILGWU—its principal union—was headed by men and had a membership consisting primarily of men. Founded in 1900, the ILGWU had almost collapsed by 1907 and struggled to stay afloat in the first decade of the twentieth century. It put little effort into organizing women workers before 1909, its leaders believing with other male trade unionists that women were passive by nature and uninterested in unionization. But the "Uprising of the 20,000"—a massive strike of young female shirtwaist makers in New York City in 1909–10—demonstrated that women could be militant strikers and could also provide the mass base of membership that the union badly needed.[2]

In the years following the shirtwaist makers' strike, the ILGWU actively recruited women workers. Recognizing that women were more effective than men in appealing to female workers, the ILGWU appointed several women as organizers to travel around the country helping to form unions and to lead strikes. In a series of strikes that hit the women's garment industry in New York, Philadelphia, Cincinnati, and Cleveland in the years 1910 to 1913, women played prominent roles, both as strikers and as organizers. The Kalamazoo corsetmakers' strike was part of this wave of strikes, and one in which women were the principal actors.[3]

The ILGWU sent three organizers in succession to lead the Kalamazoo strike: Josephine Casey, Gertrude Barnum, and Pauline Newman. Casey led the strike for the first two months, until she was arrested and jailed for picketing in defiance of an injunction. Barnum played a relatively minor role, taking over only while Casey was in jail. Newman was in Kalamazoo for the final round of negotiations and remained for several weeks after the strike was over.

This article focuses on Josephine Casey and Pauline Newman, the principal leaders. It examines the strategies they used in conducting the strike and the response of women in Kalamazoo. Casey and Newman advocated different tactics, in part because they led the strike at different stages. But their different strategies also reflected different approaches to the problems faced by women in the workplace and in American society. An examination of the Kalamazoo strike illustrates the strengths and weaknesses of Casey's and Newman's methods and in

---

2. Alice Kessler-Harris, *Out to Work: A History of Wage-Earning Women in the United States* (New York, 1982), 152, 165.

3. Louis Levine, *The Women's Garment Workers: A History of the International Ladies' Garment Workers' Union* (New York, 1924); Barbara Mayer Wertheimer, *We Were There: The Story of Working Women in America* (New York, 1977), 295–97.

doing so demonstrates the dilemmas that confronted those who attempted to organize women workers in the early twentieth century.

Josephine Casey had been a ticket-taker for the elevated railway in Chicago and then a paid organizer for the Elevated Railway Clerks. In 1911 the ILGWU appointed her to organize American-born women workers, a group the union considered particularly difficult to recruit. Casey has been described by historians as a "militant and peripatetic organizer" and "dynamic garment worker" with a "forceful and aggressive personality [that] won the confidence and allegiance of women workers." But her actions in Kalamazoo belie these descriptions. To a Kalamazoo newspaper reporter she appeared as a "charming young southern woman of most attractive personality . . . cultured, broadminded, and refined, she is of a type distinctly different from the anarchistic strike-leading individual, so often pictured as a trades union leader." Unlike many of the ILGWU's female organizers, she was American-born; this was a factor in the union's decision to send her to Kalamazoo, where the population—and the corset factory's work force—was largely native-born.[4]

Pauline Newman, in contrast, was a Russian Jewish immigrant who had come to the United States as a teenager in 1901. She went to work at the Triangle Waist Company in New York City and continued to work there until after the shirtwaist makers' strike of 1909–10, when she left the factory to become a union organizer. She had already gained experience in public speaking by campaigning on street corners for Socialist Party candidates for public office and talking to women workers outside factories to persuade them to join a union. During the shirtwaist makers' strike, Newman traveled to other cities in New York to speak to unions and women's clubs in an effort to raise money for the strikers. Soon thereafter she was appointed the first female organizer for the ILGWU.[5]

4. Wertheimer, *We Were There*, 316; Philip S. Foner, *Women and the American Labor Movement: From Colonial Times to the Eve of World War I* (New York, 1979), 477; Alice Henry, *The Trade Union Woman* (New York, 1915), 77; *LGW* 2 (June 1911): 3, and 3 (December 1912): 5–6. The first description of Casey is from Nancy Schrom Dye, *As Equals and as Sisters: Feminism, the Labor Movement, and the Women's Trade Union League of New York* (Columbia, Mo., 1980), 68; the second description is reported in Foner, *Women and the American Labor Movement*, 311, from *KTP*, 1 March 1912. Of Kalamazoo's 39,437 residents in 1910, 54.1 percent had American-born parents, and 26.7 percent were of foreign or mixed parentage; only 17.4 percent were themselves foreign-born. Blacks constituted 1.7 percent of the population (Bureau of the Census, *Thirteenth Census of the United States: Abstract of the Census with Supplement for Michigan* [Washington, D.C.: Government Printing Office, 1913], 96).

5. Pauline Newman, interview with Barbara Wertheimer, in a series of transcripts titled "The Twentieth Century Trade Union Woman—Vehicle for Social Change," by

Both Casey and Newman were members and sometime organizers for the Women's Trade Union League (WTUL). This organization of women workers and their middle- and upper-class female allies sought to organize women workers into unions, to promote protective legislation, and to achieve suffrage for women. During the shirtwaist makers' strike the league had enlisted the support of middle- and upper-class women on the side of the strikers by speaking to women's club members, settlement workers, and students at women's colleges. The spectacle of prominent society women walking the picket lines attracted publicity for the strike and gave the WTUL the opportunity to educate the public about the poor conditions of women's work. At the same time, wealthy women made much-needed financial contributions to the strike fund. This public support was important in keeping the strike going and allowing the striking workers to pose a serious challenge to their employers. In this and subsequent strikes, the appeal to public opinion was common practice.[6]

Casey's and Newman's ideas on how to go about organizing a strike were informed by their experiences with the Women's Trade Union League. Both recognized that the support of middle- and upper-class women could be valuable, although they disagreed on the extent to which the enlistment of such support should be a pivotal part of strike strategy. In addition to their shared experience as members of the WTUL, Casey and Newman had worked together as organizers for the ILGWU during the 1911 cloak- and suitmakers' strike in Cleveland. They held special meetings for the female strikers and their mothers, aided the local organizers, and attempted (with little success) to recruit local middle- and upper-class women—particularly those involved in such reform organizations as the Women's Suffrage League and the Woman's Christian Temperance Union—to the cause of the strikers. When the Cleveland strike ended in failure, Newman traveled around Michigan and Ohio seeking support from women's groups and store owners for a boycott of nonunion Cleveland-made goods.[7]

Casey was called to Kalamazoo late in February 1912 to help negotiate a contract between the Kalamazoo Corset Company and Local 82. John Dyche, general secretary of the ILGWU, had arrived there on

---

the Institute of Labor and Industrial Relations, University of Michigan, November 1976, 1–8; Wertheimer, *We Were There*, 293, 304–5; Alice Kessler-Harris, "Organizing the Unorganizable: Three Jewish Women and Their Union," in *Class, Sex, and the Woman Worker*, ed. Milton Cantor and Bruce Laurie (Westport, Conn., 1977), 152.

6. Dye, *As Equals and as Sisters*, 88–95.

7. Lois Scharf, "The Great Uprising in Cleveland: When Sisterhood Failed," in *A Needle, a Bobbin, a Strike: Women Needleworkers in America*, ed. Joan M. Jensen and Sue Davidson (Philadelphia, 1984), 146–66; Pauline Newman interview, 18–19.

February 26 and, realizing that the situation would not be easily settled, called Casey back from Toronto, where she had gone to deal with a lockout. In the year since the initial walkout in Kalamazoo, the corset workers' union had persevered, thanks to the efforts of such individuals as Homer Waterman, a resident of Kalamazoo and secretary of the Michigan Federation of Labor. Though not himself a corset worker, Waterman took such an active interest in Local 82 that an ILGWU official who visited Kalamazoo in May 1911 called him "the father and mother of this union." The official was impressed by Local 82, believing that it "is there to stay, and that it means business." He was perplexed by the behavior of some corset workers, however; one young woman, for example, arrived on roller skates to pay her dues. And when the official addressed a meeting of the union, "the members for reasons unknown to me were gathered in the back of the hall. For a near-sighted speaker it appeared as if he were addressing space instead of human beings."[8]

Such behavior can be explained by the corset workers' youth and their lack of previous experience with unions. Most were young women and may initially have been somewhat hesitant to participate in union activities. Labor activism conflicted with traditional notions of women as retiring, passive, and delicate. As Nancy MacLean has argued, women workers had to "overcome socialized norms of female submissiveness and to free themselves of restrictions to the domestic world" if they were to become active in unions. Union organizers who worked in the corset factory were successful in their efforts over the next eight months, however; when the strike began in March 1912, most of the workers in the corset factory took part.[9]

On February 29, 1912, the corsetmakers' union presented a new contract to James H. Hatfield, president of the Kalamazoo Corset Company, to replace the one that had expired the previous day. John Dyche and Josephine Casey accompanied the union's contract committee when it met with company officials. The new agreement dealt primarily with wages and hours, setting specific rates for various jobs within the factory, a minimum weekly wage for women workers, pay for pieceworkers while they were waiting for work, and a shorter work week for men to equal the legal limit of fifty-four hours for women.[10]

8. *LGW* 3 (May 1912): 9, and 2 (June 1911): 1–2.

9. Nancy MacLean, "The Culture of Resistance: Female Institution Building in the International Ladies' Garment Workers' Union, 1905–1925," *Michigan Occasional Papers in Women's Studies* 21 (Winter 1982): 7. See also Sarah Eisenstein, *Give Us Bread but Give Us Roses: Working Women's Consciousness in the United States, 1890 to the First World War* (London, 1983).

10. *KTP*, 1 March 1912.

Hatfield rejected the agreement on Friday, March 1, and fired twelve employees—seven men and five women, all active union members—for "disloyalty and inefficiency." Hatfield and other company officials met with union members again on Saturday morning but refused to reinstate the discharged workers. In response, the corsetmakers' union voted to strike. That afternoon the *Kalamazoo Telegraph-Press* published an extra edition carrying the headline "Kalamazoo Corset Company May Shut Down Factory in This City—Would Mean Heavy Loss Here." Hatfield threatened to move the entire operation of the company to a branch plant then under construction in Davenport, Iowa, if the labor dispute continued. This threat was not taken lightly by the people of Kalamazoo, for the company was a large and prosperous enterprise with a national market for its products, the Madame Grace and American Beauty corsets. It employed more workers than any other factory in town and was far and away the largest employer of women workers. If the company with the largest payroll in the city shut down, shopkeepers and providers of services would lose business and the local economy would suffer.[11]

Nevertheless, by Monday, March 4, 600 workers had joined the strike and were picketing the factory in teams. They received enthusiastic support from organized labor in Kalamazoo. The bakers' union threatened to strike if necessary in order to cut off the supply of lunches being provided by the company to nonstriking workers. Members of the electrical workers' union employed by the telephone company refused to repair telephone wires that had been cut at the factory. Resolutions of moral and financial support came from unions in Kalamazoo and neighboring towns. The Bricklayers, Masons and Plasterers Union of Kalamazoo, for example, passed a resolution on March 9 commending the corset workers for their action and sent $40 to aid the strikers. When injunctions were issued on March 11 prohibiting the

11. *KTP*, 1 and 2 March 1912. Kalamazoo was described in 1911 by the manager of the Michigan Free Employment Bureau as "a manufacturing city, located in the center of a rich farming community" (Michigan Department of Labor, *Second Annual Report* [Lansing, 1911], 71). The city's major industry at this time was the paper industry. Women were employed in the paper mills as well as in subsidiary plants that manufactured stationery, playing cards, paper boxes, and the like. Women were also employed in the manufacture of chemicals and medicines and in such traditional occupations as candymaking, laundry work, and domestic service. The Kalamazoo Corset Company, founded in the early 1890s, in August 1911 employed 1,026 persons, 835 of them female and 191 male. See Willis F. Dunbar, *Kalamazoo and How It Grew* (Kalamazoo, 1960), 133–40; Larry B. Massie and Peter J. Schmitt, *Kalamazoo: The Place behind the Products—An Illustrated History* (Kalamazoo, 1981), 133; Michigan Department of Labor, *Twenty-Ninth Annual Report* (Lansing, 1912), 115–19.

strikers from picketing the plant, members of the United Garment Workers and other unions took up the picketing until they, too, were enjoined.[12]

Casey's experience in Cleveland had taught her that when strikes became violent, public opinion could turn against the strikers; she apparently felt that the failure to enlist popular support in that strike had been due primarily to the violence that had occurred, not to a lack of sympathy for labor's cause. Therefore, she attempted to prevent a recurrence of the Cleveland events in Kalamazoo by impressing upon the strikers the importance of orderly behavior and peaceful picketing. When the corsetmakers were enjoined from picketing, she counseled them to obey the injunction, hoping to demonstrate that as responsible citizens with legitimate complaints, they deserved public support.

For the next six weeks the strikers engaged only in "mental picketing": they sang hymns and entered into silent meditation at the times of day when nonstriking corsetmakers were entering or leaving the factory. But this demure form of picketing did not achieve the intended effect; rather than impressing the citizens of Kalamazoo with the orderly behavior of the strikers and thus winning their support, it caused them to forget that there was a strike.

Other local unions, however, devised means of showing their support for the corsetmakers and keeping the strike in the public eye. They held mass meetings, arranged a dance to raise funds, staged a parade to demonstrate that the labor community of Kalamazoo was behind the strikers, and ultimately threatened a general strike.[13]

Local women's organizations, on the other hand, offered no real support. A prominent woman reportedly gave $10 to the cause in the early weeks of the strike, and the wife of a Socialist alderman created a sensation by joining the picketers and driving around the factory in her husband's automobile, but there was no organized effort on the part of non-working-class Kalamazoo women to aid the strikers. Pledges of support by prominent women and an initial show of interest in a women's auxiliary came to nothing. The oft-repeated complaints of organizers and the absence of any mention of the strike in the records of women's groups or on the women's pages of the local newspaper attest to the lack of interest. Thus, while trade unionists picketed alongside the striking corsetmakers and committees representing the ministers and businessmen of the city attempted to bring the two sides in the

12. *KTP*, 5, 8, and 11 March 1912. Local unions continued to pledge their support for the corsetmakers throughout the strike.

13. *KTP*, March–April 1912.

dispute together for negotiations, women's organizations took no public stand on the strike.[14]

This indifference came as a surprise to Casey. When the strike began, she believed that "support . . . will naturally come to us from the general public," and she predicted a quick victory for the union, counting especially on the assistance of local women. In an article that appeared in the *Telegraph-Press* shortly after her arrival in the city, Casey stated, "If the cause of labor is to win, it will be largely through the efforts of the women of the country," who in her opinion had a special sensitivity to the needs of workers: "Any woman who has ever thought seriously upon any subject recognizes the rights of labor when they are presented to her, and she sees at once that there is something economically wrong when a woman demands a waist at 50 cents when eggs are 50 cents a dozen."[15]

Perhaps because she believed that the women of Kalamazoo would naturally sympathize with their striking sisters, Casey did little at first to cultivate their assistance. She spoke to the Ministerial Alliance and visited prominent citizens in an effort to mobilize support, but she did not appeal directly to women. Soon after the injunctions were issued, however, Casey altered her strategy. At a mass public meeting to which prominent citizens had been invited, she announced that new conditions had been discovered since the beginning of the strike, necessitating additional strike demands. The corsetmakers charged that wash

14. *KTP*, 21 March and 3 May 1912. The 1912 minutes of the Ladies' Library Association of Kalamazoo—which was formed to promote "moral and intellectual improvement" in the city but was also involved in civic improvement and sanitary reform projects—allude to the need for a "thorough up-to-date YWCA building to help provide for the recreative life of our 2,000 working girls in our city" but never mention the striking corsetmakers (Board Meetings, 5 January 1912 and entries for 1912 to 1914, Ladies' Library Association Records, Western Michigan University, Regional Historical Collection, Kalamazoo). The Young Women's Christian Association, which had an industrial department and secretary to work with young women employed in the city's factories, was more concerned with their religious welfare than their material needs. The industrial secretary held noon meetings in the paper mills and helped to get a comfortable resting room for women workers put into one of the mills, but there is no evidence that the YWCA did anything to assist the striking corsetmakers (Reports of the Industrial Secretary, YWCA, Kalamazoo, 1911 and 1913; and "YWCA, 1885–1929," unpublished summary of the Association's activities, 7–8, in YWCA files, Kalamazoo). Pauline Newman thought that noontime entertainment and pleasant employee lounges were a poor substitute for decent wages and working conditions: "I am opposed to them [rest rooms, libraries, and recreation rooms in factories] because I think they are spacious devices by which the manufacturer makes a girl content with the miserable wage that he gives her. They are the instrument that prevents the organization of the women workers" (*Detroit News*, 10 March 1912).

15. *KTP*, 1 March 1912.

basins were filthy, that they had to share towels used by men with "loathesome sores," and that the foremen gave the most desirable jobs to women who submitted to their sexual advances. The foremen also neglected for several days to demand the customary payment for the thread that these women used in their work and then suggested to them "a way [in] which these girls might repay them for their act of 'kindness.'"[16]

These allegations were confirmed by several of the corset workers, who signed affidavits describing the conditions in the factory. A woman physician who often treated working girls told a WTUL investigator that "we physicians know it [the corset factory] to be an awful place for an innocent girl." She claimed that many of the corset workers had contracted venereal diseases from male workers and that "several girls . . . had taken their first step downward while employed at the factory." The investigator reported that the factory did indeed have an immoral atmosphere but was much cleaner than she had expected. Casey declared at the public meeting that although a living wage was still the primary goal of the strikers, the union would now include medical inspection of employees and improved sanitary conditions in the factory among its demands. She hoped that the "moral" fight would be taken up by the citizens of Kalamazoo.[17]

When she changed her appeal, Casey expected an immediate and forceful response from the public. She asked for the support of prominent women and attempted to organize a women's auxiliary that would seek to bring about arbitration of the strike. At the same time she began to send women strikers to cities and towns throughout the Midwest to alert women and unionists to the situation in Kalamazoo, believing that the people of the nation would pressure the corset company to negotiate.

Middle- and upper-class women in other cities had been enthusiastic supporters of labor measures. Women reformers in New York City had walked the picket lines and offered financial support to strikers during the "Uprising of the 20,000." In Chicago a board composed of labor leaders and WTUL members led the men's garment workers'

16. *KTP*, 13 and 14 March 1912; *LGW* 3 (May 1912): 12–13; Foner, *Women and the American Labor Movement*, 357; Pauline Newman, "The Story of the Corset Workers' Strike in Kalamazoo, Michigan," newspaper clipping in Leonora O'Reilly Papers, Schlesinger Library, Radcliffe College (microfilm ed., Papers of the Women's Trade Union League and Its Principal Leaders, reel 11, frame 1138).

17. "A Report of an Investigation of the Present Strike Situation at the Kalamazoo Corset Company's Factory," 17 April 1912, National Women's Trade Union League (NWTUL) Papers, Schlesinger Library, Radcliffe College (microfilm ed., Papers of the Women's Trade Union League and Its Principal Leaders, reel 4, frames 606–11).

strike of 1910–11, while other reformers organized a citizens' committee to help mediate the dispute. And in the aftermath of the 1911 garment workers' strike in Cleveland, women's clubs in Detroit, Lansing, and other Michigan cities had endorsed a boycott of nonunion Cleveland-made goods. But the women of Kalamazoo never rallied to the cause of the corsetmakers.[18]

Several factors help explain Casey's inability to arouse the sympathies of local women. First, the manner in which she raised the issue of immorality in the factory alienated some people. She turned to the question of moral and sanitary conditions in the factory as an afterthought, adopting the issue because it was brought to her attention at a time when her original strategy was not working. This strategy appeared disingenuous to the public and caused some women to discount the validity of her claims. A female physician was quoted as saying that "if the girls had walked out because of the moral conditions, if some one of their own members was their leader, if they had taken a more tactful stand, every mother in this town would have been with them."[19]

Beyond her tactical error of raising the moral issue after the strike had already begun, Casey failed to understand the particular circumstances of Kalamazoo. She had hoped to appeal to reform-minded middle- and upper-class women like those in other cities who had supported protective legislation, boarding homes, and other measures for the aid of women workers. But many of the women in Kalamazoo who fitted this description were preoccupied at the time with a statewide campaign to raise support for an equal suffrage amendment to the state constitution, which was to be voted on in the fall. Perhaps like the suffragists of Cleveland, who failed to come to the aid of striking garment workers there, the suffragists of Kalamazoo were unwilling to jeopardize their primary goal by associating themselves with striking workers.

The suffragists of Kalamazoo did express concern for working women in the abstract; their speeches emphasized the importance of the ballot for female industrial workers. Yet they viewed these women not as sisters with shared experiences but as persons needing assistance and protection. One of the suffragists stated that she did not need the ballot for herself but fought for it for the sake of other women, es-

18. Dye, *As Equals and as Sisters*, 88–95; N. Sue Weiler, "The Uprising in Chicago: The Men's Garment Workers Strike, 1910–1911," in *A Needle, a Bobbin, a Strike*, ed. Jensen and Davidson, 123–30; *Detroit News*, 2 and 10 March 1912; *LGW* 3 (May 1912): 14–15.
19. NWTUL, "A Report of an Investigation," 6.

pecially women workers. "It's pathetic," she said, "to know how many of these women do not realize how much they need the right to vote."[20]

The class position of the suffragists also militated against their coming to the aid of the strikers. Newspaper coverage of the suffrage campaign shows that Kalamazoo suffragists were part of the city's social elite—one of the leading speakers in the campaign was described as a "society matron and quite the most representative woman of the leisure class in Kalamazoo"—and that their husbands belonged to the same social and business circles as James Hatfield, president of the corset company. For these women, to support publicly the strikers would have been to betray their own class position and to jeopardize their husbands' interests and reputations.[21]

While women of like social standing in such cities as Chicago and New York had assisted striking workers, the situation in Kalamazoo was somewhat different. It was a much smaller city, having a population of only 39,000. Furthermore, only one firm was being struck, and the owner of that firm was well liked and respected in Kalamazoo. The woman who had been sent by the WTUL to investigate conditions in the factory said that James Hatfield "is the sort of businessman who holds the confidence of stockholders and general public alike." In addition to owning the corset company, Hatfield was involved in numerous other business and financial concerns in the city. In 1905, for example, he was president of the corset company, the Kalamazoo Paper Box and Card Company, and the Fidelity Building and Loan Association; a director of the Kalamazoo Trust Company and the Home Savings Bank; and a stockholder in various other firms. The 1906 *Compendium of History and Biography of Kalamazoo County* commented that Hatfield "has contributed very largely to the present prosperity and industrial importance of the city." Providing assistance to striking corsetmakers might well have appeared as a personal attack on one of Kalamazoo's leading citizens.[22]

Finally, Kalamazoo did not have a network of women reformers committed to supporting labor causes. In Chicago and New York City, such networks were already in existence when the garment workers' strikes occurred. Both cities had strong WTUL organizations; in Chicago the WTUL had solid ties with the Chicago Federation of Labor

20. *KTP*, 4 and 8 May 1912.
21. *KTP*, 4 May 1912.
22. NWTUL, "Report of an Investigation," 5; David Fisher and Frank Little, eds., *Compendium of History and Biography of Kalamazoo County, Michigan* (Chicago, 1906), 509.

and with settlement workers. Mobilizing support for strikes in these cities was made easier by the existence of these networks. In Cleveland, where no such network existed (a WTUL branch had been organized in 1909 but soon foundered), Casey and Newman were unable to arouse the support of local women during the 1911 Cloak and Suit Workers Strike. Although the appeal to public opinion was not always successful, Casey continued to believe in its efficacy, probably because of her positive experiences with the WTUL in Chicago.[23]

In the weeks following Casey's allegations of immoral conditions in the corset factory, public interest in the strike declined. The *Telegraph-Press* relegated news of the strike to inside pages under headlines proclaiming, "Strike of Corset Makers Is Devoid of Heart Agitation" and "Nothing Doing Is True Development in Labor Strike." An article in late March reported that "the strike of the corset workers grows more pinkteaish each day. Today there is absolutely nothing doing that resembles excitement." The prayer pickets and occasional public events organized by other labor unions were equally ineffective in forcing Hatfield to negotiate. He insisted that the plant was functioning smoothly and that new workers were reporting daily—thanks, no doubt, to the "girls wanted" ads he was running in the newspapers of Kalamazoo and neighboring towns.[24]

With no progress in sight, Casey again shifted her strategy. On April 21 she announced that the union would set aside the issue of better wages and hours and would instead work to make the factory a more sanitary and safe place for women to work. "This is a fight for the womanhood of Kalamazoo," Casey declared. Thenceforth she centered her appeals to the public on the vulnerability of the female corset makers to sexual exploitation in the factory.[25]

On the following day, April 22, the corset workers' union voted to defy the injunction and resume picketing. The resumption resulted in the arrest of Casey and eight others. On the advice of ILGWU general secretary John Dyche, the three men who had been arrested accepted bail and were released; the women remained in jail. Lively picketing continued despite the arrests, with members of various local unions taking turns on the picket line.

At Casey's request, Gertrude Barnum came to Kalamazoo on May 7 to lead the strike while Casey was in jail.[26] Barnum, a special arbitration

23. Scharf, "Great Uprising in Cleveland," 164.
24. *KTP*, 15, 19, and 22 March 1912.
25. *KTP*, 22 April 1912.
26. *KTP*, 22 April, 2 and 8 May 1912.

agent for the ILGWU and a friend of Casey's, joined the negotiations that were under way between corset company officials and a committee representing the union, consisting of William Stewart, president of the Kalamazoo Trades and Labor Council, and Homer Waterman, secretary of the Michigan Federation of Labor. The committee asked strikers not to picket while negotiations were in progress, as a gesture of good faith, and picketing ceased for the first time in almost three weeks on May 9. But that evening strikers "congregated in the vicinity of the factory and hissed the present employes calling them 'scabs' and 'traitors.'" Barnum then advised union members to continue picketing, but, like Casey, she urged them "to avoid all disorder or threats or violence as public opinion was sure to condemn disorder."[27]

On May 15 an agreement was submitted to the unionists which provided for a minimum weekly wage of $5 for women and girls after twelve weeks of work; charging workers no more than wholesale rates for thread; establishing a citizens' committee to investigate moral and sanitary conditions in the factory; and reinstating union members who had gone on strike. Casey thought the agreement inadequate because it did not guarantee that workers would be given back the jobs they had left; if the workers accepted the agreement, she said, they would be making a "sublime sacrifice for the betterment of moral conditions." However, she did not advise the strikers on whether or not to accept, and they were initially divided. But on May 17, after Casey and eleven other unionists were sentenced to jail terms of five to twenty days for violating the injunction against picketing, they voted unanimously to reject the proposal. Over the next few weeks members of various local unions picketed the corset factory, while Barnum tried without success to interest the women of Kalamazoo and neighboring towns in the strike.[28]

Pauline Newman arrived in Kalamazoo on June 4 to take charge of the strike when Casey was released from jail. Casey left for the East with Gertrude Barnum on June 5, planning to spend two weeks at the seashore recuperating from her imprisonment before returning to Kalamazoo to take up the fight again; Newman was to be merely an interim strike leader. As it turned out, Casey did not visit Kalamazoo again until October, for the strike was settled within ten days after her departure. Newman, however, remained in Kalamazoo for about six weeks to work with the corsetmakers' union.[29]

27. *KTP*, 8, 9, and 10 May 1912.
28. *KTP*, 15–20 May and 3 June 1912; *LGW* 3 (June 1912): 1–7.
29. *KTP*, 5 June 1912; *LGW* 3 (October 1912): 10.

Newman was in an awkward position when she assumed leadership of the strike. She had inherited a situation and a strategy created by Casey and a strike in its final stages. The corsetmakers, the ILGWU, and the townspeople were all growing weary of the strike, and negotiations between the union and the company were in progress. Newman said she felt like an outsider, having arrived so late in the conflict. Nonetheless, she assumed an aggressive stance. She said that if the strike were not settled soon, she would hold open-air meetings, stir up the whole nation, and "make things lively in Kalamazoo." She also commented that "no great cause ever won a victory without some martyrs."[30]

Newman urged the strikers to continue picketing regardless of the negotiations in progress, although local labor leaders had counseled against such action in an effort to appear as amenable as possible to the prospect of a settlement. Newman relished the picketing and took great delight in her ability to elude the police sent to arrest her, as her face was not yet known to them. She preferred the picket line to the negotiating table; as a union organizer, she said, "I am supposed to play the part of the diplomat when I would rather be the fighter. It's more natural to fight than to be diplomatic. Being diplomatic makes you a hypocrite. You say yes when you mean no, and smile when you feel like frowning. But you do it because you think some good may come of it."[31]

The strike was at a critical juncture when Newman arrived. The departure of Casey, who had won the confidence and friendship of the corsetmakers during her three months in Kalamazoo, was undoubtedly a blow to the strikers. Recognizing that their morale was low, Newman asked WTUL president Margaret Dreier Robins to come and speak to them to boost their spirits. To Newman's annoyance, Robins replied that she had to remain in Chicago for a teachers' convention. Leonora O'Reilly, vice-president of the New York WTUL and a former shirtwaist maker, did come to Kalamazoo on June 7 to speak to the strikers and investigate conditions, but her help was too little and too late. She wrote an article for the August issue of the WTUL journal *Life and Labor*—which up to this time had been silent on the strike—but by the time the article appeared, the union had signed an agreement with the company, and the strike had been turned into a boycott.[32] Had the WTUL provided greater assistance in publicizing the corsetmakers'

30. *KTP*, 6 June 1912.
31. *KTP*, 5, 6, and 7 June 1912.
32. Pauline Newman to Leonora O'Reilly, 6 July 1912, in O'Reilly Papers (microfilm ed., reel 6, frame 336); *KTP*, 7 June 1912; *Life and Labor* 2 (August 1912): 228–30.

strike and encouraging the workers in their struggle, it might not have altered the outcome but would have provided valuable psychological support to the organizers and the strikers.

As it was, Newman felt she had been placed in a no-win situation with few resources, abandoned by those she had thought most likely to support her. She joined the negotiations that were in progress, and within a few days a proposal very similar to the one that the strikers had rejected in May was presented to the union for consideration. It called for the rehiring of the strikers at their old wages—if not necessarily their old jobs—in groups of five or ten as soon as possible; a minimum wage of $5 a week for women workers after twelve weeks of employment; charging workers no more than wholesale rates for thread; and the establishment of a sanitation board or committee to investigate sanitary and moral conditions in the factory and arbitrate grievances brought against the company by former workers in connection with their rehiring. But the corset company refused to include two key union demands: that workers be given back their old jobs at the machines where they had previously worked and that the strikers be hired all at once rather than individually or in small groups. Furthermore, company officials stated that they would first rehire those workers who were least objectionable to persons already employed in the factory.[33]

Leonora O'Reilly's opinion of this proposal was that "the corset manufacturer has succeeded in getting everything and the workers take all the humiliation—while an outside Comm[ittee] refuses to have Labor's voice." She wrote to ILGWU general secretary John Dyche that she and Pauline Newman were under pressure from the conciliation committee to call off the strike, but she would not do it because with this agreement "there is no peace—or if there is it is peace at any price—the price here being sacrifice your leaders, take what you can get and be glad you are alive."[34]

Newman also seemed unhappy with the proposal but was reluctant to advise the workers on its acceptance because she had been in Kalamazoo such a short time. The conciliation committee and the Kalamazoo Trades and Labor Council pressed the corsetmakers to come to a decision, and when John Dyche arrived on June 14, he recommended that the strikers accept it. On June 15, over the protest of a large minority, the union voted to ratify the agreement.[35]

The peace was short-lived, however. It soon became clear that the

33. *KTP*, 7, 8, 12, and 15 June 1912; Leonora O'Reilly to John Dyche, 8 June 1912, in O'Reilly Papers (microfilm ed., reel 6, frames 293–96).
34. O'Reilly to Dyche, 8 June 1912.
35. *KTP*, 12, 14, and 15 June 1912; *LGW* 3 (August 1912): 4–5.

company was not living up to its part of the agreement in reinstating the strikers. Former workers were being rehired at a slow rate and on an individual basis rather than in groups. New employees were hired instead, and in one instance employees were allowed to vote on whether a woman who had gone on strike should be given work. One striker was asked to sign a paper stating that she did not belong to a union in order to get her job back. When Pauline Newman and several members of the union presented these grievances to the sanitation board on June 22, the board accepted the promise of the company's general superintendent to "try and straighten matters out in the future" and urged the union members to be patient with the company.[36]

Failing to receive a satisfactory response to their complaints, the members of Local 82 decided to renew the strike against the Kalamazoo Corset Company and ultimately turned it into a boycott of the company's products. For the next two years, several members of Local 82 traveled around the Midwest to publicize the boycott. At union gatherings and women's club meetings, these "missionaries" told of the conditions in the corset factory and the events of the strike and urged women not to buy corsets made in Kalamazoo. Pauline Newman herself went to Chicago, St. Louis, and Indianapolis that summer; when she returned to New York, she kept in touch with the corsetmakers and reported on the progress of the boycott for the *Ladies' Garment Worker*. In December 1914 the Kalamazoo Corset Company was sold at a receivers' sale; Newman and Local 82 credited the boycott with driving the company out of business. Ironically, the only victory available to the union came at the cost of hundreds of jobs for women workers.[37]

The Kalamazoo strike presents an interesting contrast in organizing styles. The different tactics and strategies used by Casey and Newman reflect different perceptions of what would be effective, but they also reflect deeply held views on the relationship between feminism and unionism. In a study of Pauline Newman and two other ILGWU organizers, Alice Kessler-Harris argued that women organizers working for male-dominated unions felt acute tension as a result of their dual roles as workers and as women. When the two roles came into conflict, their identification with the working class took precedence over their identification as women.[38] This is an accurate characterization of Newman's

36. *KTP*, 22 June 1912; *LGW* 3 (August 1912): 4–5.
37. *LGW* 3 (August 1912): 4–5; periodic references to the boycott in Pauline Newman's "Among Our Women Workers" and in *LGW*, 1912–14; Michigan Federation of Labor, *First Industrial History and Official Yearbook* (1915), 54–55; and Pauline Newman interview, 20–21.
38. Kessler-Harris, "Organizing the Unorganizable," 161.

words and actions during the Kalamazoo strike, but it does not fit Casey.

Both Casey and Newman had challenged traditional roles for women by virtue of their work as union organizers, which involved traveling alone, speaking in public, and choosing career over marriage. Both women were suffragists as well as trade unionists and had expressed their commitment to feminist as well as union concerns by joining the Women's Trade Union League. But Casey's tactics in the Kalamazoo strike conformed to norms of appropriate female behavior. She urged the picketers to be peaceful and instituted the "prayer pickets" and meditation as strike tactics; she counseled against picketing when negotiations were in progress so that the union would appear amenable to a settlement. Newman, on the other hand, favored aggressive picketing and confrontational tactics rather than a conciliatory stance. Casey's conduct of the strike emphasized the differences between men and women; Newman's approach stressed their similarity.

Furthermore, Casey made gender an issue by shifting the focus of the strike away from economic questions to moral questions. At the outset of the strike, gender-specific concerns were not at issue. The strikers, though mostly women, perceived their problems to be those of workers rather than problems peculiar to women in the workplace. The strike was initially fought for union recognition, a minimum wage, and a reduction of hours for men. When Casey learned of the sexual harassment of the female corset workers, she decided to exploit the issue in order to gain sympathy for the strikers. She thought that appeals focused on the vulnerability and exploitation of women workers would win public support. Instead, Casey was perceived as being hysterical and lacking in refinement and tact.

By publicizing the problem of sexual harassment in the factory, Casey may have demonstrated to the corsetmakers that theirs was a legitimate grievance deserving union attention. But the manner in which she phrased her appeal stressed the women workers' vulnerability and helplessness in the face of their more powerful male supervisors and thus strengthened traditional notions of women as frail, dependent, and in need of protection.

The contrasts between Casey and Newman reflect somewhat different analyses of the problems faced by women workers in American society. Like Casey, Newman recognized that women workers had certain concerns not shared by their male coworkers; for example, both believed that women workers who did not receive adequate wages were sometimes forced into prostitution or sexual liaisons with foremen or bosses in order to survive. But Newman did not think that moral issues should be made the focus of strikes. She recognized that the sexual exploitation of women workers was not unique to Kalamazoo; it existed in factories throughout the nation. As part of a larger pattern of social relations between the sexes, the problem would not be eradicated by solutions that were specific to the Kalamazoo factory. The real solution, according to Newman, was to pay women workers a living wage and then educate them to their sexual vulnerability in the workplace. In a newspaper article titled "What Is the Working Girl's Greatest Need?" she stated, "I realize that there are religious, moral, and educational problems, but I firmly believe that each of these, important as it may be, is subsidiary to the economic problem."[39]

Newman was unwilling to dilute the economic questions involved in the strike by bringing in such issues as sexual exploitation. Perhaps she understood that appeals based on women's special nature might be effective in the short run, but in the long run they reinforced a view of women as different and inferior, consigned to a lesser role in society than men.

Finally, Casey counted heavily on public support to influence the outcome of the strike. She believed, like many Progressive-era social reformers, that if injustice were brought to the attention of the public, people would naturally take action to correct it. Thus she assumed that if she publicized the "immoral conditions" that existed in the Kalamazoo corset factory, people would be outraged and demand that the company respond to the workers' complaints. Casey also assumed—rather naively—that the public would then support the workers' demands for higher wages and shorter working hours as well.

Newman was less sanguine about the power of the public to bring the strike to a successful conclusion. She doubted both the willingness and the ability of the public to influence corset company officials. Furthermore, she recognized that the support of middle- and upper-class women often came at the price of putting up with their condescending or patronizing attitudes toward women workers. Newman did not reject the tactic of appealing to the public for support, but she framed her appeal in terms different from Casey's: instead of focusing on working women's vulnerability and need for protection, she stressed their economic power as consumers. While Casey had tried to call attention to the strike by stressing the sensational aspects of the factory situation, Newman sent corset workers on the road to agitate for a boycott of the Kalamazoo Corset Company's products. Unlike the

39. *Detroit News*, 10 March 1912.

amorphous and unpredictable power of public opinion, a boycott of Kalamazoo corsets was a very real threat to the company.[40]

In the final analysis, neither Casey's nor Newman's strategy was successful. Both women were able to win the support and loyalty of the corset workers and to sustain the local union during a prolonged strike. But the strike—like many in this period—ended in defeat for the workers. Both Casey and Newman turned to middle-class women for support because they had no choice: the solid support of the working-class community of Kalamazoo had failed to budge Hatfield from his position. Maurine Greenwald, Nancy Schrom Dye, and other historians have noted the crucial role played by middle-class women who supported strikes by women workers in the early twentieth century. But as recent studies of the garment industry have shown, it was often difficult to rally middle-class women to the cause or to retain their backing during a long strike. Even when strikers did gain such support, there was no guarantee that they would win.[41]

This analysis of the Kalamazoo corsetmakers' strike, together with studies of garment workers' strikes in Cleveland and in Rochester, New York, suggests that female solidarity across class lines was often elusive during periods of labor strife. In cities where a network of middle- or upper-class female reformers with ties to the labor community had not been previously established, female strike organizers found it difficult to attract such support to their cause. Even when organizers phrased their appeals in gender terms geared specifically to women, they were not successful. Having failed to win middle-class women's support in

40. *LGW* 3 (May 1912): 13. Casey described the situation in sensational terms as part of a widely publicized prayer she composed for the prayer pickets: "Thou who didst save Noah and his family, may it please thee to save the girls now on strike from the wicked city of Sodom. Oh help us to get a living wage. Oh, Lord, who knowest the sparrow's fall, wilt thou not help us to resist when the modern devil, who has charge of our work, takes advantage of our poverty to lead us astray. . . . Hunger and cold are terrible things and they make us weak. . . . Help us to be strong. Oh, God, we have appealed to the ministers, we have appealed to the public and we have appealed to the press. But if all these fail us in our need we know that thou wilt not fail us. Grant that we may win this strike and that the union may be strong, so that we may not need to cry often, Lord, 'deliver us from temptation.' We ask this, Lord, for the sake of the little children, helpless and suffering; for the girls who may some day be mothers of children and for those girls who dislike sin, but are forced into it through poverty" (*LGW* 3 [May 1912]: 22–23).

41. Maurine Weiner Greenwald, *Women, War, and Work: The Impact of World War I on Women Workers in the United States* (Westport, Conn., 1980), and "Historians and the Working-Class Woman in America" in *International Labor and Working Class History* 14/15 (Spring 1979): 23–32; Dye, *As Equals and as Sisters;* Scharf, "Great Uprising in Cleveland"; Joan M. Jensen, "The Great Uprising in Rochester"; and N. Sue Weiler, "The Uprising in Chicago," all in *A Needle, a Bobbin, a Strike,* ed. Jensen and Davidson.

the Cleveland strike, Josephine Casey tried a novel approach in Kalamazoo. She used prayer pickets to underscore the feminine makeup of the work force and focused her appeal to the public on the issue of sexual harassment. But even this appeal failed to win over the local women. In Kalamazoo, class ties were stronger than gender ties.

The Kalamazoo strike sent a mixed message to the ILGWU. It demonstrated once again that women could be militant and dedicated union members. The women of Local 82 continued the battle long after the ILGWU had admitted defeat; as late as June 1915 the union was preparing to fight a new corset company that had been established in Kalamazoo. But the results of the strike were disappointing: the ILGWU had devoted strike funds and the energies of three female organizers to a lengthy struggle that yielded meager results. The few concessions won by the union were of little value because the company chose not to honor them, and there was no effective mechanism to ensure compliance with the agreement. The Kalamazoo strike, then, like others of this period, illustrates the great odds faced by women workers who challenged their employers by striking and forming unions in the early twentieth century. When confronting intransigent opponents like James Hatfield, who had the backing of the courts and the support of the public, workers had little chance of success.[42]

42. *LGW* 6 (June 1915): 27.

10

Seeking "a New Day and a New Way": Black Women and Unions in the Southern Tobacco Industry

Dolores Janiewski

When the fires of labor insurgency first began to glow in the southern tobacco industry in the 1930s, they were nearly extinguished by sexual and racial tensions among tobacco workers. Various segments among the people who manufactured tobacco products had worked separately from each other for more than a hundred years.[1] Racial consciousness had long stifled any recognition of common interests between black and white workers. Expectations generated by a sexually based division of labor, power, and resources dissuaded women from taking active roles outside their homes or local communities. Although emancipation and migration off the land had placed whites and blacks in a similar class position within tobacco factories scattered across the upper South, residential and occupational segregation denied them a

I thank the scholars affiliated with the Center for Research on Women at Memphis State University for their comments and criticisms on an earlier version of this essay.

1. For discussion of labor relations in the tobacco industry, see Joseph Clarke Robert, *The Tobacco Kingdom: Plantation, Market and Factory in Virginia and North Carolina, 1800–1860* (Goucester, Mass., 1965); Robert S. Starobin, *Industrial Slavery in the Old South* (New York, 1970); Nannie May Tilley, *The Bright-Tobacco Industry, 1860–1929* (Chapel Hill, N.C., 1948); and Herbert R. Northrup, *The Negro in the Tobacco Industry*, Report no. 13, The Racial Policies of American Industry (Philadelphia, 1970).

common meeting place.[2] Black women, a majority in the tobacco labor force by the 1930s, were a key constituency, but their experiences of racial, gender, and class subordination made them more distrustful of unions than any other group of tobacco workers.[3] Sparks had to be struck among black women, or the campaign to unionize the tobacco centers in Virginia, North Carolina, and Kentucky would end in failure.[4]

Black women found employment in tobacco factories in Durham, Winston-Salem, Richmond, Louisville, and small tobacco marketing towns such as Danville, Lynchburg, and Rocky Mount. In each tobacco center, patterns of race and gender relations combined antebellum traditions with postbellum innovations that responded to abolition, mechanization, and the new industrial environment. White male factory owners and managers organized and maintained a political and economic hierarchy that pinned black women to the bottom of the overlapping set of dominant–dependent relationships.[5]

Originally created to erect a barrier in "nature as well as law . . . between the black and white races," the intersecting relationships of gender and race were reconstructed in an industrial setting.[6] Since white

2. Northrup, *Negro in the Tobacco Industry;* Charles S. Johnson, "The Tobacco Worker: A Study of Tobacco Factory Workers and Their Families," 2 vols., unpublished study, Industrial Studies Section, Division of Review, National Recovery Administration, National Archives, Washington, D.C. (hereafter NRA); John W. Cell, *The Highest Stage of White Supremacy: The Origins of Segregation in South Africa and the American South* (Cambridge, Eng., 1982), 82–170. Cell relates segregation to industrialization.

3. Johnson, "Tobacco Worker," 2:412.

4. Johnson identified six centers where the manufacture of tobacco was concentrated in the 1930s: Danville and Richmond, Va.; Reidsville, Winston-Salem, and Durham, N.C.; and Louisville, Ky.

5. For explorations of the social relationships in the various tobacco centers, see E. Franklin Frazier, "Durham: Capital of the Black Middle Class," in *The New Negro: An Interpretation,* ed. Alain Locke (New York, 1968); Michael B. Chesson, *Richmond after the War, 1865–1890* (Richmond, Va., 1981); Leon Fink, *Workingmen's Democracy: The Knights of Labor and American Politics* (Urbana, Ill., 1983); Bertha Hampton Miller, "Blacks in Winston-Salem, North Carolina, 1895–1920: Community Development in an Era of Benevolent Paternalism" (Ph.D. diss., Duke University, 1981); Walter B. Weare, *Black Business in the New South: A Social History of the N.C. Mutual Life Insurance Company* (Urbana, Ill., 1973); Hugh P. Brinton, "The Negro in Durham: A Study in Adaptation to Town Life" (Ph.D. diss., University of North Carolina, 1930); and Robert Korstad, "Class, Community, and Labor Protest in the Piedmont Tobacco Industry, 1880–1950," paper presented to the Fourth Southern Labor Studies Conference, Atlanta, 2 October 1982. For studies of the tobacco hierarchy, see Dolores E. Janiewski, *Sisterhood Denied: Race, Gender, and Class in a New South Community* (Philadelphia, 1985); Northrup, *Negro in the Tobacco Industry;* and Johnson, "Tobacco Worker."

6. John Campbell, "Negro Mania—The Negro and Other Races of Man," in J. D. B. De Bow, *The Industrial Resources, Statistics, Etc., of the United States and More Particularly of the Southern and Western States* (New York, 1854), 2:203. For more theoretical analyses of

women and black women had been symbolically separated into superior and inferior beings, according to the rules of slavery, they must be differently employed in the tobacco factory. As symbols of racial purity, white women could work only where their racial and sexual "honor" could be guaranteed. Their employment must appear suitable for "respectable ladies." Employers faced no similar social imperative in the case of black women; indeed, one of them could openly boast of using "brute treatment."[7] Inculcated with the same notions of racial and sexual hierarchy as their employers, white women strove to keep their distance from those whose equal companionship was associated with degradation. Patterns of interaction developed over 300 years of racial and economic exploitation segmented the tobacco factory labor force into different and mutually antagonistic groups.

Motivated by economic advantage, antebellum tradition, and the need to assuage white sensitivities, southern manufacturers of tobacco products recruited a biracial labor force. The onset of mechanization in the 1880s brought increasing numbers of whites into the factories to operate the new machines. The growing demand for processed leaf pulled more black men and black women into the stemmeries. The spatial organization of the factory conformed to white racial views by keeping blacks confined to heavy or manual jobs in separate parts of the plant, while whites monopolized the mechanical and supervisory parts of the process in the cigarette departments. In short, a racially and sexually segmented hierarchy had been constructed.[8]

---

the use of "nature" as a way to justify social division, see Mary Douglas, *Purity and Danger: An Analysis of the Concepts of Pollution and Taboo* (London, 1966), 125–27; Floya Anthias and Nira Yuval-Davis, "Contextualizing Feminism—Gender, Ethnic, and Class Divisions," *Feminist Review* 15 (Winter 1983): 62–75; and Ronald T. Takaki, *Iron Cages: Race and Culture in Nineteenth-Century America* (New York, 1979), 47–55.

7. Orlando Patterson, *Slavery and Social Death: A Comparative Study* (Cambridge, Mass., 1982), discusses the important rules of slavery, including the insistence on "natal alienation," the sexual exploitation of female slaves, and the concern for racial purity on the part of the slaveholders; Douglas, *Purity and Danger*, 125–27, explains the reasons why caste systems guard "female purity" while treating "male promiscuity" on the part of the dominant caste as a "lighter matter." For specific discussions of the issue of "honor" in the southern context, see Jacquelyn Dowd Hall, "'The Mind That Burns in Each Body': Women, Rape, and Racial Violence," in *Powers of Desire: The Politics of Sexuality*, ed. Ann Snitow, Christine Stansell, and Sharon Thompson (New York, 1983), 328–49; and Bertram Wyatt-Brown, *Southern Honor: Ethics and Behavior in the Old South* (New York, 1982). The quotations are from *Frank Leslie's Illustrated Newspaper*, 10 February 1883; Emma L. Shields, "A Half-Century in the Tobacco Industry," *Southern Workman*, September 1922.

8. Douglas, *Purity and Danger*, 124, 127, discusses the creation of a stratified occupational hierarchy as part of a caste system where work carries a "symbolic load" and establishes the worker's position according to "varying degrees of purity." For interpreta-

Other conditions of employment corresponded to those associated with the creation of a dual labor market.[9] White workers, employed in the tobacco version of the primary labor market, experienced greater job security, better pay, and other advantages that came from employer investment in their training. Black women, hired primarily to stem tobacco leaves, found their employment more erratic; it rose and fell with the amount of leaf available. Reflecting the combination of low pay and irregular work, black women's annual wages in the mid-1930s averaged less than $500 a year, $100 below the wages paid to black men or white women and more than $200 less than the earnings of white men.[10] By hiring black women for the labor-intensive parts of the production process, tobacco companies lowered their wage costs and enhanced their ability to hire and fire at will.

Whether workers were interviewed in the 1930s or the 1970s, they expressed racial antagonisms, suspicions, and fears.[11] A black cooper, interviewed in Richmond in 1935, reported his bleak assessment of white racism: "The white people ain't going to treat you right. If you say something, then they will put you out in the street. . . . Our colored girls do more and harder work than the white girls, but the whites get more money. So many of our colored lock up with these whites, and they treat them just like slaves." An employee at the Larus Brothers plant in Richmond voiced an opinion shared by other white workers: "Everything is running smooth all the time. We have good colored folks. They stay in their place; they don't bother anybody. They works around the plant stemming, cleaning, and that sort of thing, but we aren't with them." When blacks got out of their "place" or white workers tried to push them too hard, battles sometimes broke out on the

---

tions of segmentation of the labor force, see Richard C. Edwards, Michael Reich, and David M. Gordon, eds., *Labor Market Segmentation* (Lexington, Mass., 1975). For specific descriptions of segmentation in the tobacco factory labor force, see Tilley, *Bright-Tobacco Industry*, 515–16; Michael B. Chesson, *Richmond after the War, 1865–1890* (Richmond, Va., 1981), 134–35; Robert, *Tobacco Kingdom*, 197–208; Johnson, "Tobacco Worker," 1:26; and Shields, "Half-Century," 419–25.

9. My own work suggests a segmentation by gender, class, and race which would render the term "dual labor market" inadequate but still useful. See Janiewski, *Sisterhood Denied*, 95–102.

10. Johnson, "Tobacco Worker," 2:434–38; and National Recovery Administration, "hearings on a Code of Fair Competition for the Cigarette, Snuff, Chewing, and Smoking Tobacco Industry" (1934).

11. Tobacco workers in the major tobacco centers were interviewed in 1935 for the NRA; in the 1970s, oral historians—including the present writer—conducted a series with retired tobacco workers. Some of these interviews are included in the Southern Oral History Program collection in the Southern Historical Collection at the University of North Carolina, Chapel Hill (hereafter SOHP).

factory floor. Whites deemed too sympathetic to blacks were called "nigger lovers." Blacks who spied for management became known as "white man's niggers."[12] In every factory embittered, frustrated people vented their emotions on the nearest and most vulnerable target.

Enforced silence could inflict psychological damage on those forced to work under intolerable conditions. Having succinctly described her experience as "hell," one black tobacco worker refused to say more about her years at the American Tobacco Company because she did not wish to relive the bitter past. Another woman recounted the painful wisdom that had allowed her to keep her job: she always did what she was told to do. Like many others, Annie Mack Barbee recognized that there were times for "meekness and humbling," times that came frequently for black female tobacco workers.[13]

A daughter of one black tobacco worker vividly evoked the personal and familial consequences that flowed from oppression. In her case her mother's accommodation to the white-dominated workplace led to conflict. Mary Mebane described her mother's way: "This was her routine—fixed, without change, unvarying. And she accepted it. She more than accepted it, she embraced it; it gave meaning to her life, it was what she had been put here on this earth to do. It was not to be questioned. To Nonnie this life was ideal; she saw nothing wrong with it. And she wondered in baffled rage why her daughter didn't value it but rather sought something else, some other rhythm, a more meaningful pattern to human life."[14] Later, Mebane extended her analysis to include all those scarred by "the psychological terror of segregation": "The constrictions, the restraints, the hidden threats that we lived under, that were the conditions of our lives, inevitably produced mutations in the natural human flowering. To me we were like plants that were meant to be growing up-right but became bent and twisted, stunted, sometimes stretching and running along the ground, because the conditions of our environment forbade our developing upward naturally."[15] So she explained the daily tragedies she witnessed.

A white male beneficiary of the subordination imposed upon black

12. Johnson, "Tobacco Worker," 1:226, 237; interview with two retired tobacco workers conducted by Dolores Janiewski, personal holding; Charlie Decoda Mack, interviewed by Beverly Johnson, SOHP.

13. A statement made at an American Tobacco Retirees Club, where the author asked members to aid in this research project; a black female tobacco worker, interview by Linda Guthrie, personal holding; Annie Mack Barbee, interviewed by Beverly Johnson, SOHP.

14. Mary Mebane, *Mary* (New York, 1981), 98–99.

15. Mebane, *Mary*, 177–78.

workers expressed his preference for working in a department where black men also were employed: "I'd rather work with them than with whites because you tell them to do something and they don't argue with you." White workers and supervisors could take advantage of their privileged position by verbally harassing black workers. The use of "girl," "boy," and a grown worker's first name all served to mark the superior places of whites in the factory hierarchy. Black women also became the targets of sexual advances by foremen who sought to "fumble your behind," an indignity some women accepted out of fear that they might lose their jobs if they objected.[16]

Outside the factory, workers' lives diverged still further. The spatial contours of the tobacco centers bore the visible imprint of the same forces that divided the factory labor force. On a visit to Durham in the late 1930s, Jonathan Daniels reflected on the ironic contrast between the city's image as the home of the "black bourgeoisie" and the harsh realities of black life

> even in Durham where the Negro has made money and lifted his pride. Negro insurance men and bankers work in a building in the same business section where the white offices are, but there are wide lines of railroad tracks between where the Negroes work and where they live. Indeed, Hayti [named after the black republic but spelled as it is pronounced in Durham] is almost the black ghetto complete. I rode across the tracks and by the tobacco factories. The blue and white uniforms for servants, sold everywhere by the chain store, seem almost the uniform of Negro women in Durham, where they work in the rough preparation of the tobacco, while white girls turn out the endless tubes of Chesterfields and Lucky Strikes.[17]

Formal segregationist practices in schools, churches, and public conveyances reinforced the informal barriers to social equality. A black girl who grew to adolescence in Durham in the early twentieth century reported, "Our seedy rundown school told us that if we had any place at all in the scheme of things, it was a separate place, marked off, proscribed and unwanted by the white people. . . . We came to know that whatever we had was always inferior."[18]

Gender also delimited public and private space. The streets, barbershops, and pool halls were male territory. Men patrolled the inormal boundaries that divided urban space into black and white areas.

---

16. Johnson, "Tobacco Worker," 1:311; Annie Mack Barbee interview.

17. Jonathan Daniels, *Tar Heels: A Portrait of North Carolina* (Westport, Conn., 1941), 134.

18. Pauli Murray, *Proud Shoes: The Story of an American Family* (New York, 1978), 270.

The Ku Klux Klan was only the most extreme manifestation of white male determination to control the public arena. Young males, black and white, participated in the ritual of "rocking," which threatened any intruder who ventured into alien territory with a shower of stones. The objects that were fought over in these street battles included neighborhood girls and urban space. Thus men, young and old, solidified the boundaries between "them and us" while turning women into "sexual property" reserved for the winners.[19]

Respectable women hurried through the streets between their public and private workplaces. Women who spent time on the streets risked their reputations; men were freer to indulge themselves. Churches, on the other hand, constituted female space where male pleasures were condemned. According to one historian of the blues, the street culture and church represented "two opposing world views" and mirrored the gender-based conflict that was expressed in the differences between sacred and secular music.[20] Households represented another female space; there women assumed most of the burdens of domestic labor. Surveys recorded that the average employed married woman spent three hours a day on housekeeping matters, while unmarried working women spent about forty-five minutes.[21] Some women worked past midnight, then arose at five o'clock to make breakfast and pack lunches for their families. Childbearing and child rearing responsibilities lengthened women's working days and tied them still more closely to their homes. So constrained, women found it more difficult than men to keep up with public affairs, to attend meetings, or to assume leadership roles.

Although domestic responsibilities weighed on black and white women alike, the greater proportion of black married women employed in tobacco factories added to their work loads. Social expectations encouraged young women to marry, but low wages for blacks meant that marriage and motherhood would not eliminate the need for female economic contributions. The average black family required

---

19. A blues musician, interviewed by Glenn Hinson, SOHP. For discussions of the construction of women as sexual property, see Gerda Lerner, *The Creation of Patriarchy* (New York, 1986); Mary O'Brien, *The Politics of Reproduction* (London, 1981); Ann Whitehead, "Women and Men: Kinship and Property," in *Women and Property, Women as Property*, ed. Renée Hirschon (New York, 1984); and Barbara Rogers, *The Domestication of Women: Discrimination in Developing Countries* (New York, 1979). For insights into an earlier variant of "rocking," see Natalie Zemon Davis, "The Reasons of Misrule," in *Society and Culture in Early Modern France: Eight Essays* (Stanford, 1974), 105–9.

20. Glenn Hinson, interviewed by Dolores Janiewski, personal holding.

21. U.S. Women's Bureau, bull. no. 70, *Negro Women in Industry in Fifteen States* (Washington, D.C., 1929); Brinton, "Negro in Durham," 118.

more than twice the annual wages paid to black tobacco workers to achieve the $1,500 a year needed for a satisfactory standard of living.[22] Once a woman stepped on the treadmill of private and public work, her energies easily became absorbed in the daily struggle for subsistence. As Annie Mack Barbee explained, "You never get anywhere in your goals. You just get up there and work and then it becomes habit forming. You just work, work. A lot of 'em did. . . . Once you get there and get stuck, you don't try to go nowhere, you just stay there."[23]

In the household the economic differences between black and white wages might lead to the direct subordination of a black woman to her white coworker: by virtue of her family's greater economic resources, a white tobacco worker might be able to hire a black woman to do domestic work. Here in one of the "most frequent" forms of "intercaste relationships," white women could directly express their superior position over their sister workers.[24] Here they could enforce other rituals of racial domination—including the white insistence that blacks eat separately from whites and the use of titles for whites but not for blacks—and affirm their own superiority.[25]

But racial and gender-based patterns of interaction were not the only source of identity imposed on black and white tobacco workers. In addition to corrosive racial and sexual conflict, blacks and whites alike were wounded by the "injuries of class."[26] Even the most privileged white male worker could suffer from low wages, abusive management, and other frustrating experiences. The Depression of the 1930s may have served to strengthen the employers' power, but it also nurtured a growing class consciousness on the part of the workers. Perhaps managers overplayed their hand. Certainly the growing public awareness of unions and federal protection for unionization presented tobacco workers with the possibility of cooperation across racial and gender lines.

When a team of investigators sent by the National Recovery Administration came to tobacco centers in the South, they discovered that many employees were angry about working conditions. A white woman at American Tobacco criticized the relentless demand for increased production: "They are so strict they will tear your nerves to pieces. One girl

22. Johnson, "Tobacco Worker," 1:56–65.
23. Annie Mack Barbee interview.
24. Allison Davis, Burleigh B. Gardner, and Mary Gardner, *Deep South: A Social Anthropological Study of Caste and Class* (Chicago, 1941), 443.
25. Janiewski, *Sisterhood Denied*, 41, 44–46, 47–49, 53, 108, 121, 140.
26. Richard Sennett and Jonathan Cobb, *The Hidden Injuries of Class* (New York, 1972).

had to quit with a shattered nervous system." A black woman in Durham shared the Richmond worker's opposition to company decisions: "I don't think it's right to put in them machines to take work away from us poor people." A white male fixer, perhaps employed in the same department with the black stemmer, expressed sympathy for black women "pressed to make $10 a week." Seventy miles away in Winston-Salem, a white employee accused his supervisors of using "the poor whites to whip the nigger and the nigger to whip the poor whites."[27]

Interviewed forty years later, other tobacco workers remembered crucial events that brought the idea of a union to their minds. A black man, later a union leader, remembered the way he'd received his first job in a Virginia tobacco factory. When he saw the older man who'd been summarily dismissed "crying just like a baby," he'd vowed "that will never happen to me."[28] A stemmer discovered that she could defy her "bossman" and escape punishment. Asked to inform on slow co-workers, she refused: "Listen, you don't hire me to tell you who was working and who wasn't working. You hired me to work. Now if you want to know about them people not working, you look and see for yourself, cause I ain't telling you nothing."[29] Mutual indignation and traditions of mutual defense enabled some workers to sympathize with the plight of other workers, white or black.

Louise Harris had acquiesced in conditions she described somewhat irreverently—"Preachers don't know nothing about hell; they ain't worked in no tobacco factory"—but one day she could take no more. She had tolerated a male coworker who "stooled" for managers—until he ordered her to stop singing. "Six years is six years, but this once is too often. So I'm all over him like gravy over sauce. I give him a tongue-lashing what curled every nap on his head. I sass him deaf, dumb and blind, and he takes it." Shocked by her defiance, the man accused her of involvement in a union. Unaware that such an organization existed in Richmond, Louise Harris began to search for a way out of the collective hell she'd endured too long.[30]

Other tobacco workers began the same search in the 1930s. The Tobacco Workers International Union began to stir to life after the passage of the National Industrial Recovery Act in 1933 gave govern-

27. Johnson, "Tobacco Worker," 1:224, 2:420; K. B. Wheeler, "Hearings on a Code of Fair Competition," NRA (1934); Johnson, "Tobacco Worker," 1:131–32.

28. A tobacco worker, quoted in Stuart Kaufman, "The Tobacco Workers International Union," manuscript in possession of Stuart Kaufman, Department of History, University of Maryland, College Park.

29. Mary Harris, interviewed by Glenn Hinson, SOHP.

30. "The Making of Mamma Harris," *New Republic*, 4 November 1940, 624–26.

ment sanction to the rights of workers to organize. Beginning in Winston-Salem, North Carolina, the union established a beachhead its traditional way: it signed a contract with Brown & Williamson for a union label, creating a union by managerial dictate. In Durham, where employers resisted this tactic, the TWIU shifted its attention to the rank and file. Beginning with white male workers at Liggett & Myers, it established a white local and created a cadre of activists.[31] But it faced a more difficult time attracting other workers. Black women were especially recalcitrant. One stemmer joined the TWIU local designated for stemmery workers during a wave of enthusiasm in the spring of 1934. Referring to the union organizer in the same terms she used for her employers, she reported her experiences: "The white man said it was good to join the union 'cause they would see we would have a job. . . . They told us, 'Well, if you don't join, somethin' or 'nother is going to happen next week.' . . . I didn't believe much in it, but everybody was talking so I joined."[32] Witnessing the failure of the white textile strike in September 1934, however, she and the vast majority of her coworkers dropped out of the local.

Although a black woman in Winston-Salem did not quit the union, she disliked the way her local conducted its meetings:

> They have programs at some of the meetings. They sing a song, something about the union. I don't know the words and some of them sing solos. Once in a while some of the white people come to our meeting. . . . They can do it because they don't meet on the same night the colored meet. I don't go to the meetings much. They used to meet on Friday nights, but that was pay day and most all them would be drunk, so I just stopped going. I didn't get no enjoyment or nothing out of the meetings no way.[33]

The character of the union as a white- and male-dominated organization obviously hindered black women from finding it a comfortable or trustworthy vehicle to aid them in their search for greater power in the workplace.

Fear that the meager bread could be snatched from their mouths dissuaded many black women from joining the TWIU. Such fears were particularly acute in Winston-Salem, where two previous organizing

---

31. Based on the history of the TWIU in Kaufman, "Tobacco Workers International Union"; Johnson, "Tobacco Worker"; Northrup, *Negro in the Tobacco Industry;* and the Tobacco Workers International Union Papers, Archives and Manuscripts, McKeldin Library, University of Maryland, College Park (hereafter, TWIU Papers).

32. Johnson, "Tobacco Worker," 2:414.

33. Johnson, "Tobacco Worker," 1:288.

efforts had resulted in mass dismissals by the R. J. Reynolds Company. A white machine operator described the climate of fear that caused many workers to hesitate before risking their jobs by trusting the TWIU once again: "I think we need a union of whites and blacks together. I know several who have been fired down there—they said it wasn't on account of the union, but I don't know. I understand that when they tried to form a union several years ago, Reynolds sent someone down to the union meeting to spot the faces and those people were fired. A lot of them are henpecked. They want it, but they're scared."[34] It may have been awe of white power that induced some black women in Danville, Virginia, to thwart the union drive by informing their white employers about it. The subsequent jailing of some of the union's leaders obviously exacerbated the fears already felt by many women, who reported, "You don't say union overalls down there—they'll fire you. A woman say something about union in Heaven, and got fired."[35] A Durham worker summed up his pessimism by explaining, "It would be a pretty hard job to get a union in this town because colored people have been treated so dirty." Besides, he added, "it takes a lot of money to run a union—to buck capital."[36] Despite their anger over job conditions, many workers could see no easy way to defeat their employers or to trust their fellow union members.

The organizing strategy adopted by the TWIU under its longtime president, E. Lewis Evans, constituted another barrier to black women's participation. To white male workers the TWIU offered leadership positions and active roles in the organizing drive. To black workers it offered membership in segregated locals. Although Evans insisted that black workers must be invited to join, he assured his white members that "social equality" would never be practiced under the auspices of the TWIU. As he wrote a Durham activist, the "Nigs" must be brought in or the "BOSSES will use him to defeat our general purpose."[37] In addition to racism, Evans also indicated his tendency to ignore the presence of women in the labor force he was trying to organize. When organizers faced difficulties in attracting blacks, he blamed the problem on "backward and ignorant" black workers and on antiunion attitudes among black ministers and other leaders. Refusing a Winston-Salem local's request for a black organizer, Evans explained, "It has been demonstrated that those people do not want any organiza-

---

34. Johnson, "Tobacco Worker," 1:285.
35. Johnson, "Tobacco Worker," 1:98.
36. Johnson, "Tobacco Worker," 2:414.
37. E. Lewis Evans to W. R. Culbreth, 17 August 1933, Local 176 file, ser. 3, TWIU Papers.

tion. . . . Perhaps it will be better to let them fry in their own fat for the balance of the year and, if they show some desire next year, we may ask them what they want."[38]

Writing more frankly to a white organizer, Evans agreed that blacks should never be given "any free right to do as they think they should." When black community leaders proposed a joint organizing campaign, Evans refused because businessmen "do not have the same economic basis to work from" as "our Trade Union Movement." He accused ministers of looking only for the "smile they could feel with their hands" and insisted that workers must never cooperate with middle- or upper-class allies.[39] Such views only hardened any existing suspicions felt by black leaders toward an outside, white-controlled organization such as the TWIU. The failure to attract wholehearted support from local ministers was particularly damaging to efforts to gain the loyal adherence of black women, to whom religion offered the major vehicle for collective identity.[40]

The TWIU's rejection of cross-class alliances, its racism, and its sexism left an opening for an alternative union better able to fuse the goals of black workers and unionism. Beginning in 1937 in Richmond, the "evangels of John L. Lewis" competed for black allegiance with the TWIU, which had largely ignored black workers in that city. Sponsored by the CIO and the Southern Negro Congress (an organization influenced by the Communist Party's campaign against racism), the new organizing drive held meetings in black churches, "sang spirituals and union songs," and compared the situation of "our slave fore-fathers" with the struggles of "the men and women who must still fight wage slavery." "The rapture and earnestness" of their rallies was "hardly distinguishable from that of a prayer meeting," in sharp contrast to the men's club atmosphere that had discouraged some black women from participating in the conservative TWIU's proceedings.[41] Respect for black culture and history helped the new movement to attract and keep the allegiance of black women.

When CIO organizers came south in 1937, they discovered that

38. E. Lewis Evans, quoted in Johnson, "Tobacco Worker," 2:593; E. Lewis Evans to George Benjamin, 15 October 1936, Local 179 file, ser. 3, TWIU Papers.

39. Quotation from E. Lewis Evans to H. A. McCrimmon, 22 May 1937, H. A. McCrimmon file, ser. 2, TWIU Papers. Evans gave McCrimmon his support: Evans to E. N. Ellis, 10 July 1939, Local 179 file, ser. 3; Evans to Duby S. Upchurch, 28 July 1934, D. C. Upchurch file, ser. 2, both in TWIU Papers.

40. In the Durham case, e.g., only one leading minister actively encouraged union efforts; the others remained neutral or hostile.

41. Augusta V. Jackson, "A New Deal for Tobacco Workers," Crisis, October 1983, 322–24, 330.

black women employed in the Richmond Carrington and Michaux plant had already undertaken a spontaneous strike. After negotiations produced wage increases, an eight-hour day, a forty-hour week, and recognition of the independent Tobacco Stemmers and Laborers Industrial Union, another walkout occurred at the notorious I. N. Vaughn factory. Black women won the first strike of any kind in Richmond since 1922.

It was in 1938 that Louise Harris reached the breaking point at the Export stemmery in Richmond. Having heard the word "union" from the coworker she'd defied, she found her way to a meeting sponsored by the year-old Tobacco Stemmers:

> I carried sixty of the girls from our floor. They remember how I sass this scab and they're all with me. We plopped right down in the first row of the gallery. And when they asked for volunteers to organize Export, I can't get to my feet quick enough. . . . And it ain't no time before we got seven hundred out of the thousand that works in Export. . . . But they can't fire. The boom time is on and the warehouse is loaded to the gills. And then on the first of August 1938, we let 'em have it. We called our strike and closed up Export tight as a bass drum. . . . Then this scab came up with a couple of hundred others and tried to break our line but we wasn't giving a crip a crutch or a dog a bone. I made for that head scab personal—but the cops wouldn't let me at him.[42]

The strike received support from the CIO-affiliated Clothing and Textile Workers Union, and Richmond society was shocked to see "white women out here parading for niggers."[43] Louise Harris and her coworkers won major concessions.

A new union was born. Churches were "foremost in volunteering assistance" and made appeals for the union in their sermons. Employers confronted a newly vocal group of workers. Forced to bargain, one Richmond factory owner conceded, "Times certainly changed. I remember when I used to fire a nigger for just walking into my office."[44] The strike at Export convinced the CIO to establish an official Tobacco Workers Organizing Committee. Black women had created an instrument to seek education, civil rights, and respect.

The existence of a vigorous rival challenged the TWIU to make more persuasive overtures to black workers. It also inspired the restive male workers, white and black, to challenge Evans' heavy-handed authority. First a strike against all the Liggett & Myers plants in April

42. "Making of Mamma Harris."
43. "Making of Mamma Harris."
44. Jackson, "New Deal for Tobacco Workers."

1939 signaled the new militancy of the rank and file against the staid conservatism of its aging leadership. That fall the locals forced the first convention of the TWIU in more than twenty years and took the positions of secretary and treasurer away from Evans. Finally, the insurgents forced Evans from the office of president in 1940.[45]

Yet as the 1939 L&M strike revealed, the changes in the character of the TWIU did not remove all barriers to black women's full participation. Many black women witnessed the L&M strike from the sidelines. One local that enrolled black stemmers was "not strong enough to strike."[46] The new TWIU president publicly pledged to overcome "the racial prejudice of our white members," but the union made no effort to change the segregation of occupations and the segmentation of the labor force.[47] Spurred by competition from the CIO affiliate that was organizing tobacco workers, the TWIU signed up more black workers but channeled them into segregated locals. When mechanization began to eliminate many black jobs, the union did not push for the opening of formerly white occupations or departments to the displaced black workers. As a result of union inaction and company policy, the black share of total employment fell from majority to minority status in the 1930s and 1940s.[48] Because black women's jobs were disproportionately affected, the TWIU's reluctance to end the color bar in the industry was the most significant obstacle to black women's union activity.

There were far fewer obstacles in the CIO-affiliated union. In the spring of 1942 a young organizer from the United Cannery, Agricultural, Packing and Allied Workers of America (UCAPAWA) arrived in Winston-Salem to force a breach in the antiunion wall erected by R. J. Reynolds, the city's leading tobacco manufacturer. In contrast to the experience of Durham, where the presence of the TWIU kept the rival union out, the campaign made rapid progress in Winston-Salem. By

45. *Durham Morning Herald*, 18 April 1939; quotation from Ernest Latta, interviewed by Lanier Rand, SOHP; Kaufman, "Tobacco Workers International Union."

46. Dora Scott Miller, interviewed by Beverly Johnson, SOHP.

47. W. Warren Smith, *Tobacco Worker*, 1941. Smith, however, in a letter to the president of the AFL, made clear that he did not support "social equality" (Smith to William Green, 26 August 1941, AFL file, ser. 1, TWIU Papers).

48. John O'Hare to Wilson M. Brown: "Segregation in the upper South has not disturbed us very much. This practice is left wholly to the discretion of the persons involved" ("Negro in Industry" file, ser. 1, TWIU Papers). See also Local 208 file, ser. 3; Roy G. Trice file, ser. 2; George Benjamin file, ser. 2; EEOC file, ser. 1, all in TWIU Papers. The point of view of workers who felt betrayed by the TWIU's racial policies is presented in Jean M. Cary, "The Forced Merger of Local 208 and Local 176 of the T.W.I.U. at L&M in Durham, North Carolina" (master's thesis, Duke University, 1971).

June 1943 the group of activists was poised to seize the opportunity when a spontaneous workers' action took place: 200 women stopped work at the Reynolds stemmery to protest the death of a black man denied sick leave. Their sitdown spread to include 2,000 workers by the end of the second day. When Reynolds refused to negotiate, the women turned to the UCAPAWA organizers, and a union boasting several thousand members took shape. Within a week of the initial incident, Reynolds had been brought to the negotiating table. After gaining bargaining rights in December 1943, the newly named Food and Tobacco Workers Union signed a contract with Reynolds in April 1944.[49]

The black women whose abilities were nurtured in the new union testified to its importance in their lives. Combining an emphasis on civil and workers' rights, the union transcended the narrow class consciousness fostered by its rival. Union education included black history; union activities brought workers to the ballot box, opening local elections to men and women who had been excluded. Ruby D. Jones spoke for others when she assessed the union's achievements by contrasting her life before and after the existence of the Food and Tobacco Workers Union. "You worked just like a dog and was talked to just like a dog. We didn't get no recognition or be treated like human beings until that union came in there. Even in the newspaper nobody had a Mrs. on their name until that union came. There were stores that you couldn't go into. When the union came, it was just like being reconstructed."[50] Indeed, it was the organizers' intention to reconstruct class and racial relationships in the South. Although the "woman question" was not placed formally on their agenda, a willingness to encourage black women's full participation helped to erode gender-based constraints even as they altered the balance of racial and economic power. A battle in the war to create a "regenerated South" had been waged in the tobacco industry.[51]

But victories were hard to translate into a lasting and just peace. Subordination based upon race, gender, and class was strongly entrenched. It was deeply embedded in the patterns of daily life, in the way people thought and felt, in their very definition of what was nor-

49. Robert Korstad, "Those Who Were Not Afraid: Winston-Salem, 1943," in *Working Lives: The Southern Exposure History of Labor in the South,* ed. Marc S. Miller (New York, 1980).
50. Ruby D. Jones, interviewed by Robert Korstad, SOHP.
51. Karl Korstad, "An Account of the 'Left-Led CIO Unions'" Efforts to Build Unity among the Workers in Southern Factories during the 1940s" (paper presented to the Civil Rights Institute, Duke University, 9 April 1979); Jackson, "New Deal for Tobacco Workers."

mal and natural. Women believed in the definition of their place voiced by men. Racial fears were easily rekindled. It took money to "buck capital" when companies were determined to reassert their authority. In the climate of postwar conservatism, unions could be curbed or even destroyed if they threatened too radical an assault on existing gender, race, and class relationships.

At the CIO convention in 1947, Moranda Smith, a former tobacco worker from Winston-Salem, rose to speak. Now a regional director of the FTA, she denounced legislation then being debated in Washington, soon to become known as the Taft-Hartley Act. Its backers intended to curb the powers granted to unions by the Wagner Act of 1935 and to eliminate Communist Party members from leadership positions in the labor movement. Not coincidentally, the same coalition would thwart civil rights legislation. Smith sought to inspire her audience to do battle against the forces seeking to undo the work of her union: "We want the people to walk the picket lines free and unafraid and know that they are working for their freedom and liberty. When you speak about this protection of democracy, it is more than just words. . . . Ask the people who are suffering and together you will come out with a good program where civil rights will be something to be proud of."[52] Despite the applause for Smith's passionate appeals, the CIO itself complied with the law, expelling her union for its refusal to enforce all its provisions.[53]

Three years later, as her union was confronting the forces unleashed by Taft-Hartley which allowed Reynolds to refuse to negotiate with the FTA, Smith died, a young woman in her early thirties. Her grieving colleagues testified to her courage even as they mourned the destruction of her dream:

> Because Sister Smith was determined and militant, she was chosen to serve on the union's negotiating committee. The white bossmen, who had heaped abuse and poor wages on Negro women, now had to deal with them in a respectful manner. . . . When the bossmen would speak only to the men leaders of the union, the men rejected this attempt to snub her and said, "Address your remarks to Sister Moranda Smith, she is a member of the committee." And then, much against their wishes,

52. Moranda Smith, Final Proceedings of the 9th Constitutional Convention of the CIO, October 1947, quoted in Gerda Lerner, *Black Women in White America: A Documentary History* (New York, 1973), 269–71.

53. For a general examination of the CIO, Taft-Hartley, and left-led unions, see Nelson Lichtenstein, *Labor's War at Home: The CIO in World War II* (Cambridge, Eng., 1982), 234–41.

the bosses would have to recognize her. This was a new day and a new way.[54]

Unfortunately, the old days and old ways were returning to the tobacco industry.

The TWIU, taking advantage of the opening offered by Taft-Hartley and by Reynolds' refusal to negotiate, sent black organizers to Winston-Salem. Such men as Roy G. Trice of Durham derided the FTA for "preaching social equality" and a mixture of "despotism and anarchy." Having failed in the 1948 campaign to defeat the FTA, the TWIU tried again in 1950. The votes for no union edged slightly ahead of the votes for the FTA in those elections (never again would Reynolds sign a union contract); the TWIU finished third. An exhausted Trice told the union officials that the defeat occurred because "many Negroes looked upon FTA as a God." The victory of the nonunion forces over "the false ideology on which the leftwingers thrive" was a defeat for the labor movement, for racial equality, and for the vehicle that offered black women their greatest opportunity to defend themselves.[55]

When a new generation of black tobacco workers renewed the demand for equal rights in their union and workplaces, the movement came too late to save the jobs of many black women. Gradually, after the federal government moved against racial discrimination in employment in the 1960s, the older forms of segregation began to dissolve. By then black workers, displaced by mechanization in the stemmeries, were a minority in the industry. Many black women were back in service jobs, having experienced the grim reality described by one Durham woman: "The very day we quit working up there, here comes the machines. . . . And the white man was up there putting up signs for the bathroom—'white only.' That's up there at Liggett & Myers. So the white women went up there and they didn't need to put no signs. I didn't get anything from Liggett & Myers. The mass of black women didn't get a whole lot of nothing from them." Her bitterness extended to the union, whose leaders had concurred with L&M's refusal to pull "white workers off of jobs they have held for many years in order to satisfy the desires of the colored employees."[56] She spoke proudly of

54. "Tobacco Workers Honor Fighting Union Leader," *Union Voice*, June 1951, quoted in Lerner, *Black Women in White America*, 272–74.

55. Roy B. Trice to John O'Hare, 12 November 1949 and 11 March 1950, Roy G. Trice file, ser. 2, TWIU Papers. See also George Benjamin file, ser. 2, TWIU Papers.

56. Annie Mack Barbee interview; John O'Hare to R. J. Petree (memorandum), 6 February 1962, EEOC file, ser. 1, TWIU Papers.

her individual struggles for decent treatment and "respect" from her employers, but the union had served the interests only of whites, in her experience.

Black women and their coworkers could have succeeded in creating a vehicle to serve their collective needs only by transforming racial, gender, and class relationships. Those long-enduring "habits of domination" fragmented tobacco workers into hostile and suspicious groups. After the brief interlude of New Deal liberalism, workers confronted powerful corporations armed with capital and the support of the state. The FTA agenda to build "strong democratic unions" and develop a "core of black workers to give strength to the developing movements for civil rights" challenged powerful interests.[57] Union in its most comprehensive sense eluded southern tobacco workers. The union that confined its interests to the workplace survived by putting the needs of white male workers before all others. Yet the importance of the possibilities that began to exist must also be acknowledged. The union that black women strove to build offered tobacco workers a public space where they could simultaneously address the issues of class, gender, and race. Such women as Moranda Smith voiced the hopes of many of their silenced sisters to "walk free and unafraid" in support of their just demands for "respect."

57. Korstad, "Left-Led CIO Unions."

11

Housewife and Household Worker: Employer-Employee Relationships in the Home, 1928–1941

Phyllis Palmer

In 1930 the U.S. Census recorded that approximately two million women, constituting 17.8 percent of the female labor force, were employed as private household workers. The occupation was declining in relative importance—over 52 percent of working women had been private household workers in 1870—but still ranked first among women's occupations through the 1940 census.[1] Only the job shifts of World War II and the economic changes following the war finally offered women the varied and widespread employment that ended their reliance on domestic work. The shift to other occupations was especially remarkable for black employed women, almost 50 percent of whom had earned wages from private household work during the 1920s and 1930s.[2]

I am indebted to the Radcliffe Research Scholars Program for assistance during the fall of 1983 and to the University Research Committee of George Washington University for support during the spring of 1984.
  1. Allyson Sherman Grossman, "Women in Domestic Work: Yesterday and Today," *Monthly Labor Review*, August 1980, 17–21; Bettina Berch, *The Endless Day: The Political Economy of Women and Work* (New York1982), 12–13; Alice Kessler-Harris, *Out to Work: A History of Wage-Earning Women in the United States* (New York, 1982), 270, citing George Stigler, *Domestic Servants in the U.S.*, National Bureau of Economic Research, occasional paper 24 (New York, 1946), 41, 42.
  2. Kessler-Harris, *Out to Work*, chap. 11, describes post–World War II shifts as "the radical consequences of incremental change."

The racial complexion of the domestic work force was just one more indication of the occupation's low status and, by the time of the Depression, unarguably poor pay and work conditions. Private household work was notorious for paying the lowest wages of available women's jobs and for requiring the longest weekly hours.[3] As early as the 1910s, the occupation had become a target for reformers working to improve women's work conditions. By the 1920s the poor picture presented by private household work was becoming an embarrassment to newly enfranchised middle-class women arguing for women's ability to make significant positive changes in politics and society. As the employers of the most exploited workers in the labor force, middle-class women needed to clean up their own workplaces if they were to be credible moral leaders in the society at large.[4]

Governmental intervention to raise labor standards became feasible with the election of Franklin Delano Roosevelt as president in 1932. Attempts were made to draw up a code for domestic work similar to other industry codes designed and enforced under the National Recovery Administration's "blue eagle" program (1933–34). Civil rights and women's organizations lobbied for the inclusion of domestic work under the maximum hours and minimum wage provisions of the Fair Labor Standards Act (1938). But domestic work was immune to the regulatory infection. The occupation was excluded from federal governmental action because it had no connection with interstate commerce (the rationale for suprastate regulation).[5] Practically, state and local governments tended to avoid local regulation because of its administrative difficulties; the specter of hundreds of government employees visiting thousands of homes to check on violations was a night-

3. "Studies of Labor Problems in Household Employment, by Henrietta Roelofs, Household Employment Commission of the National Board of the Young Women's Christian Association, New York City," n.d., typescript in National Board, Young Women's Christian Association Archives, New York City (hereafter YWCA Archives), reel 98.4: Household Employment Reports; Susan Strasser, *Never Done: A History of American Housework* (New York, 1982), chap. 9, esp. 169ff.

4. Ida Tarbell, "What a Factory Can Teach a Housewife," [YWCA] *Association Monthly*, November 1916, 422; "A Good Way for Women to Reform Is to Start with the Industry of Homemaking," *Women's Press* 22 (February 1928): 82; Mary Anderson, "An Occupational Analysis of Household Employment," reprinted from the Seventh International Management Congress, Washington, D.C., 1938, typescript in YWCA Archives, reel 98.4.

5. Kessler-Harris, *Out to Work*, 262, 270; Martha H. Swain, "ER and Ellen Woodward: A Partnership for Women's Work Relief and Security," in *Without Precedent: The Life and Career of Eleanor Roosevelt*, ed. Joan Hoff-Wilson and Marjorie Lightman (Bloomington, Ind., 1984), 135–52; Nancy J. Weiss, *Farewell to the Party of Lincoln: Black Politics in the Age of FDR* (Princeton, N.J., 1983).

mare version of regulations intended to advance the dream of equality.[6]

In the absence of government action, the major efforts to improve the conditions of work for domestic servants fell to associations of middle-class women, who organized to persuade their "sisters" to adopt equitable and efficient standards of household employment voluntarily. This study relies on the work of the major organizations involved in defining and disseminating standards: the Young Women's Christian Association, working through local Y's under the auspices of a Committee on Household Employment lodged with the Public Affairs Committee in the New York National Board office; and the YWCA-backed National Coalition on Employer–Employee Relationships in the Home. The coalition was founded in 1928, was renamed the National Committee on Household Employment (NCHE) after 1931, and faded out of existence in late 1941 as war employment issues took precedence.[7]

The purpose of this essay is to describe the hours of work, pay, and other conditions for women hired as private household workers during the late 1920s and 1930s; to clarify how these conditions derived from the work and familial needs and the perceptions of the employer-housewives; and to speculate about why housewives were reluctant to accept even voluntary regulation of household employment during this period. My intention is to stimulate further study of the work done in private homes, with reliance on the same questions and methods as those applied to other kinds of work.[8]

My reasons for this approach to the study of housework are four. First, until the 1950 census, household employment was the predominant wage-earning occupation for U.S. women and especially for women of color. To study domestic work with less than the rigor that labor historians, economists, and sociologists have applied to the study of

6. The problem of enforcement was cited by Clara Mortensen Beyer in an interview with Vivien Hart, Washington, D.C., July 1983, on file in the History of Women in America collection, Schlesinger Library, Radcliffe College.

7. The records of the National Committee on Household Employment are scattered. Among the sources I have used are U.S. Women's Bureau, RG 86, National Archives; YWCA Archives; Women's Trade Union League Papers, History of Women in America, Schlesinger Library, Radcliffe College (hereafter WTUL Papers).

8. Roslyn L. Feldberg and Evelyn Nakano Glenn, "Male and Female: Job versus Gender Models in the Sociology of Work," in *Women and Work: Problems and Perspectives*, ed. Rachel Kahn-Hut, Arlene Kaplan Daniels, and Richard Colvard (New York, 1982), 65–80, point out that sociologists have used a "job model" to explain men's labor force participation and a "gender model" to explain women's. Historians, similarly, often focus on work conditions to explain the behavior of male workers, while emphasizing the "family economy" to explain the behavior of female workers.

industrial, artisanal, and white-collar occupations is to demean the
women who did this work by perpetuating its invisibility as work.[9]
Second, in the United States, housework done for no wages—to take
care of oneself or of other people in a household—is still considered
primarily the responsibility of adult women. Until we pay the same
kind of attention to the work content of unpaid household-based jobs
as we do to paid employment, this work also remains invisible. It is
dismissed simply as an outpouring of women's propensity to serve
others, or romanticized as playing with children and heating up pre-
cooked meals in the microwave (or travestied as reclining in front of
the television set while eating chocolates, or fitting in laundry between
tennis lessons).[10]

The final reason for studying housework as work brings us back to
the first point. Housework has been a major division in the circumstances and historical experiences of different groups of American
women. Through the first half of the twentieth century, most white
middle-class women could hire another woman—usually a recent immigrant, a working-class woman, a woman of color, or all three—to

Third, women cannot hope to revise the way housework is performed until (a) they know what the work consists of and how it is done
and (b) they recognize the conflicting familial and social interests involved in the questions of who will do the work and according to what
standards. Even with the "wages for housework" movement of the
early 1970s and the examination of household time budgets to determine how much time the labor of caring for a household actually
requires, the work of household maintenance remains obscure. We
have measures of time spent on cooking or laundry or cleaning or child
care, but we know little about the standards for work performance, the
conditions of the work, and the relations between workers and consumers and between workers and employers, even though these people
may be kin. Until such knowledge exists, women will not be able to
transform housework; they will simply try to get paid for it or, as often
happens with cooking dinner, try to move the work out of the house.[11]

The final reason for studying housework as work brings us back to
the first point. Housework has been a major division in the circumstances and historical experiences of different groups of American
women. Through the first half of the twentieth century, most white
middle-class women could hire another woman—usually a recent immigrant, a working-class woman, a woman of color, or all three—to

---

9. Bettina Aptheker, *Women's Legacy: Essays on Race, Sex, and Class in American History*
(Amherst, Mass., 1982), chap. 6; Angela Y. Davis, *Women, Race and Class* (New York,
1981).

10. Richard A. Berk and Sarah Fenstermaker Berk, *Labor and Leisure at Home: Content
and Organization of the Household Day* (Beverly Hills, Calif., 1979), 10, argue that "we are
almost totally ignorant of how people clean their homes: how household chores are
arrayed over a 24-hour period and coordinated with one another."

11. Strasser points out (*Never Done*, chap. 15) how much home preparation of food
has been replaced not by better products or by women's collective production but by fast-
food restaurant chains.

perform much of the hard labor of household tasks. Not only was such household help denied to the women who did housework for others, but domestic servants were constrained from taking care of their own homes by their long hours away at work. American women of our era will not be able to work together on issues of mutual interest until we document, remember, and heal the historical tensions that still cluster around the performance of housework.[12]

In 1928, Lucy Carner, executive secretary of the Industrial Division of the national board of the YWCA, called a national conference on employer–employee relationships in the home. The Y was interested in household employment on both the employer and employee fronts, and many local Y's operated employment bureaus through which housewives could find workers and "working girls'" clubs for household workers.[13] The other primary mover, Mary Anderson, shared Carner's interest in improving the wages and work conditions of household workers. As director of the U.S. Women's Bureau, Anderson recognized the need to take some action on behalf of the lowest-paid women workers.

Other members of the organizing committee, on the other hand, represented the home economics establishment and thus the professional conception of housewifery: helping the housewife to be a model manager. These were Benjamin Andrews, a professor at Teachers College, Columbia University, a founding member of the American Home Economics Association, and author of a leading home economics textbook; Louise Stanley, chief of the Bureau of Home Economics in the U.S. Department of Agriculture; and Mrs. Eva von Baur Hansl, who would organize the program for the second annual conference and was an associate editor of *Parents* magazine, a publication concerned with the interests of children and of housewives-as-mothers. Mabel Thompson, an official of the Union Dime Savings Bank of New York City, the committee's treasurer, represented the professional businesswoman. Dr. Amey E. Watson was executive director of the committee and freelance fund raiser and publicist for the group after the 1928 founding meeting.

Once formed, the National Committee on Household Employment

12. Phyllis Marynick Palmer, "White Women/Black Women: The Dualism of Female Identity and Experience in the United States," *Feminist Studies* 9 (Spring 1983): 151–70, posits that contemporary misunderstandings between white women and black women are a partial consequence of white women's misappropriation and misinterpretation of the histories of black women in the United States.

13. Nancy Woods Walburn, "Elevating Housework to Professional Standing," *Woman's Press* 22 (December 1928): 856–57.

became a clearinghouse for information about wages, hours, organizing efforts, self-improvement clubs, publicity campaigns, and club activities in YWCA local chapters, in proto-unions and workers' clubs, and in women's clubs interested in housework. It operated with a commitment to reform but no clear identification with the interests of employer or worker.

Nevertheless, the major effort of the NCHE during its years of existence was to achieve formulation and widespread adoption of model contracts for the voluntary use of housewives and household workers. Initially, the major focus of this committee and of its YWCA Household Employment Committee allies seems to have been the deficiencies not of the household worker but of the housewife: "Until they themselves have mastered their jobs as home administrators, there can be no satisfactory solution of the problems of employer-employee relationships," the NCHE concluded at its second national conference in 1931.[14] Such mastery required courses in which homemakers would learn to determine the easiest and quickest way to perform a task. Failing such capacity, the NCHE recommended that the housewife hire a "trained household advisor" to assist in analyzing the needs of her home and making work plans and schedules.

Throughout the thirteen years of the NCHE's life, only Chicago was ever able to adopt and publicize a voluntary agreement. Objections to voluntary contracts kept them a constant source of debate and contention in other cities. What, exactly, were the labor standards being argued about?

The chronic arguments about model contracts were primarily about the length of the work week, whether it was possible to set hourly limits by the week, and the calculation of time off. The standard discussed throughout the 1930s was a 48-hour week for live-out workers and a 54-hour week for live-in workers (on the assumption that the live-in worker saved six hours a week in going to and from her job). If such hours seem onerous, one must realize that many women employed as domestic servants were regularly working 60-, 72-, even 84-hour weeks.

Within the 48- or 54-hour standard, a major issue was the distinction between free time and time "on call." The 1931 meeting of the NCHE voted to construe "time on call" as time when the worker was "not free to leave the house but may follow her own pursuits on the

14. "Summary of 2nd Conference, National Committee on Employer–Employee Relationships in the Home, April 13–14, 1931, New York City," typescript, YWCA Archives, reel 98.

premises. . . . Two hours on call should be considered equivalent to one hour of working time."[15] The on-call issue revealed a major difference in employers' and employees' perspectives. For the employee, "on-call" might mean afternoon phone or door answering during her only rest period between cleaning chores, cooking lunch, and preparing for the evening meal. For the live-in employee particularly, "on call" often meant watching out for the children, in essence an evening of babysitting, the most common chore imposed at the end of a regular day's schedule. Why, employees and their advocates argued, should being at home with children, but essentially unfree to leave the house or to entertain in the house, be counted at two hours of time for one hour of wages? For employers, on the other hand, the worker taking a rest from physical labor seemed to be unfairly compensated if she was paid the rate for doing work.

Time off for the worker was almost as intensely debated as how to construe hours on call. The 1931 NCHE meeting concluded that "one whole day, beginning not later than 10 A.M. and extending through the evening, or two half-days a week, beginning not later than 2 P.M. on week days and 3 P.M. on Sundays and extending through the evening, should be free." As with hours on call, employees often reported that emergencies cost them hours of the free time they were entitled to. Employers argued that the requirements of serving a family prevented guaranteed hours of free time.[16]

As local groups of YWCA employers and employees worked during the 1930s to formulate model codes, the complaint that a 54-hour week was impossible for a housewife to schedule led the Y staff and employers sympathetic to labor standards to draw up model schedules demonstrating the practicability of such codes. Model training programs were also designed, some in conjunction with state and federal relief projects, to train workers to schedule themselves and to demonstrate to their housewife employers better ways of organizing household tasks.[17] The Philadelphia Institute on Household Occupations, formed by a public-spirited group of Philadelphia YWCA women with the aid of the director of School Extension, who furnished teachers'

15. Dr. Benjamin Andrews, *Household Employment Bulletin No. 1,* July 20, 1933, RG 86, Box 927, National Archives; "The Servant Problem," *Fortune,* March 1938, reports the "on-call" debate.

16. RG 86, Boxes 924 and 925, National Archives.

17. Swain, "ER and Ellen Woodward"; Phyllis Palmer, "Housework and Domestic Labor: Racial and Technological Change," in *My Troubles Are Going to Have Trouble with Me: Everyday Trials and Triumphs of Women Workers,* ed. Karen Brodkin Sacks and Dorothy Remy (New Brunswick, N.J., 1984), 80–91.

salaries, ran a program for three years (1936–39) and issued a report
including representative work schedules.

The schedules developed by the Philadelphia project were not, the
final report insisted, simply theoretical. Rather, each one was the result
of a plan devised by a trained worker to fit the needs of the particular
household in which she was employed. What follows is one day of a 48-
hour live-in week designed for the care of a house of ten rooms and a
family of two adults and one child.

Monday*

Laundry			
Own lunch			
Daily cleaning downstairs	}	10:30–2:00	210′
Wash dishes			
Take clothes in			
Finish cleaning downstairs	}	2:00–4:30	150′
Clean bathroom			
Cook and serve dinner at 6	}	4:30–6:00	90′
Wash dishes and kitchen floor	}	6:00–7:00	60′
			510′

*Employer prepares breakfast and does upstairs work (8½ hours).

This worker had all day Wednesday off, but on Sunday she put in a full
nine hours, during which she cooked and served breakfast to give the
housewife a break and sorted the laundry for Monday's washing.

In order to work out this schedule, which came in at 48 hours per
week, the employee's mealtime was deducted. The employer, as the
report said, made "concessions," revealing what employers saw as their
appropriate tasks in the employer–employee division of labor. Since
the employer wanted the heavy parts of the housework handled by the
employee, she took it upon herself to make her own breakfasts and to
assume responsibility for the upstairs bedmaking and straightening up.
The schedule for the remainder of the week indicates that the employer does none of the heavy cleaning, cooking for weekday meals,
laundry, or dishwashing. Indeed, even child care is sometimes relegated to the household worker, who is requested to stay with the child
in the evening while the employer and "her husband go out." This
employer did consider the evening's home attendance as overtime and
paid the worker accordingly until 10:00 P.M., after which the servant
could go to bed—provided the child cooperated in not demanding
attention thereafter.

The plan for another household, this one with a young baby, raises a problem that seems common to these schedules: they make no allowance for emergencies, or even for the disruption of children wanting to play or needing help. What follows is the schedule as printed for 11:00 A.M. to 6:15 P.M. six days a week (including 15 minutes of the worker's time for lunch), with the understanding that the additional six hours to make a 48-hour week are "to be applied to evening employment when the employers want to go out."

Daily Duties	*Weekly Duties*
Marketing	*Monday*—Family washing
Washing breakfast dishes and sometimes dinner dishes from night before	*Tuesday*—Family ironing
	Wednesday—Thoroughly clean living room and 2 bedrooms
Preparation of lunch	*Thursday*—Thoroughly clean kitchen, den, and bathroom
Take baby for walk	
Daily straightening of house	*Friday*—Whatever mending necessary
Baby's laundry	
12:00–12:30 Baby's orange juice	*Saturday*—General cleaning and weekend preparations
2:00–2:30 Baby's milk	
4:00–4:30 Baby's orange juice	
Get dinner ready (do not serve)	

This schedule, like many others, was predicated on the idea that the baby would make few demands outside "the fixed points [that] are the baby's feeding time. All other duties revolve around and are adjusted to them." The employer, for her part, "assumes responsibility for the baby and the family before breakfast, before the worker comes in at 11:00, and after she leaves at 6:00 in the evening, so that she can secure the services of a competent worker who goes ahead on her own assuming full responsibility for the house and baby while she is there. The employer has . . . part-time employment outside her home during these hours."[18]

These two schedules are apt illustrations of the major expectations for domestic workers during the 1930s: to take over the heaviest physical labor of a household, or to take on enough of the responsibilities for a household so that the more highly educated employer might use her skills more fully in professional employment or voluntary activities. The need for a surrogate housewife was especially great in households

18. Both schedules appear in "Final Report of the Philadelphia Institute on Household Occupations, August 1939," Box 3, WTUL Papers.

with young children in an era that provided hardly any services or care for them outside the home.[19]

Model schedules such as those developed by the workers and teachers in the Philadelphia Institute describe a workday that requires steady and demanding labor, but they were apparently a definite improvement over the work loads actually demanded by many employers during the 1930s. Evidence collected by YWCA household workers' clubs and contained in pleas to the Department of Labor and to Mrs. Roosevelt and the president reveals the backbreaking drudgery, coupled with extensive responsibility, that characterized household labor in the 1930s. The presence of the Roosevelts in the White House and the publicity given New Deal labor standards led thousands of workers to write to government bureaus. These letters, collected in the National Archives, were intended—as the correspondent often stated—to tell officials in Washington about conditions and events they might be ignorant of: the realities of existence in other parts of the country.

The most poignant stories during the early 1930s came from southern black women, who were facing the harshest regional economic and political situation: they were the earliest group to find that the Depression gave employers the power to pay lower wages for longer hours of work. In many southern towns the wage reduction was exacerbated by the unwillingness of local officials to certify black families for relief, so that any job offer had to be accepted to bring money into the family. Unemployment rates in the South were much higher for black men than for white men. By the mid-1930s, unemployment among black adults in some areas was running between 30 and 40 percent, double the rate of white adult unemployment.[20] Without access to relief, the situation of black families was desperate. One consequence was lower wages and longer hours of domestic work.

Two problems plagued black female domestics in particular during the first years of the Depression: loss of jobs and lowered wages for the jobs still available. When white women workers were laid off from *their* jobs, "they dismiss[ed] their domestic help, either desiring or being forced to do the housework themselves."[21] As a result, black women

19. Kessler-Harris, *Out of Work*, chap. 9; Elyce Rotella, *From Home to Office: U.S. Women at Work, 1870–1930* (Ann Arbor, 1981), 17–26; Margaret O'Brien Steinfels, *Who's Minding the Children? The History and Politics of Day Care in America* (New York, 1973), chap. 2.

20. Harvard Sitkoff, *A New Deal for Blacks: The Emergence of Civil Rights as a National Issue: The Depression Decade* (New York, 1978), chaps. 2, 3.

21. Mary Anderson, "The Plight of Negro Domestic Labor," paper presented to the Conference on the Position of the Negro in Our National Economic Crisis, Howard University, May 1935, RG 86, Box 927, National Archives.

were ready to work for pittances; even so, their hold was precarious because of competition from white women laid off from their factory, clerical, or professional jobs. As Mary Anderson reported in her speech to the 1935 Howard University Conference on the National Economic Crisis, black women's unemployment rates in domestic service (the major occupation for black women) were twice those of white women in locales where both races were represented in domestic work. The consequence by 1935 was—as Anderson said, citing a Norfolk, Virginia, periodical—that "four dollars per week is the average wage for a woman with hours running from 7 A.M. until 9 P.M., in some cases, with the one-half day off on Thursday. In most cases, the domestic has to pay $1.25 a week for street car or bus transportation out of the meager $4 a week."[22] It is worth noting from this account that black women were working much longer hours than the 54- or 60-hour weeks recommended for live-ins; in addition, they were traveling to their homes for the night. Whose choice this was, the worker's or the employer's, is unclear. The important thing to note is that the low cash wage was not supplemented by the provision of room and board.

Surveys of conditions for both black and white workers in southern areas were made by racially mixed YWCA groups during the mid-1930s. In Louisville, Kentucky, the Interracial Household Employment Committee collected stories from its members. Two of these stories give some sense of how grueling domestic service was, for black or white women.

King, Mildred Lois (white)
Hours: 6:45 a.m.–8 p.m.—4 in family (1 difficult, ill child)
Work required: all cooking, cleaning, children's laundry, nursing every
  afternoon
Wages: $5.00 per week and room and board
Off time: ½ day Thursday and every other Sunday
Problems: Too much work expected by employer. Every meal must be
  served formally. No free time in day from child. Must rise sometimes
  with child at 5 a.m.—and stay up remainder of day.

Gertrude Hunter (colored)
Hours: 6:30 a.m.–9 p.m.—9 in family (1 is invalid)
Work required: housework and entire care of children, sewing and mending, laundry of bedding, bathroom supplies, and tea towels
Wages: 1924 (3 children in family)—$11.50 per week and room and
  board

22. Anderson, "Plight of Negro Domestic Labor."

1935 (6 children in family)—$7.50 per week and room and
board
Off time: 12 noon to midnight on Thursday and every other Sunday
afternoon
Problems: Has to fill in very often when the cook doesn't arrive. Children
are disrespectful. 2 to 3 times a year (for a week or ten days) both
adults go away and Gertrude has entire charge of house, no extra
help and unable to leave house.[23]

Additional evidence indicating that white women's working conditions were often determined by the standard set for less powerful black
women comes from a survey compiled by a mixed committee of seven
white and seven black girls selected by the 1934 Southern Industrial
Conference to design questionnaires. These questionnaires were sent
to 34 white associations, of which 22 replied, and to 34 black branches,
of which 4 replied. The results are skewed, because "many towns in the
south have practically no white household employees—and several
YWCAs in the South have no Household Employees in Industrial
Clubs." With these limitations, they found that whites were working
longer hours each week than were blacks—71.5 hours versus 66 hours.
The very slight difference in pay also pointed to minimal racial differences in wages and hours: $6.44 a week for whites versus $6.17 a
week for blacks. But 83 percent of the white women were "living on the
place," versus 45 percent of black women; the vast majority of white
women were given a room, while the majority of black women were
paying for housing.[24]
   A number of the letters to Washington indicate that exploitation
was not confined to the South. From Waterville, Maine, a report came
to the Department of Labor that "housewives here and in neighboring
towns are importing girls from French-Canada for domestics and are
holding them in slavery—worse, in fact, for they are not supported
properly. . . . One girl is doing all the work in a seven-room house, does
the washing and ironing and the mending as well. She receives $3 a
week out of which she pays for a room."[25] A domestic from Cleveland
wrote to President Roosevelt: "When they hire you they tell you there is
no washing or cooking, just ironing and general housework. After they
have you a week or so they give you everything including washing and
ironing. Then the man want you to wash the carpets, and also there

23. YWCA Archives, reel 97.
   24. YWCA Archives, reel 98.
   25. Jo Pattengall to Boris Stern, *Labor Information Bulletin,* Bureau of Labor Statistics,
February 1940, RG 86, National Archives.

[*sic*] car everyonce a week. They expect the maid to work from 8:00 o'clock in the morning till 12:00 o'clock in the evening. Still they think they pay her too much."[26]

Household workers were chagrined when federal legislation intended to assist hard-up workers did not include them. In addition to being excluded from the 1938 wage-and-hours provisions of the Fair Labor Standards Act, domestic work was not covered by the unemployment provision of the Social Security Act—nor was agricultural labor. A letter from California expressed frustration at "[Senator Robert Wagner's] reason for excluding this class of workers. . . . He says the means of determining unemployment in these categories [farm workers and domestic workers] is difficult. As a houseworker for 9 years, I had no difficulty in knowing when I was out of work. . . . There should be some reward for the folks who grow our food and the ones who have to dish it out,—and wash the dirty dishes."[27]

The enlightened leaders in the NCHE supported both social security coverage for domestic workers and their inclusion in state maximum hour and minimum wage laws. The middle-class constituents of the NCHE and the YWCA were, however, unable to draw up satisfactory model contracts or to agree to lobby state legislatures on behalf of domestic workers. Why were white middle-class women employers so unsympathetic to regulatory attempts, even in the form of model contracts, that such contracts were adopted only at the end of the decade, and then only in Chicago?

My conclusion is that housewives felt so put upon by endless unpaid work that they wanted desperately to extricate themselves. Thus it was in their interest to pay low wages for such labor; they had an incentive to perpetuate the low social esteem and presumed low economic value of housework. On the other hand, the social position that a wife derived from her husband rested partially on the performance of wifely duties, and so she pushed for a high quality of housework, child care, and family relations. Caught in the conflict between society's denigration of housework and evaluation of women on its competent conduct, housewives did not challenge the middle-class norm of housework; rather, they projected their dilemma onto the women less powerful than themselves whom they employed. The housewife employer kept the benefits of the housewife position and pushed as many of the

26. Emelia Gajinak to President Roosevelt, 21 April 1940, RG 86, Box 925, National Archives.

27. Pauline Risto, Household Training Department, San Bernardino Trade Schools, to Mary Anderson, 5 September 1940, RG 86, Box 926, National Archives.

penalties as she could onto another woman: the working-class white or black domestic.

Numerous commentators recognized that the housewife's treatment of her domestic was a reflection of her own treatment. As one said, "Many employing housewives never can reconcile themselves to *paying* another woman for doing that which she did for so long and never got a salary for."[28] The *New York News* printed a column, "The Cruel Housewife," explaining that the "majority of home women, even in this century, get nothing for their labor except a few clothes and the food they eat. . . . You can't expect brilliant economic reasoning from a class that has never shared in economic profits. Most of these women were reared in the tradition that the wife, the mother, the home maker, the person who cleans and dusts and washes and irons and scrubs and sews, and is supposed to raise an excellent family between while, shall receive for all this no regular stipulated wage. . . . And as they have received, so they give."[29]

A major factor in middle-class women's treatment of their servants, then, seems to have been their own sense of the unfairness of the demands placed on them—demands that, if they had enough money, they could simply slide over to another woman. Here lies the explanation, I think, for much of the disagreement over hours, which was the point at which employers balked when faced with the notion of model contracts. As one Brentwood, Los Angeles, housewife put it, "Wages and environment and choice of employer, they can all be controlled, but hours *no!!*" She explained:

> A good household worker enjoys her work *like a good housewife* and doesn't think in terms of hours, but in terms of how tired she is at the end of the day. Perhaps there have been twelve hours, off and on, of light, ordinary tasks that anyone does around the home. She doesn't need that at all, whereas 8 hours of heavy cleaning, polishing, vacuuming, and window-washing would leave her exhausted. When there are children, there is a twenty-four hour schedule for the lady of the house, who doesn't complain about it but who does ask the helper to keep ears open for children on occasional evenings when the employers are asked out. Are these hours to be regulated? They are a matter for cooperation not regulation.[30]

28. Mrs. Chauncy Leggett Turner to Mrs. Roosevelt, 3 October 1941, RG 86, Box 924, National Archives.

29. Mrs. Walter Ferguson, "The Cruel Housewife," in "One Woman's Opinion," *New York News,* 7 April 1933, RG 86, Box 326, National Archives.

30. Louise R. Levinson to Louise Stitt, Women's Bureau, 13 January 1941, RG 86, Box 924, National Archives (my emphasis).

The woman who could write this does not have her own identity separated from that of the woman she has hired to work for her. This equation between what is expected of "the lady of the house" and what she can expect of the person she hires has an endearing anti-industrial quality, but it is unrealistic to expect another woman to do the work of the "lady of the house" without receiving any of the employer's perquisites.

Middle-class employers wanted servants who would serve in the uncalculating and wholehearted manner expected of the middle-class wife and mother herself. Middle-class women defended the virtue of a "personal relationship" between maid and mistress instead of the business relationship implied in contracts. In a dialogue, "Do Servants Need a Code?" presented in a 1934 issue of *The Forum,* Dr. Amey Watson of the NCHE started the debate by saying that the committee was advocating for household employees "a contractual relationship and not a personal one. . . . Our relations to our husbands and children of course are personal, and we still think of our servant as a personal relationship."

Dr. Mary Fisher, a psychologist at Sarah Lawrence College, replied: "Yes, indeed, only we must make sure that it is a civilized personal relationship within a contractual relationship. In the home it can't be on a purely labor basis. The home, *if it means anything,* means that there can be personal, friendly relationships. Any household employee who is outside such a relationship is immediately going to be at a great disadvantage." Eva von Baur Hansl, also of the NCHE, supported the point with a letter from a "german girl" who had written saying, "I want someone to notice, to CARE whether I come or go! . . . If a home is to be as impersonal as a factory or an office, I won't work in one any more. Then I will study stenography, become an office boss, and get away from all the hateful pots and pans!!"[31] (One might add that many wives would gladly do the same.)

Employers consistently refused to adopt business standards of set hours and organization for the work of the household, apparently because of the endlessly expansive demands made on women, primarily by their husbands and children. Faced with demands for three

31. *The Forum,* July 1934. This entire issue is devoted to the debate, which allegedly took place at a dinner meeting attended by the following controversialists: Mary Anderson, Women's Bureau; Dr. Benjamin Andrews, Columbia University Teachers College; Mrs. Wayne Babcock, Philadelphia Council of Household Occupations; Mrs. Richard Boardman, Scientific Housekeeping, Inc., New York City; Dr. Mary Fisher, Sarah Lawrence College; Emma H. Gunther, Mrs. Eva von Baur Hansl, and Dr. Amey Watson, National Committee for Household Employment; Frieda Miller and Nelle Swartz, New York State Department of Labor; Mrs. Douglas Moffat, New York League of Women Voters; Mrs. Paul Reynolds, Westchester County Council on Household Employment.

hot meals daily, laundered and ironed clothes, clean bathrooms, and neatly made beds, her attendance at social functions and the provision of entertainment for friends and business associates in the evenings, a middle-class woman who could hire another woman to work in the house wanted from her the same undaunted and complete responsiveness to these needs as was expected of the wife and mother herself. In fact, as became most obviously true for those women who were willing to claim the right to use their education and skills outside the home, the middle-class woman who could afford to hire help was looking for a clone: a woman who could do things as she herself did them, for the hours that were expected of her, and with the credit for finding such a paragon going to her, "the housewife."

Even when employers recognized the justice of workers' requests for more regular schedules and better planning, they could not take the responsibility for controlling their families' desires and needs; even when women could be persuaded of the reasonableness of a particular set of work standards, the "emergency" provision was always added. The notion of contract could be accepted only with a clause that required the employee to change her schedule in case of some unforeseen need. (No wonder corporations have been surprised during the 1970s and 1980s by managerial workers' requests for policies that take account of family needs; such an expectation was unprecedented in American business, where the manager's wife and her domestic were the ones who rearranged a schedule to take care of household contingencies.)

In 1938, after seven years of efforts to get voluntary agreement on a model contract, the YWCA National Committee on Household Employment could still argue about whether or not to include household workers in legislation proposed in the New York State legislature for a 60-hour maximum week. The arguments for household workers' inclusion were that the law would (1) meet the need for regulation of hours, (2) bring workers under workmen's compensation, (3) give employment agencies backing to raise standards, and (4) benefit general housekeepers by giving employers some sense of the number of hours worked each day. These seemingly compelling arguments were met by the counterarguments of the employer members of the committee: (1) housework cannot be regulated like factory work, because emergencies such as sickness arise in a household; (2) the bill might be called unconstitutional on the grounds that it invaded the sacred rights of the home; (3) enforcement would be difficult; (4) members with small children might find it difficult to limit their servants' time to 60 hours.[32]

32. "Minutes of Meeting, January 7, 1938," typescript, YWCA Archives, Reel 97.

Faced with the conflict between the interests of its employer constituents and its reform endeavors for working-class members, a subcommittee made two recommendations. First, the legislation should make clear that time for meals was not considered working time. Second, the YWCA should work with the New York Women's Trade Union League, the bill's sponsor, to reword the bill. For the moment, the convenience of the Y's middle-class employing members won out over the committee's obligation to "working girls." The decision illustrated the YWCA's chronic division of interests and its ultimate siding with the more powerful group.[33]

The nationwide, multicity, years-long commitment by the NCHE and the YWCA affiliates resulted in no tangible gains. In 1941, wages and conditions remained as they were in 1928. Federal labor legislation specifically excluded domestic workers, and hour-and-wage laws passed by various state legislatures during the reform euphoria of the Depression decade rarely covered domestic workers. Proto-unions, formed often from YWCA industrial girls' clubs, had generally faded from existence.

Less easy to ascertain is the impact of the necessarily interracial effort on the YWCA's continuing commitment to racial justice in the United States. The focus on domestics in the association's study sessions enabled middle-class white women to confront racial stereotypes and petty acts of unintentional bigotry, and clubs for domestic workers gave an economic rationale to interracial work in girls' industrial clubs. Perhaps the household employment work of the 1930s laid the groundwork for the YWCA's more aggressive integrated club policy at the end of World War II.

The efforts of the YWCA and NCHE did result in the collection of data about the attitudes of housewives and domestic workers toward housework and about the way the work was performed. In the face of persistent ideals of domestic privacy and of housewife autonomy, the Y mobilized thousands of women to write up accounts of work in their homes and to interview their neighbors and colleagues. What those household stories revealed was the demanding and expansive nature of housework. What the stories failed to change was the middle-class feeling that the only solution was to pass on as much of the work as possible to another woman.

33. Faye Dudden, "Why Not Domestic Service? The Twentieth Century," paper presented to the Sixth Berkshire Conference on the History of Women, June 1984, makes the helpful point that much of the YWCA material about household employment makes confusing reading because it simultaneously represents the viewpoints of employer-housewives and of employee-domestics.

12

"This Work Had a End": African-American Domestic Workers in Washington, D.C., 1910–1940

Elizabeth Clark-Lewis

> The living-in jobs just
> kept you running; never stopped.
> Day or night you'd be getting
> something for somebody. You'd
> serve them. It was never a
> minute of peace. . . .
>
> But when I went out
> days on my jobs, I'd get my
> work done and be gone. I guess
> that's it. This work had a
> end.[1]

When African-American women migrated from the rural South to the urban centers of the North to work as live-in servants, few imagined they were beginning an escape from restraints imposed by race, gender, and class. But escape they did, and this essay examines the transition of twenty-three such women as they moved beyond live-in

Research for this essay was supported in part by a Smithsonian Institution postdoctoral fellowship.
   1. Dolethia Otis, interviewed by author, September 1982. All names used are pseudonyms.

household servitude to self-employment during the first three decades of this century. It also demonstrates that as their roles changed, they experienced a new freedom to exercise control over their own lives, and their perceptions about themselves and their relationships to others underwent a significant change. It is important to recognize, however, that these changes occurred within a restrictive cultural environment.[2]

An urban scholar noted in the last decade of the nineteenth century that "household service now drew the despised race to the despised calling."[3] A variety of historical circumstances were responsible for the household employment revolution this scholar perceived during the years between 1900 and 1930, a revolution that has received very little scholarly attention because service work is outside the market and has historically been poor women's work. Few social scientists have asked why, in the twentieth century, this employment has gone from a white "golden age" to an African-American "problem era," from the age of the white "servant girl" to the African-American "cleaning woman."[4]

National census employment data for the years between 1900 and 1930 reveal the largest employment increases for white women in clerical, sales, and factory occupations. Simultaneously, the number of native-born white women in household service work *fell* by 40 percent. Poor migrants, from abroad or from rural areas, had historically provided servants for urban households unable to acquire native-born white women servants. When foreign immigration slowed to a trickle after World War I, an important source of new white servants was eliminated. Within the first two decades of the twentieth century, household work lost its importance as an occupation for white women. By contrast, the number of African-American female household workers *increased* by 43 percent. Nationally, during the 1900–1930 period,

2. For a full discussion of this employment transformation, see Elizabeth Clark-Lewis, *This Work Had a End: The Transition From Live-in to Day Work* (Memphis, 1985). For the purposes of this paper, females employed on a daily basis primarily to clean private family homes will be referred to as household workers. However, no adjustments will be made to any terms within direct quotes.

3. Isabel Eaton, "Special Report on Negro Domestic Service," in W. E. B. Du Bois, *The Philadelphia Negro* (New York, 1899), 136–37.

4. Bettina Aptheker, *Woman's Legacy: Essays on Race, Sex, and Class in American History* (Amherst, Mass., 1982), 112; Ann Oakley, *The Sociology of Work* (London, 1974), 96; Evelyn Nakano Glenn, "The Dialectics of Wage Work: Japanese-American Women and Domestic Service, 1905–1940," *Feminist Studies* 6 (1980): 432–71; Susan Strasser, "Mistress and Maid, Employer and Employee: Domestic Service Reform in the United States, 1897–1920," *Marxist Perspectives* 1 (Winter 1978): 52–67; Daniel Sutherland, *Americans and Their Servants* (Baton Rouge, 1981), 6.

the southern exploitive system triumphed: African-American women were forced into a "servant caste."[5]

Surveys of specific northern urban centers found that the sharp rise in the number of African-American household workers had three sources: the new, large-scale migration of African-Americans to urban centers outside the South; the fact that African-American women were twice as likely as white women to be employed; and discriminatory policies that barred African-American women from 86 percent of employment categories. By 1926 the predominance of African-American migrant women in household service in Washington, D.C., was well established. During the early twentieth century, the District of Columbia experienced the largest percentage increase in African-American population in the eastern United States. More important, in 1900, 54 percent of the employed African-American women in the District were working in domestic service; by 1930, that figure had risen to 78 percent.[6]

Expanded employment opportunities lured a stream of migrants to the urban North, where they moved into segregated communities that coalesced around churches, schools, philanthropic institutions, and businesses. But because of antimigrant biases in the established African-American communities, only rarely could the newcomers find work in businesses owned by African-Americans or in the segregated schools of the communities where they settled. Disproportionately young, female, and poorly educated, they found themselves in urban centers where the pattern of racial segregation combined with class and gender restrictions to limit the jobs available to them. In overwhelming numbers the female migrants became household workers.[7]

Early social scientists enumerated the statistical (but none of the

5. U.S. Department of Commerce, Bureau of the Census, *Negro Workers in the United States, 1920–1932* (Washington, D.C., 1935), 294, 297, 300, 303–4, and *Fifteenth Census of the United States, 1930—Population Bulletin and Summary* (Washington, D.C., 1934), 6; Joseph Hill, *Women in Gainful Occupations, 1870–1920* (Washington. D.C., 1929), 38, 59, 90, 96, 105, 117; Du Bois, *Philadelphia Negro*, 434.

6. Records of the Government of the District of Columbia—General Files and Records of the National Council of Negro Women, RG 351, National Archives; Records of the Bureau of Human Nutrition and Home Economics—Servant Living Needs (Colored), RG 176, National Archives; National Committee on Household Employment, *There Must Be a Code of Standards* (Washington, D.C., 1974); Mary Waggoman, "Wartime Job Opportunities for Women Household Workers in Washington, D.C.," *Monthly Labor Review* 60 (March 1945): 575–84; Grace Fox, "Women Domestic Workers in Washington, D.C.," *Monthly Labor Review* 54 (February 1942): 338–45.

7. George E. Haynes, *Negro Migration* (Washington, D.C., 1919); Ray S. Baker, "The Negro Goes North," *World's Work* 34 (July 1917): 315; Florette Henri, *Black Migration* (Garden City, N.Y., 1976), 53–60.

qualitative) changes that household work underwent as a result of the large influx of African-American women seeking this employment in areas outside the rural South. In recent studies, social historians have analyzed the forces that have shaped household work, described the reasons why different groups entered household work, and observed the change in the character of this employment with the advent of each group. The hypotheses developed by these historians are important, but they need to be tested at the local level; moreover, they do not emphasize the impact of this employment on the lives of the workers themselves.[8]

Washington, D.C., is an excellent locus for a case study of African-American household workers. Large numbers of migrants were attracted to Washington, a burgeoning commercial center with a demand for unskilled labor and a benign racial image reinforced by articles in nationally distributed African-American newspapers. In 1883 one paper asserted that "Washington has become a town with very free negro and white mixing at social activities. The two also live in racially integrated areas."[9]

In order to understand Dolethia Otis's statement, "This work had a end," it is necessary to examine the context from which these women emerged and the manner in which the shift from "servant" to "employee" was made. Using an interdisciplinary cultural approach, I have attempted to explore important dimensions of their occupations, learning directly from them their attitudes concerning the sociology of work. The conditions under which they were reared and the system of meanings, values, and aspirations they developed before their employment as household workers provides a background against which their adult lives can be more fully appreciated and understood.

In the South, during the late nineteenth century, girls were quickly incorporated into the work routine of their households. "By four you'd do field work; by six you'd be doing small pieces in a tub every washday and bring all the clear water for rinsing the clothes. By eight, you'd be able to mind children, do cooking, and wash. By ten you'd be trained up. Really, every girl I know was working-out by ten. No play, 'cause

8. David Katzman, *Seven Days a Week* (New York, 1978), ix; Alba Edwards, "Comparative Occupational Statistics for the United States, 1870–1940," in the Sixteenth U.S. Census, 1940, *Population* (Washington, D.C., 1943); Allyson Grossman, "Women in Domestic Work," *Monthly Labor Review* 103 (August 1980): 18; "Women and Child Labor," *Monthly Labor Review* 15 (July 1922): 116–17.

9. Constance Green, *Washington: A History of the Capitol* (Princeton, N.J., 1962), and *The Secret City* (Princeton, N.J., 1967); Waggoman, "Wartime Job Opportunities"; "Notes from Washington," *National Negro Register* 3 (June 1883).

they told you: life was to be hardest on you—always."[10] This brief statement by an eighty-six-year-old migrant worker from Virginia reveals much about the early lives of African-American women born in the rural southeastern United States during the late nineteenth and early twentieth centuries.

Fourteen of the twenty-three women I interviewed grew up on farms owned by their parents; nine lived on share-tenant farms. Nearly all were reared in extended family households consisting of mothers, fathers, grandparents, siblings, and other relatives. They were all born between 1884 and 1911. Each household included at least one former slave; thus every woman in the study vividly recalled hearing firsthand descriptions of the degrading conditions of slavery. Further, the women were able to cite beliefs held by those former slaves regarding patterns and practices that enabled slave families to survive under the harshest of circumstances.

Family support, according to all of the women interviewed, was a focal point of rural churches. In addition to religious instruction, churches provided the only mutual aid, educational, and recreational activities available to African-American families in the rural South. After the family, the church was the most important means of individual and community expression.[11]

The education of all of the women in the study had been severely limited by the need to help support the family, which they recognized as their primary responsibility by the age of seven. They worked first on the family farm, caring for the youngest children and serving as apprentices to older girls and women. Each of the twenty-three women recalled her mother's leaving home for residential (live-in) employment in white households in the surrounding area and recognized that independently employed children were an important part of the family's survival strategy.[12] "Like everybody, by eight years old I went in to work with Mama," said Bernice Reeder in discussing the short period of outside tutelage which preceded a girl's first employment as live-in servant to a white family. She was alone on her first job, "at just nine

10. Naomi Yates, interviewed by author, 15 September 1982; Stewart Tolnan, "Black Family Formation and Tenancy in the Farm South, 1900," *American Journal of Sociology* 90 (September 1984): 305–25; Lawrence Levine, *Black Culture and Black Consciousness* (New York, 1977).

11. Melvin Williams, *Community in a Black Pentecostal Church: An Anthropological Study* (Pittsburgh, Pa., 1974), 8–10; Carter G. Woodson, *The Rural Negro* (Washington, D.C., 1930), 150–78.

12. Christine E. Bose, "Household Resources and U.S. Women's Work: Factors Affecting Gainful Employment at the Turn of the Century," *American Sociological Review* 49 (August 1984): 474–77.

years old! I was so scared," she continued. "Nobody cared you were a child. . . . You was a worker to them."[13] The economic constraints faced by African-Americans in the rural South in the late nineteenth and early twentieth centuries made such early labor an unavoidable and accepted part of family and community life.

It was essential that girls learn young to meet the three-part training criteria developed by African-Americans in rural areas of the South. Each girl child was first required to become proficient in child care and housekeeping duties for her extended family. She then learned to perform household duties, under the supervision of adult kin, in the homes of whites in the surrounding communities. Finally, following this period of tutelage, she undertook housekeeping tasks alone in the homes of local southern white employers. By the age of ten, the women in this study told me, they also had to show clearly that they had the maturity to take another step: to travel to Washington, D.C., where sisters and aunts who worked as live-in servants (and sent money home) needed support in the form of child care and housekeeping by younger family members.

These girls made the journey north by train. None had ever been out of her home state before. Twenty were taken to the train station by a male relative; all left their places of birth in the early morning, traveled alone, and were met by other relatives upon arrival in Washington.

When sharing reminiscences of their northbound journey, the women always described the feeling of freedom they experienced. "When you got on the train," Velma Davis exclaimed, "you felt different! Seem like you'd been bound up, but now this train untied you. It's funny . . . like being untied and tickled at the same time!"[14] The girls understood that their first obligation was to carry on the rural-based family survival strategy in the homes of kin who served Washington's white households as live-in workers. The only significant change in their lives, initially, was the move to the North.

Many studies that investigate the importance of the northern migration emphasize only the contribution southern women made to the child care and the financial stability of the northern household. Other studies suggest that the real benefits of migration went to the rural southern families in the form of money sent home monthly by kin residing in the North. These arguments tend to polarize the rural–urban relationship; neither acknowledges the dual/multiple roles play-

13. Bernice Reeder, interviewed by author, 18 March 1981.
14. Velma Davis, interviewed by author, 20 July 1982.

ed by both northern and southern relatives. When rural families (lacking financial resources) permitted their young women to migrate out of the South to assist relatives residing in the North, migration was seen as a continuation of the survival/support culture developed in the South. All segments of the African-American family operated under the assumption that older members of the kin group assisted younger ones for the very basic purpose of ensuring the survival of the family's young people and of the family as a whole in both North and South.

Urban kin gave support to the migrant in several ways, if we may judge from information provided by the women interviewed. They paid all of her travel expenses to Washington, helped her adjust to urban life, and found employment for her within twelve months. In all the cases studied, the women were hired where their kin had contacts; in twenty-one of twenty-three cases, the coresident kin acquired employment for the migrants in households where they themselves were currently living. The girls migrated originally to provide support only to their urban kin; once they themselves became employed, however (after an average of one year), they were expected to assume responsibility for meeting the needs of both the urban and rural segments of the family.

As newly hired live-in servants, these female migrants learned that their primary role was to serve the mistress of the house, not just to complete the assigned tasks—a departure from the way they had worked in southern households. In the South, these African-American household workers had received daily task assignments from the white male head of the household. Migrants stressed that in Washington they slowly learned a new employment reality. Through trial and error, and with the advice of the more experienced earlier migrants, they learned to act in response to the needs of the wife rather than the husband.[15]

Each of the twenty-three women was dismayed to learn that uniforms were mandatory in the District of Columbia. The wearing of uniforms was perceived by all as the major difference between their servant *work* in the South and their servant *role* in Washington.[16] For these women, the uniform objectified the live-in servant and determined her fate in the workplace. The home was the white mistress's stage and major realm of influence, and the uniform legitimized her power. Ophilia Simpson recalled that "them uniforms just seemed to make them know you was theirs. Some say you wore them to show

15. Katzman, *Seven Days a Week*, 155, 214–15.
16. Peter Berger and Thomas Luckmann, *The Social Construction of Reality* (Garden City, N.Y., 1966), 89–92.

different jobs you was doing. Time in grey. Other times serving in black. But mostly them things just showed you was always at their beck and call. Really that's all them things means!"[17]

Tasks assigned and directions given to the household staff were perceived by the migrant woman as the white woman's means of expressing her power, which she exercised principally on migrants. When Velma Davis lived in with a Chevy Chase family, the treatment she experienced differed from that accorded servants not born in the South. "She knew you was from down home, working to help them survive, so, that woman just plain ran us to death! People from up here could leave, so she'd be more careful with all them 'cause they'd quit on her. But for me it was a job that kept me up here . . . it wasn't hard like the field jobs . . . and I could keep money going home. It was a for sure help—a blessing."[18]

Despite the fact that each woman (and her family in the rural South) desperately needed the income her labor generated, within seven years these women were actively trying to leave the "servant life." There were several aspects of live-in employment that they all disliked. The uniform formalized the serving of the family for long hours, which they could not control. The wife as the authority figure had little respect for their needs. Worse still, they were forced to live in small quarters completely isolated from the African-American community.[19]

But it was the question of church participation that first stimulated more than half of those interviewed to seek a change. Not being able to attend regular services on Sundays and generally feeling left out of the continuing life of their churches became for these women a potent symbol of the restrictions of live-in labor. "Even working-out down home, you'd go to church," Costella Harris explained, bedridden at eighty-six after a lifetime of household employment in Georgetown. "Everybody did," she continued slowly. "Now, most came just to hear the Word. But some came to keep from being in a kitchen somewhere. . . . Church gave you six, not seven days of work. But up here you never saw inside any church on Sunday, living-in."[20]

Painful as all these restrictions were, however, they were probably not sufficient by themselves to lead the women to reject live-in servant work. The *ability* to make the change emanated from the phenomenon known as "penny savers clubs." Twenty-one of the twenty-three wom-

17. Ophilia Simpson, interviewed by author, 12 July 1982.
18. Velma Davis interview.
19. Aptheker, *Woman's Legacy*, 122; E. R. Haynes, "Negroes in Domestic Service in the United States," *Journal of Negro History*, October 1923, 384–442.
20. Costella Harris, interviewed by author, 15 November 1982.

en actively associated themselves with such mutual benefit associations, which sponsored social gatherings and provided sickness and death benefits to members. The organizations—begun by poor migrant working women who barely sustained themselves economically—were citywide, but active membership in each one was restricted to persons from specific states (or regions of a state) in the South. Although rarely mentioned in the literature. the penny savers clubs served as a vital economic base for the female migrant.[21] After an average of six years of saving, the women were able to develop the important economic leverage they needed to leave servant life.

The role of the church and of the penny savers clubs in first awakening the desire for change and then facilitating the process of that change cannot be overestimated. The clubs permitted the women, during the transition from live-in service to household day work, to maintain financial security for themselves and their kin in the rural South. No woman left live-in work until she had saved enough money to maintain herself and send money monthly to rural kin. The concern all these women had about the continuity of support to their southern families equaled or exceeded the concern they had for their own circumstances. They sought to find a less circumscribed economic and employment environment without abandoning one of the original motivations for leaving their rural families—relief of the family's economic distress.

The women soon identified laundresses as critical figures in their search for autonomy. Laundresses served as role models: unlike the other staff members, they did not belittle the migrant woman's desire to gain household work on a nonresidential basis, and they alone knew the categories and rules related to operating within several households simultaneously. The laundress also brought information about households that were seeking the services of women on a live-out basis for one or two days a week.[22] All but two women in the study acted upon the advice of a laundress when they located and acquired their first jobs as household day workers, and even those two had found the laundress to be the *only* staff member who supported their ambition to escape live-in work.

The women saw six major benefits to the shift from live-in servant to household day worker. First, as indicated by the language they used

21. One Mississippi penny savers club is documented in Records of the Government of the District of Columbia—Blue Plains Industrial School (Colored), 1927, RG 351, National Archives.

22. "A Washerwoman," *Independent* 57 (November 1904): 1073–76; Katzman, *Seven Days a Week,* 84–86.

to describe their experiences, their work seemed more their own. They spoke of their earlier jobs in depersonalized language because they sought detachment from their employers and a buffer against the employers' insensitivity to them as workers and African-Americans. References to their lives as live-in servants were characterized by the frequent use of "you." Here, for example, are some of Virginia Lacey's comments: "You was brought up here . . . you better never blink," and "You was worked to death."[23] Velma Davis recalled, "When I say 'my job,' I mean a job I got and I'd keep if they acted decent. 'They job' is for them; a job that you did and did, more and more—from one thing to another, early to late, and you worked! It's hard to tell what I mean."[24]

Second, the previously isolated African-American women began to make contact with one another amid their newly flexible working conditions, encountering many others like themselves. The structure that had created social marginality among African-Americans in Washington was slowly being dismantled; the women's isolated and restrictive living circumstances were relegated to an oppressive past. Bernice Reeder said that during twelve years as a live-in servant she had always believed that eventually she would have an opportunity for a better life. "Every working day," she said, "I knew in myself me living in it wouldn't be for long. And it wasn't just me. *All* us came here to do better!"[25]

Third, as the women changed jobs, they moved to rooms in boardinghouses and began to adopt a sharply different lifestyle. The other girls in the house where Velma Davis became a boarder "was all doing day-work, too," and "soon I was doing just about everything with them. I just liked being with these girls [who] was single, nice."[26] After the move from live-in servant work, Velma Davis said that she did not see her family for long periods of time. She said that it was when she moved to the boardinghouse that she began to feel she had finally left home. In 1919, Beulah Nelson took a room in a house where there were other boarders like herself. She said, "I lived there for three years, and I didn't see my brother much at all." She described the parties she and the other female boarders were allowed to host, and told me, "Them was my best days, and that's how I met my husband!"[27]

Having left the kin-directed live-in world, coboarders and other

23. Virginia Lacey, interviewed by author, 27 July 1982.
24. Velma Davis interview.
25. Bernice Reeder interview.
26. Velma Davis interview.
27. Beulah Nelson, interviewed by author, 14 August 1982.

commuting household workers became guides, role models, and mediators for other women who followed them into their changed environment. It was with this new group that they forged and maintained ties of emotional dependency. Amy Kelly said she received much valuable advice and support from other roomers. "And if I ever got done wrong or anything—they'd tell me what to say to the woman . . . them girls was good to me." It was only after being around other young women working "days" that she was sure her "live-in days was done."[28]

Fourth, their places of work changed. Employers usually hired someone other than their former live-in servants to work as daily household employees. The women acknowledged this policy; thus, in communicating their new plans to their employers, they understood that future employment in that household would not be considered. "People who had a full staff only wanted full-time live-in workers," contributed eighty-one-year-old Helen Venable, whose roots were in Alabama. "When you said you wanted to work days, you left there. She told you, you'd not be able to come back. It was okay, 'cause you'd got all set."[29]

Fifth, each woman indicated that turning to day work produced a subtle change in her relationship to the white women for whom she worked. Virginia Lacey described the new experience with an employer this way: "She'd meet you at the door, tell you how she wanted her house done, and she'd be gone. You did the work without her in the way, slowing you up. On a day job we all knew how to get everything done—but, in your own way. Having anybody around will make you work slower."[30] The household day worker was able to dictate her own pace, set her own priorities for tasks, and organize the process by which she completed designated chores.

The women all agreed that working efficiently was impossible when they were frequently interrupted and spoken to by an employer. They felt that they knew how to perform their tasks well and that they did not need to be monitored. "When I got work by the days, I'd work my way," explained Velma Davis. "Nobody'd be looking over your shoulder, saying what you was to do. What was the need leaving Sister and everybody if I was only going to work back with somebody else watching me? People took to day work to finally get to work by theyself."[31] She said she wanted nothing more to do with live-in work once she left Bradley Boulevard, where she had been a servant.

28. Amy Kelly, interviewed by author, 22 June 1982.
29. Helen Venable, interviewed by author, 21 July 1982 and 9 September 1982.
30. Virginia Lacey interview.
31. Velma Davis interview.

Finally, all of the women stressed that as they moved out of live-in work, they shed their uniforms and other symbols of their identities as live-in servants. Each had felt locked into a narrow and constricted role by the need to wear uniforms of "black for this" and "gray for that." Discarding that badge of their station in life clearly disaffiliated them from their previous work. Octavia Crockett, though very ill and weak, was eager to tell me that "when I got my first day job, I told them right off that I wasn't wearing a uniform. Them things are what really makes you a live-in . . . I had my own work dresses and all. They is just as nice."[32]

Virginia Lacey agreed: "I'd go to whatever house I'd have to be to work at. I change to my work clothes and then clean the house. . . . I never liked to be in the uniform. I guess serving in a uniform made you be back on staff. And you wasn't, so you'd just not want to wear that uniform." She paused for a moment, reflecting. "Wearing your own clothes—that's like you being your own boss! You was on your own job for a day and pay, then go home."[33]

Some scholars and artists who are sensitive to the problems of domestic service have tended to view negatively the bags in which day workers carried their clothes.[34] But these women took pride in the fact that they "carried work clothes" to their jobs; they felt that the bags were symbols of personal freedom and in that sense were positive. In fact, Marie Davis reported that workers often called them "freedom bags"; she observed, "When I got to carry clothes, I was finally working in what I wanted to. No black or gray uniforms or castoffs from the whites down home. I was proud to put my stuff in a bag at home. I guess I wanted to finally show I didn't wear a uniform. I wasn't a servant."[35]

As servants in uniform, the women felt, they took on the identity of the job—and the uniform seemed to assume a life of its own, separate from the person wearing it, beyond her control. As day workers, wearing their own clothes symbolized their new view of life as a series of personal choices rather than predetermined imperatives. "Living-in, you had no choices about nothing. But working out you'd be able to pick homes, days, and kinds of work you didn't do. You'd have some say in it," Bernice Reeder pointed out. "That's better."[36]

32. Octavia Crockett, interviewed by author, 3 May 1984.
33. Virginia Lacey interview.
34. Turner Brown, *Black Is . . .* (New York, 1969), 68–69; Louise Mitchell, "Slave Markets Typify Exploitation of Domestics," *Daily Worker*, 5 May 1940; Carter G. Woodson and Lorenzo Greene, *The Negro Wage Earner* (New York, 1969), 230–31.
35. Marie Davies, interviewed by author, 3 August 1982.
36. Bernice Reeder interview. Cf. the findings of Katzman, *Seven Days a Week*, 221.

A new identity was gained. Gone was the identity to which they were born or which had been ascribed to them; this new one they had *achieved* on their own, and their newly acquired friends and associates validated this achieved status.[37] As Bernice Reeder explained, "Once you got some work by the day and got around people who did it, you'd see how you could get ahead, get better things. You'd see how to get more and more days, some party work, extra sewing, stuff like that."[38] Velma Davis agreed: "When I started working days, other people [other household day workers] would show you how to get a few extra dollars. In this town you could make more money, and they'd sure show you how."[39]

The women's transformed identities and modified employment modes led to several other changes in the African-American community. For one, the women's interest in the penny savers clubs waned. Most studies trace the weakening of the mutual benefit associations to the widespread unemployment of the Great Depression—an economic crisis that had begun by 1926 in African-American urban communities. Jessie Blayton, for example, stressed that the economic depression of 1926 to 1929 taxed all African-American savings associations' resources by creating a great demand for benefits at the same time that their members found it harder to keep up with their dues. Gunnar Myrdal suggests that alternative forms of life insurance provided the benefits previously gained only through mutual benefit associations. These observations are both partly true, but there are other factors to be considered as well. Although the associations continued to exist after the fall of the stock market, household day workers perceived them as institutions serving the needs of live-in servants. The day workers transferred their money to banks, in part because their new jobs gave them the opportunity to do so.[40] As Eula Montgomery remarked, "I'd have used them [banks] earlier, but with that woman you never got time to go to a place like that. I know I didn't."[41] Minnie Barnes verified this point: "I used a bank as a day worker because it was on my streetcar line home."[42]

37. Ward Goodenough, "Rethinking 'Status' and 'Role': Toward a General Model of the Cultural Organization of Social Relationships," in *Cognitive Anthropology*, ed. Stephen Tyler (New York, 1969), 314.

38. Bernice Reeder interview.

39. Velma Davis interview.

40. Edward Denison, *Economic Growth in the United States* (New York, 1961), 2–4; Jessie Blayton, "The Negro in Banking," *Bankers Magazine* 4 (December 1936): 511–14; Gunnar Myrdal, *An American Dilemma* (New York, 1944), 316–17.

41. Eula Montgomery, interviewed by author, 15 September 1982.

42. Minnie Barnes, interviewed by author, 12 July 1982.

"Most of the women," explained Helen Venable, "felt them clubs wasn't for workers; it wasn't for . . . people getting their money on payday or getting paid every week."[43] The savings clubs, like uniforms, were viewed as symbols of the servant role. Marie Davis said, "The banks was better than clubs. They was for servants; banks was for people with jobs."[44] The women wanted to deal with established savings institutions, as other salaried employees did, and using a bank was a public acknowledgment of their new status as independent workers.

The waning of the mutual benefit associations did not, however, mean the decline of support for rural kin. On the contrary, economic assistance typically increased after the transition to household day work. In speaking of the support she provided her relatives still living in the South, Velma Davis said, "I didn't miss a month. . . . That's why I got myself set before I left live-in. I never missed sending my share home."[45] If anything, the women adhered even more strongly to their premigration beliefs concerning kinship obligations. However, the earlier belief that the reciprocal support/obligation system operating inside kin networks should be carried on through community economic associations such as penny savers clubs no longer had meaning.[46]

The level of these women's participation in the African-American churches of Washington also changed significantly. Live-in servant work had greatly restricted their attendance and involvement in church activities. Velma Davis recalled, "Living in? You never dreamed of going to day service. Sundays, you'd be out of there [the live-in household], if you was good, by four or five."[47] Regular participation in daytime church services was also an indication of status. "Big people, like government messengers, or people working in a colored business office, that's who'd be regular at Sunday day services," Eula Montgomery said. Individuals who worked in those types of jobs, she pointed out, had their Sundays free; they could also, therefore, "be on the church's special committees."[48]

Live-in service had limited all aspects of interactions with other church members. Eula Montgomery went on: "If you lived in a room in the attic, how could you be in any of them clubs? You couldn't bring

43. Helen Venable interview.
44. Marie Davies interview.
45. Velma Davis interview.
46. Cf. the kin support arrangements in Tamara Hareven, *Family Time and Industrial Time* (New York, 1982), 142–53; Elizabeth Bott, *Family and Social Network* (London, 1971), 249.
47. Velma Davis interview.
48. Eula Montgomery interview. See Williams, *Community*, 33–47, for an excellent analysis of Afro-American women in urban churches.

nobody over there. . . . You never got to be in a fellowship. That was
for people who got off on Saturday and Sunday. They had a nice place
to have people over to—not no kitchen." She also explained the contrast between the professed religious beliefs of employers and their
practices in relationship to live-in servants: "Now, they'd get up and go
out to Sunday morning church. . . . He'd act like Sunday was such a
holy day around there. He made it clear Sundays was a day of rest. But
us? We'd work like dogs just the same. We didn't get no rest on that
day."[49]

The day-of-rest philosophy obviously did not apply to live-in servants; it simply underscored the contradiction between the concern for
the family's beliefs and the lack of concern for the servants' religious
needs and rights that existed in the homes of employers of all faiths.
"Jews," said Virginia Lacey, "would have them big dinners and tell they
childrens all about getting saved from slavery and death. But they'd not
a bit more care . . . if you got to see the inside of any church."[50]

Regular church attendance, achieved through less confining employment, was accompanied by more leisure-time activity. A married
couple could go to morning church services, and in summer they could
go out for picnics, Dolethia Otis pointed out.[51]

Participation in church and leisure activities was viewed, not surprisingly, as representative of the attainment of *better* work; according
to Nellie Willoughby, a migrant from Virginia, "it showed you had
work you didn't live at."[52] It did not mean that these women did *easier*
work. The point was that the work they did—even if more strenuous—
permitted some previously unavailable free time. Bernice Reeder cited
the laundress as an example: "She'd have four washes to do. Then
she'd have them heavy irons for ironing time. She worked, but she'd
still be able to get to church. She was on so many boards. . . . She
worked real hard for six days, but every Sunday she was off. Then, too,
she had evenings to herself."[53] The washing and ironing constituted
backbreaking labor; the live-in servants recognized this fact. But as live-
out work it offered a number of advantages, the most often stated of
which was that it allowed the worker to develop new social roles.

All of the women interviewed asserted that household day work was

49. Eula Montgomery interview.
50. Virginia Lacey interview.
51. Dolethia Otis interview.
52. Nellie Willoughby, interviewed by author, 28 July 1982.
53. Bernice Reeder interview. Women migrants and lighter work are discussed in
Kelly Miller, *Race Adjustment* (Miami, Fla., 1969), 171.

directly responsible for their ability to participate in the churches. The result of this change was wider church membership. Previously, working-class women had not been well represented in the African-American churches. "Most women down at Mason Street Baptist who were real active," said Helen Venable, "were educated good and had jobs like teaching. As people got more away from live-in you saw a lotta different people in all the things that church has. Then more and more people got in the church's clubs or work."[54]

The growth of African-American churches in Washington, then, was a direct consequence of the steady influx of these working-class (former live-in) women.[55] They strongly supported church expansion because their participation in the church activities further separated them from the stigma of servitude.

Contemporary scholars who have studied household service employment during the first three decades of the twentieth century have recognized how the "service" institution changed during that period.[56] The changes in the racial and employment structure of household work dominate the generalized studies of that era. Most scholars, however, have failed to recognize how household service workers changed important institutions in the twentieth century.

Live-in servant work imposed countless burdens upon African-American female migrants to the District of Columbia before the Depression, yet "service-class" women developed and controlled philanthropic organizations that allowed them eventually to escape the boundaries of live-in servant employment. Although the African-American women quoted here remained in household service work all their lives, they restructured its salient features and created more freedom for themselves.

Reformers who rely only on archival records may view household service work as "a dead end."[57] Scholars all too often see household workers as merely products of change, never as its causes; as objects of

54. Helen Venable interview.

55. E. Franklin Frazier, *The Negro Church in America* (New York, 1971); A. H. Fauset, *Black Gods of the Metropolis* (Philadelphia, 1971); "The Black Church," *Black Scholar* 2 (December 1970): 3–49.

56. Lois Helmbold, "The Impact of the Great Depression on Black and White Working Class Women's Lives and Relations," paper given at the Sixth Berkshire Conference, June 1984; Karen Tucker Anderson, "Last Hired, First Fired: Black Women Workers during World War II," *Journal of American History* 69 (June 1982): 82–97; Katzman, *Seven Days a Week*, 226–79; Sutherland, *Americans and Their Servants*, 182–99.

57. Katzman, *Seven Days a Week*, 11; Lucy Maynard Salmon, *Domestic Service* (New York, 1897), 141–42n.

events, not as their subjects; as passive reactors, not as active forces in history.[58] The words and lives of these women refute such views. Orra Fisher's response sums up best what the women expressed when asked about the progress and the success they have seen in their lives:

> I worked hard to serve God and to see that my three girls didn't have to serve nobody else like I did except God. I satisfied to know I came a long way. From a kitchen down home to a kitchen up here, and then able to earn money, but live with my children and grands. Now Jesus took me every step—that's real.
>
> But look at me, with more than I ever dreamed I'd have. And my three, with houses, and jobs. My girls in an office, and the baby—my son—over twenty years in the Army. I get full thinking about it. I had it bad, but look at them.[59]

58. Henri, *Black Migration*, x.
59. Orra Fisher, interviewed by author, 2 August 1982.

13

"He Isn't Half So Cranky as He Used to Be": Agricultural Mechanization, Comparable Worth, and the Changing Farm Family

Corlann Gee Bush

We are the owners of a "Caterpillar" Thirty Tractor and you just can't imagine how much time and labor it saves. Before we had our tractor we farmed with 30 or 40 head of horses and mules and had four or five hired men to cook for all summer long and one, sometimes two, all winter. Now I have only two men in the summer and none at all during the winter.

I used to be tied down at home all the time cooking for a bunch of hired help and many times had to have a hired girl, which I don't need now since we have the "Caterpillar." It gives me more leisure time and I enjoy life more now than I ever have before.

And the most important thing of all is that [since] my husband doesn't have to get up so early in the morning and tend to a bunch of horses before breakfast and work until late at night feeding and unharnessing, he isn't half so cranky as he used to be.[1]

In this passage from a letter written to the Caterpillar Tractor Company, Mrs. David Harding is discussing a little-studied but important aspect of agricultural history: how mechanization affected the work relationships of individuals within the family unit. She is also describing the different effects that the same technology, the crawler tractor,

1. Caterpillar Tractor Company, *At Last We Wives Can Have Vacations,* pamphlet distributed by Hofius-Ferris Equipment Co. (Spokane, c. 1936), 5–6.

had on her life and her husband's. In doing so she raises interesting questions about the direct effects of that technology on men, its primary users, and its cross-over effects on women, its secondary or indirect users.

The purpose of this article is to analyze the direct and cross-over effects of mechanized tractors on the "comparable worth" of men and women on family farms in the Palouse region of northern Idaho and eastern Washington.[2] The family farm is an excellent model for such a study because it is a stable unit of production that allocates resources and divides responsibility in order to accomplish common objectives. Unlike the factory or corporation, the family farm is small enough that adjustments made in response to new technology are immediate and observable. In other words, one can trace the patterns of change and response within a representative yet limited universe.

Similarly, the Palouse region is the perfect area within which to study agricultural mechanization. The Palouse (the name is derived from the French for "grassy meadow") is a unique topographical region located in the northwestern United States, between the western foothills of the Bitterroot Mountains and the semiarid plateau of the Columbia Basin. The typical Palouse countryside is characterized by dense rolling hills with very steep (80- to 90-degree) northeast slopes and more gentle (20- to 40-degree) southwest slopes. Composed of up to 250 feet of loess, windblown dust derived from the eruption of volcanoes in the Cascade Mountains, the Palouse Hills were a pioneer's dream and a farmer's nightmare: the soil was fertile, contained no rocks, and was suitable for dry land farming, but the hills were so steep that they could not be cultivated by then-conventional means.

From earliest settlement in the 1860s through the end of the nineteenth century, farmers in the Palouse were engaged primarily in subsistence agriculture, farming the flatter bottomlands, pasturing their livestock—especially hogs—on the grassy slopes, and hoping for a technological breakthrough that would allow them to plant and harvest the steeper hills surrounding them. That breakthrough came in the form of the fluid or equalizing hitch invented in 1892 by Peter Schandoney.[3] By the early 1900s this device had made its way to the Palouse,

---

2. I have used considerable license in applying the term "comparable worth" to the work of women and men in farm families. Individuals within these families did not then, and do not now, think of their work in terms of its "equity" or "worth." Such terms are analytical and ahistorical at best; however, no other language better allows us to talk about the common components of work or describe the relative value of jobs.

3. Thomas B. Keith, *The Horse Interlude: A Pictorial History of Horse and Man in the Inland Northwest* (Moscow, Idaho, 1980), 67.

where it opened the hills to crop production and set up the conditions that make the Palouse the perfect microcosm in which to examine the effects of technological change on gender roles within the family.

The history of American agriculture is, everywhere, the study of the change from subsistence to mechanization to commercialization.[4] In the Palouse, unlike other areas of the country, this evolution is a current event, close enough in time to study from original sources.[5] Many children of early settlers survive, and excellent written and oral sources abound. Further, changes in Palouse agriculture have been directly tied to specific changes in farm technology which are well documented in advertisements, brochures, and the literature of the Cooperative Extension Service.

Yet, in important ways, Palouse agriculture has changed very little since the early 1900s: it is and has been family-dominated and oriented to commodity production for external markets. Subsistence farms are, by definition, family farms, but the reverse is not necessarily true: in 1980 over 80 percent of Palouse farms are still under family or family-corporate ownership.[6] Because the family has continuously been the primary unit of ownership and production in the Palouse, the shift to agribusiness ownership which has compromised family farming in other parts of the country has had little effect here. Changing ownership is thus not a variable that needs to be factored into this analysis of changing farm technology. Market orientation can likewise be ex-

4. As Susan Strasser points out in *Never Done: A History of American Housework* (New York, 1982), 67, farm families have never been either totally independent of the market economy or totally subsumed by it. During the late nineteenth century, subsistence farms on the Palouse bought goods (shoes, coffee, tea, kerosene) and sold surplus produce (butter, eggs, wheat, pork) to miners in northern Idaho and to workers on the railroads. To call such farms "subsistence" operations obscures the extent to which they were dependent upon and involved in the market economy. Likewise, to call contemporary farms "commodity-production" operations obscures the extent to which the farm family provides its own food and labor. Nonetheless, there are marked differences in the orientations of the two types of farm to the market economy. I use the term "subsistence farm" to mean one that tends to provide as much as possible for the needs of the family, with surplus sold only on local markets; a "production-oriented" or "commodity-production" farm is one that tends to concentrate on growing crops on a large scale for shipment to national or international markets.

5. Among these sources are the Latah County Oral History Project and the (Idaho) Rural Women's History Project (transcripts available at the archives of the University of Idaho, Moscow); the Whitman County Oral History Project (transcripts available at the Whitman Historical Society, Pullman, Wash.); and the Washington Women's Heritage Project (transcripts available at the Washington State University Library Archives, Pullman).

6. 1982 Census of Agriculture, Idaho, State and County Data, vol. 1, pt. 12, 4, 159–61.

cluded. The crops that grow best in the Palouse are soft winter wheat, dried peas, and lentils. Since there is a limit to the amount of noodles, pea soup, and lentil chile that can be consumed by local residents, most farm produce has been shipped to national and international markets since the completion of the railroads and improvements in farm technology broke Palouse agriculture out of its subsistence phase in the late 1890s and early 1900s.

Thus, such variables as ownership of production and market orientation, which could complicate an analysis of the effects of changing technology on farm families, are excluded by the nature of Palouse agriculture itself. In addition, although the standard stages of agricultural development are evident in the Palouse, the transition from one stage to another was rapid, widespread, and technology-generated. One specific invention, the Schandoney hitch, which changed Palouse agriculture from a local to a national market orientation, did so for almost all farmers within a ten-year period. Similarly, the Caterpillar tractor with an internal combustion engine that did not stall out on steep hills was perfected by the 1930s;[7] within ten years, very few Palouse farmers were using horses. Thus the connections between machinery and work are comparatively easy to discern and study.

In sum, if it is possible to analyze something as evanescent as how an individual's work changes in response to technological innovation, if it is possible to construct from that analysis a more generalizable understanding of the relationship of technological change to gender roles, it will be possible to do so with farm families in the microcosm known as the Palouse.

It is a truism that the most profound technologies have been the simplest—consider the horse collar, the stirrup, the waterwheel, and Peter Schandoney's cloverleaf hitch.

Forged out of a solid iron rod, easy and inexpensive to produce, the Schandoney hitch looks like a slightly elongated three-leaf clover, no more than 12 inches wide and no less than 12 inches long. It was hitched along the center line between the two spans of each team of horses, attached with clevises to the ends of each (three-horse) tripletree, then connected by a chain to the center of the preceding tripletree. Because it used leverage to distribute the load equally among all horses, the Schandoney hitch gave much greater flexibility and stability in maneuvering large teams than the fixed or "dead" hitch that preceded it. Under the dead-hitch system, lazy horses allowed others to pull more of the load; horses on the outer edges of a team pulled more

7. Keith, *Horse Interlude*, 167–68.

weight than those toward the center. Pulling up steep hills caused undue strain on lead horses; braking caused strain on the wheel horses. As a result, 32 horses furnished far less than 32 horsepower, the minimum required to haul a heavy, ground-powered combine through the fields.[8]

Before the invention of the Schandoney hitch, farmers had tried to solve this problem either by using larger animals or by adding horses to their teams. Unfortunately, horses weighing over 1,500 pounds sank to their fetlocks in the soil, while Palouse wheat horses at the ideal weight of 1,200–1,450 pounds[9] were too light to pull a combine on a dead-hitch system. On the other hand, the mere addition of horses only increased the teams' unwieldiness and proved no more efficient.

The cloverleaf hitch was a blessing for both farmers and horses. Now farmers could hitch together teams large enough to generate one horsepower per horse; and because the load was equally distributed, farmers could get more work from each animal without harming it. By 1920 it was not uncommon to see five separate combines harvesting one wheatfield at the same time. Each combine was pulled by thirty-three to forty-four horses and required five to nine men to operate it. Among them were the teamster, who drove the horses; the header man, who adjusted the height of the sickle bar; the "sack-jig," who filled the sacks with grain; one or two sack-sewers, who whipstitched the filled sacks; the roustabout, who rode a saddle horse alongside the team, ran errands, and functioned as troubleshooter; the mechanic, who kept the machinery in running order; and a barn man, who supervised the feeding, watering, and care of horses and harness.[10]

A large farm harvesting with four or five ground-powered combines might use 132 to 220 horses and mules and employ 25 to 35 hired hands for the operation, all under the supervision of the farm operator. An astonishing 10,000 itinerant workers were hired to harvest crops in 1920.[11]

Hired hands were paid a minimal wage plus "food and found" (board and room). Women supplied the food portion of this wage and benefit package. They fed an average of twenty-five men—including husbands and relatives—five meals a day for a minimum of ten days to

8. Kirby Brumfield, *This Was Wheat Farming: A Pictorial History of the Farms and Farmers of the Northwest Who Grow the Nation's Bread* (New York, 1968), 120.

9. Keith, *Horse Interlude*, 37.

10. Keith, *Horse Interlude*, 87; see also Brumfield, *Wheat Farming*, 61–63, 128–32.

11. Susan Armitage, "Pacific Northwest Farm: Women and the Frontier Tradition," paper presented to the American Farm Women in Historical Perspective Conference, 1984.

a maximum of four weeks.[12] Breakfast was served just before sunup, and a snack of sandwiches and lemonade was taken to the men at midmorning. A large sit-down dinner was served about 1:30 while the men rested during the heat of the day; another snack was taken out to the fields in the late afternoon; and supper was served around sunset. During harvest, women worked from 3:00 A.M. to 10:30 P.M., an average of one and a half to two hours longer than the men. With five meals to wash up after, cleaning up was as demanding as cooking and far less rewarding. Women never put just-washed dishes in the cupboards but simply reset the tables for the next meal. Because women baked bread as often as five times a day and pies at least once, their woodstoves were always hot. For this reason, most women cooked in sheds or shanties away from the main house. Obviously, women did not get to rest from the heat of either the day or their cookhouses.

Just as neighboring farmers combined and pooled horses and equipment, farm women often pooled their pots, pans and labor. A woman would be in charge of the cooking operation while the workers were harvesting on her farm. When they left, she would often go to a neighbor's home to help cook the meals for the harvest crew there. Despite such sharing, there was never enough help, so work in the cookshack provided summer jobs for many local teenage girls.

Just as her farmer-husband was responsible for all the complicated planning, management, and supervisory tasks of the harvest operation, the farm wife was responsible for equally complex tasks in her own arena: organizing the work of the neighbors and hired girls who helped her, planning all the menus, and ensuring that there was enough food for each meal. Being prepared for the harvest often meant stretching last year's food to feed this year's crew, putting in a garden with both early- and late-bearing crops, canning early produce, raising chickens, gathering eggs, milking cows, making butter, and buying what could not be produced at home. These were challenging tasks that demanded management skills at least as sophisticated as those required of her husband.

Obviously, farming—especially harvesting—during the era of horse and human power was difficult business. Palouse farm operations were a curious mixture of self-sufficient subsistence farming and large-scale cash-crop commodity production. Both men and women on these farms performed some work that was production-oriented and

12. This composite view of the farm woman's responsibilities during harvest is drawn from the recollections of Wayve McBride Comstock, Roberta Nygaard, Betty Smith, and other women interviewed in 1975 and 1976 as part of the Rural Women's History Project (RWHP). See also Brumfield, *Wheat Farming*, 67–70.

other work that was subsistence-oriented. Men simultaneously managed the production operation and contributed to family subsistence; women generally managed the subsistence operation and helped out with production tasks when necessary. For example, men's production work was the management of the cash crop that brought in the money needed to pay hired hands, pay taxes, buy seed and equipment; their subsistence work included the growing of hay crops, caring for the horses and cattle, repairing harness and machinery. Women planted large gardens, canned the produce, milked cows, raised chickens and small animals, and sold the surplus for "butter and egg" money. These activities cut expenses, provided food that the family would otherwise have had to buy, and supplied women with their only source of cash. In addition to these subsistence activities, they managed a complicated harvest cooking operation that, by partially substituting for wages, contributed to the profitability of the farm.

Such was, in fact, the preferred economic survival strategy for farmers on the Palouse throughout the first three decades of the twentieth century: raising market crops for cash, growing subsistence crops to cut expenses. It is especially important to note that men and women played equally crucial roles in the economic survival and growth of these family farms.

Despite the productivity and profitability of the large-scale harvest operation, many farmers wanted relief from the personnel management tasks that the enormous harvest crews imposed on them. Some farmhands were highly skilled laborers who hired on with the same farmer year after year, but many were unskilled laborers who needed jobs but had little loyalty to their work or their employer. The tasks of identifying each man's skills, organizing the workers, and supervising them were formidable, especially for farmers with little managerial expertise.[13]

The farmers' desire for a technological solution to their problems with horses and hands was continually thwarted by the lack of a reliable internal combustion engine that would be inexpensive to operate and would not stall out or tip over on the steep Palouse hills. Unfortunately for farmers who felt burdened by heavy supervisory responsibilities, their horse operations were efficient and productive. A report of the Wheat Growers Economic conference in 1926 found that wheat farms of less than 1,000 acres produced wheat at less cost with horses alone than with tractors and horses.[14] Only on farms of more than 1,000

---

13. Keith, *Horse Interlude,* 121; Brumfield, *Wheat Farming,* 44.
14. Brumfield, *Wheat Farming,* 164–65.

acres were tractors found to be as profitable as horses, and even then horse operations were found to be "efficient and [they] need not necessarily be converted to tractor operation."[15] So despite the difficulties, inconvenience, and hard work of operating large-scale farms with horse power and hired hands, wheat farming in the Palouse remained labor-intensive and horsepower-dependent into the 1930s.

While the convergence of several factors (including war-induced labor shortages and access to petroleum products) were required before crop production in the Palouse could be completely mechanized, the most important influence was the development of a tractor with a reliable engine and stable traction. The Caterpillar or crawler tractor was just such an innovation; it did not stall out or tip over, and its traction system distributed the load evenly, thereby increasing both stability and maneuverability. In addition, a crawler tractor could be hitched to the plows, seeders, and combines a farmer already owned, in effect substituting one power source (diesel fuel) for another (horses).

Despite the obvious labor-saving advantages of crawler tractors over horses, farmers had to think about more than just the requirements of their production operation if they wanted to buy a tractor. Tractors cost money that would immediately be diverted from the family itself, particularly from improving the standard of living of the women and children. As a farm family could afford a crawler tractor or a refrigerator but not both, women had to be convinced that investing in a tractor would be to *their* benefit. Enterprising corporations such as the Caterpillar Tractor Company set out to show that the purchase of crawler tractors would actually help farm women at least as much as investment in kitchen appliances. *At Last We Wives Can Have Vacations* was one example of such an attempt. This "tractor tract" set out to demonstrate—in the wives' own words—how a crawler tractor, her husband's technology, actually improved a woman's quality of life:

> There are so many ways that I am benefited by the "Caterpillar" Tractor that I do not know where to begin. . . . When we farmed with horses, I did most of the milking in the working season, because there was no time to lose—now I help milk if I want to. No hurry. . . . We are also able to buy things for our home that we have wanted for a long time—one a power washer, another a radio, both a great pleasure. We are planning very much on buying a home of our own very soon, if wheat doesn't go too low.[16]

15. Brumfield, *Wheat Farming*, 165–66.
16. Mrs. F. R. Johnson, quoted in *At Last We Wives*, 9–10.

Now when a picnic comes along my husband can't say, "Oh, the feed is about gone. Can't take a day off for anything until this work is done." Or if the family wants to go to the Lake for a few days, we don't need to worry about the tractor getting into somebody's field of wheat, or doing without a drink. We get our work out of the way in good time now, so if I need some help in the yard he has time to do some of the heavy spading and cleaning.[17]

As these women and the other contributors to *At Last We Wives* remind us, nothing—not electric ranges, refrigerators, or washing machines—changed the lives of Palouse farm women as dramatically or as quickly as the crawler tractor. One year the harvest required, say, sixty-six horses and eighteen hands; the next it was mechanized and required no horses and five hands.

But the labor savings and freedom from personnel supervision so long desired by her husband left the farm wife without a context for her own management skills. Once a (largely unrecognized) contributor to the production operation, the farm woman was reduced from co-manager to farm wife. It is one of the paradoxes of technological change that she saw her freedom from harvest cooking as a gain that far outweighed her loss of status and autonomy:

I must say that up to now it is the most wonderful thing that has ever been used on our farm. It is not only convenient for the men, but for the women as well. It certainly saves a great amount of work and expense. There isn't always a meal to cook for hired help as before, which occupies the biggest part of a woman's time during the day. This also means that a woman has her weekends free. The men benefit as well, for there aren't any chores to do every day of the year.[18]

The farm might no longer need hired labor at all. Hiram Drache estimates that each tractor displaced three to five farm workers;[19] in the Palouse, I believe this figure to be closer to seven to nine workers, the average size of a combine crew. The first workers to be laid off were the 10,000-plus itinerant laborers who had flooded into the Palouse each summer, but even local hands were gradually displaced as farmers realized that they could meet their reduced and deskilled labor requirements from within their own families. As a result, the farm wife

17. Mrs. O. L. Fletcher, quoted in *At Last We Wives*, 7–8.
18. Mrs. Con Fink, quoted in *At Last We Wives*, 13.
19. Hiram Drache, *Beyond the Furrow: Some Keys to Successful Farming in the Twentieth Century* (Danville, Ill., 1979), 47–48.

became the farm's unpaid and unacknowledged "hired hand"—doing chores, driving grain trucks, going to town for parts, and keeping books, but making few of the operational decisions: that responsibility remained with her husband and the professionals he hired. Roberta Nygaard explains:

> In the days when I was growing up there were no books kept. There wasn't any income tax in those days. But since we've had books, and there's a terrific amount of bookkeeping on a farm nowadays and especially in the partnership my husband is in . . . Of course we have our income tax done by an accountant but then I have to get the books ready. Oh, you just can't imagine the bookkeeping there is.[20]

A closer look at what happened as a result of the switch to tractor operation reveals that men traded personnel supervision for increasingly complex operations management, while women swapped sophisticated operations management for "helping out." It would be comforting to believe that as women became more involved in the "outside" farm work, they became more integral to the farm's management, participating in the decision-making and gaining recognition for their contributions. In fact, however, the reverse seems to be the case. A farm wife's new tasks were merely added to her old ones: since she was already going to town for groceries, she could stop off and pick up a part; since she was already keeping a record of her household expenses, she could keep the farm's books too; since it was so much easier to cook in her modern kitchen and she had fewer to cook for, she could drive the grain truck. "Pretty soon [my sons'] wives kind of took over and started driving the bulk truck," Wayve Comstock relates, "but even nowadays, the whole family, the farms are so big, the whole family has to do all the work they can. They can't hire because wages is so high. . . . That was one of the things that was a little different in my life."[21]

As the farm mechanized, indebtedness grew, and the margin of error narrowed. Farming became increasingly risky, not because of the danger of being kicked by a horse or run over by a combine but because the wrong decision coupled with a bad year could threaten the survival of the farm itself. The farm wife's work, on the other hand, became less complex and less demanding, as the context in which she had had autonomy disappeared. Still busy performing myriad tasks even though freed from the heavy labor of harvest cooking, farm wom-

20. Roberta Nygaard, RWHP interview, 1975.
21. Wayve McBride Comstock, RWHP interview, 1975.

en in the Palouse failed to recognize that they no longer played a vital role in the farm's economic survival.

Such was the paradox of farm mechanization. It made everyone's work easier and life better, but it also loaded men's roles while eroding women's. The absolute standard of living improved absolutely, but the comparable worth of women's work relative to men's actually decreased.

Four factors contribute to an understanding of how the comparable worth of men's and women's work changed in response to agricultural mechanization: financial contribution, complexity, discretion over one's time, and diversity.[22] Changes in the first three factors have a direct effect on the value of the work; changes in the last, diversity, have an inverse effect.[23]

Financial contribution is defined as both income earning and expense cutting. Although they have the same function—maximizing the family resources—income production is a more valued activity than expense reduction. In a market economy, the value accorded to work is determined by the amount of money it earns; activities aimed at cost reduction are never as visible or as highly valued as cash-producing activity, even if the amount saved is equal to the amount earned.

On Palouse farms during the horse-farming era, the subsistence activities of both men and women were aimed at reducing costs. However, the farmer's commodity production work was, overall, more valued than his wife's harvest cooking because he could turn his labor into cash while she could only claim to have reduced expenses. Thus the farm woman's crucial financial contribution to the farm was obscured because it was an expense-reduction activity directly connected to her traditional domestic role as cook, housewife, and nurturer.

A revisionist history of American industrialization would show the 1920s to 1960s as the decades when the market economy completed its "hostile takeover" of women's domestic production—forcing women, particularly farm women, out of "business" and into less competitive and ever more marginal economic activity. Eggs, milk, and butter became cheaper and more widely available in stores than when they were

22. The factors were suggested by and much modified from the components—knowledge and skills, mental demands, accountability, and working conditions—used by Hay Associates in the job factor analyses they perform in pay equity studies. See *The Comparable Worth Issue: A BNA Special Report* (Washington, D.C., 1981), 45.

23. Corlann Gee Bush, "The Barn Is His, The House Is Mine: Agricultural Technology and Sex Roles," in *Energy and Transport: Historical Perspectives on Policy Issues* (Beverly Hills, Calif., 1982), 235–59.

provided by women's domestic labor. Store-bought clothes became cheaper and more stylish. It became less expensive to buy a case of applesauce than to can the applesauce oneself. And even though store-bought applesauce, butter, and shirts were inferior in quality to their homemade counterparts, the savings in time and the freedom from drudgery seemed to more than compensate farm men for their loss of self-reliance and farm women for their loss of centrality.

Farm families thus became firmly locked into the market economy, engaged in the pursuit of the cash necessary to buy the products and goods once provided by their own labor (with the costs of processing, preservation, and transportation added on). In this shift lies the reason that farmers so consistently over-produce: they need more and more cash because they must sell their produce in a buyer's market and buy goods and services in a seller's market.

Complexity is the term used to describe the number of separate variables that must be considered in order to perform a task or make a decision. Running a large-scale commodity-production enterprise was a complex undertaking for Palouse farmers even during the horse-farming era, and it was made more so by the advent of the crawler tractor. Contemporary farmers have to decide not only which crop varieties to plant but also which fertilizers, pesticides, and herbicides to apply, which equipment to buy, which marketing and amortization strategies to use, how to service their debts, and whether or not to participate in government allotment, marketing, or soil conservation programs. In contrast, the complexity of the tasks their wives performed decreased. With few hired hands, there was no major cooking operation to manage, and the number of variables involved in their work was dramatically reduced. The farm wife's food operations, which once required her to make complex management decisions about the procurement, preservation, and processing of food for large numbers of workers, now were reduced to the tasks necessary to feed her immediate family. In general, since the more complex an operation, task, or decision, the more value it is accorded, women's work lost worth as their husbands' gained it.

Discretion over time refers to the extent to which an individual can control the way she spends her time and the degree to which she can make demands on the time of others; conversely, it is the degree to which one is independent of the demands of others. (This analysis considers time to be a resource comparable to labor or money in that it can be allocated or demanded according to the needs and requirements of the enterprise.) The more discretion a person has over her time and the more control over others' time, the higher the comparable worth of the work she does and the more crucial she is to the survival of the farm as an economic unit.

No aspect of the life of the Palouse farmer has changed more than his discretion over his own time. It used to be the essence of horse farming that one was at the beck and call of others: livestock needed to be fed, stables cleaned, and harness mended; cows needed milking; calves, foals, and lambs had to be watched carefully during and after birthing; crops needed to be harvested when they were ripe. Indeed, one of the reasons Mr. Harding was cranky was that as a horse farmer, he had so little control over his time.

The tractor changed this situation dramatically. Farmers no longer had to care for horses, and harvesting crops was no longer the race against time it once had been, since one tractor-pulled combine could harvest in a day what it took two horse-drawn combines to harvest in a week.[24] (Modern self-propelled combines can harvest the same field in hours.) Thus, freed from endless chores and some of the demands of livestock, farmers had more discretion over their own time.

Horse farmers may have been at the beck and call of their animals and crops, but women were at the beck and call of their husbands. Women prepared meals to facilitate men's work and served them on men's schedules. In addition to doing their own chores, women were often expected to help their men, while reciprocal assistance was almost never given. Indeed, women's domestic work is known for its interruptibility: it can be picked up, worked on, put down, left, and picked up again later. All of women's handwork is so regarded, as are washing clothes, ironing, and cleaning house. Even baking and cooking are to some degree interruptible. Only during harvest did women have some measure of control over their time and, of course, the time of their neighbors and hired girls. Women who were cooking five meals a day were too busy and their work was too important to be constantly interrupted. They were left largely alone to manage their own time.

Paradoxically, the tractor actually increased men's control over women's time and thereby made women's work less crucial. Because women were no longer doing their own production-related work of cooking for harvest crews, they were "free" to help out the men. Women today are given driving and "go-fer" tasks: they drive grain trucks to the elevators, they go to town for spare parts, they do the banking, they pick up tools and take animals to the vet. Driving and errand running are important; the tasks need to be done; someone has to do them, and they are congruent with the work women are already engaged in—

24. Brumfield, *Wheat Farming*, 167–68.

shopping and bookkeeping. Yet such work is intermittent and still highly interruptible, focused on "helping out" rather than managing. Driving and errand running are not nearly so crucial or so autonomous as harvest cooking used to be.

Diversity means the extent to which work is comprised of different components and activities. In diverse farming operations, a variety of crops are grown and a number of marketing, income-producing, and expense-reduction strategies are used. Subsistence or commodity-subsistence farms are generally more diverse than full commodity operations. In general, the greater the diversity, the less the risk and the less crucial the work.

During the horse-farming era, most Palouse farms combined commodity production and subsistence activities. Farmers planted in a three-stage crop-rotation system, alternating wheat, peas or lentils, and summer fallow. They also hunted wild game, planted hay and forage crops, bred and sold horses, and kept milk cows and beef cattle in small herds. In addition, many farmers worked as custom cutters for nearby farms or ran steam threshers. Their wives grew large gardens, canned or preserved the produce, sewed the family's clothes, and earned butter and egg money. Wayve Comstock continues her story:

> That was one of the things that was a little different in my life than in some others, we did have a lot of help, because it took a lot of help in those days to get the work done. It took five on the thresher crew and we hired a man to stay with me when the crew was away, and we had a lot of relatives that worked for us part time. And I was home with three little children, real small, and I had the chores to do, and the shop-keeper to wait on—he would come and get vegetables and butter and those fryers that I raised—and I also canned fruit in two-quart jars for the cookhouse and we had our own eggs. We had all the stuff we could possibly get from home to feed the people we got 'cus it cut down on the expenses, and nobody was making any money except a few like us that did extra jobs like thrashing and harvest. You can see how busy we were, very busy, but it was a happy life and we made it pay.[25]

All these activities made the Palouse farm of the 1920s an extremely diverse and stable operation. The failure of any part of the enterprise meant hardship but did not threaten the loss of the farm.

After the coming of the tractor, farmers started divesting themselves of subsistence activities by selling horses and cows and devoting all their acreage to commodity production. More money was earned,

25. Comstock interview.

and such an operation may have become more efficient, but the farm lost its diversity and its subsistence base, becoming more vulnerable to the vagaries of national and international markets. From the mid-1930s on, crop failure, overproduction, or low prices jeopardized the survival of many Palouse farms to a degree unknown before. The successful farm may have been more successful than ever, but there were unexpected negative consequences: there were fewer and fewer farms; the individual farmer's work became more crucial; and he lived under greater stress.

In contrast to their husbands, farm women continued to be very busy with very diverse work: they worked double days during the "horse interlude," they worked double days in the 1940s and 1950s, and they work double days today. Farm women today are unpaid, on-call farm labor: they manage the family's consumption; they are concerned with the style and appropriateness of clothing and home furnishings; they have become gourmet cooks and gracious entertainers. Women's work is (as Sarah Elbert asserts elsewhere in this volume) so diverse as to be invisible and so varied as to be worth less than the more single-minded, production-oriented work of their husbands.

The Caterpillar tractor spelled the end not just of horse farming in the Palouse but of an era of rough comparability in the worth of men's and women's farm work. Men's work as autonomous managers and decision-makers became increasingly crucial to the survival of the farm; women's work became less crucial because women performed more tasks requiring less skill and independence. One contemporary farm woman states, "I would say that a rural woman learns very young in life that she has to make it on her own. She can't depend on her neighbors to do little things for her, [and] you have to learn how to really work with your husband or with your mother or whoever is in charge. You've got to learn very young to get along with them and to make it."[26]

The horse interlude in the Palouse was a time when the scale and scope of farming were so great that it was impossible for farmers to exercise simple control over all phases of their operations. "Simple" control, as Richard Edwards defines it, is the control exercised by a single entrepreneur or business owner over all phases of the production or labor process.[27] The boss hires, fires, defines the work to be done and sets the pace of that work. Palouse farmers exercised simple

26. Rebecca Kellom, RWHP interview, 1975.

27. Richard Edwards, *Contested Terrain: The Transformation of the Workplace in the Twentieth Century* (New York, 1979).

control over farm production—including the labor of their hired hands, wives, and families—*except* during harvest. Then the work was so complex, the scale was so great, and the demands were so intense that simple control was no longer possible.

Farmers coped with the increased demands of harvest by temporarily surrendering some of their simple control and relying on "technical" control, that is, control exercised by the nature of the work itself.[28] In other words, the machinery and the structure of tasks to be performed dictate how workers work. That was true of the Palouse wheat harvest: horse-drawn combines were machines that required their operators to perform discrete tasks in specific ways; horses and hitching systems required precise, highly formalized handling; hired hands required quantities of high-protein, high-carbohydrate food at particular times. The most any farmer could do was to exercise simple control in hiring the "best" men he could and finding the "best" place for each hand to work. The fields, horses, and machines dictated the rest. The most a farm wife could do was to work like hell and hope the food held out.

When the crawler tractor took over, it allowed—indeed required—farmers to reexert simple control over the harvest labor process. In other words, the autonomy over the food service operation that the farmer had vested in his wife was recalled and his control over her labor reestablished.

By reducing labor requirements and making work safer and less time-consuming, the Caterpillar tractor worked to the absolute advantage of both men and women on Palouse farms. Both gained ease and free time. Yet it also dramatically altered their status relative to one another. The farmer gained greater control over his time and his wife's labor. Relative to her husband and her previous status, the farm wife lost status as she lost technical control over a vital aspect of the enterprise.

That women either did not notice or did not mourn this loss of relative status testifies to several ironic truths about gender, technology, and patriarchy. First, farm women's lives were hard; they performed more work than men for longer hours and less pay and recognition. Any invention that promised relief was welcomed without reservation. Second, when a woman is under the "simple" control of her husband, any activity or purchase or machine that makes him less "cranky" has a direct and positive effect on her well-being. When he is in a good mood, her working conditions improve; when he is in a bad

28. Edwards, *Contested Terrain*.

mood, they deteriorate. This is why so many women during the horse-farming era, women who had never read *At Last We Wives*, agreed to the purchase of a Caterpillar tractor before they got a washing machine; this is why so many women today let their husbands purchase a personal computer when they really need a new vacuum cleaner—they want peace.

In addition, when a woman marries a farmer, she marries an enterprise and a lifestyle. Women willingly sacrifice their own desires and status in order to increase the net worth of the farm and facilitate its intergenerational tranfer.[29] Women on horse farms saw tractors and combines as more likely to accomplish these goals than would washing machines and refrigerators. Further, most farm women (correctly) assumed that they would eventually acquire these domestic conveniences with the cash derived from a more profitable farm.

Finally, farm women did not notice or object to their declining comparable worth because invisible work is *invisible,* even to the laborer. Despite their crucial contribution to the wage-benefit compensation of hired workers, farm women did not see themselves as the autonomous, productive comanagers they truly were. They never saw themselves as exerting technical control over a labor process that was essential to the farm's economic success. They did not consider their work to have worth comparable to their husbands'. When the context that made their work crucial disappeared, they did not realize that they had lost anything of value.

Palouse farmers and their wives seem never to have considered the subtle patterns of inequity they set in motion when they traded their horses for tractors. Then, it seemed enough "to farm more acres in the same time—and of course more acres means more wheat. Wheat in turn means more money—more money means more vacation trips with friend hubby and family, and also better home furnishings, and the Caterpillar tractor is to blame for it all."[30]

29. See Sarah Elbert's article, chap. 15 in this volume.
30. Mrs. Arthur Mumau, quoted in *At Last We Wives*, 8.

· *Part 4* ·

1940–Present

14

Wins and Losses:
The UAW Women's Bureau after
World War II, 1945–1950

Nancy Gabin

Employed during World War II as a riveter at the Ford Motor Company's huge River Rouge complex in Dearborn, Michigan, Gwendolyn Thompson was laid off from her job in June 1945. She, like other discharged defense workers, wanted to return to the comparatively well-paid jobs in the auto industry, and she reported promptly to her employment recall in the winter of 1946. Thompson was accustomed to hard work, but she found her new job unusually heavy and difficult. As a leader of the women's committee in her United Automobile Workers (UAW) local, Thompson recognized her experience as just another attempt by plant management to harass female employees out of their jobs. Nevertheless, she told Mildred Jeffrey, director of the UAW Women's Bureau, that she was seriously considering quitting. Jeffrey pleaded with Thompson not to surrender and to "hang on," both for her own sake and for that of other women who needed her leadership to assert their own rights and interests. Thompson took Jeffrey's advice. She called the company's bluff and retained her right to postwar employment at the River Rouge plant. She sought the first of several offices she would hold in Local 600 and extended her activities in behalf of women. In 1948, with the assistance of the Women's Bureau, she and women from other locals established a women's committee for the Detroit region of the UAW; after its creation in 1950, Thompson also served on the bureau's National Advisory Council.[1]

Thompson's story indicates the important role played by the UAW Women's Bureau in the immediate postwar period. The first of its kind among American trade unions, the agency was created in March 1944 to meet the needs and serve the interests of women, whose share of the UAW's membership had increased since 1939 from 7 to 28 percent.[2] The establishment of the Women's Bureau reflected not only the greater presence of women in the war-converted automobile industry but also their newly enlarged role and influence in the auto workers' union. When reconversion to peacetime production threatened to erase the gains made by women during the war, the Women's Bureau supported a campaign to mobilize resistance to sexually discriminatory layoffs and to extract a pledge from the international leadership that women's right to postwar employment in the auto industry would be respected. After reconversion, the bureau strove to sustain and nurture the activism that had first developed among female auto unionists during the war years. At a time of widespread reaction against the independence exhibited by women defense workers, the UAW Women's Bureau served as a beacon to women auto workers, encouraging them to pursue the goal of gender equity that they had adopted during the war and reconversion periods.

The actions and achievements of the UAW Women's Bureau from 1945 to 1950 offer a contrast to the standard view of the experience of American women in the 1940s. Noting the massive withdrawal of women from basic industries during reconversion and the postwar revival of the ideology of domesticity, scholars have emphasized the impermanence of the advances made by women workers during World War II. The principle of gender equity in the labor market and the workplace, according to these writers, quickly lost whatever approval it had gained during the war and remained out of favor until the feminist movement revived it in the 1960s. Recent work has begun to explore the years

1. Katherine Lowrie to Frieda Miller, 13 March 1946, U.S. Women's Bureau Papers, RG 86, box 1416, Lowrie folder, National Archives; Mildred Jeffrey interview, 52, in "The Twentieth-Century Trade Union Woman: Vehicle for Social Change," Oral History Project, Institute of Labor and Industrial Relations, University of Michigan, Ann Arbor (hereafter cited as TUW Oral History); UAW *Fair Practices Fact Sheet* 2 (March–April 1948): 2.

2. R. J. Thomas to all Regional Directors and Local Union Presidents, 22 April 1944, War Policy Division—Women's Bureau Collection, box 5, folder 10, Walter P. Reuther Library, Archives of Labor and Urban Affairs, Wayne State University, Detroit (hereafter cited as ALUA); Gladys Dickason, "Women in Labor Unions," *Annals of the American Academy of Political and Social Science* 251 (May 1947): 72.

between 1945 and 1960, revealing the survival and vitality of feminist goals and purposes. Although these studies have modified our understanding of the postwar era, they overlook the trade union as an arena for female activism. The UAW Women's Bureau sought with some success to sustain the momentum of the war years and the reconversion period despite the postwar consensus on woman's place. By integrating issues of concern to women into the union's agenda and establishing a presence for women in the union leadership and international hierarchy, the bureau counteracted the devastating impact of reconversion and ensured the survival of gender-conscious protest.[3]

The establishment of the Women's Bureau indicated the extent to which World War II had changed gender relations within the UAW. The massive influx of women into auto plants made male UAW leaders more attentive than they had been before the war to the concerns of female workers. The UAW's advocacy of child care facilities, maternity leave provisions in contracts, and union counseling programs encouraged women to regard the union favorably. Taking advantage of wartime circumstances, women leaders, whose numbers also increased during these years, pressed the UAW to fulfill its role as ally and assist them in challenging sexually discriminatory employment practices as well. Male unionists on the whole were less receptive to demands for equal pay for comparable work, equal seniority regardless of sex, and job classifications based on the content of the operation rather than the sex of the operator; but women leaders, acting in their capacity as local officers, accomplished some of their collective bargaining goals late in the war.[4]

3. Published studies of women workers during and after World War II include Karen Anderson, *Wartime Women* (Westport, Conn., 1981); D'Ann Campbell, *Women at War with America* (Cambridge, Mass., 1984), 101–61; William Chafe, *The American Woman* (London, 1972), 135–95; Alan Clive, "Women Workers in World War II: Michigan as a Test Case," *Labor History* 20 (Winter 1979): 44–72; Susan Hartmann, *The Home Front and Beyond* (Boston, 1982), 53–99; Ruth Milkman, "Redefining 'Women's Work': The Sexual Division of Labor in the Auto Industry during World War II," *Feminist Studies* 8 (Summer 1982): 337–72; Karen Beck Skold, "The Job He Left Behind: American Women in the Shipyards during World War II," in *Women, War, and Revolution*, ed. Carol Berkin and Clara Lovett (New York, 1980), 55–75. New explorations of women in the late 1940s and 1950s include Hartmann, *Home Front and Beyond*, 143–61; Alice Kessler-Harris, *Out to Work; A History of Wage-Earning Women in the United States* (New York, 1982), 300–311; Leila Rupp, "The Survival of American Feminism: The Women's Movement in the Postwar Period," in *Reshaping America*, ed. Robert Bremner and Gary Reichard (Columbus, O., 1982), 33–65.

4. For a more detailed treatment of women and the UAW during World War II, see Nancy Gabin, "Women Auto Workers and the United Automobile Workers' Union (UAW-CIO), 1935–1955" (Ph.D. diss., University of Michigan, 1984), 56–120.

Organized just as the demobilization of the female labor force began, the Women's Bureau soon was at the center of a controversy over
women's rights, union responsibilities, and managerial prerogatives.
Although many women withdrew from the labor force voluntarily,
those who wanted to keep their better-paid jobs in the auto industry
after the war suffered harassment at work, discrimination in layoffs
and recalls, and violation of the rights guaranteed them in collective
bargaining agreements. The Women's Bureau worked in conjunction
with activist women in the locals to protest the treatment being accorded female auto workers. From the fall of 1944 through the summer of 1946, these women pursued all opportunities to register their
protest: they urged other women to contest unfair practices, held in-
formational meetings and conferences, formed women's committees in
locals where there were none, filed grievances and appeals, organized
picket lines outside plant employment offices, and pressured the UAW
leadership to defend the hard-won principle of seniority and safeguard
women's right to exercise seniority in transfers, layoffs, and recalls.
Despite these efforts, most women did not gain access to postwar jobs
in the auto industry. In June 1946, just as the auto industry was beginning its tremendous postwar expansion, the number of women employed in production had fallen from a wartime peak of 208,000 to
60,800, and their share of the auto labor force stood only 2 percentage
points higher than the figure for 1939.[5]
Although several factors help to explain the meager results of the
women's protest movement, the principal cause was the absence of any
fundamental change during the war in the structure and organization
of work in the auto industry. The sexual division of labor, codified in
sex-based job classifications, wage rates, and seniority agreements, historically had confined women to a small number of lower-paid jobs in
auto plants. The successful integration of women into "men's" jobs
during World War II had the potential to widen women's access to
employment. Neither employers nor male unionists, however, wanted
wartime exigencies to alter permanently the sexual composition of the
auto labor force. Early in the war period, before the great influx of
women into the plants, both sides negotiated for the preservation and
extension of the sexual division of labor so that women would hold
"male" jobs only for the duration of the war.[6] The challenge to these

---

5. Nancy Gabin, "'They Have Placed a Penalty on Womanhood': The Protest Actions
of Women Auto Workers in Detroit-Area UAW Locals, 1945–1947," *Feminist Studies* 8
(Summer 1982): 373–98; U.S. Bureau of Labor Statistics, *Handbook of Labor Statistics,
1947* (Washington, D.C., 1948), 18.
6. Milkman, "Redefining 'Women's Work.'"

arrangements which some activist women initiated before the end of the war was simply too little, too late. Only a massive and sustained upheaval in the sexual division of labor could have ensured job opportunities for senior women workers. UAW men might have been willing to defend women's right to exercise seniority in transfers, layoffs, and recalls, but they were not interested in undertaking the larger fight. Numerically and politically weak, women alone could not effect a transformation in the sexual division of labor in auto plants.

Despite its inability to prevent the restoration of prewar patterns of occupational segregation by sex, the Women's Bureau did have a certain degree of success during the reconversion period. First, the campaign against sexual discrimination in layoffs and recalls consolidated the informal and loosely organized network of local women activists which had developed during the war. Mildred Jeffrey, director of the bureau from its inception until 1948, claims that the mobilization of the women's network was one of its most important accomplishments, both because it increased the visibility of women in the UAW and because it provided a resource for collective action after reconversion.[7]

Second, women leaders gained from the reconversion experience a clearer understanding of the arbitrary and discriminatory character of the sexual division of labor. Lillian Hatcher, assistant director of the Women's Bureau in the 1940s, remembers that "we began to look a little differently at the whole question of equal job rights for women . . . when the . . . layoffs and recalls came and there were all sorts of innuendos about not calling back women because allegedly there weren't any jobs open that they could perform." According to Hatcher, women leaders realized that "to say that she wanted to be classified forever as a female worker was hurting the working woman . . . because there were many jobs that were tagged male occupations that women could perform as well as any other person."[8]

A resolution adopted by the delegates to the 1946 convention was another achievement for the Women's Bureau and other female activists within the union. It sought to codify the wartime gains made by women and to incorporate the lessons of reconversion into union policy and practice. Urging the UAW to fulfill the democratic promise of industrial unionism and defend the right of the female membership to equal treatment and equal opportunity in the auto industry, the women asked the union to reaffirm its position against such employment practices as unequal pay for equal work and sexually discriminatory

7. Author's interview with Mildred Jeffrey, 1 August 1983.
8. Lillian Hatcher interview, 83, TUW Oral History.

layoffs, recalls, and discharges. The resolution went further, instructing the UAW to expand its definition of discrimination based on sex
and publicly declare its opposition to the inclusion in contracts of separate seniority lists for women and men. Finally, the resolution reme-
died a major weakness in the UAW's approach to the problem of sex
discrimination by making the International Executive Board (IEB) responsible for the implementation of the agreed-upon policies rather
than leaving it wholly to the discretion of local union officers.[9]

In June 1946 the IEB granted the Women's Bureau, which had
been in limbo since the dissolution of the War Policy Division, permanent status by incorporating it into the newly established Fair Practices
and Anti-Discrimination Department. William Oliver, codirector of the
department, explained that although the unit was principally concerned with the employment problems of black workers, it would give
"special emphasis . . . [to] women's problems in the automobile industry since it is unquestionably the largest single minority group within
the jurisdiction of the UAW-CIO."[10] The action by the IEB indicated
the extent to which the war and reconversion had altered both gender
relations and the role and status of women within the UAW. Before
1942, women were a marginal presence not only in the plants but in the
union as well. By according women the status of a minority group, the
UAW acknowledged the existence of discrimination based on sex in the
auto industry and provided women with a legitimate platform for extending their gains. The consolidation of the women's network, the
introduction of a critique of the sexual division of labor, the codifica-
tion of antidiscrimination policies, and the institutionalization of an
advocate of women's rights offset the losses sustained by women during
the reconversion period.

In a report to the IEB in December 1946, the Women's Bureau
assessed the progress made by the union toward the elimination of
sexual discrimination in the auto industry. The presence of 63,900
women in the plants, the greater extent of equal wage rates, and the
preservation of the bureau itself offered "proof of a job well done."
The report noted, however, that there were "many problems to be
licked." Citing the persistence in some contracts of dual seniority lists
and sex-differentiated wage scales, the absence of provisions for mater-

9. *1946 UAW Convention Proceedings* (Detroit, 1946), 328–29.
10. Second Quarterly Report of the Fair Practices and Anti-Discrimination Department, 1946, UAW Fair Practices and Anti-Discrimination Department—Women's Bureau Collection, box 2, folder 17, ALUA.

nity leaves, and the limited availability of upgrading and promotional opportunities for women, the bureau criticized the "laxness" of union officials in eliminating discrimination from collective bargaining agreements and in enforcing those contract clauses that protected women's right to fair and equal treatment.[11]

The Women's Bureau stated the problem more forcefully in an April 1947 report on the status of women foundry workers in the auto industry: "No one but a blind fool would believe that in the UAW-CIO prejudice against women working, against equal pay, against women holding the same or comparable jobs as men, against women's participation on an equal basis with men in the local union has been eliminated." Emphasizing the importance of educating male unionists "as to the rights of women to work and hold a job," the report observed that the bureau "*alone cannot solve all of these problems. It will take the united support and mobilization of all forces within our union to change the one factor which is most difficult—the question of changing human nature.*"[12]

The Women's Bureau, however, was not sanguine about the prospects for a thoroughgoing postwar challenge to sexual discrimination by union men. Its own limited resources and power attested to the general indifference of the still male-dominated and male-oriented UAW to the principle of sexual equality. The bureau was composed of just two people in this period—Jeffrey was the director until Caroline Davis replaced her in 1948, and Hatcher served as assistant director—and lacked the power to implement or enforce the UAW's official antidiscriminatory policies; it had to rely on the powerful regional directors to effect change at the local level. With just a few exceptions, the attitude of these men toward the efforts of women unionists to be treated equally with men ranged from a lack of interest to disapprobation. Raymond Berndt, director of Region 3 (Indiana), indicated his understanding of the role of women in the UAW in his opening remarks to a regional women's conference. Explaining that local UAW offices and halls "should be dressed up to the point where we are in a position to invite all civic leaders . . . [in] for discussion," Berndt informed the women that it was their special responsibility to clean up the premises. Other regional directors were hostile rather than conde-

---

11. Fair Practices Department Report, 10 December 1946, 17–19.
12. "Conditions Affecting the Equal Status of Women Foundry Workers," n.d. [April 1947], 3, 15, Walter P. Reuther Collection, box 21, Fair Practices Department 1946–47 folder, ALUA.

scending toward women, approving contracts that contained sexually discriminatory clauses and obstructing appeal procedures.[13]

The antagonistic relationship between the Women's Bureau and several regional directors reflected the undercurrent of tension in regard to gender relations within the UAW in the postwar period. To a certain extent the directors' criticism of the bureau's activities stemmed from an ongoing struggle within the union over spheres of authority rather than a limited commitment to sexual equality. Concerned to remain free of interference by international headquarters in Detroit, regional directors tended to regard the Women's Bureau staff, which was appointed by Walter Reuther, with suspicion; they protested as a matter of principle when the bureau bypassed the chain of command and dealt directly with a local union. Jeffrey recalls that Richard Gosser, director of Region 2B (Toledo), often complained to Reuther that she had "jumped over the fence." The defense of prerogatives by regional directors, however, also concealed an aversion to conflict and controversy and a fear of exposure. Dorothy Haener, who became active on behalf of women during reconversion, is more cynical about the motives of regional directors, claiming "there was really a reluctance . . . on the part of the regions always, to have us come in and get involved in what they called 'the woman's problem' because they really felt that we tended to incite people."[14]

The Women's Bureau decided that the initiative for preserving and extending earlier gains lay with women themselves. Its limited powers meant that the elimination of the disparity between policy and practice was to a great extent contingent upon women's own efforts at the local level. The bureau also recognized that unless the female membership evinced interest in obtaining equal rights and opportunities, the international leadership would have little reason to insist that male unionists adhere to union policies. "The best we could do," explains Jeffrey about this period, "was to work with the women, to try and get them activized and militant, very demanding in their own local unions, and as they did that to be supportive of them."[15] Hoping to sustain the momentum of the movement among women in the UAW for equal rights, the Women's Bureau devoted its energy and resources in the

13. Report of Women's Conference, 24 April 1948, Fair Practices Department—Women's Bureau Collection, box 5, folder 3, ALUA; Nancy Gabin, "Women Auto Workers and the UAW-CIO in the Post–World War II Period: 1944–1954," *Labor History* 21 (Winter 1979–80): 5–30.
14. Mildred Jeffrey interview, 63; Dorothy Haener interview, 64, TUW Oral History.
15. Mildred Jeffrey interview, 63.

years from 1947 to 1950 to increasing female participation in the local unions and encouraging women to act individually and collectively in defense of their interests as workers and union members.

As it confronted the task of mobilizing a rank-and-file women's movement, the bureau was encouraged by the efforts of activists in several UAW locals to sustain gender-conscious protest in the aftermath of reconversion. The Local 154 Women's Committee, for example, mounted a successful campaign in 1947 to include an equal-pay-for-equal-work clause in the local's contract with the Hudson Motor Car Company. Enforcing an arbitrary sexual division of labor, Hudson was paying women in jobs classified as "female" 90 cents an hour but paying men in comparable operations classified as "male" an hourly rate of $1.20. Women employed in "men's" jobs were the victims of the most blatant discrimination: they received $1.11 an hour, while their male counterparts received $1.60. To demonstrate support for the principle of equal pay, the women's committee held meetings that were attended by hundreds of female employees. The all-male bargaining committee bowed to pressure and included an equal-pay clause in its list of demands. Although jobs remained separately classified as "male" and "female," the new agreement equalized wage rates for work performed by both sexes.[16]

The action taken by the Local 653 Women's Committee in the winter of 1946–47 to protest the arbitrary dismissal of 150 female employees at the Pontiac Motor Division of General Motors also demonstrated the vitality of feminist principles in the immediate postwar period. The scarcity of male labor in the summer of 1946 forced the company to hire women. Regarding this as a temporary expedient, management fired all the women on the grounds of inefficiency in December, just a few weeks before their probationary period was to expire. Although the women technically were ineligible for union protection, the local—at the urging of Della Rymer, a member of the local executive board, chair of the women's committee, and veteran of the reconversion struggles—filed a grievance on their behalf. When plant

16. The Local 154 Women's Committee also wanted a single seniority list and elimination of sex-based job classifications, but the local bargaining committee did not support these demands. The supplemental agreement drawn up in February 1948 did provide that in the event of a plantwide layoff, male and female occupational groups would be considered interchangeable. See Local 154 Proposed Contract, 29 December 1944; Proposed Agreement between Local 154 and Hudson Motor Car Company, n.d. [July 1947]; and Local 154 Supplemental Agreement, 13 February 1948, all in Norman Matthews Collection, box 14, Local 154 folder, ALUA; Agreement between Local 154 and Hudson, 13 February 1948, Emil Mazy Collection, box 37, folder 3, ALUA; and "Dorothy Scott of Hudson," *Ammunition* 5 (September 1947): 9–11.

management rejected the complaint, the women's committee marshaled support for the discharged women, holding public meetings at the Pontiac YWCA, issuing press releases condemning management's action, and seeking the support of community women's organizations and the Pontiac City Council. The UAW's General Motors Department and Region 1B office submitted an appeal to Ralph Seward, the union–management umpire. Noting that the mass dismissal had not been occasioned by a reduction in force or "any individual misconduct or inefficiency on their part," Seward asserted that the action stemmed solely from the renewed availability of a male labor supply. Seward informed GM that "an employee's sex alone does not constitute good cause for discharge" and ordered the women reinstated. The UAW's Fair Practices Department hailed Seward's decision as "the first real victory toward the elimination of discrimination against women in industry."[17]

The Women's Bureau embarked on a program designed to inspire women in other local unions to imitate the efforts of those in Locals 154 and 653. Regional women's conferences, attended by groups of 50 to 140 women, were a central feature of this program. As an educational device, they alerted women to the character and consequences of sex discrimination and acquainted them with international policies protecting their right to fair and equal treatment. The conferences also offered guidance in filing grievances and appeals, organizing local women's committees, and seeking election to local office. In addition, the conferences served as a forum where women could meet, express concerns, and exchange information. Providing a uniquely supportive environment, they engendered a sense of purpose and solidarity among women in the UAW.[18]

To reach women who did not attend the regional conferences, the Women's Bureau featured articles about women activists in such UAW publications as *Ammunition* and *Fair Practices Fact Sheet*. The women

17. *Detroit News*, 12 February 1947; Fourth Quarterly Report of the Fair Practices Department, 9 June 1947, 10–11, Fair Practices Department—Women's Bureau Collection, box 2, folder 18, ALUA; *Fair Practices Fact Sheet* 1 (March 1947): 4, and 1 (May 1947): 1; "What Happens When 150 Women Are Fired," *Ammunition* 5 (May 1947): 1–4; and Umpire Decision E-81, 19 March 1947, in *GM Umpire Decisions* (Detroit, n.d.).

18. The first regional women's conference was held in Region 2B (Toledo) in December 1945. By 1950 the Women's Bureau was holding women's conferences in all regions of the UAW; in many regions, they were convened on an annual basis. Information about the conferences may be found in Fair Practices Department—Women's Bureau Collection, box 5, folder 3; Fair Practices Department Reports to the IEB; Women's Bureau Reports to the UAW Conventions; and issues of *Fair Practices Fact Sheet*, all in ALUA.

selected for recognition were all active in their local unions, both as elected officers and as volunteers on special interest committees; many were also committed to challenging sexually discriminatory employment practices. Betty Jaskierny, for example, merited attention not only because she was the first woman elected to a top office in Local 490 but also because she was the first officer to have demanded the upgrading of female employees. An article in *Ammunition* similarly praised Dorothy Scott for her role, as fourth vice-president of Local 154, in seeking to win equal pay for women employed at the Hudson plant. By her own account, Dorothy Haener first was inspired to become involved in the union during reconversion when Kaiser-Frazer refused to recall wartime women workers in line with seniority.[19]

Intended to inspire self-confidence as well as admiration, the stories about women activists emphasized not just their exceptional achievements but the traits they shared with all women. The article about Scott, for example, sympathetically described the leader's shyness and reluctance to speak at the Local 154 general assemblies. "Part of my work with the women of the local," Scott explained, "is a struggle with myself." Articles about married women always mentioned how many children they had and lauded their willingness to combine domestic responsibilities with union activities. Camille Gordon, recording secretary and member of the bargaining committee of Local 837, kept house for her husband and five children and also was active in her church and PTA. Gordon's activism, the *Fair Practices Fact Sheet* remarked, "is striking evidence that one can combine motherhood and trade unionism." As the article about Gordon suggests, another purpose of the biographical features was to counter the notion that employment and participation in union affairs were unfeminine pursuits. Stella Ulrich, for example, worked "to provide a fuller life for her children" and was "one of the thousands of women in the auto industry who have successfully combined their activities as mother and trade unionist."[20]

The efforts of the Women's Bureau to promote and cultivate activism among women auto unionists bore results. With the bureau's encouragement, ten female delegates to the 1947 UAW convention drafted a resolution reaffirming the union's commitment "to further women's struggle for equal opportunities in the auto industry" and mandating the convocation of annual women's conferences in all re-

19. *Fair Practices Fact Sheet* 2 (January–February 1948): 2; "Dorothy Scott of Hudson," *Ammunition* 5 (September 1947): 9–11; "How Dorothy Haener Got on the Fair Practices Committee," *Ammunition* 6 (November 1948): 29–31.

20. "Dorothy Scott of Hudson," 11; *Fair Practices Fact Sheet* 3 (March–April 1949): 2, and 3 (May–June 1949): 4.

gions. Since the resolution did not make it to the convention floor for
debate and ratification, it was referred to the IEB for approval. Despite
the support of Emil Mazey, the UAW secretary-treasurer, the resolution was strongly opposed by several regional directors, who, with the
four top officers of the union, constituted the IEB. Speaking for the
opposition, Richard Reisinger initially argued against the resolution
not in principle but in the interest of economy. In subsequent statements, however, the director of Region 2 (Cleveland) revealed that his
opposition reflected an insensitivity to the extent of sexual inequality in
the plants: "Now there are problems, I assume, in some regions," Reisinger remarked, "and some where there aren't." Objecting to the
calling of women's conferences "where they may not be necessary,"
Reisinger added derisively that the resolution would benefit "every
little minority group that wants to have a conference." The resolution
was rejected by the IEB because it lacked the unanimous support of the
board members.[21]

Offended and dismayed by the board's action, women in several
Detroit-area locals organized a regional women's committee to drama-
tize the issue of women's rights within the UAW. The formal an-
nouncement of their organization was, despite their anger, conciliatory
in tone. Established "for the purpose of giving to the women workers . . . a medium through which they may discuss their mutual problems," the Region 1-1A Women's Committee, the group stated, would
seek to resolve those problems "in a manner amicable to the best interests of the trade labor movement." In contrast to Reisinger, the
directors of Regions 1 and 1A offered the women support and cooperation. "We want this committee to have full freedom to plan its own
program," asserted Norman Matthews, codirector of Region 1. "We
want this committee to bring in ideas and suggestions to improve working conditions and the status of women generally both in the union and
in the plant."[22]

In June 1948 the sixteen members of the Region 1-1A Women's
Committee submitted a proposal to the IEB for the establishment of
similar committees in all the regions. Anticipating an unsympathetic

21. *Fair Practices Fact Sheet* 2 (January–February 1948): 8; Minutes of the IEB, 796–
99, UAW IEB Collection (processed), box 10, March 1948 folder, ALUA. The ten
women included Scott, Jaskierny, Rymer, Caroline Davis, Nettie Nielson of Local 247,
Mildred Szur of Local 174, Evelyn Siterlet of Local 684, Eloyse Rivers of Local 365,
Helen Moore of Local 602, and Zita Bowens of Local 195.

22. Second Quarterly Report of the Fair Practices Department, 7 June 1948, 10, Fair
Practices Department—Women's Bureau Collection, box 2, folder 19, ALUA; *Fair Practices Fact Sheet* 2 (March–April 1948): 6.

response, the committee linked the particular problems then being experienced by women auto workers to the general concerns historically shared by all American women. In view of "the progress and achievements women have made since the first Women's Rights Convention in Seneca Falls, New York, in 1848 and acknowledging their present role as citizens, trade unionists, workers and home-makers," the proposal stated, it was incumbent upon the IEB to "recognize the complexities of women workers' responsibilities." The regional women's committees were to serve several purposes. They would enable women leaders to discuss problems and recommend policy to the regional directors, stimulate the participation of rank-and-file women in union activities and political action, channel information on women's problems from the Women's Bureau to the regional offices, and "give increased recognition of the women's contribution to the Union." The IEB not only approved the proposal but subsequently sanctioned the establishment of a National Advisory Council to the Women's Bureau. Composed of representatives of the regional women's committees, the National Advisory Council met annually to hear reports of regional problems and activities, discuss mutual concerns, and evaluate union policy and practice.[23]

The formation of regional women's committees and the establishment of the National Advisory Council gave women increased visibility within the UAW and institutionalized a communication and support network for women unionists. The group of women who had campaigned for changes in UAW policy during the war and spearheaded the movement protesting discriminatory layoffs and recalls after the war did not emerge intact after reconversion, however. The membership lists of the regional women's committees and the National Advisory Council nevertheless indicate the continuity between wartime and postwar female activism in the UAW. Such women as Emma Murphy, Della Rymer, Gwendolyn Thompson, Gertrude Kelly, and Jennie Taylor survived the ravages of reconversion and made valuable contributions to the Women's Bureau as it sought to promote and cultivate collective action among women in the late 1940s.

The network of activists that acquired formal institutional status within the UAW in the period from 1947 to 1950 also included women who had not participated in the wartime campaigns. Dorothy Scott, for example, attended the first national UAW women's conference sponsored by the Women's Bureau in December 1944 as a Local 154 dele-

23. Women's Committee Proposal, n.d., Fair Practices Department—Women's Bureau Collection, box 5, folder 8, ALUA.

gate but did not become actively involved in her local women's committee until 1947. Dorothy Haener attributed her interest in women's
rights to actions taken by Kaiser-Frazer and Local 142 during reconversion. Kaiser-Frazer, which bought the Willow Run, Michigan,
bomber plant from the Ford Motor Company in 1945, refused to
honor an agreement with Local 50 giving hiring preference to former
bomber plant workers. Women's rehire rights were most conspicuously
violated. Women had worked at the Ford plant as drillpress operators,
inspectors, and tool-crib attendants, but Kaiser-Frazer wanted women
for "female" jobs only. Ignoring women's seniority rights, the company
hired men with no history of employment with either Ford or Kaiser-
Frazer for jobs that women were eminently capable of performing; it
restricted women to sewing machine operations and small parts assembly. Haener had worked at the bomber plant and been minimally active
in Local 50 during the war. Hired as a clerk by Kaiser-Frazer in 1946,
she led an organizational drive among the clerks and engineers. After
the group joined Local 142, Haener won election to the local's bargaining committee and, over the objections of men who had supported her
campaign, demanded that Kaiser-Frazer recall former Ford female
employees to "male" jobs. "The men were very angry at me," Haener
recalls. "It was a terribly awakening experience for me. I really believed
all this stuff we preached and believed that everybody was going to do
it." The unwillingness of male unionists to defend the interests of wom-
en workers dismayed Haener but also inspired her to greater activity.[24]

The establishment of the regional women's committees and the
National Advisory Council helped to offset the resistance of the regional directors to the goals and purposes of the Women's Bureau after
reconversion. The all-female bodies provided the office with direct
access to the local unions and a means of circumventing hostile directors. The reinvigoration and expansion of the female leadership network also enhanced the status of the UAW's antidiscriminatory policies, lending additional legitimacy to the bureau's intents and purposes.

24. "Dorothy Scott of Hudson," 9–11; "How Dorothy Haener Got on the Fair Practices Committee," 28–31; *Fair Practices Fact Sheet* 3 (September–October 1949): 2; Dorothy Haener interview, 29–34, 37–38, 46. Of the eleven members of the first Region 1-1A
Women's Committee, seven had participated in wartime campaigns; the other four were
new to the Detroit-area network. Of the thirteen members of the first National Advisory
Council, seven had started their activity during the war and six became active participants after the war. Biographical data have been culled from a variety of sources, including attendance lists of women's conferences, UAW convention delegate rosters, reports
of meetings, articles in UAW publications, local union records, and oral histories.

The evidence of rank-and-file interest in challenging sexual inequality also attested to the influence of the Women's Bureau and the effectiveness of its programs. The bureau received an increasing number of unsolicited complaints of discriminatory employment practices, and several local unions requested the assistance of the bureau during contract negotiations. Having increased the visibility of women and issues of concern to them, the Women's Bureau petitioned Walter Reuther in 1949 to strengthen efforts to put policy into practice and to abolish sex discrimination in auto plants under contract with the UAW. Encouraged by Reuther's offer of support and cooperation, the bureau inaugurated a campaign to extend equal rights and opportunity to all women in the auto industry and the UAW. Reflecting on the history of women in the UAW, Lillian Hatcher identifies the early 1950s as the time "when we were really down to [the] serious business of eliminating discrimination as it might have been directed in contracts."[25]

Despite the successes of the late 1940s and the optimism of the Women's Bureau in 1950, the principle of gender equity made little headway during the 1950s. The ad hoc victories and individual or local advances were important, but the separate and unequal status of women in the automobile industry remained essentially unchanged during the first postwar decade. Nor did women gain greater access to power within the UAW in the 1950s. With the exception of a few departments devoted to out-of-plant matters and community service activities, all international and regional union offices were directed by men, and women did not sit on the IEB until the 1960s. Women also were denied participation in collective bargaining above the local level.[26]

The limited progress made by women after 1950 raises questions about the efficacy of the strategies adopted by the Women's Bureau. Gender-specific organizing clearly was effective in mobilizing women auto unionists and promoting female collective action. In such male-dominated environments as the auto industry and the UAW, women's groups and conferences at the local and regional levels protected women from male criticism and gave them the confidence to assert themselves. The very existence of the Women's Bureau within the interna-

25. Lillian Hatcher to William Oliver and Caroline Davis, 28 April 1949, box 5, folder 8; Oliver to Walter Reuther, 26 May 1949, box 6, folder 8, both in Fair Practices Department—Women's Bureau Collection, ALUA; Lillian Hatcher interview, 32. Information regarding complaints and requests received by the Women's Bureau in the late 1940s is found in the Fair Practice Department reports to the IEB and the bureau's reports to the UAW convention.

26. Nancy Gabin, "Women and the United Automobile Workers' Union in the 1950s," in *Women, Work and Protest*, ed. Ruth Milkman (Boston, 1985), 259–79.

tional hierarchy also conveyed the idea that women's rights were a legitimate issue. The slow pace of change after 1950, however, suggests that gender-specific organizations may have posed an obstacle to the achievement of sexual equality. The UAW leadership, for example, tended to use the Women's Bureau, the National Advisory Council, and the regional women's committees as window dressing rather than to fulfill the union's rhetorical commitment to gender equity. Instead of seeking to minimize that problem, the bureau unwittingly exacerbated it. Jeffrey, Davis, and Hatcher may have been too obsequious with international leaders, especially with those who, like Walter Reuther and Emil Mazey, were supportive of efforts to promote female activism and advance the principle of gender equity but were willing to sacrifice these ends in the interests of the male majority.[27] The Women's Bureau, moreover, relied on bureaucratic solutions to problems that also required local agitation, education, and organization. Its limited resources and the importance of female institution-building make understandable the bureau's emphasis after World War II on establishing the regional women's committees and the National Advisory Council, but more direct means of mobilizing rank-and-file women might well have undermined the IEB's self-defensive posture.

These criticisms do not discredit the efforts and achievements of the UAW Women's Bureau in the immediate postwar period. The withdrawal of women from auto plants during reconversion and the preoccupation of male union leaders with defending wartime gains, fighting antilabor legislation, and resolving internal conflicts made it unlikely that any attention would have been paid to women's issues in the late 1940s without the perseverance of the Women's Bureau. Its accomplishments also made the UAW's relations with women better than those of most other unions in the years following World War II. Although the disparity between policy and practice frustrated women auto unionists, the UAW's official commitment to gender equity offered them a legitimate platform for contesting discrimination by employers and unionists alike. The regional women's committees, the National Advisory Council, and the bureau itself, moreover, gave UAW women a presence and an opportunity that women in other unions lacked.[28] Despite the conservative ideological climate of the postwar

27. Gabin, "Women Auto Workers," 199–200.

28. Although attention has been paid to women and organized labor during World War II and reconversion, little work has been done on the subject for the late 1940s and the 1950s. The few extant studies indicate that with the exception of the UAW and the United Electrical Workers, the principle of sexual equality was not advanced by unions in this period. See Philip Foner, *Women and the American Labor Movement from World War I to*

years, the Women's Bureau managed to sustain the momentum of the war years and ensure the survival within the UAW of gender-conscious protest.

_____

the Present (New York, 1980), 394–416; Hartmann, *Home Front and Beyond,* 64–70; Melissa Hield, " 'Union Minded': Women in the Texas ILGWU, 1933–1950," *Frontiers* 4 (Summer 1979): 59–70; Ruth Milkman, "The Reproduction of Job Segregation by Sex: A Study of the Changing Sexual Division of Labor in the Auto and Electrical Manufacturing Industries in the 1940s" (Ph.D. diss., University of California, Berkeley, 1981), 317–32.

15

Amber Waves of Gain: Women's Work in New York Farm Families

Sarah Elbert

Signing her works "A Farmer's Wife," Marietta Holley used an upstate New York rural dialect and local color to popularize "wimmen rites" in the 1880s and 1890s.[1] Her heroine, Samantha, expostulated on the contrast between a farmer's day and his wife's endless round of chores:

> Now when a man ploughs a field, or runs up a line of figgers, or writes a serming, or kills a beef critter, there it is done—no more to be done over. But sposen a woman washes up her dishes clean as a fiddle, no sooner does she wash 'em up once, than she has to, right over and over agin, three times three hundred and 65 times every year. And the same with the rest of her work, blackin' stoves, and fillin' lamps, and washin' and moppin' floors. and the same with cookin'. Why jest the idee of paradin' out the table and teakettle 3 times 3 hundred and 65 times

I gratefully acknowledge the help of Doug Reynolds—who provided the title of this essay—and the advice and support of Gould Colman, Joan Jensen, Cornelia B. Flora, Sue Armitage, Corlann Bush, and Bob Green.

1. Marietta Holley wrote twenty novels featuring Samantha between 1873 and 1914. Among the best known were *My Opinion and Betsey Bobbett's* and *Samantha on the Woman Question*. The passages quoted here are reprinted in W. Elliot Brownlee and Mary M. Brownlee, *Women in the American Economy* (New Haven, Conn., 1976), 113–15. See also Jane Curry, ed., *Samantha Rastles the Woman Question: The Humor of Marietta Holley* (Minneapolis, Minn., 1983).

every year is enough to make a woman sweat. And then to think of all the cookin' utensils and ingredients—why if it wuzzn't for principle, no woman could stand the idee, let alone the labor, for it haint so much the mussle she has to lay out, as the strain on her mind.[2]

Her friend Betsey Bobbett, a spinster, tried to present the notion of "woman's highest speah" as some compensation to Samantha. Woman's job, she said, was to "soothe lacerations, to be a sort of poultice to the noble manly breast when it's torn with the cares of life."[3]

Social scientists since the turn of the century have continued to discuss farm women more or less in terms of the debate between Samantha and Betsey. A great flow of literature documents the changing tasks of farm women, enumerating them and clocking the hours women spent on household work and farm work. Policy makers, reformers, and organized farm women themselves have sought a variety of means to upgrade the living standard of farm households, and thereby to reduce the backbreaking labor, loneliness, and drudgery of American farm women.[4]

The family farms that survive today have to a great extent the same domestic comforts as urban households of comparable class and region. Social Darwinists argue that the contemporary farm woman's education, home appliances, and familiarity with the latest social trends testify to the survival of the fittest farming families. From 1960 to 1970 alone, the farm population shrank from 15.6 million to 8 million. The hardy survivors made it, if the prescriptive literature was correct, partly because the gender division of labor on farms became more like that of urban households. Farm wives supported the management decisions of their husbands, properly raised children to follow their fathers' lead, and themselves benefited from the resulting efficiency. Or, to put it another way, those farms that could do so became capital-intensive survivors and thus produced more with less labor; farm income rose, and farm wives realized their "highest speah."

Something nevertheless remains puzzling about this comfortable, progressive explanation. The survival of the family farm seems anachronistic in a system dominated by large-scale corporate production.

---

2. Brownlee and Brownlee, *Women,* 113–14.

3. Brownlee and Brownlee, *Women,* 113–14.

4. Recent summaries and reviews of this literature include Polly A. Fassinger and Harry K. Schwarzweller, "The Work of Farm Women: A Midwestern Study," in *Research in Rural Sociology and Development,* ed. Harry K. Schwarzweller (Greenwich, Conn., 1984), 2:37–60; and Peggy J. Ross, "A Commentary on Research on American Farm Women," in *Agriculture and Human Values* 2 (Winter 1985): 19–30.

This essay briefly reviews the literature on gender relations in American family farming and then focuses on the changing relationships of work and family in twentieth-century American agriculture. Two case studies are drawn from a panel of twenty farming families in upstate New York who were interviewed regularly from 1967 through 1982 to illustrate the contemporary coordination and control of family labor on the farms.[5] Some explanation for the persistence of family farming within a large-scale corporate system lies, I believe, in the unique relationship between the character of agricultural production and the gender hierarchy of farm households.

Farming families are not, of course, homogeneous units; they vary in commodity production, acreage, sales, and region as well as in ethnicity, life-cycle stages, educational background, and the like. The former attributes are usually referred to as "structural" aspects of family farms, the latter as "personal" aspects of farming families. Moreover, we need to look at "his" farm and "hers." From the colonial period to the present, men and women on farms have reported different things about their joint enterprises, and they have reported the same things in different ways. Regardless of the size of the operation, however, most contemporary farming families report that women perform an average of 25 percent of the total (couple's) hours of farm work in addition to about 70 percent of the household work.[6] Needless to say, men's farm work is concentrated in a consistent pattern of "male" tasks, and their housework hours are spent not in endless daily rituals but in sporadic tasks, such as plumbing repairs and carpentry. Farm couples' involvement in household labor is more gender-segregated than their division of farm labor. At least since the mid-nineteenth century this appears to have been a general pattern on America's family farms. Women cross over more frequently; they perform, when necessary, a number of "male" farm chores and play a great variety of roles on the farm, in the home, and in off-farm work. The *multiple* work roles of farm women partially explain their "invisibility" as farmers.[7]

As Carolyn Sachs points out, farm women's "invisible" contribution

5. Cornell University Farm Family Documentation Project. The final collection of tape-recorded interviews, 591 typed and indexed transcripts of interviews, farm and financial statements, and all correspondence between researchers and farming families constitute a permanent documentary collection housed in the Department of Manuscripts and University Archives, Olin Library, Cornell University. For a more detailed summary of the study by two frequent interviewers, see Gould Colman and Sarah Elbert, "Farming Families: The Farm Needs Everyone," in Schwarzweller, *Research in Rural Sociology and Development*, vol. 1. I thank JAI Press for permission to reprint materials from this study. The same authors are at work on a book about farming families.

6. Fassinger and Schwarzweller, "Work of Farm Women."

7. Fassinger and Schwarzweller, "Work of Farm Women."

to farm production and their primary responsibility for the reproduction of households have helped some family farms to survive the increasing domination of agribusiness.[8] To keep women on the farm today, I will argue, farm ownership and off-farm work, as well as farm and household tasks, will have to be more egalitarian. Farm men and farm women are remarkably persistent across time in articulating two goals: intergenerational transfer, the passing of family farms on from one generation to the next; and improving the net worth of family farms to ensure that transfer. Multinational industries and vertical integration of the agricultural sector do threaten the livelihood of American farming families. On the other hand, women are gaining considerable technical expertise in agricultural colleges; they are more than willing to organize politically; and they have worked successfully for community property and reformed estate tax laws throughout the country. Farm families are smaller than they used to be; farm women's productive years have increased. If family farms become more gender-equal enterprises, farm women may become the only female group who have been able to pass on land, skills, and viable cooperative enterprises to their children.

Family labor on family farms persists in the face of gradually intruding industrial farming for several important reasons. First, farm operations take place sequentially in the course of the production cycle. Only one operation can be performed at a time. As Max J. Pfeffer succinctly puts it, "each of the operations of plowing, harrowing, planting, cultivating, and harvesting cannot be performed until the preceding operation has been completed and the natural processes of crop growth have taken place."[9] There is a gap between the total production time of agricultural commodities and the labor time expended in agricultural production. In industry an owner/manager may employ workers in simultaneous and different stages of production; for example, car engines and car bodies can be produced at the same time in different locations on the factory floor, continuously employing a stable work force on the production line. Farmers, on the other hand, depend on a skilled, stable work force who may be inactive for periods within each production cycle.

In the late nineteenth and early twentieth centuries farmers had regular hired hands and seasonal harvesting crews. Farm women, assisted by female kin, neighboring women, and hired "girls," fed the

8. Carolyn Sachs, *Invisible Farmers: Women in Agricultural Production* (Totowa, N.J., 1983), and "Women's Work in the U.S.: Variations by Region," *Agriculture and Human Values* 2 (1985): 31–39.

9. Max J. Pfeffer, "Industrial Farming," *Democracy* 3 (Spring 1983): 37–49.

production workers. And, as Corlann Bush points out in this volume, farm women raised their own produce and canned and stored the food that fed their families and the hired workers. Year-round workers were necessary to care for draft animals used in production and to help in raising feed for those animals. Most of that scene has disappeared, displaced by the expensive machinery, fuel, herbicides, pesticides, and commercial hybrid seeds (inputs) needed to ensure high production. The debt-to-asset ratio has become a vital concern on all farms but particularly for young farm families who do not have much equity. Ordinarily, farm income cannot quite cover principal and interest payments in the early years of a farm loan. Young farm wives at the early stage of their family cycle find themselves also involved in the early stages of the farm firm; they are responsible for a variety of farm chores and often do off-farm work as well to help pay loans and meet current household expenses.

If a farm prospers, it may well move through stages of business development, each with its clearly defined mode of labor control. Richard Edwards, in *Contested Terrain: The Transformation of the Workplace in the Twentieth Century,* identifies an industrial model of modes of control and coordination of the labor process as firms develop.[10] Even though its sequential production makes agriculture different from the industrial assembly line, the modes of labor control and coordination at various stages of a farm enterprise's development are strikingly similar to those Edwards describes. He posits that "simple control" is usually exercised by a single entrepreneur, often with the help of foremen or managers. The boss wields power personally, often sets the pace himself, hires and fires, and uses "incentives and sanctions in an idiosyncratic unsystematic mix." As tendencies toward concentration of economic resources increase, the scale of production enlarges, and production becomes more complex and specialized. "Simple control" is then deemed less effective, and more formal "structural systems" of control are devised by large firms. These systems can be "technical," when control is built into the physical structure of the labor process (assembly line), or "bureaucratic," when the control rests in a hierarchical impersonal social structure ("company policy") marked by precise titles and job descriptions.

If a farm succeeds economically, it generally does so as a result of an increase in the scale of operations and often of a shift from simple control to bureaucratic, technical, or even corporate control. In such

---

10. Richard Edwards, *Contested Terrain: The Transformation of the Workplace in the Twentieth Century* (New York, 1979).

cases it is not only machines that displace wives and children from their places in a primary, labor-intensive stage of farm operation but new forms of labor control and coordination that the owner-operator deems appropriate to an expanded operation. A farmer may assert that the farm does not "require" the services—and, incidentally, the challenging authority—of a farm wife at her mature life-cycle stage, when she may be newly freed from child care responsibilities. Grown children may find that they can no longer confront their father directly. Their demands can be rejected by impersonal arguments and even by hired technicians, managers, or a "system" that rules out the participation of people who lack "formal education" or the personality qualifications deemed appropriate for farm management. An owner may find an impersonal mechanism useful at any time, but reliance on it is an especially striking manifestation at the expanded bureaucratic or corporate stage of farming, when it coincides with a new stage in the family's life cycle.

It is important to remember that farm family members feel themselves to be a permanent unit bound by ties of affection and kinship; they often submit to a high degree of control during peak production without threatening strikes or slowdowns. Farming is complicated by the vagaries of the weather and the risks associated with both crop production and the maintenance of healthy, high-producing dairy herds, poultry flocks, and so on. Farm workers, when they are family members, accept the fact that they must be available at odd hours, during inclement weather, and especially at planting and harvesting seasons. While children are growing up, they frequently hope to remain attached to the family farm as adults. Household and workplace are not separate, and interdependence is a key factor in labor coordination during the early stages of the farm enterprise. Whether it remains so, and under what circumstances, is problematic, as the following case studies indicate.

The consciousness of commitment to the farm and identification with the rural "way of life" on the part of family members was best described by one farm wife, Meg Lewis, in an early interview when she happily observed that "the farm needs everyone."[11]

Meg and Ted Lewis were both born during the Depression and grew up on family farms in the same upstate New York county. Ted, seven years older than Meg, knew her brother in high school; they

---

11. The following case studies are drawn from the Cornell University Farm Family Documentation Project. All names, places, and some details have been altered to ensure the privacy of respondents.

were friendly rivals in 4-H cattle judging. Meg was a tomboy, by her own account, tagging after her brother and happiest driving the family's team of horses. One old snapshot shows brother and sister hosing down the brand-new tractor that replaced their team when Meg reached her teens. The next family album pictures show her in a trim suit and pumps, her shining hair newly styled in a "feather cut." Soon Ted Lewis appears alongside Meg; they were married when she was just eighteen. As the only son of a general farmer, Ted reasonably expected to succeed his father. Meg assumed, correctly, that her family's farm would go to her brother.

The elder Lewis, however, was in no hurry to pass on the four-generation home farm to the young couple. They lived with Ted's aunt nearby for a year while he worked as his father's hired man. Meg, having taken the high school's business course, went to work in the office of a nearby Sears store. Their earnings bought a small farm about thirty miles from Ted's homeplace. With a mortgage, marginal land, and dairy cows accumulated during Ted's 4-H years, they set out to convert their labor power into capital. Within the next three years, with the help of Meg's father, they rebuilt their old house and outbuildings and were able to sell out at a profit.

The next step was to buy a hilltop farm within sight of Ted's old home, where they could use some of his father's machinery and trade their labor. He knew the land and the neighbors; and Meg, now with two small sons in tow, had a ready-made babysitter in her mother-in-law. Ted's mother helped with the children, got her daughter-in-law a sewing machine, and made it clear that supporting one's husband in his work was the goal of a good farm wife. Meg worked alongside her husband to build their new house, remodel the barn, and improve crop production. They did not borrow money to build their home but saved their credit to be used for farm improvements that would make money. Twenty years later, when Ted's father died, the homeplace acres were added to the hilltop farm holdings.

Meg became the expert on calves and herd bloodlines. For the next twenty years she was the first one up in the morning, checking the stock and returning to wake her husband and children for breakfast, which she prepared. Each morning she fed calves and helped milk cows, cleaned the milkhouse, dumped milk from milking pails to cans, brought in the "house milk," and then worked on farm records and bookkeeping in the afternoon. Somehow she also managed to do all the housework and laundry, cook, can, and sew clothes for herself and her daughter, Linda, born four years after the second son. Each evening Meg was back in the barns to feed "her" calves, help with the milking, and shake down hay for the cows. This, of course, was only the winter routine; in spring and summer she "drove tractor," too, and helped bring in 1,500 bales of hay. Consistently she trained the children in farm chores, coordinating their labor and her own with the tasks and the pace Ted set.

Meg affectionately described Ted as the "boss" when he came into the kitchen (as she was finishing the decorations on his birthday cake) and announced that the hay was ready. She said, "I don't pay attention to the hay. He comes in and says it's ready, he says which field I'm to go to, and I go. He tells me how it's been raked and so I know how to bale it. And it was exactly nine when I set foot in the house again. I usually don't bale beyond seven, but that was the last of the hay and it looked like rain, so I just stuck right with it." She was proud of being able to fulfill the norms he set and proud also that he "talked everything over," by which she meant that he used her as a sounding board. Ted made no decisions about culling the herd without her, admitting that she knew the cows better than he did. He also made equipment purchases with an eye to what she felt comfortable using. Meg kept the books and records according to her own system. She also did the income tax each year and constantly read farm journals, clipping advice for Ted.

Child rearing was Meg's domain, too. In addition to riding herd on the boys to do chores as their father wished, she made sure that Linda filled in on housekeeping and cooking when her mother's labor was needed at farm chores. Above all, Meg's time and labor were at her husband's disposal; her authority over the children was unquestioned as long as she was his adjutant.

The family's hierarchy and process became more evident as the children grew up and intergenerational transfer loomed. By the time the older boy was seventeen, his father clearly favored him as the next farmer; both parents, but his father in particular, pressured him to come home directly after school for farm chores. He had some interest in after-school sports and clubs, but such activities were clearly put in second place. During summer work—spraying herbicide, plowing, and milking—he was given more responsibility until it was clear that his chores involved commitment to the farm operation at large. His younger brother seemed to sense that his own chores were just chores; he did not accumulate heifers of his own, and he spoke about becoming a veterinarian. He also became a star wrestler on the high school team; after some 400 matches by the end of his senior year, he reported that his parents had attended only one. Linda assembled milking units and shook down hay after school, but her parents were far more lenient in granting her hours away from the farm than they were with her brothers.

The dairy operation simply could not support three more farmers; Doug, the elder son, would replace his father, and a way would have to be found for the farm to support Meg and Ted's retirement too. Ted, counting on his family labor force, tried vegetables and then put in acres of berries, hoping to diversify and so make room and income for everyone. But he found himself strung out, falling behind in one set of operations or another. The children, after all, had school responsibilities, and often the crop that fed the cows had to take precedence over practices that were vital to establishing fruit crops. The dairy operation, Ted knew, was the family's stable income. Meg simply could not manage to coordinate children's labor, housework, farm errands, calves, veterinarians, milk dealers, and bookkeeping for dairy *and* vegetable *and* fruit operations.

Meg and Ted expected their children to go to college, but they could not afford tuition for them. The family's cash income was never more than $10,000 a year. They could have borrowed against the farm, but borrowing for such a purpose would have violated twenty years of principle and practice. Loans, based on the operation's net worth, were taken out only to improve production; college loans would have reduced net worth and threatened Ted's ability to borrow for farm improvements. Doug milked night and morning, was paid as a hired man, and did his college homework on Sundays, but he did graduate from an agricultural college nearby. His brother, Bob, was discouraged from leaving home to accept an athletic scholarship because his labor was necessary at home, particularly during the years when Ted was trying to diversify. Meg still assumed that Ted would find a way to keep the entire family on the family farm.

Bob went to a community college, paying his own way but gradually feeling more and more disheartened as it became apparent that there was no real partnership possible for him on the home farm. Finally he left the area, taking a job as a milk inspector; when he married, he found his own way toward veterinary medicine with the help of his working wife. Linda, who also paid her own way through community college, recalled being aware that each child was valued chiefly in terms of his or her relationship to the farm. She said, "When Doug graduated he got a new car, and then Bob graduated and they helped him get a used car; I got a ten-speed bike. I know that in some families all the kids would have gotten the same thing, but not ours." She added later, "Farming's been hard on all of us."

It was hardest of all, perhaps, on her mother. When Ted gave up the vegetable and fruit crops, he had already bought a diesel tractor to make diversified production more efficient. Meg was not consulted or considered in its purchase, and she did not feel comfortable driving it. A chopper was used with the tractor to cut up grass for silage, eliminating much of the hay that Meg used to bale. Then Doug took over many of her dairy operations. At first she was pleased, she said, to have the time to "get my hair done like other women." But then Ted, without any discussion with his wife or with Bob and Linda, transferred the farm from himself to Doug. It was not a partnership but another sole proprietorship. Ted rented the land and buildings to Doug and sold him the herd and machinery, payment to be made with a percentage of the milk check each month. That was when Meg discovered that her name had never been on the farm deed.

Ted had developed a solid community network during his dairy farming years. He was on numerous planning and dairy boards; he was able to get a real estate license and easily sold several unused "brush" lots off his own land. He then branched out to sell hobby farms to suburban young couples while Meg, who still considered herself a farmer's wife, retreated into hurt silence; "They took the farm away from me," she announced later. She wanted to go on with both barn and housework, expecting Doug to follow her advice on the cows and to value her expertise. As an agricultural college graduate, however, Doug quickly found his own priorities and his own advisors in the dairy service people, who could tell him what other successful dairy farmers were doing.

Linda finally got her mother to apply for a secretarial job, and Meg began working part time for the first money of her own she had received in twenty years. She is still working as a secretary. Doug married an agriculture student and pays her a wage for barn and field work. She invests in cows, buying into her husband's herd. They live across the road from Meg and Ted in an apartment attached to the new machinery shed. Doug has been able to expand the herd, and he has a pipeline milker that takes the milk directly from the cows to the refrigerated bulk tank—no more pails to carry and dump. He also has a silage unloader, a luxury he especially values, remembering the years when he and his brother put on boots and four pair of socks to go up into the silo on freezing winter mornings. His improvements are the result of his own hard work and competence; they also reflect the fact that his parents improved their net worth and passed on a local reputation for hard work and efficiency.

Meg likes her new daughter-in-law and strongly supports her demand for pay and equity. She doesn't think the "girl quite measures up as a housekeeper" but admits that "I don't wait on my husband hand and foot any more either. If I'm sitting down and he wants something, he can get up and go to the counter himself." Her daughter and son-in-law have a more egalitarian marriage. They share housework and earning a living. Linda and her husband built their own house and dream of someday having a self-sufficient farm, raising organic produce. In the meantime they both have to go off-farm and earn wages.

Meg and Ted Lewis never got to the "bureaucratic" or "corporate" business stages. The control Ted exercised was "simple"; he worked as hard as or harder than other family members and set the pace as the boss. Ultimately his authority was that of owner-operator, and he felt he had to use it. "Someone had to be boss, and I had the expertise," he said. His wife and children identified not so much with him as with the farm—it, not Ted, needed everyone. The hierarchical control of family labor occurred in a familiar cultural context in which the roles of father and property owner reinforced each other.

It is important to emphasize, however, that the larger structure of agriculture strongly affected the decision-making process of the farming family. The Lewises' hilltop land was not considered productive by agricultural experts, and their herd of thirty-five cows was not large enough to be efficient by agribusiness/agricultural college standards. Nevertheless, the Lewises limed, contour-plowed, and manured their fields, getting an excellent yield with intensive labor and a felt need to improve their resources for generational transfer. Again, by working together and parceling out chores to children as they grew up, Ted Lewis, his wife, and his son knew each cow they milked; they hand-adjusted the feeding mixtures, culled the herd carefully, and produced an unusually low bacteria count and an unusually high protein content in their milk. Since processing plants mix this "good" milk with the less nutritious bulk milk for sales, the Lewis farm enjoyed a good reputation among service people; the driver who picked up their milk drew his own "housemilk" from their load. Their herd had less mastitis and fewer uterine prolapses than the average; both Ted and Doug produced more pounds of milk per man than much larger, more "efficient" operations. Dairy farmers also count on money from the sale of culled cows for beef. The Lewises knew that animals picked up for auction often waited miserably with full udders for several days before they were slaughtered. Ted took their cows in himself to avoid this cruelty. And looking at a Holstein named Glorious, he commented, "That family has been with us from the day we started to farm."

Ted Lewis used what economists call "human capital" to avoid going deeply into debt and to ensure the farm's survival. He bought used equipment, such as a refrigerated milk tank that did not have automatic washing gear, and Meg did not complain about her additional chore of washing it down. His sons unloaded silage by hand, and he and they "drove tractor" from an unheated cab in below-zero weather—a heated tractor cab would have cost another $2,000 to install without raising production or "efficiency." Meg was angry about government price supports, which she felt really benefited larger producers who had gone deeply into debt to manage big herds and bigger bulk production. The price supports bailed out the big equipment, fertilizer, and feed companies, to whom larger farmers were indebted; they benefited neither small, high-quality producers nor consumers. It was a vicious cycle and one that the Lewises deliberately avoided—but at a terrible human price.

Less than two hours' drive from the Lewis farm, the Clavel Brothers Corporation also produces milk on an efficient 300-cow dairy operation. Adam and John Clavel, graduates of a notable agricultural college, stay in close touch with their alma mater's farming experts. They joined their father's 125-acre Castle Rock Farm in the late 1940s. Its excellent land produced diversified crops: milk, chickens, apples, beans, oats, and hay for regional markets. John Clavel, Sr., survived the Depression by fully using his family's labor, as John, Jr., remembered: "He was a driver, he was a worker, yeah, a man with a lot of grit and determination."

Within ten years the brothers prospered enough to buy out their father. Their modern management principles included an avowed intention to "keep the women out,"[12] following the commonly shared belief of agricultural experts that "women are more emotional than men and will tend to disrupt rational decision making if they are partners or corporate voting stockholders."[13] Both sons met their city-raised wives in college. Anne, who became Mrs. John Clavel, Jr., was a registered nurse, fully employed at a large urban hospital, during her

---

12. For studies of the relationship of women's housework, farm work, and off-farm work and decision-making, see Eugene Wilkening, *Farm Husbands and Wives in Wisconsin: Work Roles, Decision Making and Satisfaction, 1962–1979* (Madison, Wis., 1979); and Eugene Wilkening and Denton E. Morrison, "A Comparison of Husband and Wife Responses Concerning Who Makes Farm and Home Decisions," *Marriage and Family Living* 25 (August 1963): 349–51.

13. It should be emphasized that not all male farmers take such advice and that the corporation form of family farming can be chosen with perfectly equitable intentions and results. This essay does not discuss the many such successful operations but chooses instead to concentrate on some of the worst problems in family farming in order to illustrate common tensions and conflicts within households and between household values and goals and the larger agricultural sector in the United States.

husband's wartime naval service. A photo of her, uniformed and smiling, still sits on her husband's neatly organized desk. Adam met Carrie Johnson, a home economics student, at a college dance; they married shortly after her graduation, and Adam began work on the home farm.

Both women accepted their husbands' ownership and labor control. They contributed their time and energy to the farm, explaining their subordination as part of their husbands' recollection of "bad old times" when their mother-in-law aged before her time doing housework and raising her children in a drab home that lagged far behind the barn in modern improvements. Anne romantically remembered her first summer on the farm as a bride: "We lived in the cabin the first summer we were married, which had no running water or electricity, but it was a very, very beautiful place. We went down to the river every night swimming and picnicking, and it was just lovely." The next year the young couple moved into a house on the rented farm next to their homeplace. John worked both places with his father and brother, and by 1948 they were able to buy the rented farm with John's Navy savings and Anne's small inheritance from her father. When their first daughter was born, Anne recalls, "I still didn't know the difference between hay and straw." She learned that her first contribution to farming consisted in "waiting on money" for the restoration of their house, while every bit of her inheritance and John's savings and profits went into land and equipment.

Carrie later chose a contractor-built house with help from plans published in the *Farm Journal.* Its 1950s ranch style features such farm adaptations as a "mud room" between the house and barn, where rows of rubber boots line up beneath tidily hung barn suits, heavy jackets, and caps. In the first decade of her married life, the mud room was also where customers came to buy baskets of freshly picked apples.

Clavel sons and daughters ran errands between the houses and the thirty-cow dairy barn, where Guernseys stood in stanchions—mild red cows, smaller than today's predominant Holstein breed. Carrie remembers them affectionately as personable, handsome animals. In the mid-1950s the small Guernsey herd was replaced with forty Holsteins; then thirty more of the large black-and-white cows were added as both families prospered and saved on household expenses to build up the farm. By the early 1960s the brothers were carefully investigating the new free-stall system of dairy production. They visited other farms, consulted extension agents and college professors, and settled on an industrial plan for their own dairy operation. Anne was crucially involved in the plans because cost accounting, the heralded means of identifying practices that best reduced production costs, required pre-

cise record-keeping, and Anne assumed that duty. The Clavels participated in an experimental accounting service, run by the college, where-
in their farm accounts could be compared with those of other farms in
the project. Anne recorded any farm detail having cost implications:
putting fuel in the tractor, picking up spare parts, treating sick animals.
She paid the bills and managed the flow of cash. She was paid for her
work, and she used the money to "buy out" of cleaning house: considering the housework her responsibility, she paid for cleaning help out
of her earnings. Although she reported only part of her working hours
as the farm's employee, she was in fact on duty twenty-four hours a
day: "If I'm there I take the messages, I go on errands. And if somebody wants something looked up, I find it for them just like that."

Anne and Carrie had large families by current standards; each bore
and raised five children. Living within shouting distance of one another, the two sets of cousins were raised quite differently. Anne was a
strict disciplinarian, proud of her immaculate house and equally proud
of her successful husband. She was his "helper," never even mention-
ing her own financial investment in the farm. Her success was in his
success, and she felt they were a smoothly functioning partnership with
John as chairman and herself as "executive officer." Carrie's household
was a more relaxed one for Adam and their children, largely because
Carrie herself did all the work in it. Her children recall with some
embarassment their mother's willingness to pick up after them and to
tolerate their home decorating schemes for their own rooms. Most of
all she accommodated to their father's grueling daily schedule: up for
4:30 A.M. milking and out again to check the herd before bedtime at
9:30 P.M. The oldest children helped in the barn and orchards and
were paid for their work. But the youngest of Carrie and Adam's
family never ran along the old path between house and barn; in fact, by
the time he came along, the barns were no longer anywhere near the
farmhouse. He did, however, go with Carrie when she worked as a
volunteer with the children of the migrant laborers who picked apples
for the Clavels. Carrie thought migrant pickers were "trying to get
ahead" by leaving their home villages. She took Chris, the youngest
boy, with her so that "he gets the experience along with the other kids.
He's been very sheltered, and it took a little adjusting."

Both Anne and Carrie registered the same gentle complaint about
those years: "lack of time, you know—the men worked such long hours
that we had very little time off to do things as a family." Corporate
farming later brought them real vacations, "a whole month every other
year," at the cost of earlier labor-intensive family farming.

The Clavel farm is now run on a schedule that carefully regulates labor, cows, machinery, and capital. It follows an industrial rhythm that ignores seasons. Unlike the Lewises' cows, which winter in the barns and move to the hilly pastures for the spring and summer, the Clavels' cows are confined in a steady-state 365-day operation. They do not eat baled hay, but rather get their roughage from corn or hay harvested as silage and stored in two giant, vertical silos, 30 feet in diameter and 80 feet high. Cows are assembled in four small herds, each fed a ration adapted to the amount of milk produced.

Huge free-stall barns house the herd; the animals can move freely within the barn, but they never see a pasture. Food is supplied by a motor-driven conveyor; a crowding gate (electrified wire) moves cows to the milking parlor, where a dozen cows can stand in two lines above the milkers' pit and the milking machines. The herdsmen can quickly examine udders and hook and unhook mechanical milking equipment without bending or lifting. Once the animals are drained, they move back into the barn, where large motor-driven fans circulate the air without human labor. The model of factory production is inescapable to the visitor's eye. Indeed, the new barns, situated out of sight of the Clavels' house, reinforce the separation of farm and family. There are separate calf, heifer, and milking-cow barns and procedures; raising heifers, once the work of wives and children on the home farm, is now contracted out to small neighboring farms whose owners simply did not have the capital or the luck to modernize and expand as the Clavels did. Five hundred acres now support a first-rate milking herd of 300 Holsteins.

Only one third-generation Clavel—Adam and Carrie's eldest son, George—has been allowed to join the family corporation, formed ten years ago. He is college trained and served his apprenticeship on a large corporate dairy farm in Arizona. His father and his uncle judged him the most skilled, experienced, and stable of all the children. Anne and Carrie had no voice in the selection of a successor. John, Jr., and George meet with neighboring dairymen regularly at the village diner to agree on a neighborhood price for hired labor. They are a family corporation worth several million dollars.

Adam died of cancer just as George came home to the farm with his wife, Jessie, an English major whom he met in college during the 1960s. Carrie still lives in her *Farm Journal* model house; she is active in church work and travels to see the other children scattered about the country. She believes the Lord has been good to them all and feels grateful that before Adam died they had joined a charismatic evangelical church that reinforced their commitment to the Christian ideal of the husband as head of household. Husband and wife are one, she says, and that one is the husband.

Anne is a good deal less content. John is also active in the evangelical church, and he prays with his group of "Full Gospel Businessmen" for his wife's conversion. But she has become a reader in the local Episcopal church, strongly supports the right of women to become priests, and—having been replaced as farm bookkeeper by a computer accounting firm—has found part-time work off the farm. Anne's bitterness is not easily concealed; her children, she says, have had their farm taken away from them. Living in communities several hours distant from her, they will not work on the home farm without some authority in decision-making, and for their father they would constitute a potential labor problem. He insists that the farm "requires a more streamlined operational system to prosper and provide for everyone."

The orchard was bulldozed long ago because, as Ted Lewis also found out, the coordination of labor required to produce both fruit and milk was too time consuming, and the need for labor in peak periods of production often pitted one enterprise against another. In addition, equipment for one operation had to be tailored or outfitted for the other enterprise. The Clavel brothers felt that permitting family members to get involved with animals or become too "nostalgic" about orchards was simply not good business. They did not, moreover, want to be involved in the "personal" problems of workers' families, which might sometimes lower their efficiency on the job. To the Clavels, hired workers, each responsible for only one part of the total operation, are selling their labor-time; what happens after working hours is not their employers' business. The men who run the milking machines from a pit see only udders as several hundred animals move through the milking parlor. They are hardly concerned with which cows go to slaughter or how long they wait. There is, in this "family" corporate enterprise, a clear distinction between farm and family. The "modernization" process is complete.

American farm families, like many farmer and peasant families all over the world, make choices within the context of the household, and they are influenced by their households' needs and goals as well as by the resources available.[14] Resources consist not only of land, water,

14. Christina H. Gladwin, "A Theory of Real-Life Choices: Applications to Agricultural Decisions," in *Agricultural Decision-Making: Anthropological Contributions to Rural Development*, ed. Peggy F. Bartlett (New York, 1983), 46–47.

credit, and family labor; they also include information and expertise. Farm households, however, are part of a larger industrial capitalist system that plays a crucial role in determining which enterprises survive as family farms and which members of a farming family can stay in the enterprise. Very few American farm families can help all of their children to remain in farming, even though they have fewer children than they used to.[15] Long-term observations of the way family members decide who will remain a farmer and who will volunteer to leave reveals a long-term, subtle, and painful decision-making process. Farming families depend upon a warm sense of mutuality to maintain work discipline and promote generational continuity. Such traits conflict with the emotional distance evidenced by proponents of modernization, who see the decline in the farm population as a manifestation of natural evolution.

Farm women remain "invisible" because their access to resources remains indirect, through husbands and fathers. In 1980 the National Farm Women Survey, commissioned by the Department of Agriculture, conducted telephone interviews with 2,509 women who were identified by the agricultural census as either farm operators or wives of farm operators; while the farms were not necessarily family farms, 88 percent of the women reported that their families owned at least some of the land they farmed.[16] Sixty percent of the farm women identified themselves as wives, mothers, or housewives; 5 percent stated that they were farm wives, and 4 percent listed themselves as farmers or ranchers.[17] Changes in the reporting data will make farm women even harder to find and classify after 1983, because unless they report themselves as farm operators and managers, they will be listed under the category "other farming, forestry and fishing operations."[18] A woman who identifies herself as a farmer or farm operator must list farming as her *principal occupation*, thereby publicly subordinating her work as a homemaker and mother.

Even if a growing awareness of their right to name themselves as farmers should prompt farm wives to claim such status, the common pattern of labor control/coordination linked to sequential production

15. See Ingolf Vogeler, *The Myth of the Family Farm: Agribusiness Dominance of U.S. Agriculture* (Boulder, Colo., 1981); and Ann Foley Scheuring, *Tillers: An Oral History of Family Farms in California* (New York, 1983).

16. Calvin Jones and Rachel Rosenfeld, *American Farm Women: Findings from a National Survey* (Chicago, 1981). A "family farm" uses less than 1.5 (hu)man-years of hired labor (census definition).

17. Jones and Rosenfeld, *American Farm Women*.

18. Kathleen Scholl, "Classification of Women as Farmers: Economic Implications," *Family Economics Review* 4 (October 1983): 8–17.

and family development cycles renders such self-classification unlikely. Changing the prevailing gender pattern, marked by male ownership of farmland in men's productive years and women's ownership of farmland when they are older widows, would depend partly on making housework and child care more gender-equal.[19] Male farmers might then find it difficult to gain and keep their status as the indispensable authorities on their farms.

Some farming families do make room for all the family members who want to be involved in the enterprise; they may, for instance, coordinate on- and off-farm work or manage the production of diverse but compatible commodities. Such fortunate developments depend in large part on the personal and structural characteristics of each enterprise and on larger developments in the system of American agriculture. The evidence supplied by this panel of New York State farming families suggests that more gender-equal families, for the most part, display a pattern of joint ownership in land and enterprise from the beginning of a marital pair's settlement on their farm. The consistent participation of contemporary women in farm work positively affects their decision-making power.[20] Women are more likely, moreover, to farm throughout their productive years when they have equal access to expertise, experience, and credit, and when other family members are willing to share child care and housework. This kind of equitable coordination may well be a key factor in enabling family farms to stay in business and pass their farms on to those younger farmers who want to continue the business and the farming way of life.[21] In the immediate past, farm wives have often contributed their

19. See Carolyn Sachs, "Women's Work in the U.S."; and Cornelia B. Flora, "Women and Agriculture," *Agriculture and Human Values* 2 (1985).

20. Fassinger and Schwarzweller, "Work of Farm Women."

21. Linda Schotsch, "Who Will Farm in Five Years?" *Farm Journal* 109 (March 1985): 13–19, reporting on the recent farm crisis, finds middle-sized farms in the central region and young farmers in particular to be most in danger of going out of business. More off-farm income helps, the article notes, and farm wives are the people most likely to contribute their off-farm income to meet debts and household expenses. Judith Kalbacher, "Women Farm Operators," *Family Economics Review* 4 (1983): 17–22, reports an increase in women actively involved in farm tasks and notes the difficulty in identifying women as farmers because the agricultural census provides information on only one person per farm: namely, the person who does most of the farm work and/or makes most of the managerial decisions; partners and comanagers are not individually identified. More than half the farms operated by women are in the South, Kalbacher notes, for several reasons: women operators tend to be older (over sixty), and there are more minority farmers there; a higher percentage of black farmers and other minorities are women, and they and other older Americans are located disproportionately in the South. Grain and dairy farming are dominated by men, and these farms are not concentrated in the South. Both Schotsch and Kalbacher regard middle-sized farms as those whose

best years to both farm work and household work, only to find their places taken by sons or by hired workers. Their reward in such situations is a mixed blessing: they have played a major part in ensuring their children's future but have done so at the price of displacing themselves when they are still able and vigorous.

---

income from farm products is between $40,000 and $200,000; such farms account for 38.5 percent of American agricultural output, and there are 580,000 of them. Some 1.7 million units produce below $40,000 in sales; they include part-time or "hobby" farms and are most dependent on off-farm income for survival. The 112,000 largest farms, producing $200,000 or more in sales, account for 50 percent of U.S. output.

16

By the Day or Week: Mexicana Domestic Workers in El Paso

Vicki L. Ruiz

In a controversial series, journalists for the *El Paso Herald Post* wrote that even though Mexican women seeking domestic employment in Texas "risk being overworked, swindled, and even sexually abused, they come to El Paso by the thousands, taking off their shoes, rolling up their pants and wading the Rio Grande in the early morning hours."[1] Segmented by class, gender, and ethnicity, Mexican women workers have historically occupied the bottom rung of the economic ladder.[2] Marginalized members of the work force, they have also been marginalized in academic scholarship. Their day-to-day struggles for survival and dignity have gone largely unrecorded in the annals of Chicano history, labor theory, women's history, and border studies. While some scholars decry the paucity of research materials available to document

I am grateful for the help provided by my research assistants for this project: Sylvia Hernández, Julieta Solis, and Anna Montalvo. ¡Gracias por todo!

1. Michael Quintanilla and Peter Copeland, "Mexican Maids: El Paso's Worst-Kept Secret," in *Special Report: The Border* (*El Paso Herald Post*, Summer 1983), 83.

2. Denise Segura, "Labor Market Stratification: The Chicana Experience," *Berkeley Journal of Sociology* 29 (1984): 57–91; Mario Barrera, *Race and Class in the Southwest: A Theory of Racial Inequality* (Notre Dame, Ind., 1979), 131, 151; Vicki L. Ruiz, "Working for Wages: Mexican Women in the American Southwest, 1930–1980," Working Paper no. 19, Southwest Institute for Research on Women (Tucson, 1984), 1–4.

the lives of Mexican women, an important resource is as accessible as the nearest tape recorder. Oral history not only increases the visibility of minority women but fosters understanding and appreciation as well. Oral interviews, housed at the Institute of Oral History, University of Texas at El Paso, form the core of this study.[3]

The situation of Mexicana domestics in El Paso provides one of the more dramatic examples of the impact of economic segmentation among women of color in the United States. In providing an overview of this significant, specifically female, segment of the labor force along the border, this essay examines a number of key issues: the centrality of women to the border economy; the nature of exploitation attendant on what has historically been termed "women's work"; and the question of ethnicity and women's employment in a border town.

El Paso is one of the most impoverished cities in the United States. In per capita income, only five other urban areas (of a total of 303) rank lower than this border community. More important, El Paso has the dubious distinction of having the lowest per capita income of any city with a population in excess of 100,000. The city also has a reputation as a minimum-wage town, yet 15 percent of El Paso County households earn less than the minimum wage of $6,968 a year.[4] Unemployment here, furthermore, exceeds both the national and state averages. While unemployment figures hovered around 7.1 to 7.8 percent for the state of Texas and for the nation as a whole during the winter of 1985, El Paso's joblessness rate approached 12 percent.[5]

An ethnic dimension complicates the earnings and employment patterns in a city where 63 percent of the population has been classified as of "Spanish origin." A representative Anglo head of household, for instance, earns $20,400 annually; a Hispanic counterpart's yearly income averages $12,600. Eight-five percent of El Paso residents whose income dips below the poverty level are Mexican. Conversely, Anglos compose 81 percent of persons earning $50,000 or more per year.

3. The Institute of Oral History at the University of Texas, El Paso, has the largest collection of taped interviews (over 700) dealing with the U.S.–Mexico border. A significant number of these interviews focus on the lives of Mexicana and Mexican-American women workers, many of whom were interviewed as part of the institute's Border Labor History Project. From August 1983 to May 1985 I served as director of the Institute of Oral History.

4. John Rebchook, "El Paso Is a Minimum Wage Town" and "The Poor in El Paso," in *Special Report: The Border* (*El Paso Herald Post*, Summer 1983), 74, 66.

5. "Labor Force Estimates for Texas Counties—Feb. '85," prepared by the Economic Research and Analysis Department, Texas Employment Commission. The El Paso figure is 11.9 percent, or 24,175 unemployed persons actively seeking work.

Forty percent of Hispanic workers hold blue-collar jobs, while 47 percent of Anglo employees fill high-level professional positions.[6]

The economic situation in Ciudad Juárez, directly across the border, appears even more dismal. Despite the absence of reliable employment figures for El Paso's sister city, a safe estimate places joblessness at between 10 and 15 percent of the area's work force. Salaries for blue-collar operatives are extremely low in comparison with those in the United States. In the "twin plants" (*maquiladoras*),[7] the take-home pay for line personnel averages 523 pesos a day ($3.48 in 1983), a wage set by the Mexican government. With such a low pay scale, it is not surprising that thousands of Juarenses (both men and women) cross the Rio Grande in search of employment. In fact, a typical El Paso domestic worker can earn almost five times the wage garnered by her peers in the *maquiladoras*. Twin-plant employers, however, hold out the promise of business- and government-sponsored social service benefits, the lure of which prove more attractive to workers than the actual pay.[8] As a twenty-year-old Mexicana *maquila* worker remarked, "If I didn't work here, I don't know if I would have a job. Maybe I would be a maid."[9] The choice for many Juárez women seems clear: employment as *trabajadoras* (workers) in the twin plants or as maids in either Ciudad Juárez or El Paso.[10]

How many women work as domestics in El Paso? There are no reliable estimates. According to the 1980 census, 1,063 El Paso women identified themselves as maids in private homes. This figure is very low, for it does not include Juárez commuters with work permits or the undocumented women who compose the bulk of the city's domestic labor force. Nestor Valencia, director of the City Planning, Research, and Development Department, stated, "If only 10 percent of El Paso's

6. Peter Copeland, "Border Ambiente," and "The Two Cities of El Paso," both in *Special Report: The Border (El Paso Herald Post*, Summer 1983), 12, 21.

7. Many multinational corporations have constructed facilities on both sides of the U.S.–Mexico border in order to lower their labor costs. A "twin plant" is thus one that has a twin on the other side of the border. See María Patricia Fernández-Kelly, *For We Are Sold* (Albany, 1983), for an insightful glimpse into life in the *maquiladoras*.

8. Interview with economist Jeffrey T. Brannon, 27 March 1985, conducted by the author; Debra Skodack, "Border Business: Twin Plants Give Boost," *Special Report: The Border (El Paso Herald Post*, Summer 1983), 68–69; *El Paso Herald Post*, 8 April 1985. The extent to which these promises of benefits are realized is currently the subject of considerable controversy.

9. Skodack, "Border Business," 69.

10. Employment in the El Paso apparel trades is considered a step up from domestic work, in both pay and prestige. Most maids seem to view sewing slacks at Farah as a "good" job.

households had maids, that would be more than 13,400 maids and a significant employment sector."[11] Although an accurate measure is impossible, probably more than 10 percent of El Paso homemakers hire domestic help. Perhaps as many as 15,000 to 20,000 women are private household workers.

The salaries of Mexican domestics are sadly deficient in comparison with those earned in other parts of the nation for similar work. In El Paso a daily maid (a woman who comes in to clean once a week) earns an average of $15 a day, while a live-in household worker receives from $30 to $60 a week. Some employers, however, offer no more than $80 a month for live-in services. The ready availability of domestic help at bargain-basement prices has led to the commonly heard comment: "The best thing about El Paso is the cheap maids."[12]

Domestic workers are so welded into the city's lifestyle, particularly for middle- and upper-income families, that many homes contain areas identified as "maid's quarters." These accommodations vary from large, light, airy rooms with a separate bath and entrance to a small bed nestled against the washer and dryer. It is very fashionable to have domestic help. As one person observed, "Once you get a microwave, the next status item is a maid." Not only Anglos employ household workers; Mexican-Americans and Mexican nationals who live in El Paso hire them too. In fact, many working-class homes benefit from live-in labor; Mexican-American factory operatives frequently hire domestic help.[13] The ready availability of Mexicana maids is not attributable solely to the recent economic crises in Mexico; Mexican domestic workers have played important roles in El Paso's economy at least since the turn of the century.

According to a sample of 393 families taken from the 1900 census, only twenty-three El Paso homes had live-in maids; of those families, only one had a Spanish surname and was, in fact, the family of the Mexican consul. Many Anglos, however, hired Mexicanas as day servants.[14] Elizabeth Rae Tyson, a native of El Paso, explained: "Every Anglo American family had at least one, sometimes two or three ser-

11. Quintanilla and Copeland, "Mexican Maids," 86.

12. Quintanilla and Copeland, "Mexican Maids," 83–84, 86; El Paso Shopping Guide, 21 December 1983; El Paso Herald Post, 26 March 1985; El Paso Times, 9 April 1985; personal observations by the author.

13. Quintanilla and Copeland, "Mexican Maids," 83, 86; interview with Mr. M., 8 June 1983, conducted by the author; personal observations by the author. Real estate brokers frequently mention "maid's quarters" in advertising their listings.

14. Mario T. García, Desert Immigrants: The Mexicans of El Paso, 1880–1920 (New Haven, Conn., 1981), 254n.

vants: a maid and laundress, and perhaps a nursemaid. . . . The maid came in after breakfast and cleaned up the breakfast dishes, and . . . last night's supper dishes . . . did the routine cleaning, washing, and ironing, after the family dinner . . . washed dishes again, and then went home to perform similar service in her own home."[15] These Mexicanas worked from 7 A.M. to 5 P.M. for $3 to $6 a week.[16]

Domestic labor provided the most common form of employment for Mexican women during the first half of the twentieth century. In 1919 the U.S. Employment Bureau opened an office in El Paso. According to the historian Mario García, bureau personnel expended large amounts of time and energy in placing Mexican domestics in area residences. In November 1919, for example, 1,740 Mexicanas applied to the agency for employment assistance and 1,326 found work. During the 1930s and 1940s, the Rose Gregory Houchen Settlement House, operated by the Methodist church, also found jobs for Mexican women as domestics. Staff members operated an informal bureau that endeavored to locate Christian homes for Christian women. The settlement also provided child care and medical services to the people of El Segundo, a poor, predominantly Hispanic neighborhood.[17]

In 1933, in the midst of the Great Depression, many El Paso housewives were horrified to learn that more than 500 domestics had organized themselves into the Domestic Workers Association—in other words, they had formed a maids' union. These women, led by the political and labor activist Charles Porras, had banded together because they simply could not support their families on the then-average wage of $1.75 a week.[18] Porras recalled: "I organized the Domestic Workers Association—all women, local from *here*. Mind you, $3 a week! I wouldn't let them take a nickel less; and they had to get carfare. . . . You'd be surprised to see the number of women, I mean the upper class women *here* that went to the Immigration outfit and tried to get me deported . . . [or] arrested because I was getting these women to stay away from them."[19]

15. Mary Wilson Barton, "Methodism at Work among the Spanish-Speaking People of El Paso, Texas" (master's thesis, Texas Western College, 1950), 15.

16. García, *Desert Immigrants*, 77.

17. García, *Desert Immigrants*, 60; Vicki L. Ruiz, "A History of Friendship Square: Social Service in South El Paso" (manuscript, 1983), 37–38.

18. *El Paso Herald Post*, 23 September 1933; interview with Charles Porras, 18 November 1975, conducted by Oscar Martínez (on file at the Institute of Oral History, University of Texas, El Paso). My thanks to Mario García for providing the news clipping.

19. Charles Porras interview. During this period in other sections of the United States, domestic workers did generally earn $3 a week. See Lois Rita Helmbold, "Class

Although these Mexicanas received financial and organizational support from a few area locals affiliated with the American Federation of Labor, the maids' association appears to have been short-lived.[20] Community hostility to the union, as well as rampant unemployment on both sides of the border, ensured a ready supply of domestic servants for El Paso middle- and upper-income housewives at any wage these homemakers deemed suitable.

In 1953 Anglo housewives formed an organization of their own, the Association for Legalized Domestics, in response to the McCarran-Walters Immigration Act, which placed controls on the flow of Mexican nationals into the United States. The Association for Legalized Domestics sought the assistance of the Immigration and Naturalization Service (INS) in contracting (legally) for the labor of Juárez women. Members of this organization desired the importation of domestic help along the lines employed by Southwest agribusiness to recruit Mexicanos to work as farm labor under the *bracero* program. Maids, classified as "non-immigrants," would be contracted to specific employers with specific conditions.[21] The proposed "bracero maid" contract comprised the following provisions:

1. The non-immigrant must be asked for by name and must be between the ages of 18 and 35.
2. The non-immigrant must supply the prospective employer with an acceptable health certificate. . . .
3. Non-immigrants must supply the prospective employer with a certificate from Mexican authorities stating that they are free of any civil or criminal record. . . .
4. Non-immigrants must have character references. . . .
5. The contractor must pay a minimum salary of $15 a week.
6. The contractor must provide acceptable living quarters and food. . . .
7. The non-immigrant . . . must have at least one and one-half days of rest per week, at which time the non-immigrant is free to leave the premises and return to Mexico.

Conflict and Class Cooperation among Women during the Depression," paper presented at the Fifth Berkshire Conference on the History of Women, Poughkeepsie, N.Y., June 1981.

20. *El Paso Herald Post,* 23 September 1933.

21. *El Paso Times,* 25 September 1953; *El Paso Herald Post,* 12 October 1953; Rodolfo Acuña, *Occupied America: A History of Chicanos,* 2d ed. (New York, 1981), 144–50. One of the most comprehensive accounts of the bracero program is Ernesto Galarza's *Merchants of Labor: The Mexican Bracero Story* (Charlotte, N.C., 1964).

8. The non-immigrant may visit Mexico within a limited area designated by the Immigration and Naturalization Service. . . .

9. A $10 fee must be paid by the prospective employer to the [INS]. . . .

10. Non-immigrant domestic working visas will cost the prospective employer $41.50. This sum will be paid to the U.S. Consular Service.

11. The contract may be terminated by either employer or employee and employee returned to Mexico at any time. . . .

12. The contract and working period . . . is for a period of one year and may be renewed at that time for a fee of $10 providing the U.S. Labor Department states that no qualified domestics are available in the United States. . . .[22]

Mexican-American household workers vehemently protested the proposal. In a letter to a local advice columnist, one El Paso maid stated that an ample supply of domestic help was available on the Texas side of the border. Local housewives preferred women from Juárez, she asserted, because they would work for lower wages: "We charge $3 a day and most ladies want to pay just $12 or $14 a week." The columnist responded by chiding the woman for not accepting the pay scale offered by El Paso homemakers; she did, however, recognize the magnitude of the household tasks assigned to many domestics. "I think that the amount of work . . . and the hours have a lot to do with the wages," the columnist wrote. "That $14 and $12 a week can be too little when a maid is expected to do everything but breathe for her employer."[23] Reflecting conventional attitudes of the 1950s, she rebuked housewives for their reliance on household workers: "I think American women could do more housework than they are doing these days. . . . I believe that a good healthy tiredness from housecleaning and cooking a mighty good meal for their family or digging in the garden would stave off more nervous breakdowns than all this hub-bub and how-dya-do over civic . . . duties. I have heard doctors say so."[24]

As it turned out, the controversy generated by the Association of Legalized Domestics became moot when the Department of Justice refused to consider a bracero-type program for Mexican maids.[25]

This formal organization among El Paso homemakers stands out as

22. *El Paso Herald Post*, 12 October 1953.
23. *El Paso Herald Post*, 15 and 30 October 1953.
24. *El Paso Herald Post*, 30 October 1953.
25. *El Paso Herald Post*, 9 and 18 November 1953.

an isolated case. Typically, the regulation of household labor takes place on a one-to-one basis between *patrona* and maid within the confines of a private residence. The experiences of the Mexicanas in domestic service have ranged from rewarding, fulfilling employment to sexual abuse. While one woman proudly displays pictures of the Anglo children she helped rear, another recounts how she was sexually harassed and even assaulted by her employers' husbands.[26] Subtle day-to-day humiliation, however, often leaves the deepest scars. As the domestic worker Enriqueta Morales recounted:

> There are those that treat me very well. I feel even as if I were one of the family. And with others, it was very different. They humiliated me. With some, they give something to eat . . . they sit you down at the table and everything. As we sit together, we eat, we talk—it's all the same. And others, well, it's different. They only give you a sandwich and a glass of water. And that's all they put on our plate. [They say] "Look, this is your lunch." In time, you may be given a glass of tea, even a soda. Or sometimes, they didn't give me any lunch. That hurts.[27]

Many domestics provide a variety of services for little pay. One employer, while entertaining friends, instructed his Mexican maid to wash all of the guests' automobiles. The book *Your Maid from Mexico: A Home Training Course for Maids* encourages Mexicanas to "always . . . find new ways to help and please your employers." These little extras range from hairstyling to sewing to shining shoes. The routine duties of most household workers include cleaning, babysitting, cooking, even gardening, for a mere $30 to $60 a week. Little wonder, then, that many El Paso women emphatically declare, "I couldn't live without my maid."[28]

Many *señoras* have little understanding of the everyday realities facing the women they employ. Although written over twenty years ago, the following excerpt from *Your Maid from Mexico* reflects the apparent ignorance and patronizing attitudes characteristic of many contemporary El Paso homemakers:

26. Michael Quintanilla, "Legal Maid: She Devotes Her Life to Others," *Special Report: The Border* (*El Paso Herald Post*, Summer 1983), 88; interview with Rocío, 29 May 1979, conducted by Oscar Martínez and Mario Galdós (on file at the Institute of Oral History, University of Texas, El Paso).

27. Interview with Enriqueta Morales, 14 June 1979, conducted by Oscar Martínez, Mario Galdós, and Sarah John (on file at the Institute of Oral History, University of Texas, El Paso).

28. Quintanilla and Copeland, "Mexican Maids," 84; Gladys Hawkins, Jean Soper, and Jane Pike Henry, *Your Maid from Mexico: A Home Training Course for Maids in English and Spanish* (San Antonio, 1959), 6, 8; personal observations by the author.

You girls who work in homes can soon become more valuable to your employers than girls who work in offices, stores, or factories because our homes . . . are closest to our hearts. . . . Remember, as you learn new skills day by day, you are not only learning how to become a better wife and mother . . . but you are learning to support yourself and your family in a worthwhile career in case you must be the breadwinner.[29]

In fact, some women believe that they are doing Mexicanas a favor by hiring them. As one poorly phrased classified advertisement stated: "Permanent live-in child carer of 3 in exchange for private room and food."[30] This potential employer obviously did not feel compelled to offer any sort of monetary remuneration. Middle- and upper-income residents, in particular, often have definite opinions concerning domestic workers. Mike Trominski, a deputy director of the INS, succinctly summed up common sentiments: "People think that it is a God-given right in El Paso to have a wet maid that they can pay a few dollars and will do anything they want."[31] Such employers, whether Anglo or Mexican-American, are generally unappreciative of the household services they enjoy. At social functions, some women swap maid stories that begin: "My maid is so stupid that . . . " This denigration of intelligence has not been lost on the domestic worker, even though she often cannot speak the language of her employer. Describing her communication with her Anglo *patrona*, one Mexicana poignantly revealed: "She didn't know any Spanish and I no English. But she has learned much from me. I believe I have learned very little from her because, well, Mexicans, we aren't, well, I'm not so intelligent."[32] The low self-esteem of this woman is undoubtedly the product of years of prejudice and humiliation. INS official James Smith sums it up: "It's human nature—the abuse and the exploitation."[33]

The superior attitudes assumed by many *patronas* can reach preposterous proportions. Some women, perhaps unwittingly or perhaps deliberately, forget to pay their housekeepers at the end of the day or week. When the maids ask for their wages, these employers act offended, as if to convey the message: "Just who do you think you are?" In addition, *patronas* sometimes believe that they are entitled to regulate the private lives of their domestic workers. When one Mexicana

29. Hawkins et. al, *Your Maid from Mexico*, 2.
30. *El Paso Herald Post,* 26 March 1985.
31. Peter Copeland, "INS Checks Maids' U.S. Entry," *Special Report: The Border* (*El Paso Herald Post,* Summer 1983), 89; personal observations by the author.
32. Enriqueta Morales interview.
33. Quintanilla and Copeland, "Mexican Maids," 84.

who cleans several homes in the Coronado area (a middle- to upper-middle-class, largely Anglo neighborhood) informed her clients that she was pregnant with her second child, she received mixed responses: two of her employers offered maternity leaves with pay, but another callously issued an ultimatum: "Get an abortion or lose your job." In Señora Chavarría's words, "I tell her, I get other work."[34]

Blatant discrimination can even be detected in the classified sections of El Paso's newspapers and shopping guides. Advertisements appearing under "Domestic Help" frequently contain such phrases as "must be clean," "neat appearance," and the ubiquitous "some English necessary." A few area women refuse to hire Mexicanas. One recent advertisement noted: "Wanted: European housekeeper."[35]

An Anglo businessman offered the following reasons why he and his wife are delaying parenthood:

> The major dilemma would be what to do with the child. We don't really like the idea of leaving the baby at home with a maid . . . for the simple reason if the maid is Mexican, the child may assume that [the] Mexican is its mother. Nothing wrong with Mexicans; they'd just assume that this other person is its mother. There have been all sorts of cases where they [the infants] learned Spanish before they learned English. There've been incidents of the Mexican maid stealing the child and taking it over to Mexico and selling it.[36]

This winding statement reveals the (at best) ambivalent attitudes that many Anglo El Pasoans harbor toward Mexicans and their culture.

However, life may not be any easier for maids employed by Mexican-Americans. Some women assert that Hispanics treat them worse than Anglos do. "Mexican women; they are the worst," one woman stated simply. Many prefer to work for newly arrived Anglos. Perhaps newcomers to the area (often first-time *patronas*) feel a bit guilty about hiring Mexicanas at such bargain rates; as a result, they may be more considerate and appreciative of their household workers.[37]

Of course, strong, harmonious relationships can develop between a

34. Interview with Martina Hernández, 29 November 1983, conducted by Sylvia Hernández (on file at the Institute of Oral History, University of Texas, El Paso); interview with Mónica Santos de Chavarría, 13 December 1983, conducted by the author.

35. *El Paso Times*, 20 February 1984; *El Paso Herald Post*, 17 February 1984; *El Paso Shopping Guide*, 21 December 1983, 14 February 1984.

36. Interview with Robert Lyons, 23 July 1984, conducted by Mary Ann White (on file at Institute of Oral History, University of Texas, El Paso).

37. Interview with María Cristina Carlos, 20 June 1979, conducted by Oscar Martínez (on file at Institute of Oral History, University of Texas, El Paso); interview with Mrs. C., 1 June 1983, conducted by the author; personal observations by the author.

Mexican domestic worker and her El Paso employer. When one Mexicana's infant became ill with severe diarrhea, for instance, she called her *patrona*, Mrs. C., who escorted the mother and baby to Thomason General Hospital. During the early-morning hours, both Mr. and Mrs. C. waited with the mother until the child was examined and treated, then drove the woman and her infant home. This display of genuine concern may be uncommon, but it does indicate that the relationship between a private household worker and her employer need not be one of humiliation, callousness, or exploitation.[38]

Economic necessity propels Mexican women into domestic labor. Many live-in maids have their own families in Ciudad Juárez; their own children are generally cared for by relatives. Typically they visit their families on weekends. Younger women, some recruited from the interior of Mexico, often stay with a family for months at a time. A youthful Mexicana may enter domestic service in order to earn money for her family or to save for her own marriage. "I go home about once every month," one eighteen-year-old stated. "Sometimes I stay a week. . . . Most of the time I go home for the weekend. I miss my family. . . . Sometimes I miss them too much."[39]

"Commuter" maids of all ages form the majority of the live-in domestic labor force in El Paso. These women wade across the river early Monday morning, catch a Sun City Area Transit (SCAT) bus, work all week, and then return home for the weekend. While their pay remains low, it is enough to provide food, clothing, and shelter for their families in Ciudad Juárez. In fact, their earnings are comparable to those earned by white-collar Juarenses.[40]

The prize-winning poet Pat Mora has clearly captured the divergent worlds of the Mexicana employee and her Anglo employer in a poem tited "Mexican Maid."

> Would the moon help?
> The sun did,
> changed fhe *señora*'s white skin
> to red, then copper.
> "I'm going to take a sun
> bath, Marta, sun bath, *sí?*"
> Marta would smile, nod,

38. Mrs. C. interview.

39. Quintanilla and Copeland, "Mexican Maids," 84; personal observations by the author; Michael Quintanilla, "Illegal Maid: She Plays Cat and Mouse with La Migra," *Special Report: The Border (El Paso Herald Post,* Summer 1983), 87.

40. Quintanilla and Copeland, "Mexican Maids," 84–86; Jeffrey Brannon interview.

> look at her own dark skin
> and wish
> that she could lie
> outside at night
> bathed by moonlight,
> lie with her eyes closed
> like the *señora* wake to a new skin
> that would glisten white
> when she stepped off the dusty bus
> at the entrance to her village.[41]

It is important to remember that not all domestics internalize the negative attitudes imposed upon them. Even if they experience psychological and physical abuse, many retain their sense of humor, their pride, their integrity. When María Cristina Carlos left her job in a private home to work in a tortilla factory, her employer refused to pay her for her final two weeks' work. Adding insult to injury, the *patrona* then spread the rumor that her maid had robbed her. With rising indignation, Señora Carlos demanded, "But just who had robbed who?"[42] Another woman recounted how her employer's husband had offered her $20 if she would take off her clothes and dance on the dining room table. Although trembling inside, she managed to reply, "I'm not looking for that kind of work. There are many places where you can see women dance and for less money."[43]

The issue of household labor is not confined to employer–employee relationships; domestic workers make significant contributions to the city's economy. Nestor Valencia, director of the city planning office, remarked, "It's an industry that is part of the fiber of the community." In fact, the Sun City Area Transit depends on domestic workers for at least half of its riders. One SCAT official even claimed, "If they ever cracked down on domestic help, especially illegals, we would lose our ridership." By midafternoon in this West Texas community, the suburban bus stops are thronged with Mexicanas, some wearing old sweaters in the winter and holding umbrellas in the summer, some sitting on benches, others on hard pavement. The city bus system is so clearly identified with its Mexican clientele that the Border Patrol routinely boards SCAT vehicles to check the citizenship documents of the passengers.[44]

---

41. "Mexican Maid," reprinted from *Borders*, by Pat Mora (Houston, 1986), 36.
42. María Carlos interview.
43. Rocío interview.
44. Quintanilla and Copeland, "Mexican Maids," 84, 86; personal observations by the author.

The apprehension of undocumented maids is not a high priority for the INS, however. While the Border Patrol will take women into custody at the river or from city buses, these officials will not search private residences. The rationale for this policy centers on the fact that domestic work is not a lucrative position coveted by U.S. citizens. INS Deputy Director Mike Trominski bluntly pointed out, "It doesn't make sense looking for one illegal maid in Eastwood when we could be removing an alien from a good paying job." Still, commuter maids are routinely picked up near the river and driven back to Juárez. Border Patrol agents apprehend some women so frequently that they call them by name. "Norma, again?" they asked, after detaining one woman for the third time in a single day.[45]

Mexicana domestics have developed elaborate strategies for crossing the U.S.–Mexican border. Some will time their routes precisely to arrive at a border bus stop at the same time as the scheduled bus. Rocío remembered that once when she and several other women were crossing the river near a Border Highway bus stop, the driver purposely held his vehicle for them; and after they had boarded, he offered each of them a tissue to wipe their mud-streaked legs.[46]

Others prefer to cross before daybreak and then depend on catching rides to the downtown plaza, where they can board SCAT buses to all parts of the city. However, women dread accepting rides from strangers (often "coyotes," who demand a small *mordida* [bribe] for their services); indeed, they could be and have been sexually assaulted. "Tu cuerpo es tu morida" (Your body is your bribe) may not be an uncommon phrase among coyotes. Because of their dubious status in the United States, these rape victims do not report the incidents. Women also fear crossing the four-laned Border Highway and the six lanes of Interstate 10. The gangs of Mexican and Mexican-American youths who congregate on both sides of the river pose another threat. In view of all the hazards involved, many Mexicanas cross in groups and often with family or friends.[47]

Household workers with some knowledge of English and of El Paso may take a more direct approach: they cross at one of the three bridges

45. Quintanilla and Copeland, "Mexican Maids," 83, 85; Copeland, "INS Checks Maids," 89; Quintanilla, "Illegal Maid," 87.

46. Interview with Esperanza Avila, 10 May 1979, conducted by Mario Galdós and Sarah John (on file at Institute of Oral History, University of Texas, El Paso); Rocío interview.

47. Esperanza Avila interview; interview with Irene González, 12 October 1979, conducted by Mario Galdós and Virgilio Sánchez (on file at Institute of Oral History, University of Texas, El Paso); Quintanilla, "Illegal Maid," 87; Mónica Santos de Chavarría interview.

and declare their citizenship as "American." One woman who has used this tactic remarked that she preferred Anglo to Mexican-American immigration officials because the former tend to ask fewer questions.[48]

Another government service agency concerned about the role of domestic workers in the El Paso economy is the local branch of the Social Security Administration. By law, if any person pays another person more than $50 for services over a three-month period, both parties must pay 6.7 percent of the weekly wages in social security taxes. Even if the employee is undocumented, the employer must still pay the tax. The reasoning behind this regulation is simple: after forty to fifty years of service, a domestic worker who has received wages on a cash-only basis throughout her life is often left with nothing in her declining years. Yet even if her *patrona* has paid into the social security system, she still cannot collect benefits unless or until she has legal resident status in the United States. This law is flagrantly violated. Many employers are reluctant to deduct the taxes and to keep the appropriate records. Domestic workers, too, tend to be unwilling to give up any of their meager, hard-earned wages. "I want my money now," one Mexicana stated flatly.[49]

Another piece of legislation ignored by most *patronas* is the minimum-wage law. Few Mexican domestics receive the $3.35 an hour to which they are entitled, regardless of their citizenship or residence. The average daily wage of $15 for a woman who cleans once a week for six to eight hours translates into $1.88 to $2.50 an hour. The hourly wage of a live-in maid earning $30 to $60 a week is considerably less. Interestingly, social security was not extended to private household workers until 1952, and these women were also excluded from minimum-wage legislation until 1974.[50]

As long as high unemployment and a surplus labor pool persist on both sides of the border, El Paso homemakers will continue to employ Mexican household workers at bargain wages. Economic segmentation and sexual exploitation are likely to continue as long as Mexicana household workers face a quadruple whammy—class, gender, ethnicity, and citizenship. Their dubious status in the United States compounds the barriers confronted by working-class women of color. Fur-

48. Rocío interview.

49. Peter Copeland, "Social Security Head Went on Warpath," *Special Report: The Border (El Paso Herald Post,* Summer 1983), 89; Quintanilla and Copeland, "Mexican Maids," 84; Quintanilla, "Illegal Maid," 87.

50. Copeland, "Social Security," 89; *El Paso Herald Post,* 26 March 1985; *El Paso Times,* 9 April 1985; Alice Kessler-Harris, *Women Have Always Worked: A Historical Overview* (Old Westbury, N.Y., 1981), 84.

ther research by historians and social scientists is needed before we can comprehend fully the economic contributions and experiences of Mexicana domestics on the U.S.–Mexico border. Though frequentjy victimized, Mexicana domestics are not victims but women who meet each day with integrity and endurance. As one woman puts it, "I go where I have to go. I do what I have to do."[51]

51. Personal observations by the author.

17

Working Women's Consciousness: Traditional or Oppositional?

Cynthia Costello

Recent historical research has focused long-overdue attention on the combined impact of class and gender on working women's actions and consciousness. Louise Tilly's study of nineteenth-century working women in the cotton, textile, and tobacco industries of France demonstrates that the household division of labor was a critical factor in determining women's participation in collective action.[1] Thomas Dublin's research on nineteenth-century Yankee mill girls shows that the combination of a patriarchal farm background and the new social relations in which the mill girls found themselves—both in the mills and in the boardinghouses—provided the basis for the mill girls' participation in the Ten Hour Movement and the Female Reform Association.[2] And

The research for this paper was supported by an American Association of University Women Frances Perkins Endowed Fellowship, a Business and Professional Women's Foundation Research Grant, and a predoctoral fellowship from the Smithsonian Institution. I am grateful to the Women's Oral History Project—to Sue McGovern, Ruth Powers, Joanne Whelden, Barbara Melosh, and particularly Catherine Loeb—for initiating and collecting several of the interviews with strike participants at the Trust. Special thanks are also owed to Sara Cooper and Dale Trelevin at the Wisconsin State Historical Society for sponsoring the Women's Oral History Project.

1. Louise A. Tilly, "Paths of Proletarianization: Organization of Production, Sexual Divisions of Labor, and Women's Collective Action," *Signs* 7 (Winter 1981): 400–417.

2. Thomas Dublin, *Women at Work: The Transformation of Work and Community in Lowell, Massachusetts, 1820–1860* (New York, 1979).

Sarah Eisenstein's study of turn-of-the-century working-class women demonstrates that working women's consciousness was contradictory, forged out of their critical negotiation with both the dominant Victorian ideology and the alternative feminist ideology of the period.[3]

This essay examines the interplay between class and gender in the lives of contemporary working women. Based on oral history interviews, the analysis highlights the contradictory character of collective action for fifty-three office workers who initiated a strike action against their employer in September 1979.[4] Caught between their work and family identities, between an older notion of themselves as nonconfrontal and a newer notion of themselves as entitled to certain rights at work and at home, these women were responding to sex-discriminatory working conditions. By enabling the women to challenge the conventions and restrictions of their everyday lives, the strike resulted for most of them in a transformation in their consciousness as working women. And for many, the strike reverberated well past its conclusion, influencing the women's feelings about their employer, other workers, their families, and themselves.

The office workers were employees of the Wisconsin Education Association Insurance Trust (the Trust), a company founded in 1970 by the Wisconsin Education Association (WEA) to provide insurance coverage for school system employees. As the arm of the largest union in the state, the Trust was an unusual insurance company. Appointed by WEA, the members of the Trust's board of trustees were mostly former teachers. The fact that the Trust's managers reported to a union-appointed board of directors prevented them from implementing blatantly antiunion policies. At the same time, however, the Trust's status as an "arm of a union" did not protect the company from competitive pressures. Constrained to function according to insurance industry standards (otherwise, WEA would switch to a major carrier), the

3. Sarah Eisenstein, *Give Us Bread but Give Us Roses: Working Women's Consciousness in the United States, 1890 to the First World War* (London, 1983).

4. Most of the data for this paper were derived from six semistructured interviews with managers (including questions on managerial policies, decisions, and attitudes; specific managerial responsibilities; and the strike), and twenty-two in-depth oral and thirty-seven short written interviews with strikers. Every woman who was on strike was asked to participate in the oral history interviews; because several of the women who refused were known to be critical of the strike, there is some selection bias. The oral interviews, averaging two to four hours, were semistructured and covered the following topics: work and family history, union background, work and family attitudes, working conditions at the Trust, the strike, and poststrike working conditions. The short written interviews included demographic questions, as well as questions on work and family history, union background, and extent of strike participation. Additional materials for this article—union newsletters, grievances, and labor contracts—were provided by the United Staff Union.

Trust organized its work process according to a traditional, patriarchal hierarchy and managerial mentality.

In the first ten years of operation, the two male managers at the Trust set policies and directed the work of the five female claims adjusters, who performed the entire range of manual tasks involved in claims adjusting: opening the mail, setting up the file for the insured, deciding on the claims payment, and typing the insurance checks. In 1975, two female supervisors were hired to deal with the "communication problems" that had developed between management and nonmanagement employees. This move was not particularly successful. That same year, the nonmanagement employees decided to join the United Staff Union, the state local of the National Staff Organization, an independent union representing employees of teachers' unions.

During the term of the first union contract—from the fall of 1975 until the fall of 1977—the Trust grew significantly, adding new benefit plans to existing teacher contracts. Management responded to growth by hiring twenty additional employees, by expanding the managerial hierarchy, by rationalizing the claims process, and by dividing its employees between two separate locations. The billing, accounting, and data processing departments were housed in one building, the claims and clerical departments in a second building along with the two top managers. Responsible for the allocation of tasks and the monitoring of employee performance, the department managers and supervisors had a decisive influence on the tenor of office relationships. In the first building, managers fostered a work atmosphere that granted significant autonomy to union employees, encouraging casual, friendly interactions both during and after work hours. Satisfaction with working conditions in these departments was therefore greater than in the claims and clerical departments, where supervisors closely monitored the work of their subordinates, discouraging even work-related conversation.

The geographical separation between the two buildings posed a barrier to communication among the Trust women, causing problems as the union entered its second negotiation in the fall of 1977. The union representatives were dissatisfied with the management proposal for a reduction in leave time and wages. They also resented the attitude of the management negotiator, who, as bargaining team members recalled, justified the low wage proposal as "sufficient for secondary wage earners working for pin money."[5] The union team recom-

---

5. There is no way to assess objectively what Trust managers actually said. Throughout the interviews, the union women referred to comments and attitudes of the top

mended that its membership reject the contract and consider a strike. But in the absence of strong interdepartmental ties and a shared assessment that working conditions were unacceptable, the Trust women could not reach a consensus. They voted against a strike. Weakened by the vote, the union negotiators accepted the contract.

Six months later, the Trust management moved their forty union employees to a new building. With the move came new sex-discriminatory work rules that clearly demarcated the rights of male managers from the rights of female employees. Management installed a time clock, then issued individual and group reprimands for tardiness of as little as one minute; directed the union employees to use the side door and the stairway, reserving the front door and the elevator for themselves; and instituted a rigid schedule, requiring the women to take staggered breaks and lunches by department. To separate the women within departments, management erected carrels.

To many of the women, the sex-discriminatory work rules indicated that management was trying to establish two classes of employees at the Trust: male managers and female employees. Their comments described the male managers as a privileged caste who looked down on their subordinates as "uneducated" and "secondary" wage earners. As one woman put it: "The attitude that there were two classes of people started at the top and filtered down . . . the elevator, the fact that management had two Christmas parties [one for themselves and one for the women] . . . all these things added up to a sharp division between management and union."

The educational backgrounds of the Trust women varied: all had high school diplomas; 30 percent had some college education, and 11 percent had college degrees. Two of the women were registered nurses. Many of those without a formal higher education had acquired technical skills by working in medical and dental offices; others learned such skills on the job. Particularly for the claims adjusters, whose jobs required them to interpret X rays and make decisions about complex insurance claims, management's allusions to their "replaceability" were insulting.

In the year leading up to the strike, several incidents heightened the Trust women's frustration with managerial policies and attitudes: management refused to grant leave time to a union steward who wanted to visit her dying father; suspended a second woman with two children

---

managers that they found particularly offensive. For the purposes of this article, the determination of the accuracy of managerial statements is less important than the shared understandings about those statements among the office workers.

for going home in the middle of a snowstorm; and denied time off, even without pay, to a third woman who needed to visit her asthmatic daughter in the hospital, stating (as several women recalled) that "women who have responsibilities for their children should stay home like our wives do." These incidents struck the Trust women as bitterly ironic. When management needed to legitimate their low wages or lack of promotional opportunities, they defined the union women as "mothers" and "wives." But when the women requested time to fulfill their family responsibilities, management denied their requests. For many of the Trust women, these attitudes reflected the fact "that the Trust employees were all women and upper management all men. . . . These men had no sympathy for working mothers and wives."

A common understanding of the problems at the Trust began to emerge as the union women prepared for the 1979 contract negotiations. The union formed committees and selected eight women for the bargaining team. After coming up with the motto "WEA'RE WORTH IT!" (a reference to their employer, WEA), the union ordered T-shirts and buttons, which all the women wore on bargaining days. And to transmit reports about the upcoming negotiations, the bargaining team published a newsletter, *As the Trust Turns*. Through both serious and humorous articles, the newsletter communicated information across departments, validating the union women's right to "stand up to management."

With the commencement of negotiations on August 1, management's bargaining behavior played a central role, as one woman stated, in "feeding the discontent of the women and helping to foster unity." Management's contract offer included the elimination of the salary schedule (which guaranteed semiannual raises), a reduction in leave time, and the elimination of seniority rights for layoffs. The union's proposal called for expanded fringe benefits, union input into work rules, and language clarification. Through newsletter articles, bargaining team members communicated to their coworkers the conflicts and differences that developed at the bargaining table.

A central theme was management's insensitivity to the needs of working women: "[Management has] no empathy or even insight into the problems that we, as women, face when combining jobs and homemaking. And they seem to tie in this lack of empathy with the fact that we are all 'clerical' workers. If ignorance is bliss, they are damn tranquil!! Regardless of the job title—be it teacher or clerical worker— women do have distinct problems which need attention and addressing in a contract!!"

Also controversial was the proposal for salaries—"Management suggests TAKING AWAY salary increments! . . . We were reminded by management that we were not negotiating a teacher's contract. We do not have an identity problem. We know we're not teachers, but we're not second class citizens, either!!"—and for union input into work rules (such as access to the elevator and the front door): "Management seems reluctant to include certain employee rights as part of the contract. WE disagree. Second only to monetary gain, human rights and principles are sacred issues!!!"

Union meetings became an important tool for the forging of clerical strategies. Before the bargaining began, few of the Trust women had attended general membership meetings with any regularity. In principle, these meetings were designed to address the interests of the three bargaining units of the United Staff Union—the professional staff (the lawyers who bargained teacher contracts for the WEA), the clerical support staff for the professionals, and the women who worked for the Trust. In practice, the priorities of the mostly male professional staff usually took precedence. In numbers, the professional staff constituted a minority: the membership of the USU included twenty-five professionals, twenty-five support staff, and fifty-three Trust women. Partly because they felt that the male professionals looked down on them as "only clericals," the Trust women had stayed away from general membership meetings. But the union meetings for the Trust bargaining unit were different. Most of the clericals described these meetings as spirited, well run, and democratic. Many declared that "their" union meetings contributed to Trust-wide discussions of working conditions and feelings of solidarity.

As the September deadline for the expiration of the 1977 contract approached, management and union reached a stalemate. The Trust women reported that the management team refused to sit across the table from the union women, negotiating instead with the male union representatives. This behavior underscored the belief of many Trust women that "management had no respect for the union women, simply because they were women."

In car pools on the way to work and by phone at night, the Trust women talked increasingly about the impasse in bargaining and how a strike might affect their work and family lives. Some felt excited about the challenge of a strike. Others worried about what a picket line might require: "I had no idea what a strike would be like. I disliked the idea of a strike immensely. I didn't feel I wanted to quit though. I felt I could go along with a strike." Some felt confident that their families could accommodate a strike, but family situations provoked anxiety for others: "The anticipation of the strike made me nervous because we were expecting a baby and I was trying to get the bills out of the way."

On September 14 the Trust management issued production standards for the claims adjusters, stating that a failure to meet them would result in discharge, and instructed supervisors to monitor the actions of their subordinates more closely. The union newsletter reported that the Trust management had "joined the ranks of the Ayatollah Khomeni." Some of the union women reacted by slowing down their work. Others openly discussed plans for a strike in front of their supervisors. On the Friday afternoon before the strike vote, the union women packed up and removed all their personal and work-related materials from their carrels.

Two nights later, all fifty-three women gathered at the Sheraton Hotel. Unknown to the Trust women, the two male negotiators for the union team agreed that evening to accept management's outstanding bargaining proposal. When the union women found out, they were furious. It was not their understanding that the male negotiators had the power to accept a contract offer without the women's approval. The Trust women decided to go ahead with the strike vote. One of the bargaining team members described the results: "We decided to tally out loud how many 'yeses' and how many 'nos' as far as the strike vote was concerned. It kept going yes, yes, YES!! I get goosebumps just thinking about it now. And after it was all counted, everybody just cheered and hugged each other. There was a mixture of happiness and 'I'm scared to death' in the room."

Carrying picket signs made the night before, all the union women gathered at dawn on October 1 for a mass rally. The administrators called off work for the day. With the target of their protest absent, the Trust women had time to organize into picket shifts and plan for the days ahead.

The women felt confident that their strike action would result in gains. Most assumed that without the claims adjusters, clericals, and billing clerks, the Trust would be unable to conduct business as usual. But management had prepared for the strike also. For several weeks preceding the strike, computer programmers had been writing programs to short-step the claims process: eliminating the steps normally taken by adjusters to validate procedures and payments, Trust management had set up a fast-track system for processing claims. While many errors were made, this system allowed managers and supervisors to perform the bulk of the work normally processed by union employees.

Unaware of management's initiatives, the union women experienced the first weeks of the strike as an exciting and empowering time, a time when norms were suspended and new kinds of behavior encouraged. In the first week, confrontations with management were mostly verbal. Well-liked supervisors were given preferential treatment, but managers and supervisors who had harassed union women found themselves the objects of insults and ridicule. Freed from the constraints of the workplace hierarchy, the women found that the strike provided opportunities to assert themselves and act in new (and sometimes unexpected) ways. One woman reported:

> There were women who came up with fantastic ideas. All the women got militant occasionally. From the youngest, single woman to the oldest, all got crazy occasionally. . . . All the women got loud and rowdy, held up nasty signs, and said things they wouldn't usually say. I myself said something really nasty to the top manager when he bumped me with his car. I was shocked as were the other strikers. The manager's eyes bugged out when I insulted him. But all the other strikers laughed.

For some of the women, the more aggressive aspects of the strike provoked acute discomfort—in particular, the insults yelled at management, the margarine spread over managers' cars, the eggs and tomatoes thrown at managers, and the glass spread across the driveway. One woman in her late fifties described her ambivalence: "The strike was quite traumatic for many of the women. Several were not happy with picketing and did not want to picket but they did. I myself felt in very alien territory. I couldn't act as vociferously as the others." A second older woman resolved her uneasiness with the marching and screaming on the picket line by sitting off to one side in her lawn chair. She summed up her skepticism about the outcome of the strike in the comment "It's a man's world." Other women, both young and old, remembered feeling uncomfortable about the violent activities that occurred on the picket line.

For some, family situations proved a source of tension. While the single women were free of the demands of husbands and children, their independence had a cost: they had no one to rely on if strike funds ran out or dismissals followed the strike. The single mothers were even more vulnerable: the strike threatened their ability to provide not only for themselves but for their children. While the union promised strike funds for several weeks, one divorced mother who collected welfare to augment her minimal salary stressed the "high costs" of the strike. And the reactions of husbands had a decisive influence on married women's experience. Some reported supportive spouses who totally endorsed the strike, increasing their household and child-care contributions to fill in when necessary. But other marriages were strained by the strike. The one woman interviewed who left the strike after the first week attributed her decision to family pressures: "I had been raised in a management household and all of a sudden things were so confusing. My husband helped me decide to leave. With a new baby, it was hard. My husband said, 'You have to leave.'"

Many women who stayed through the strike discussed the "emotional pressures" that resulted at home. One woman, who had just supported her husband through a two-month strike of his own, described the unexpected and unsettling impact of her strike on their family life: "My husband was fed up. I lived strike 24 hours a day and was gone a lot at meetings. My husband did much of the child care, housework, and cooking. I was worried about my marriage but felt I couldn't give up the strike. I've never gone through anything so stressful in my life." A second woman reported similar tensions in her home. Not a union man himself, her husband kept asking when the strike would be over. Anxious about their mortgage, he told his wife that she would have to take a part-time job. She did, but with picketing and bargaining responsibilities, her marriage suffered.

Some of the women reacted to their husbands' objections with assertive claims about their right to participate in the strike. In response to her husband's demand that she quit, one woman countered, "I don't care if you like it or not. I'm in this strike and will be until the end. And there isn't much you can do about it." And remembering the numerous times she had adapted her life to her husband's needs, a second woman asserted, "I didn't stand in your way when you moved me around the country, and damn it to hell, don't you stand in my way now."

Whatever their family situations, the strike provided an opportunity for the union women to share their personal lives and develop close ties with coworkers. On warm days, some women brought their children to the picket line, an act that, according to one woman, "management resented because it made them look bad." No longer segregated by department, the women formed strong friendships and commitments on the picket line: "Before we were divided into upstairs and downstairs. . . . [On strike], you got to know all sides of people. People shared their personal lives. You had to talk about something happy to distract you from the strike. You would talk about your kids and your husband." Bargaining team members were not required to picket, but one strike leader showed up every morning to boost morale. For her, "the new friendships were the best part of the strike." Another woman expressed her friendship commitments even more strongly: "As the strike progressed," she recalled, "the issue became not only gaining a good contract but also protecting my friends."

The developing unity of the Trust women brought with it clear norms for strike participation. Each woman was expected to do her part; in some cases, disapproval was directed at those thought to be shirking their duties; one single mother whose child care responsiblities prevented her from picketing regularly felt unsupported by other union members. Had any woman crossed the picket line and returned to work, more severe sanctions would have resulted. According to one of the strikers, "We would have killed her." One of the two women who left the strike near the beginning discovered the extent of her coworkers' resentment when she reapplied for her job after the strike. The union women made it so uncomfortable for her that she withdrew her application.

The picket line helped to solidify the relationships among the union women, and management's strike behavior contributed to a heightened sense of "us" versus "them." During the first few weeks the management bargaining team refused to bargain altogether. "They had the attitude," reported one woman, "that they would punish us bad little girls for striking." When the management team returned to the bargaining table, they responded to the union's demand for female representation at all bargaining sessions by calling in an outside mediator. For many of the Trust women, such actions reflected an attitude that, as one woman put it, "we were just a bunch of dumb little women who didn't know what we were doing" and contributed to the women's belief that management would go to great lengths to avoid recognizing the legitimacy of the union's demands.

The striking women faced other challenges as well. Publicity was a problem: the strike received little newspaper or television coverage.[6] Gaining support from other unions and community groups also proved difficult. While a few other labor unions—a local nurses union, The American Federation of State, County, and Municipal Employees, and a teacher's union (Madison Teacher's Incorporated)—helped out on the picket line, extensive support from the community's trade unionists and feminists was not forthcoming. The union women felt that their own inexperience was partly responsible for the low level of support.

---

6. Two years earlier a bitter strike had taken place at the major Madison newspapers (owned by Madison Newspapers Incorporated). This may partially explain the low level of newspaper coverage for the Trust strike, although the fact that it was a women's strike may also have been a factor.

Some of their initiatives, however, revealed a sophisticated approach to strike strategy and politics. The most unique tactic involved Jane Fonda in a ploy to inform the members of WEA about the situation at the Trust.[7] A month into the strike, the union women discovered that WEA had invited Jane Fonda to be the keynote speaker for its yearly convention in Milwaukee. The Trust women contacted Fonda, who agreed to incorporate into her address a statement prepared by the strikers. Before 5,000 teachers, Fonda concluded her speech by asking:

> And what if I told you that there are 53 women who work for an insurance company who, like Blacks in the days when they had to sit at the back of the buses, aren't allowed to walk in the front of the building and take an elevator to their offices. They have to come in a back door and walk up the back stairs. So little respect is given them by management that there is one supervisor assigned to every five clerical workers; that the supervisors follow them and time them even when they are in the restrooms; follow them when they are off duty to be sure that their private time is spent the way the secretaries have said it was going to be spent; that these skilled workers, some of whom have worked for a long time as clericals, get as a starting pay $3.08 an hour . . . when half of these women support families by themselves? And what if I told you that they're your employees?[8]

According to the union women, the president of the WEA and the management of the Trust were furious: Fonda's comments were both unexpected and embarrassing. But for the Trust women, the Fonda speech was a high point of the strike: it resulted in more publicity, increased support from WEA members, and—perhaps most important—confirmation that the strike was a legitimate action.

The impasse in bargaining began to undermine the union's confidence that the strike would soon be resolved. Many of the women had anticipated a strike of several weeks' duration, at the most. As time wore on and strike benefits expired,[9] several took part-time jobs. The majority of the women continued their picketing responsibilities, but, as one woman described it, periods of demoralization set in: "At times, we thought we should go back to work. People were getting on each other's backs, and towards the end we didn't feel united. It looked like

---

7. The Trust women reported that until this time they received uneven responses from teachers: some supported the strike; others ignored it.

8. Memo provided by the United Staff Union.

9. Strike benefits of $100 a week were provided for the first four weeks of the strike. After that time, low-interest loans were available through the United Staff Union.

management could win at times. But then, it would switch to the union side."

The bargaining team recognized that if the strike persisted into December, some of the union women might abandon the effort; they therefore recommended to the membership on November 23 that the union accept the contract proposed by the mediator. The women agreed and returned to work on November 28.

The contract embodied gains in the area of improved grievance language and strong union input into work rules but a significant loss in the elimination of the salary schedule. In management's view, the union had lost the strike. In the estimation of many of the Trust women, however, the union had won. To understand the women's assessment, we have to examine how the strike changed their attitudes toward their employer, other workers, their families, and themselves.[10]

By enabling the union women to challenge the restrictions of work and family, the strike resulted for many of them in greater self-confidence, outspokenness, and independence. Many gained an enhanced sense of self-worth: "The strike taught me that I can be proud of myself for myself. I needn't apologize for lack of a label or because I'm 'only a housewife' or 'only a claims adjuster.'" And another insisted that "I will no longer be put down just because I'm a woman."

Many of the women expressed great pride in their collective accomplishments during the strike. "I feel really good about myself," stated one woman. "Whenever anybody brings up anything about the strike, I feel really excited. I think, 'We really did something. WE, not I.' It could never be an 'I' or 'me.' WE, WE, it has to be everybody. Without all of them, nobody could have done anything."

A second woman emphasized the satisfaction gained from successfully carrying off an "all women's action": "The biggest thing I wanted [was] to show [that management was] cold and male chauvinist. . . . And also just to show the people that we were women and we can do it. We didn't need men to help us. I was very proud to be part of it . . . being women and doing it on our own. And we put up a hell of a fight for so long!"

For some women, new-found independence translated into a more assertive stance in relation to their husbands. Although noting that she looked forward to spending more time with her family after the strike,

---

10. To objectively measure the impact of the strike on the women's consciousness, one would need to conduct two interviews, one before and the other after the strike. Since all the interviews were collected after the strike, I have only one measure, which—though biased as an indicator of objective changes in consciousness—is an accurate reflection of the women's perceptions of the changes.

one woman declared that "my husband now knows that I will not back off if I feel strongly about something." A second woman, when asked whether her life had gone back to normal, replied, "There is no returning to normal because I am a different person. I am less self-abnegating in relation to my family." A third woman discovered that her increased assertiveness "has created some problems. I'm a lot more assertive and have a lot more outside interests like the women's movement. I'll say something when I think things aren't fair, and my husband is used to my saying nothing." The strongest statement of change in her family life was offered by a fourth woman, who reported that the strike transformed her from a "dutiful" wife into an independent woman:

> I realized after the strike that I don't have to wait on my husband because he is a man. If I'd had an experience like the strike at the beginning of my marriage, I would have made my husband see that he had to share the housework. I am now more independent from my husband. I won't wait on him or accept being put down as a woman. . . . My new independence has caused a lot of stress in my marriage. But I feel it is important to keep asserting myself.

Heightened feelings of individual self-worth were linked for many to a new commitment to standing up for their rights in the workplace as well. A number of the participants expressed a strong conviction that working women have the right to take action in the face of demeaning working conditions. One woman emphasized that she had learned to stand up to management: "Before the strike, I would have done whatever I was told, not thinking I had the right to say otherwise. Now, I do realize that . . . if you are not getting treated equally and fairly, you do have the right to say otherwise. . . . I learned not to be afraid. . . . [Before], I felt like I was stepping on pins and needles all the time. . . . I learned I didn't have to take that anymore."

A second woman echoed her coworker's conviction: "At the strike's end, the union women felt proud of ourselves. We proved that we wouldn't take harassment, that we would take action if pushed around. . . . I now recognize the power in numbers. I feel the strike will have a lasting impact on my future work life. I would stick up for my rights."

The strike left some of the women with a greater consciousness of the class distinctions between management and union personnel. As one woman explained: "I now feel that my job is just as important as anyone else's. The Trust could probably get along without the supervisors but not without the people who do the actual work. It's very possible that the strike made me feel that all the jobs at the Trust are equally important." And a second woman offered a similar critique of management's greater privileges: "The supervisors and managers don't have to punch in and out, they receive pensions, and don't have to pay for coffee. They come and go when they want. They think they are better than we are. That is wrong. Union employees are the ones who help management get their paychecks."

The class consciousness of the union women was fused, for many, with a gender consciousness about the male-dominated hierarchy at the Trust. One woman attributed managerial behavior to sexist attitudes: "Management is always trying to make sure their employees know their place is one step below. . . . The problem with the male managers is they are trained in the double standard." For another woman, the managerial hierarchy at the Trust was inextricably bound up with patriarchy: "Management thinks that women are all lower class and that really hurts. I think this is a male-female issue. They treat them this way due to their attitudes about women." And, echoing the sentiments of her coworkers, a third woman underscored the "chauvinism" of male management:

> If there were more men as union employees, it would be harder for management to get away with things. . . . Management would not expect men to take abuse. The management is very male chauvinistic and has the attitude that "woman's place is in the home" and that if women don't like the conditions at the Trust, they should leave. I disagree. Union women have the right to have a job and reach the top also.

From opposition to the patriarchal behavior and attitudes of Trust management, the women extended their experience to a greater identification with the organizing efforts of other working women. Typical of their remarks was this statement: "Since the strike, I feel more supportive of other strikes. I don't pay that much attention to strikes though. I would feel differently if it was an all-women's strike. I discuss strikes with my girlfriends who have experienced strikes." With one exception, all the women supported the nurses' union in Madison (the United Professionals), which had come close to striking soon after the Trust action. As one bargaining team member put it, "I was even let down when the nurses didn't strike because I identified with the nurses strike as a women's struggle."

Greater ambivalence was expressed over support for the labor movement as a whole. Slightly less than half the women (45 percent) stated that they supported all labor unions and labor actions. The comments of one woman typified their views: "I am supportive of labor actions—of any strike. I supported the bus strike [by the Teamsters] in Madison. I don't think anybody would strike unless they were out to fight for what they wanted. I think that's right."

Among the other 55 percent, poststrike attitudes toward unions and labor actions were mixed. Several women felt that strikes were appropriate only under certain circumstances. One asserted, for example, that "there are jobs where people should not strike because a lot of people would be hurt." Another argued that in the current economic crisis, workers should not strike over monetary demands.

Of the women who qualified their support for the labor movement, the majority disapproved of "big labor"—of what they described as highly paid, male labor unions. Some women felt that the demands of such unions as the Teamsters and the United Automobile Workers contributed to inflation and gave "small unions like the United Staff Union a bad name." When asked if she supported the 1980 Teamsters' bus strike in Madison, one woman replied: "I wasn't opposed to the strike, but I couldn't help but compare it to our strike at the Trust. For example, when you compare wages, you can't help but conclude that the bus drivers are better paid because bus driving is a male occupation. I also felt some envy for all the publicity they received."

A second woman expressed stronger disapproval: "I felt critical of the bus strike. I was not supportive of their wage demands. I just cannot support a union on strike for a 20 percent wage increase. I would feel happy with the wages those workers have now. I felt they were out of line."

And a third woman was strongly critical of both the Teamsters' strike and "big labor":

> I was not crazy about unions when I started at the Trust and I am not crazy about them now. A union is needed at places like the Trust. In general, unions were very helpful when they first started. In the last fifteen to twenty years, unions have created problems in the economy with their wage demands. I would like unions more if money weren't always the primary issue. If the UAW hadn't constantly demanded higher wages, they might not be accepting cutbacks now. I went out on strike for the working conditions, not the money . . . I did not support the bus drivers.

Some of those who criticized "big labor" were inconsistent in their views. One woman who argued that certain unions shouldn't strike later qualified her statement: "With the economy the way it is, the union is probably the best thing the Trust women have going for them. . . . There are a lot of people critical of unions but there are also a lot of people out of work. If they had been in a union when the business closed, they might have received some compensation." And having contrasted "good" with "bad" unions, a second woman voiced support for both the local Teamsters' strike and the national strike by the Professional Air Traffic Controllers Organization (PATCO).

What is the explanation for the ambivalent feelings of the Trust women toward labor unions? The consciousness of working women—like that of working men—is often inconsistent and contradictory, combining elements of the dominant belief system and an explicit or implicit critique of that system.[11] Michael Mann has suggested that workers are more likely to express oppositional values in areas that reflect their direct experience (for example, in relation to their own workplace) and hegemonic values in areas more distant from their own experience (for example, in relation to the "capitalist system").[12] For the Trust women, the direct experience of the strike became the basis of a strong identification with all working women's struggles. Support for the "labor movement as a whole" required a more abstract commitment.

This framework provides an explanation for the variation in levels of support for the labor movement. Of the ten women who expressed unambivalent support for unions, eight came from backgrounds where their fathers, their husbands, or they themselves had belonged to a union. Through their family networks, these women had access to pro-union attitudes and values. Previous contact with unions, however, did not translate into consistent support for the labor movement. Of the twelve women who expressed reservations about trade unions, five came from union backgrounds. This suggests that while indirect contact with labor unions through family members facilitated a pro-union identification, it was often insufficient to counter the dominant media (mis)representation of the labor movement.

There is a second interpretation of the Trust women's views about the labor movement. For many of the women, the central characteristic distinguishing "good" from "bad" unions was the gender of their membership. Most of the women indicated support for small unions representing *female* workers in low-paying jobs, but expressed criticism of

11. For analyses of the ambivalent character of working-class consciousness, see John Westergaard, "The Rediscovery of the Cash Nexus," in *The Socialist Register*, ed. Ralph Miliband and John Saville (London, 1970), 111–38; Michael Mann, "The Social Cohesion of Liberal Democracy," *American Sociological Review* 35 (1970): 423–39; and Howard Newby, *The Deferential Worker* (Harmondsworth, England, 1979).

12. Michael Mann, *Consciousness and Action among the Western Working Class* (London, 1975).

large unions representing *male* workers in high-paying jobs. Their encounters with the male domination of the professionals over the United Staff Union gave the Trust women direct experience with gender hierarchy in the labor movement. The distinction drawn between "male" and "female" unions may have reflected, in part, an extension of their own experience to a critique of sexism within the labor movement as a whole.[13]

The analysis of the strike at the WEA Insurance Trust suggests the complex meanings and consequences of women's involvement in collective action. First, it points to conflict as an important aspect of women's relationship to work and family. The focus on conflict reveals the ways in which these clericals were actors, attempting to gain control and self-respect, rather than passive objects of managerial strategies and familial constraints. Faced with working conditions defined by patriarchal management attitudes, as well as a hierarchy of surveillance and control, the women at the Trust responded by initiating a strike action. For many of the women, the strike was not easy. It required that the single mothers risk financial hardship, that the married women challenge traditional power relationships with their husbands, and that all the women confront conventional expectations about proper feminine behavior. While these pressures caused a significant level of discomfort for some of the women, a commitment to "seeing the strike through" overrode the misgivings of all but a few.

Second, the analysis highlights how closely participation in oppositional actions and critical consciousness are linked. The process of participating in the strike led to the solidification of the women's relationships and a growth in their critical consciousness. By taking action, the women at the Trust promoted further thought. Shared sensibilities about rights and goals, only partially formed until the collective action brought further understanding, were forged on the picket line.[14] The

13. For historical analyses of sexual hierarchy within the labor movement, see Alice Kessler-Harris, "Where Are the Organized Women Workers?" in *A Heritage of Her Own,* ed. Nancy F. Cott and Elizabeth H. Pleck (New York, 1979), 343–66; Heidi Hartmann, "Capitalism, Patriarchy, and Job Segregation by Sex," in *Capitalism, Patriarchy, and the Case for Socialist Feminism,* ed. Zillah R. Eisenstein (New York, 1979), 206–47; and Ruth Milkman, "Organizing the Sexual Division of Labor: Historical Perspectives on Women's Work and the American Labor Movement," *Socialist Review* 10 (January–February 1980): 95–150. See Sharon Hartman Strom, "Challenging 'Woman's Place': Feminism, the Left, and Industrial Unionism in the 1930's," *Feminist Studies* 9 (Summer 1983): 359–86; and Roslyn L. Feldberg, "'Union Fever': Organizing among Clerical Workers, 1900–1930," *Radical America* 14 (May–June 1980): 53–67, for analyses of the ambivalent relationship of labor unions to female clerical workers.

14. See Temma Kaplan, "Female Consciousness and Collective Action: The Case of Barcelona, 1910–1918," *Signs* 7 (Spring 1982): 545–66.

central element of this "shared sensibility" was a consciousness of working women's rights. From opposition to the patriarchal behavior and attitudes of the Trust management, many of the women extended their experience to a greater identification with feminist issues and the working women's movement.

But as dramatic as the strike was, it would be a mistake to misinterpret the conclusions that the Trust women took away from their experience. Like other participants in collective action, the union women incorporated the lessons of the strike into preexisting ideas about work and family. On the basis of their encounters with managerial sexism and harassment, the union women developed a particular interpretation of working women's rights: the right to oppose blatantly discriminatory management practices and to demand respectful treatment on the job. For many of the women, however, a consciousness of work-based rights did not extend to a more general identification with the labor movement (or the women's movement). It is important to address the ways in which this particular consciousness of "working women's rights" may be insufficient to challenge more sophisticated managerial initiatives and strategies.

Managers have available to them a wide array of strategies to control their work force. If derogatory comments and surveillance tactics provoke organized resistance, managers can implement a "human relations" approach, deploy computerized technologies, or institute internal labor markets to fragment women's work culture and quiet dissent.[15] In the face of such managerial initiatives, office workers need a conception of "rights" that includes rights of control over the technological and social organization of work.

One might draw the conclusion from this analysis that office workers initiate collective actions only in the face of blatantly coercive, dis-

15. For analyses of managerial strategies in the office workplace—from Taylorism to office automation—see C. Wright Mills, *White Collar* (New York, 1951); Harry Braverman, *Labor and Monopoly Capital: The Degradation of Work in the Twentieth Century* (New York, 1974); Evelyn Nakano Glenn and Roslyn L. Feldberg, "Proletarianizing Clerical Work: Technology and Organizational Control in the Office," in *Case Studies in the Labor Process*, ed. Andrew Zimbalist (New York, 1979), 51–72; Jane Barker and Hazel Downing, "Word Processing and the Transformation of the Patriarchal Relations of Control in the Office," *Capital and Class* 10 (Spring 1980): 64–97; Anne Machung, "Word Processing: Forward for Business, Backwards for Women," in *Women's Toils and Triumphs at the Workplace*, ed. Karen Sacks and Dorothy Remy (New Brunswick, N.J., 1984), 124–39; Mary C. Murphree, "Office Technology: The Changing World of the Legal Secretary," in Sacks and Ramy, *Women's Toils and Triumphs at the Workplace*, 140–59; and Judith Gregory, "Technological Change in the Office Workplace and Implications for Organizing," in *Labor and Technology: Union Responses to Changing Environments*, ed. Donald Kennedy, Charles Craypo, and Mary Lehman (University Park, Pa., 1982), 83–102.

respectful, and sexist working conditions. Such a conclusion would sell short the experience of the women who participated in the strike at the Trust. In many ways, the strategies of the Trust women reflected both the extent and the limits of the women's movement. It is partially because feminists have validated women's right to protest sex discrimination in the workplace that the Trust women were able to mobilize for this strike. But the working women's movement is still in its infancy. If office workers like the women at the Trust are to translate their consciousness of "working women's rights" into more far-reaching organizing strategies, they require a strengthened working women's movement capable of providing the institutional support, the financial resources, and the ideology to underwrite such efforts.[16]

16. For discussions of the working women's movement, see Roberta Goldberg, *Organizing Women Office Workers: Dissatisfaction, Consciousness, and Action* (New York, 1983); David Plotke, interview with Karen Nussbaum, "Women Clerical Workers and Trade Unionism," *Socialist Review* 10 (January–February 1980): 151–59; and David Wagner, "Clerical Workers: How 'Unorganizable' Are They?" *Labor Center Review* 2 (Spring–Summer 1979): 20–50.

Contributors

CAROL GRONEMAN is Professor of History at John Jay College of Criminal Justice, City University of New York, and former Executive Director of the New York Council for the Humanities. She is co-author of *Corporate Ph.D.* (Facts on File Publishers) and Chair of the Board of the Institute for Research in History.

MARY BETH NORTON is Professor of American History at Cornell University. She is the author of *Liberty's Daughters: The Revolutionary Experience of American Women, 1750–1800* (Little, Brown) and co-author of *A People and a Nation* (Houghton Mifflin), an introductory American history textbook.

MARY H. BLEWETT has taught at the University of Lowell in Massachusetts since 1965. In the early 1970s she shifted her focus from twentieth-century political history to nineteenth-century social history, concentrating on class, gender, and protest among industrial workers in New England.

CORLANN GEE BUSH completed research for her article while employed by the University of Idaho. She is currently Human Resources/Affirmative Action Director at Montana State University, where she hopes to be able to expand her research on agricultural technology and gender roles to include the effects of irrigation systems and computers on the work of ranch men and women.

ELIZABETH CLARK-LEWIS, a native of Harrisburg, Pennsylvania, is Professor of History at the Alexandria campus of Northern Virginia Community College. Currently she is a postdoctoral fellow at the Smithsonian Institution.

CYNTHIA COSTELLO is the study director for the Committee on Women's Employment and Related Social Issues at the National Academy of Sciences. She is currently at work on two projects: a book on clerical workers and collective action in the insurance industry, and a research project on home-based clerical work in the finance and high-tech industries.

SARAH ELBERT teaches history at the State University of New York, Binghamton, and is currently Visiting Professor at California Polytechnic State University. Author of *A Hunger for Home: Louisa May Alcott's Life and Work* (Rutgers University Press), she is working on "Lad: A Dog," a study of the natural world in modern children's literature.

CHRISTIE FARNHAM is Assistant Professor of Afro-American Studies and former Director of Women's Studies at Indiana University. She has published articles on the black experience in slavery and Reconstruction.

NANCY GABIN is Assistant Professor of History at Purdue University. She is writing a book on women and the United Auto Workers from the 1930s to the 1970s.

JANET GOLDEN is Assistant Director of the Francis C. Wood Institute for the History of Medicine. She is working on a book about wet-nursing.

DOLORES JANIEWSKI is currently teaching Southern history at Mount Holyoke College, where she is also analyzing the symbolic expression of gender and race in southern ideology. Her first book, *Sisterhood Denied: Race, Gender, and Class in a New South Community* (Temple University Press) was published in 1985.

KAREN M. MASON is a graduate student in history at the University of Michigan; her dissertation deals with women reformers and their political activism in Chicago, 1900–1930. She is also coauthor (with Carol Lacey) of *Women's History Tour of the Twin Cities* (Nodin Press).

NANCY GREY OSTERUD teaches history and gender studies at Lewis and Clark College in Portland, Oregon. Her essay is part of a larger study of relations among women and men in a rural community from the mid-nineteenth to the mid-twentieth century.

PHYLLIS PALMER, Director of the graduate program in Women's Studies at George Washington University, has written on relations between black women and white women in the women's movement and is currently at work on a book about housework and household employment in the interwar United States.

KATHY PEISS is Associate Professor of History and Women's Studies at the University of Massachusetts, Amherst. Her recent book is *Cheap Amusements: Working Women and Leisure in Turn-of-the-Century New York* (Temple University Press).

VICKI L. RUIZ is Assistant Professor of History at the University of California, Davis. Recently she was awarded an American Council of Learned Societies/Ford Foundation Fellowship to continue her research on the heritage of Mexican women in the Southwest.

ANN SCHOFIELD is Associate Professor of American Studies and Women's Studies at the University of Kansas. She is working on a study of female labor activism.

CAROLE TURBIN is Assistant Professor of Sociology and Women's Studies at the State University of New York's Empire State College and was on the faculty of Vassar College from 1978 to 1980. She has published articles and is currently working on a book on the interrelationship of nineteenth-century women's work, family life, and labor activism.

LAUREL THATCHER ULRICH teaches history at the University of New Hampshire. She is the author of *Good Wives: Image and Reality in the Lives of Women in Northern New England, 1650–1750* (Alfred A. Knopf).

Index

Library of Congress Cataloging-in-Publication Data
"To toil the livelong day."
    Papers presented at the Sixth Berkshire Conference on
the History of Women held at Smith College June 1–3,
1984.
    Includes index.
    1. Women—Employment—United States—History—19th
century—Congresses.   2. Women—Employment—United
States—History—20th century—Congresses.   3. Women—
United States—Economic conditions—Congresses.
I. Groneman, Carol.   II. Norton, Mary Beth.   III. Berkshire
Conference on the History of Women (6th : 1984 : Smith
College.
HD6095.T6   1987   331.4'0973   86-47975
ISBN 0-8014-9452-4 (pbk.:alk. paper)
ISBN 0-8014-1847-X (alk. paper)